THE EMERGENCE OF
PROVINCIAL NEW HAMPSHIRE,
1623–1741

THE EMERGENCE OF PROVINCIAL NEW HAMPSHIRE, 1623–1741

DAVID E. VAN DEVENTER

The Johns Hopkins University Press
Baltimore and London

To My Mother

This book has been brought to publication with the generous assistance of the Andrew W. Mellon Foundation.

Manufactured in the United States of America

The Johns Hopkins University Press, Baltimore, Maryland 21218
The Johns Hopkins University Press Ltd., London

Library of Congress Catalog Card Number 75-33758
ISBN 0-8018-1730-7

CONTENTS

Part IV: The Transformation of Society

MAPS

TABLES

PREFACE

This monograph analyzes the development of society in colonial New Hampshire through a detailed examination of its creation and its changing characteristics in the seventeenth and early eighteenth centuries. It is my hope that this intensive study of a small frontier colony's societal development can serve as a model for understanding societal development in the larger, more complex colonies.

In a study of this nature the date of termination is always somewhat arbitrary. I chose 1741 because of the two spectacular political and economic decisions made by the British government regarding New Hampshire at about that time: the separation of the New Hampshire and Massachusetts executive and the resolution of the Massachusetts-New Hampshire boundary dispute, which more than tripled New Hampshire's land area. As the culmination of more than two decades of agitation on the part of New Hampshire leaders, these two events symbolized both an end and a beginning. They brought a gradual decline in the influence of Massachusetts in New Hampshire affairs, and they ushered in an era of territorial and population expansion and provincial localism. Nonetheless, I have discussed societal developments after 1741 when I found that some of the long-term economic and social patterns could not adequately be explained without exploring the evidence of the 1740's.

The major questions posed in this study relate to the problems and opportunities facing those colonists who came into northern New England. What was the nature of the Piscataqua frontier? What economic and social opportunities and problems confronted these settlers? How did they seek to develop the opportunities and solve the problems? What

values guided them in their activities? What social structure, economic
interests, values, and institutions dominated New Hampshire society by
the 1740's and how and, to some extent, why had these factors modified
earlier patterns?

The introductory chapter discusses the salient features of the Piscataqua environment and the earliest settlements between the Merrimack
and Piscataqua Rivers, analyzing the adjustment by the first inhabitants
of these towns to frontier realities. Part II is concerned with the colonists' early problems and achievements as they sought to fulfill the
promise of the land and its resources. It analyzes the methods of land
distribution and timber utilization among the towns, the dangers posed
by the Masonian proprietary controversy and the French and Indian
wars, and the impact of the Massachusetts-New Hampshire boundary
dispute and of land speculation upon land usage.

Part III details developments in trade and commerce, particularly the
extensive economic expansion that occurred during the early eighteenth
century. It discusses the settlers' responses to the internal threats of
capital scarcity, labor shortages, an inadequate medium of exchange,
inflation, and indebtedness and to the external threats posed by wars,
the Navigation Acts, English mercantile competition, and economic
competition from Massachusetts merchants. Included are analyses of
the permanent economic interests of the colony and of its import and
export trading patterns in the seventeenth and eighteenth centuries
(based upon the manuscript Piscataqua Shipping Returns).

Part IV analyzes the transformation of the four Piscataqua villages
into a relatively mature provincial society. Preoccupied with a search for
social order and stability, the settlers at first used the church, the family,
the town meeting, and the law within the context of an intimate community setting—the town—to perpetuate cherished values. But by the
1690's the towns as units of social organization were no longer able to
resolve effectively the divisive problems and conflicting values among
the inhabitants. Consequently, during the early eighteenth century the
provincial government supplanted the town as the more important
sociopolitical institution, and its leaders developed a more complex
system of values capable of solving the problems disrupting New Hampshire's expanding society. The expansion of overseas trade, the impact
of the war era from 1689 to 1713, the creation of new towns and parishes,
and the presence of royal government in the colony all worked to promote these social changes. As this final section also reveals, the New
Hampshire social order gradually was changing from a relatively cohesive system of social arrangements and values toward an order based
upon social, economic, and religious individualism. Throughout most of

New Hampshire's early history and even into the 1740's, economic and social opportunities continued to abound, and avenues to the very top of its political, economic, and social structure remained open.

Because I believe that historical explanation, at its best, can be as accurate as a working hypothesis in the sciences, I have included most of the evidence which shaped my conclusions in the body of my explanations and notes; colleagues can thus more easily find whatever errors exist in my samples of evidence and in my logical connections between evidence and conclusions. It may be that this inclusion excessively clutters my explanations at times, but I see it as an important aspect of historical methodology. In transcribing materials from manuscripts and printed sources, I have retained original spellings. Original punctuation has been altered only when necessary for clarity. Superscript letters have been brought down to the line. Paper currency designations refer to local New Hampshire paper unless otherwise labeled.

The use of dates in this study requires some explanation. England did not begin using the Gregorian calendar until 1752. During the seventeenth century it used the Julian calendar, in which the new year began on Lady Day (or the Feast of Annunciation), which occurred on March 25. Hence, in this study any date between January 1 and March 24 will be given with the Julian calendar year followed by the Gregorian calendar year, such as February 1640/41.

In publishing this study, a revision of my dissertation, I wish to acknowledge with deep appreciation the invaluable guidance I received from Jack Greene, who excited my interest in colonial history very early in my graduate career and who perceptively supervised the development of the original dissertation. I appreciate, too, the many excellent comments of Edward M. Cook, Jr., and of Jackson K. Putnam, who read the manuscript in an early stage of revision.

My gratitude also goes to a number of librarians, particularly the personnel at the Massachusetts Historical Society, New Hampshire State Library, New Hampshire Historical Society, Western Reserve Historical Society, and Western Reserve University Library. I am especially grateful to Miss Dorothy Vaughan at the Portsmouth Public Library and Mr. Daniel Griffin at the New Hampshire Historical Society, who graciously allowed me to photograph a variety of manuscripts in their library collections. I appreciate the assistance of Professor Robert C. Calhoon, who helped me obtain valuable source material from the British Public Record Office in London. John B. Buzas provided indispensable aid in constructing maps and technical assistance in the design of the tables. I also wish to acknowledge the photographic laboratory at California

State University, Fullerton, for the use of its facilities. My thanks go to Ann Fensler, who helped type the manuscript, and to the readers and editorial staff at the Johns Hopkins University Press for their valuable recommendations and encouragement.

A final note of gratitude is extended to my wife, Elaine, for her suggestions and forbearance, and to my daughter, Laura, for proofreading.

PART I

BEGINNINGS

CHAPTER I

A FRONTIER FOR ENGLAND AND MASSACHUSETTS BAY COLONY

The Piscataqua Environment

Between 1623 and 1641 immigrants from England and Massachusetts Bay Colony established four small settlements along a sixteen-mile strip of the northern New England coastline. This strip extended southward from the Piscataqua River to an imaginary line three miles north of the Merrimack River, the northern boundary of Massachusetts. These small towns—Dover, Strawbery Banke, Exeter, and Hampton—were the nucleus of what became in 1679 the royal province of New Hampshire.[1]

Until 1740, the bounds of this frontier province constituted that part of New England "lying and extending itselfe from three Miles Northward of Merrimack River or any part thereof unto the Province of Maine with the South part of the Isles of Shoals."[2] Throughout the early colonial period, New Hampshire's western boundary was generally considered as following the meandering course of the Merrimack River, west for forty miles, then north and northeast for sixty miles to its source near Lake Winnipesaukee. The entire area of New Hampshire thus amounted to no more than some 2,400 square miles.[3] But in 1740 a Privy Council decision clarified this vague phrasing so favorably to New Hampshire that it ushered in a new era for the colony.[4]

Impressed by the abundant fishing resources of upper New England, the earliest English visitors to the New Hampshire region had stressed the importance of the Piscataqua River, the Isles of Shoals, and the Maine coast.[5] The Isles of Shoals, four miles off the New Hampshire and Maine coast, though rock-strewn and barren, provided the necessary warm and sunny weather for drying and curing haddock and codfish. Unlike Newfoundland, they provided a year-round fishing season.[6] The Piscataqua River, with its freshwater source and saltwater mouth, teemed with a great variety of fish. In 1708 George Vaughan, a New Hampshire fish merchant, listed twenty-six varieties, including cod, haddock, perch, flounder, sturgeon, herring, salmon, alewife, pike, trout, bass, and shellfish such as crabs, cockles, and oysters.[7]

Furthermore, the Piscataqua River was but the end product of a complex and beneficent river system. Originating in a "pond" northeast of present-day Wakefield, forty miles from the coast and flowing southeastward, the Salmon Falls River, known below the falls as the Newichewannock River, combined with the Cochecho River at Dover and a western branch (formed from the waters of the Winnicot, Exeter, Lamprey, Oyster, and Back Rivers and of two inland tidal bays—Great Bay and Little Bay) at Dover Neck to form, for the last seven miles to the Atlantic, the Piscataqua River. From Dover Neck seaward, the Piscataqua's rapid currents, adequate depth, and tidal waters insured year-round navigation; and with the tide rising into all these bays and rivers as far as the lower falls of each river, there existed the means for a unified communication and transportation system, favorable to trade and commerce.[8] These elements plus an excellent harbor[9] and such abundant fur-bearing animals as beaver and marten attracted Ferdinando Gorges, Captain John Smith, Captain John Mason, David Thomson, and Edward Hilton to the Piscataqua region before 1630.[10]

At first these earliest colonizers, preoccupied with fish and furs, paid little attention to other qualities of the area. They failed to grasp the economic significance of the dense and silent forests they encountered —large stands of white, yellow, and pitch pine; black, red, and yellow oak; spruce; cedar; maple; white and black ash; plus a variety of others. Nor did they immediately attend to the agricultural possibilities.[11] Perhaps the rather forbidding coastline—a combination of rocks, sand, tidal creeks, small coves, and marshlands—coupled with dense, boulder-strewn forests reinforced their original trading intentions; yet from the 1640's onward New Hampshire was destined to be primarily a province of small farmers.

During the next one hundred years settlement generally followed the geographic face of the region. Beyond the coastal area of marshland, low hills, and plains were upland ridges and rough hills which were inimical to easy tillage.[12] Once cleared, the richest lands—meadows along the banks of rivers—could support grain crops, while the low, widespreading hills might serve as pasture land for cattle, sheep, and goats. Even the unsightly marshlands performed valuable functions by providing rich supplies of food for wildlife and "salt hay" for animal fodder.[13] That the obstacles faced by the farmer in cultivating the land were legion is attested in part by the slow progress of colonization westward. Abundant trees and rocks, a relatively cold climate, and a short growing season played their part in limiting the settlers' advance to only about thirty miles inland in a hundred years.

Creation of Four Communities

Between 1623 and 1641 Englishmen of varied and diverse backgrounds entered this environment.[14] Two main sources—the Council for New England of Plymouth, England, and Puritan Massachusetts Bay Colony—provided the stimulus and the settlers in this colonizing process.

The Council for New England, organized in 1619 by Ferdinando Gorges in Devonshire, sought the establishment of feudal principates in New England. Obtaining title to the lands between the fortieth and forty-eighth parallels, its forty gentleman patentees, using the lure of monopoly rights to trade and fish, hoped for an avid West Country merchant participation that would provide the main financial support necessary for colonization. When this source of capital failed, the council began granting lands to various groups and individuals, including Gorges, Mason, David Thomson, and Edward Hilton. Ultimately, in 1635, because of merchant dissatisfaction with the meager profits of colony planting, the council portioned out all its land assets to privileged individuals and dissolved.[15] Two permanent settlements in New Hampshire developed from these grants: Dover and Strawbery Banke.[16]

Dover owes its origin to a patent given a London fishmonger, Edward Hilton. He received an informal grant from the council and between 1623 and 1628 established a small colony at Dover Neck, seven miles up the Piscataqua.[17] In March 1629/30 the council formalized his patent by granting him "all that part of the river Piscataquack called or known by the name of Hilton's Point with the south side of the said River, up to the fall of the River, and three miles into the Maine Land by all the breadth aforesaid."[18] By that time Hilton and his settlers, at their own cost, had transported cattle, built some houses, planted corn, and were engaged in fishing, possibly in conjunction with West Country fishermen on the Isles of Shoals.[19]

Meanwhile, in 1629, Captain Mason, Gorges, and seven London merchants, desirous of tapping what they hoped would be a rich fur trade near Lake Champlain and Lake Ontario, received some indefinite grants of land near Lake Champlain and a provision that they could choose 1,000 acres of any ungranted lands convenient for their plans.[20] This group, the Laconia Company, believed that the lakes could be reached by sailing up some of the New England rivers. Their agents chose the Piscataqua as their base of operations, establishing themselves on the site of David Thomson's improved lands at Little Harbor. From here these agents, led by Governor Walter Neale, established two small settlements and trading posts—one at Strawbery Banke south of the Piscataqua and the other at Newichewannock Falls on the north side of the Piscataqua opposite Hilton's patent[21]—and began exploring the river's upper reaches for a water passage to the lakes. By 1631, these forty or so "servants," realistically appraising their environment, had built a saltworks and "Great House" and had turned to fishing, wine-making, lumbering, and farming. In November 1631, the Laconia Company secured a patent to the lands in its possession on the Piscataqua and also rights to the Isles of Shoals and fishing "thereabouts."[22] Even the merchants had altered their original plans and now thought in terms of establishing "a great Nursery for Shipping and Mariners."[23]

Yet, by December of 1633 the merchants had become so discouraged by the small returns, the failure to find an outlet to the lakes, and the failure of a fishing voyage that they recalled Neale to England and began withdrawing from the enterprise.[24] In 1634 Mason and Gorges bought out the shares of those who withdrew and divided the lands northeast of the Piscataqua River (in Maine) between themselves, leaving the lands lying southwest of the Piscataqua in the "common and undivided ownership" of the company.[25] The company's servants were discharged, but Mason enthusiastically sent over some carpenters and others who built two new sawmills to serve as a base for a lumber trade.[26] With the Council for New England collapsing under royal attack, Mason and Gorges devised plans in early 1635 to divide all the lands under council control into provinces and to surrender the charter to the king, persuade him to confirm these grants, and have him appoint a general governor for the whole territory. Consequently, in April 1635 Mason obtained a grant from the council encompassing all his earlier grants. This grant was called "Newhampshire."[27] But Mason died later that year before the Crown could confirm his grant, and nothing more was done either toward its confirmation or for the stranded settlers.[28]

Thus, the settlements south of the Piscataqua remained undivided among the Laconia proprietors, who abandoned the Strawbery Banke settlement after Mason's death because they were themselves on the brink of bankruptcy.[29] Dissolution of the council and bankruptcy of the Laconia Company left both Strawbery Banke and the Hilton patentees at Dover without legitimate authority and, in fact, almost completely autonomous.[30]

Unlike Dover and Strawbery Banke, the town of Exeter, established in 1638, had primarily religious origins. Its founder, the Reverend John Wheelwright, brother-in-law of Anne Hutchinson, arrived in Boston from England in June 1636 with a reputation as an able preacher and

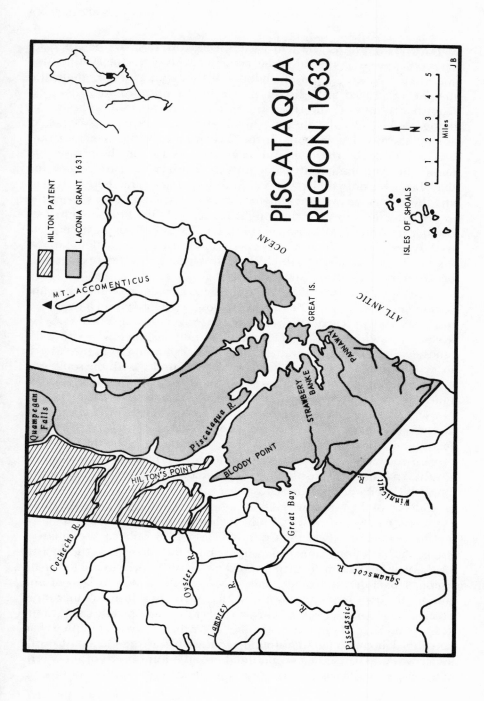

PISCATAQUA
REGION 1633

HILTON PATENT

LACONIA GRANT 1631

MT. ACCOMENTICUS

OCEAN

ATLANTIC

ISLES OF SHOALS

Miles
0 1 2 3 4 5

N

GREAT IS.

PANNANAY

STRAWBERY BANKE

BLOODY POINT

Piscataqua R.

Quampegan Falls

HILTON'S POINT

Cochecho R.

Oyster R.

Lamprey R.

Great Bay

Winnicutt R.

Squamscot R.

Piscassic R.

JB

some renown because he had been silenced in 1632 by the Anglican bishops. Almost immediately he became involved in the Antinomian controversy. Mrs. Hutchinson endorsed his preaching and recommended that he be elected an assistant pastor in the Boston church, but ex-Governor Winthrop succeeded in defeating this attempt, although by doing so he split the Boston church further. Seeking reconciliation among the warring factions in the Boston church, the General Court declared a fast in 1637; but Wheelwright seized upon the occasion to launch an Antinomian attack against the Puritan ministry, suggesting that they were only under a covenant of works and "the more holy they are, the greater enemies they are to Christ."[31] After Winthrop's reelection as governor in May 1637, he sought to reconcile the Boston church by ridding it of the Hutchinson faction. He had Wheelwright brought to trial for sedition in October. Wheelwright refused any retraction, protesting his innocence, and was finally banished from the colony in November on grounds of contempt and sedition.[32]

In the spring of 1638, Wheelwright led his friends and followers, some twenty families, into the Piscataqua region, where they purchased lands from an Indian chief, Wehanownowit, Sagamore of Piscataquacke. Wehanownowit was given the right to "hunt, fish, and fowl" within the lands deeded. He in turn granted them lands extending from the "Merrimack River to the Patents of Piscataquacke, bounded with the south east of Piscataquacke patents and so to go into the country northwest thirty miles so far as the east line."[33] This grant directly conflicted with the Massachusetts charter but not with the patents granted to Dover or to the Laconia Company. By the summer of 1639 there were at least thirty-five men living in Exeter by the "Falls of the Pascataquack" on the Exeter (or Squamscot) River. Their newly formed civil compact acknowledged loyalty and authority to the king but "according to the libertys of our English Colony of the Massachusetts."[34]

The last of the four towns, Hampton, was established under the direct supervision of Massachusetts. Probably because of the valuable salt marsh in the region, the General Court in early 1636 ordered a plantation established at Winnacunnet and a house built there to serve as the nucleus of the new settlement. It then granted a township there to the Reverend Stephen Bachiler and others and appointed three men to lay out and apportion town lands among the settlers.[35] In June 1639, Winnacunnet received town privileges,[36] and in September the townspeople changed the town name to Hampton.[37] Unlike the other towns, Hampton had undefined bounds, but the Bound House built at the General Court's order was one-half mile beyond the three-mile limit north of the Merrimack River, while most of Hampton was situated even farther northward.

The settlement of Hampton by Puritan churchmen represented a clear attempt on the part of Massachusetts to enlarge its sphere of influence.[38]

Thus, by 1640, there were four separate and unrelated settlements in New Hampshire, each originating from England or Massachusetts.[39] All faced a generally similar frontier environment but reacted to it according to their own needs and interests as they interpreted them. An examination of the peculiar needs and points of view of each, as well as of the general characteristics of this frontier environment, reveals the main elements of historical change in New Hampshire society during the first stages of settlement.

Adjustments to Frontier Realities

Strawbery Banke's earliest settlers came directly from southern and western England, seeking profits from fish and furs and bringing royalist political attitudes and Anglican religious beliefs incompatible with those of their Massachusetts neighbors.[40] From their first arrival, however, they were preoccupied with obtaining food. Of necessity, they turned to agriculture.[41] Nor were the Laconia Company's dreams realized in the Piscataqua environment, as their factor at Piscataqua, Ambrose Gibbons, did not hesitate to inform them:

You complain of your returnes; you take the coorse to have little. A plantation must be furnished with cattle and good hire-hands, and necessaries for them, and not thinke the great lookes of men and many words will be means to raise a plantation. Those that have bin heare this three years, som of them have nether meat, money nor cloathes—a great disparagement. I shall not need to speak of this; you shal heare of it by others. For myself, my wife and child and 4 men, we have but ½ a bb. of corne; beefe and porke I have not had. . . . I nor the servants had nether mony nor clothes. I have bin as spare as I could, but it will not doe. . . . You may, perhaps, thinke that fewer men would serve me; but I have sometimes on C [100] or more Indians, and far from neybers. These that I have I can set to pale in ground for corne and garden. I have diged a well within the palizado, where is good water. . . . More men I could have, and more imploy, but I rest thus until I heare from you. The vines that were planted will come to little.[42]

And a year later:

Your Wor'shp have donne well in setting forward your Plantacon, and for your milles they will prove beneficial unto you, by God's assistance. I would you had taken this coorse sooner. . . . I perceive you have a great mynd for the lakes and I as great a will to assist you, if I had 2 horses and 3 men wth me, I would by God's helpe soone resolve you of the cituation of it, but to live there myself. . . . I have paled in a piece of ground and planted it. . . . I hope there will be 8 or 10 quarters of corne. . . . If you did send a shippe for the Western Islands of 6 score tunne or thereabouts for cowes and goats, it would be profitable for you. A stock of iron worke to put away wth boardes from the mill will be good.[43]

The servants never had remarkable success with the fur trade: planting corn and raising cattle took much of their time. But they found time for fishing, wine-making, lumbering, and setting up an ironworks.[44] Edward Godfrey at Little Harbor had charge of the fisheries and by 1632 owned six large shallops, five fishing boats, and thirteen skiffs.[45] As the above letters show, Gibbons carried on a fur trade with more than one hundred Indians, but so few profits were available without further investments in servants' wages that both he and the company became discouraged.[46]

Mason's death and the collapse of the Laconia Company by 1636 left its agents at the mercy of their wage-hungry servants. By 1638 Gibbons and others had acquiesced in the division of Strawbery Banke among its inhabitants, who then established a civil government under an elected governor, Francis Williams, and an Anglican church under Richard Gibson's ministry.[47] As a consequence of these events, the Strawbery Banke settlers, holding their land without legal authority, lived in fear of outside interference in their local affairs from several sources—the Crown, proprietors, or Massachusetts.

Hampton's settlers, mainly East Anglian Puritan farmers under the direct jurisdiction of Massachusetts, stood in stark contrast to those of Strawbery Banke.[48] Migrating first to Massachusetts, and supported by the General Court, they looked to that body to assert its jurisdiction in the Piscataqua region in order to thwart attempts by both Exeter and Strawbery Banke to challenge Hampton's land titles.[49] The General Court's approach in this controversy with Exeter (which claimed its lands by right of purchase from the Indians) emphasized that Indians had "a natural right" only to lands they improved, "so the rest of the country lay open to any that could and would improve it," and thus claimed the disputed lands "as within our patent, or as vacuum domicilium."[50] When Exeter stubbornly refused to accept such arguments, the court sent explorers up the Merrimack River, found that it ran north as well as west of Exeter's bounds, and notified Exeter "that though we would not relinquish our interest by priority of possession for any right they could have from the Indians, yet seeing they had professed not to claim any thing which should fall within our patent, we should look no farther than that in respect of their claim."[51] The General Court here implied for the first time that Massachusetts' bounds encompassed not only the land three miles north of the Merrimack, but any area between the Merrimack's source in the back country and the Atlantic coast. This assertion forced Exeter to acquiesce in Hampton's land claims through fear that Massachusetts might carry out its veiled threat and assume jurisdiction over Exeter lands as well. Undoubtedly, the same considerations stopped challenges from Strawbery Banke claimants. Hampton stood alone among the four towns in its enthusiastic support of the power of Massachusetts in the Piscataqua region.

The town of Hampton also differed in more subtle ways. Existing under Massachusetts' jurisdiction gave it a sense of religious and political stability, a unity of purpose, a feeling of security unmatched in the other towns. It enjoyed the advantages of authorized political, judicial, and religious institutions as well as the knowledge that its civil and religious salubrity was a concrete concern of the General Court.[52] Its people did not experience the painful adjustments in economic purpose that slowed the progress of Dover and Strawbery Banke; they settled quickly along the Hampton River and utilized the fertile salt marsh and meadow lands for raising cattle, Indian corn, wheat, and rye.[53] From the first, the town impressed visitors as a prosperous and growing community.[54]

Exeter had its own special niche. Like Hampton, its settlers were East Anglian farmers; the majority—including William Wentworth, founder of a dynasty of New Hampshire commercial and political leaders—were from Lincolnshire. But their Antinomian religious beliefs differentiated them from the majority of Bay Colony Puritans. They found themselves not only in religious disagreement with Massachusetts Puritans and Strawbery Banke and Dover Anglicans but also in economic controversies with Massachusetts and the other three towns. The settlers had established themselves on the Exeter River as an agricultural community raising cattle, swine, and Indian corn. To such a community adequate meadows were a necessity, though few were present. Naturally enough, they began seizing meadows (in direct competition with the other three towns) and improving them wherever they could be found. Because of the support of Massachusetts, Hampton had little trouble warding off such encroachments, so that after 1639 Exeter engaged in a competitive scramble for meadow lands with Dover and Strawbery Banke. The town's isolated religious and political position placed it at a decided disadvantage in this situation.[55]

That still other problems were inherent in Exeter's isolation was indicated by its attempts to form a civil compact in 1639. There was no problem in establishing the form of government, but sharp disagreement arose over how much emphasis to give "that due Allegiance which we owe to his Highnesse" the king. After rejecting two different civil compacts in less than ten months, a majority finally agreed in May 1640 that they were subjects of Charles I with all "the liberties" of Massachusetts and bound to obey the "godly and christian laws" of England and such laws "according to God" enacted among themselves.[56] Exeter, like Strawbery Banke, feared outside interference from any source.

Dover's situation, more complex than the others, made it the center of controversy in the 1630's. Originally settled by West Country fishermen interested primarily in trade, Dover had become by 1630 an agricultural community planting corn and raising cattle.[57] But Dover Point had a sandy surface, and the settlers needed meadows. They soon began ferrying their animals across the river to the fresh and salt meadows at Bloody Point. By 1632, they had taken possession of the nearby meadows and forests and had built houses on this upper part of the newly issued Laconia Company patent.[58] One of these squatters, Captain Thomas Wiggin, had personal connections with Governor John Winthrop of Massachusetts and was a Puritan himself. In October 1631, after a murder in Maine, Wiggin had written Winthrop suggesting that Massachusetts should extend its law over the whole upper New England region; but Winthrop "thought best to sit awhile."[59] The following spring, news spread about the Laconia grant; Governor Neale appeared on Bloody Point and proclaimed the Laconia Company's jurisdiction. Neale and Captain Wiggin had a heated argument there, but both retired without resorting to swords.[60]

Shortly afterwards, Wiggin returned to England resolved, with the help of Massachusetts authorities, to place the Hilton patent into the hands of "honest men" friendly to Puritan Massachusetts. At Winthrop's urging,[61] Lord Say, Lord Brook, and others purchased the Hilton Patent from the Bristol merchants and sent Wiggin back with a group of Puritan settlers as governor and manager of the new company. On his arrival Wiggin again offered Winthrop and Massachusetts jurisdiction over crimes committed on the Piscataqua; but Winthrop again, after significant hesitation, refused.[62] Wiggin's new settlers soon aroused the hostility of Edward Hilton and most of the earlier Dover settlers. Many of this latter group now moved permanently across the river to Bloody Point and southeastward, squatting on lands included in the Laconia Patent.[63] Thus, the Dover settlers, controlled by new patentees, divided into two camps, roughly along Anglican-Puritan lines; yet both factions infringed on the nearby Laconia grant and elsewhere when valuable lands beckoned.[64]

One of the main points of dispute between these two groups was whether or not Massachusetts should assume jurisdiction over the Piscataqua. This conflict had important economic undertones. From the point of view of Wiggin and the Puritan patentees, Massachusetts promised to be a potent ally, especially in their project to deprive the original settlers of some choice territory. Even more pronounced economic motives inhered in the "Anglican" position. Many Anglicans were settled on lands for which they had no title; but because none of the patentees of the Council for New England had any governmental or jurisdictional rights, squatter rights could not be challenged, for no legal courts could exist to hear such cases. If Massachusetts extended its jurisdiction over the entire region, the Bay Colony courts could hear such cases; then Dover squatters might lose lands to either the new patentees or Massachusetts, and the land distribution at Strawbery Banke might be overturned.[65]

Into this volatile situation came the disquieting news from England that John Mason had died, the Laconia Company and the Council for New England were dissolving, and religious conflicts were intensifying. As anxiety and uncertainties increased, Dover, divided against itself, exploded. The patentee's governor, Wiggin, was overthrown; and by 1638, an Anglican minister, George Burdett, had replaced him.[66] The next year the people of Dover chose a Puritan hostile to Massachusetts, Captain John Underhill.[67] Then, in 1640, new political changes took place when a rumor spread that Underhill was negotiating with Massachusetts to bring the Piscataqua under its jurisdiction. The situation was apparently so dangerous that Governor Francis Williams at Strawbery Banke felt compelled to enter the fray, insuring a temporary victory for the anti-Massachusetts groups.[68] Thus, the complexities of the Dover situation coupled with Massachusetts interest in the Piscataqua and royal preoccupation elsewhere had brought Dover to the brink of anarchy.

Seeking compromise and stability, some of the inhabitants signed a civil compact known as the Dover Combination in the summer of 1640. In this document they pledged their loyalty to the laws of England "together with all such orders as shall be concluded by a major part of the freemen of our Society."[69] Earlier in March or April, most of the signers had written a letter to the governor of Massachusetts, Thomas Dudley, repudiating Underhill, and holding out hope for the future:

Truth it is we do very well approve of your judicious ways, and shall be very joyful, you please God to enlarge us, that we may be free from other engagements and promises which some of us are obliged in to the owners or patentees, from whom under his Majesty's Letters Patents we enjoy our free liberty, which causeth us not for present to submit to any other government than that which we have already entered into combination to observe according to the King's Majesty's laws, *until such time as the owners come over to us, which we suppose will be about three months hence,* and then our propositions considered as the Lord shall direct us, we will labor more to satisfy you.[70]

Three elements in this merit special attention: their desire for stability and order ("your judicious ways"); their desire for more land ("you please God to enlarge us"); and, as the final twist to an already perplexing situation, their request that they be released from their promises to the

Puritan patentees who had financed their way to Dover with Captain Wiggin.

At this point the Massachusetts leaders felt that the time was ripe for negotiating. They sent three men to the Piscataqua to reconcile differences and to obtain consent from the leading men in the towns for an extension of Massachusetts' jurisdiction over the Piscataqua River. The continuing preoccupation of the king with domestic matters and news of the impasse between king and Parliament indicated to Massachusetts leaders that there probably would be no royal interference with this extension, but they proceeded cautiously. They purchased part of the Hilton patent from the English Puritan patentees and obtained an absolute conveyance of jurisdiction from them over the entire Hilton grant.[71] This grant, as originally intended, comprised only the upper Piscataqua. Massachusetts then read a new meaning into this patent by interpreting the words "the ryver Pascataquack" in such a way as to include Strawbery Banke within its bounds.[72] Still unsatisfied with the strength of this claim, the General Court hesitated until October 1641. Then, instead of asserting jurisdiction on the basis of either the Hilton patent or the consent of the inhabitants, it revived the approach used successfully against Exeter in 1639 and based its claim on the Massachusetts Charter: "Whereas it appeareth that by the extent of the line (according to our patent) that the ryver of Pascataquack is within the jurisdiction of the Massachusetts and conference being had (at several times) with the said people and some deputed by the General Court for the settleing and establishing of order in the administration of justice there. It is now ordered . . . with the consent of the inhabitants of the said ryver . . . that from henceforth the said people inhabiting there are and shall be accepted and reputed under the government of the Massachusetts."[73] The General Court clarified this vague phrasing later: "Our patent, according to the express terms therein contained without any ambiguity or color of other interpretation, lies between two east and west parallel lines drawn from the most southernly part of Charles River and the most northerly part of Merrimack, with three miles advantage upon each. . . . All those eastern plantations . . . are comprehended within our northerly line."[74] In other words, the northern boundary extended to a line three miles north of the source of the Merrimack River, Lake Winnipesaukee, encompassing all the settled areas of Maine and New Hampshire.

Why did the Piscataqua inhabitants acquiesce in this extension of Massachusetts' jurisdiction? They did so in part because Massachusetts offered them stability and security without destroying the local status quo and interests, and in part because they had no satisfactory alternative. Massachusetts smoothed the way by promising them the continuance of all "liberties of fishing, planting, felling timber as formerly enjoyed in the said river." It promised them exemption from all taxation, except for charges particularly beneficial to themselves, and extended its judicial system to the Piscataqua. By appointing Anglicans Edward Hilton and Francis Williams to the new court with the other four Puritans and by permitting local nomination of associates and assistants, Massachusetts insured that many shades of opinion would be represented. It also recognized to some extent the existing town combinations by allowing those holding office under them to remain in authority for the moment. The court also extended to the Piscataqua inhabitants the right to send two deputies to the General Court; and when the question arose concerning the qualifications for suffrage, it ordered "that all the present inhabitants of Pascataquack, who formerly were free there shall have liberty of freemen in their several towns to manage all their town affairs and shall each town send a deputy to the General Court though they be not at present Church members."[75] Besides these liberal concessions, the court exempted Edward Hilton's estate from any taxation[76] and evidently gave informal promises that it would protect the Piscataqua settlers, Anglican and Puritan alike, from the Hilton patent claimants.[77] By 1643, the Bloody Point area plus 400 acres of nearby uplands had been added to Dover's bounds, an ample reward for its acceptance of Massachusetts' jurisdiction.[78] Yet even with these varied concessions Strawbery Banke's inhabitants very reluctantly accepted the inevitable, remaining unfriendly to Massachusetts.[79]

Exeter, too, undoubtedly preferred to ignore Massachusetts' new jurisdiction, and actually did so for two years. By 1643, however, both Dover and Hampton had benefited in meadowlands at Exeter's expense, while the Hilton patentees, thwarted by Massachusetts' protection of Dover and Strawbery Banke, now sought land within Exeter bounds. In early 1643 Exeter sent a petition which the General Court spurned because Exeter did not show enough respect to Massachusetts' charter claims.[80] In May, Exeter's inhabitants humbly accepted their fate and petitioned again, asking that its bounds be settled, as "we shall not be able to subsist to be a Town except this honored Court be pleased to relieve us," and asking for three commissioners "to put an issue to small differences amongst us."[81] In September the General Court received them into its jurisdiction under approximately the same terms as the others; however, it did not grant Exeter the privilege of sending a deputy to the General Court.[82]

By 1643, all the towns destined to be part of New Hampshire had come under the political jurisdiction of Massachusetts but not entirely under its influence.[83] Two of these towns were already over ten years old, while the other two were slightly under five. Despite differences in attitudes, the settlers in each of them had reacted similarly to the general features of the Piscataqua frontier.

The most important characteristic of this frontier was its abundant economic opportunity. Land, lumber, fish, and furs—these resources promised opportunities for profit. But at this early stage of settlement, when survival was the primary concern, the land loomed as most important. Thus, the dominant economic drive among the settlers of the 1630's was a constant search for meadows, marsh, and planting lands; and agricultural pursuits—raising cattle and corn—absorbed most of their energies. Even the very few who had other concerns also plowed and planted: Ambrose Gibbons, the Laconia Company's fur-trading agent, is a prime example. Through 1641, then, the New Hampshire frontier supported an undifferentiated agricultural society. Its lumber, furs, and fish were yet to be profitably exploited by its settlers. Those who did attempt specialization in these areas faced other discouraging economic problems—a lack of fluid capital and a high cost of labor. The Laconia Company's experience illuminates these problems.

Another feature characterizing New Hampshire, less important in this period, was its Indian population. Thousands of Indians roamed the forests of the Piscataqua region, most of them indifferent and peaceful, some friendly and helpful. Several Algonquian tribes lived near Lake Winnipesaukee and at least two near the Piscataqua—one at Newiche-wannock Falls, another at Squamscot Falls on the Exeter River—where they hunted, fished, and planted.[84] Both Strawbery Banke and Exeter had friendly contacts with the Indians, exchanging clothing, blankets, corn, and tools for meat and furs.[85] Not until the 1670's, as settlements expanded and encroached upon Indian hunting lands, did warring Indians significantly influence the directions of New Hampshire frontier development.

Economic opportunity and Indians were present to some extent in all the English frontier colonies at this time, but the Piscataqua region undoubtedly had far more than its share of another common feature of frontiers—lawlessness—primarily because the region lacked both legal governments and courts. Little evidence has survived concerning brutality, immorality, and drunkenness in this period, though the court records after 1643 are full of such problems.[86] But the evidence clearly shows that land grabbing was practiced by all the towns and, for that matter, by Massachusetts, which justified such practices through a philosophy that the land "lay open to any that could or would improve it."[87] This lack of law and order not only encouraged such activities by the inhabitants but openly invited unscrupulous adventurers into the region, especially to Dover and Strawbery Banke. In 1632, Strawbery Banke's Walter Neale appealed to Governor Winthrop for military aid against sixteen pirates along the Piscataqua.[88]

By the late 1630's Dover, Strawbery Banke, and Exeter's inhabitants had reacted to such conditions by establishing civil compacts. But when such compacts provided neither impartial judges in cases concerning property controversies nor adequate enforcement techniques, all three towns acquiesced in accepting the stability of the Massachusetts judicial system. Massachusetts justified its purchase of the Hilton patent in terms referring to these conditions on the Piscataqua: "And . . . also the inhabitants residing at present within the limits of both the said grants have of late and formerly complained of the want of some good government amongst them and desired some help in this particular from the jurisdiction of the Massachusetts Bay, whereby they may be ruled and ordered according unto God both in church and commonweal, and for the avoiding such insufferable disorders whereby God hath been much dishonored amongst them."[89] In such an environment of conflicting values and interests, security and order had emerged as paramount values among the settlers.

From 1641 until 1679 the New Hampshire colonists benefited so greatly from their connection with the Massachusetts judicial system that they showed great reluctance to abandon it when the crown converted them into a royal province. Forced to rely upon their own initiative, they reenacted most of the Massachusetts judicial system in their continuing search for order and stability after 1679.[90]

The changing attitudes of powerful and interested outsiders toward the valuable Piscataqua region constituted a final continuing frontier reality for the inhabitants of the four New Hampshire towns. The two most potent outsiders with whom they dealt in their first hundred years were Massachusetts Bay Colony and England.[91] The push and pull between these two powers fundamentally influenced New Hampshire political, social, and economic practices throughout the colonial period. Taken under Massachusetts' authority in 1641 because of royal preoccupation elsewhere, the New Hampshire towns remained in this status until 1679, when, once again against the wills of most of the inhabitants, they were torn from Massachusetts by the Crown and made into a royal province through the influence of anti-Puritan English merchants, Crown officials, and interested land speculators at the royal court. After 1679, the people of New Hampshire moved slowly and gradually away from dependence upon Massachusetts' authority toward dependence upon the mother country's authority in economic and political affairs. They never totally escaped the influence of either until the American Revolution. Under these continuing influences, then, the New Hampshire colonists sought their own political, economic, and social identity.

By 1641, the fewer than nine hundred settlers in the Piscataqua region had only begun to tap the abundant opportunities available to them.[92] With external stability relatively assured, they could begin in earnest to put into practice the values of each community. They faced the future expectantly in their quest for economic prosperity and social stability.

PART II

THE PROMISE OF THE LAND

CHAPTER II

THE PROMISE OF THE LAND: UTILIZATION OF BASIC RESOURCES

Distribution of the Land

To the vast majority of the New Hampshire settlers the land, with its attendant resources, constituted the most attractive and readily exploitable commodity in the Piscataqua frontier. Once the issue of lawful authority had been tentatively resolved through the acceptance of the jurisdiction of Massachusetts, the settlers accelerated the distribution of their land. In town meetings they elected selectmen or townsmen, whose primary function was to parcel out land in a manner acceptable to the electorate.[1] The formulas for land distribution differed from town to town according to each community's needs, resources, and values. Nevertheless, the four towns followed a general pattern in their land grants. The earliest years (the dates varying from town to town) saw the original founders obtaining land for themselves and their families and establishing somewhat restrictive rules toward newcomers. This was followed in the 1650's by a relaxation of the rules, as all the towns offered attractive land grants to outsiders in an attempt to recruit new settlers who could help provide local economic growth and security. In the 1660's, however, as available land became scarce in three of the four communities, town land grants to newcomers ended, with the consequence that new settlers henceforth had to purchase their way into each town. A somewhat similar pattern of restriction, relaxation, and restriction occurred in the timber usage policies of the towns. Finally, although there were variations from town to town, the town grants were generally given to individuals according to their economic and social status and their willingness to serve the public in each community.

In their first land division, the Hampton freemen awarded fifteen grants, varying from 80 to 300 acres, to the original founders of the town. The largest grants (300 acres) went to the minister, Stephen Bachiler, and the associate pastor and teacher, Timothy Dalton. The second largest grants (250 acres) were given to the minister's son-in-law and to the town representative to the Massachusetts General Court; the remaining grants were also based upon the wealth, social status, and perceived abilities of each recipient.[2]

Freemanship in Hampton was a highly valued and responsible status. Until 1647, only freemen could hold town offices and vote for town officials. To qualify for freemanship, one had to belong to the church and take an oath of loyalty and service to the commonwealth. The high valuation accorded to freemen can be seen in the fact that in the town's second land grant (1640) fifty-three men who were not freemen (over 75 percent of the male inhabitants) received only 10 acres each for house lots, while Robert Tuck, a new freeman, received 100 acres.[3]

When land was granted for a cow commons in Hampton, however, the criteria changed. After two years of controversy, the freemen in 1645 granted 200 acres of cow commons in 147 shares to fifty-eight people on the basis of individual need and projected actual usage. John Moulton, one of the earlier 250-acre grantees and the fourth richest person in the town in terms of town grants, petitioned the Massachusetts General Court to set this land division aside because it was based neither upon wealth as mirrored by tax rates nor upon the number of children per family.[4] Apparently, the number of cattle an individual possessed, an indication of his agricultural potential, was most important to the freemen who portioned out the cow commons. The ox commons granted in 1649 went to the same people in the same proportions. But as production of cattle for export to Massachusetts became more profitable to the town's economy, ownership in the cow commons emerged as the general basis for all further large land grants in Hampton.[5]

Ownership in the cow commons became more restricted after 1662, when the town required that any individual admitted as a town inhabitant must possess "one share of commonage, at least, according to the first division, and land to build upon."[6] Thus, after 1662, every inhabitant necessarily was a freeholder possessing at least one share of the commons as a stake in the town and as a basis for future land grants. Thereafter, any new inhabitant would generally have to buy his way into the town.[7]

The increasing restrictiveness of land distribution policies in Hampton is illustrated by the establishment of the new township of Kingston, which was granted to people outside the town from the western area of Hampton's commons by the New Hampshire lieutenant governor and council in 1694. This action enraged some of the Hampton community.

King William's war thwarted any settlement of this area for a time, but in 1700 demands for some commons grants at the "new plantation" from the outsiders and some Hampton townspeople brought a quick response from Hampton's leaders. On November 18, 1700, the Hampton freeholders voted that only freeholders "in this town" could attend freeholders' meetings; that only commoners "according to the first grant of shares of the cow commons" could vote in disposing of commons lands; and that the common lands in the "new plantation" should be granted on the basis of holdings of cow commons, with those owning "above one share" receiving two shares, those owning one share receiving one share, and those twenty-one years of age who were born and reared in the town receiving one-half share, "excepting those persons who claim a right in Kingston by virtue of any grant from the Lieutenant Governor and Council." This vote illuminates the conflicts and tensions both within and without the town over land grant policies. On the one hand, Hampton's relatively stringent control over its common lands persuaded some of the land-hungry inhabitants to look outward toward the Crown-favored proprietary claimant for succor; on the other hand, the land at Kingston lay within Hampton's bounds and, from the freeholders' point of view, should have fallen under their authority. They felt it should not have been given to outsiders as had been the case. Thus, Hampton's freeholders sought primarily to protect town rights to unimproved commons from outside jurisdiction and secondarily to receive assurance that the townspeople would be the beneficiaries according to their proportionate cow commonage (a crude measure of economic status) in the community.[8]

Exeter's religiously zealous inhabitants shared many of the same goals with the Hampton settlers but utilized somewhat different means. They adopted a religious government in which the settlers elected three elders who served as magistrates, carried out all executive and judicial functions "according to the righteous will of God," and enacted town orders and laws subject to the inhabitants' consent.[9] In these early years freemanship meant little at Exeter (unlike Hampton), for none of the early elders were freemen. Evidently, though, there were a few freemen; five of them elected military officers for the town in 1641.[10]

But the town gave no favors to freemen in apportioning the valuable meadows, marshes, and uplands. All meadows were divided into four equal parts, with the first three parts apportioned according to the number of cattle owned by each inhabitant and the fourth part divided into equal lots for those who had no cattle; the "upland lots for planting" were given on the basis of the number of persons and cattle in each family; and the marshes were divided among all the inhabitants, with those owning cattle receiving proportionately larger shares.[11] Family size

and herd size—the practical needs and agricultural potential of each
family—guided Exeter's approach to land policy.

Other values also entered into Exeter land policy. When new marsh
lands were found in 1643, the town rewarded individual initiative by
voting that marshes of less than twenty acres belonged to the finder
"forever," but marshlands of twenty acres or more became town property
with the finder receiving a double portion.[12] The inhabitants granted
their minister, John Wheelwright, eighty acres of upland instead of the
normal portion; and when he left Exeter for Maine after Massachusetts
assumed jurisdiction over Exeter, the town conditionally granted him a
large tract of marshland in a vain attempt to woo him back.[13]

With Wheelwright gone and the town in danger of disintegration,
Exeter openly recruited immigrants between 1643 and 1709 by granting
them anywhere from 10 to 100 acres of land after their decision to become
settled inhabitants in the town. The amount of the grant varied with the
financial and social worth of each new settler. More than the other New
Hampshire towns, Exeter used conditional land grants to lure valued
craftsmen and others into the community. The last such grant was given
to John Light, a feltmaker and shopkeeper, in 1705.[14] The town exemplified its strong community cohesiveness by granting the sons of inhabitants at least thirty acres of land within the town when they were ready to
set up for themselves. Exeter's dangerous frontier location and its abundant lands played an important role in its open-handed land policy toward
newcomers.

When it came to granting the common lands or new areas to the town
inhabitants, the principal basis for division was the proportion of tax
each individual paid in support of the minister; this proportion was in
turn based upon his taxable property or "ratable estate."[15] There were,
however, some exceptions to the general practice. In March 1681/82, the
town promised to grant ten acres of "meadow/marsh" to anyone who
would clear that much swampland in areas belonging to no one else.[16]
There were also many special grants to ministers, important town leaders,
lumberers, and any others whom the town thought deserving.[17]

By 1709, Exeter had granted all but "two miles of the west end of the
township" from its seventy-square-mile area. Demands arose for a division of this last commons, but in 1714 the town decided to lay it out as a
"perpetual commonage." Nevertheless, the pressures of the younger
generation and of newcomers seeking their share of the commons finally
brought a distribution of all remaining common lands in 1725, giving
each inhabitant enough land for at least a small farm.[18] Although the
town ordered these grants to be "divided in proportion," the order must
have been loosely interpreted. Each newcomer received 20 acres, sons of

inhabitants received at least 30 acres, and inhabitants received anywhere from 30 to 300 acres, based upon their "ratable estates."

From 1640 to 1725, then, Exeter's settlers gave and sought opportunities with their abundant town lands, utilized them in a comparatively equalitarian fashion, and based their grants upon the individual's social and economic worth to the town. The third, restrictive stage in land grants did not occur in Exeter until after 1725.

The methods utilized by Dover's settlers in parceling out their lands are none too clear. Their earliest extant town records begin in 1647 and include grants from 1642 onward, but in the 1630's Thomas Wiggin had granted lands to his Puritan followers. In addition, some settlers had purchased lands from the Indians, and the original Hilton patentees held land as well. Moreover, the Strawbery Banke settlers claimed the same lands at Bloody Point. These explosive land controversies had moved Dover's settlers toward acceptance of Massachusetts' authority and jurisdiction over the towns. It was no accident that when Massachusetts did assume jurisdiction over the four towns, its agreement dealt primarily with the Dover settlers and rewarded them well with land.[19] In 1643, Dover received the Bloody Point area: "All the marsh and meadow ground lying against the Great Bay on Strawbery Banke side . . . together with 400 acres of upland ground adjoining"—most of the land Dover settlers had sought.[20] Thus, many of the best lands must have been occupied long before the town records speak of any land grants.

The Dover town records do reveal, however, that until 1665 each inhabitant received a grant of upland, marsh, commonage, and a house lot—an attractive recruitment measure. The earliest recorded land division gave twenty-acre lots to twenty-three inhabitants in 1642.[21] In 1648, another division of six acres each went to twenty people, fifteen of whom had not received land from the grant of 1642.[22] In 1652, an ox and cow commons was granted to all the inhabitants of Dover Neck, and by 1661 this commons had been divided equally among the twenty-seven men who lived there.[23] These are the only instances of multiple land grants given in the records; all others were single grants to individuals.

Between 1642 and 1655 the town gave forty-two individual grants ranging from 3 acres to 500 acres. A willingness to serve the community was the value rewarded in these grants, for the largest grants generally went to freemen, lumberers, and church and town leaders. Of the ten people who had received over two hundred acres from the town by 1660, nine were freemen. In the tax list of 1648, largely a reflection of land ownership, out of fifty-seven people taxed, eight of the top twenty, eight of the middle twenty, and two of the bottom seventeen were freemen, revealing the generally well-to-do status of freemen.[24] Dover's freemen had no monopoly on voting or on holding public office; nevertheless, 75 percent of those holding the office of selectman between 1647 and 1656 were freemen, and freemen alone could elect the deputy to the Massachusetts General Court.[25] On the other hand, eight out of the ten people who had amassed more than two hundred acres in town grants by 1660 were also lumberers owning sawmills. In fact, most of the large single grants had been given to these individuals for mill usage, but only after they had become freemen.[26]

Evidences of strong discontent over Dover's land grant practices appeared between 1656 and 1661. In March 1655/56, the town meeting ordered that no new grants be given until the existing ones were laid out and until each inhabitant had received his share of the commonage. The record of this meeting also stated that each inhabitant had received grants of "land, timber, and rivers" and confirmed those grants; it concluded by ordering that no new grant be given after March of the next year without the consent of every inhabitant. But in February, a town meeting ordered that "whereas the town is debarred from making grants of land . . . the Selectmen or such as the town shall depute shall have power to grant land according as occasion shall require."[27] Thus, a shift in power occurred here, as land grants passed from direct to indirect control of the townspeople. At this point the question of suffrage became important. Some freemen contended that under Massachusetts' jurisdiction only they could elect town officers and hold public office. Another question also was at stake. Good land had become scarce: should every inhabitant's permission be required for each new town grant of commons? The selectmen issued at least seventeen grants between 1656 and 1658, but town confirmation of them was postponed from meeting to meeting as these issues intensified.

In December 1658, the selectmen took matters into their own hands and ordered that all ungranted commonage on Bloody Point belonged only to Bloody Point inhabitants and could not be granted without their consent. In March 1658/59, the selectmen extended this principle by giving similar local control over commonage to the settlers of the Dover Neck, Oyster River, and Cochecho areas.[28] Aware of the mounting tension, they also drew up a statement for consideration at the next town meeting: "We propound this to your consideration whether by a unanimous consent we were legally chosen as formerly other townsmen were before us, and that all our legal acts shall be ratified and confirmed, and that you look at us as legal Selectmen for the town of Dover as being for the year 1658. This is voted by the major part of the town to pass for an act."[29] When the townspeople met in June 1659, their first action dealt with the franchise: "Voted that all the inhabitants of this township of Dover that have taken their oath of fidelity have their free vote in choice of their Selectmen and all other officers concerning the town affairs, and that the former act of the choice of Selectmen made the 17th day, 4th month, 1657, in point of time is nullified and of no effect."[30] (Though the town records contain no information about this 1657 meeting of the selectmen, suffrage had evidently been restricted to freemen at that time.) The townsmen then voted out three of the five selectmen as well as the town clerk and ordered the new selectmen to obtain the town books and show them to whomever they wished for correction of any defects before returning them to the new clerk, Deacon John Hall. Finally, the townsmen drew up a more democratic, less restrictive policy of land distribution by voting "that the present Selectmen have power with the *main part* of *all* our inhabitants in *every* of our respective places to grant land as they see fit with the consent of the *major part* of our inhabitants in every of our several respective places."[31] Thus a clique of the earlier inhabitants found themselves thwarted in their attempts to control town policies and restrict future land grants.

The underlying significance of this series of events is not entirely clear from the available evidence. Either the settlers reiterated pre-1657 values or a peaceful revolution occurred. Probably the former took place, as a majority of the townspeople thwarted an attempt by a combination of some pro-Massachusetts settlers (including freemen) and some other settlers to maintain the status quo in town land holdings and gain permanent dominance in town politics and land policies. At any rate the crisis clarified three Dover approaches: relative newcomers and the majority of townspeople desired a more liberal land grant policy, the power to grant lands lay in the hands of the selectmen and the majority of inhabitants, and the ultimate political authority in the town lay with the inhabitants rather than the freemen.

The clique of freemen and older settlers had one last alternative before them. They sought a ruling from the Massachusetts General Court on the question of "whether or not all that have taken the oath of fidelity have liberty to choose."[32] Evidently, news of the suffrage law of 1658—which authorized those who had taken the oath of fidelity, were twenty-four years of age, and owned a £20 ratable estate to vote—quieted the controversy, for nothing more appeared on this issue.

The political and economic decisions of 1659 paved the way for new land grants. For the next six years new grants were so plentiful that in August 1665, the town found it necessary to curtail them, granting only cow commonage to new inhabitants, "the town not being of a capacity to give accommodations as heretofor."[33] After 1665, new settlers would need enough money to purchase their way into the town, while the sons of the first generation who had not received land grants would have to rely upon the extensive grants received by their fathers but not yet surveyed. Henceforth Dover's inhabitants gained land either through inheritance or purchase of pre-1665 grants rather than through distribution of new commonage.

This scarcity of land for newcomers played at least a small part in the gradual decline of Dover's political and economic influence in the Piscataqua region through the colonial period.[34] And it played a decisive part in the Dover land scandal of 1729–31, when the New Hampshire General Assembly found that at least fifty-four land grants had been fraudulently written into the Dover town records between 1694 and 1729.[35]

In the 1640's, the predominantly Anglican settlers of Strawbery Banke paid dearly for their aloof and isolationist attitudes toward Massachusetts as they found themselves deprived of both the relatively good agricultural lands near Bloody Point and any political prominence in the Piscataqua region. But by the early 1650's two new factors which fundamentally changed these attitudes made an appearance: these were the immigration of a number of aggressive, dynamic Puritans into Strawbery Banke and the appearance in 1651 of an English claimant to the land there in the person of Joseph Mason.[36]

Mason's arrival and his immediate commencement of lawsuits against three Maine settlers sparked a spirited revolt against Massachusetts among some of the Strawbery Banke settlers. In October 1651, the Massachusetts General Court received an aggressive, sullen petition spelling out Strawbery Banke's grievances. The petition suggested that since "you [Massachusetts] accepted of the ordering and governing the said petitioners by way of their petition and by stretching of the Line . . . that you would be pleased to give order for the laying out of our township for want of which we deeply suffer." It also demanded that courts be held at Strawbery Banke as well as at Dover and that the town be allowed two magistrates and some assistants. Finally it demanded: "Whereas Mrs. Mason has here an agent who lays claim to some of lands we inhabit, in behalf of Capt. John Mason's heirs; that you would be pleased to maintain the same unto us against any that shall hereafter oppose us, if by stretching of the Line the lands be within your jurisdiction; if not, then to leave both our persons, lands, and all freely to ourselves, as formerly we were before you took us into your Government, to maintain our own rights, or to submit ourselves to those to whom it may appear justly due."[37]

The Massachusetts leaders had not been caught unawares by events at Strawbery Banke, for in August they had written Thomas Wiggin, the leading Massachusetts supporter in the Piscataqua region, that rumors had spread that the Strawbery Banke settlers were about to "set up a new Government . . . contrary to their engagements and oaths." Wiggin was asked to investigate the situation, send them a list of the leaders involved, and send the leaders themselves to the General Court to answer for their

rebellious behavior.[38] Apparently, it was Wiggin's appearance at Strawbery Banke that forced the town's petition to the Massachusetts government.

The Bay government responded by confirming to Strawbery Banke all
the land between Hampton and Strawbery Banke "not already granted to
towns or persons (Swampscot patent excepted)" and granting the town
one court a year plus three associates to hear lawsuits involving property
worth less than £2.[39] In May 1652, the General Court clarified its claim to
the Piscataqua region by voting that the northern boundary of its charter
was a line "from the Northernmost part of the river Merrimack and three
miles more north where it is to be found . . . and thence upon a straight
line east and west to each sea."[40] The Court also authorized a survey
committee to find the Merrimack's "most northerly part." In October, the
committee reported that Lake Winnipesaukee was the river's source.[41]
Acting upon this information, the General Court asserted its *political*
jurisdiction over the entire Piscataqua region on the basis of its charter,
yet it did not explicitly assert jurisdiction over the land itself.

Acting under the dictates of these events and motivated by their
continuing drive for good land, Strawbery Banke's settlers petitioned
again in May 1653, spelling out in no uncertain terms why they sought an
enlargement of their boundaries. They maintained that "the quality of
the land we live upon is so bad, it's incredible to believe except those who
have seen it. . . . Some are constrained to remove from want of land to
accommodate them with their stocks." All the other towns had been
"bounded," yet Strawbery Banke, "the first of any in these parts," had
not; "this neck of land which we live upon . . . is far less than any
neighboring town about us." They concluded by asking for some of the
Squamscot patent lands and for a change in their town's name from
"Strawbery Banke" to "Portsmouth"—"a name most suitable for this
place, it being the River's mouth and as good [harbor] as any in this
land."[42] The supplicating tone of this petition was strikingly less arro-
gant than that of the 1651 petition, an indication that changes were
occurring at Strawbery Banke.

One of the key changes had taken place in April 1652, when the town
leaders changed their form of town government so that it more closely
conformed with that of the Massachusetts towns by vesting land-granting
powers and all other powers in the "townsmen," or "selectmen," elected
by the inhabitants.[43] At the same time, however, the inhabitants restricted
the selectmen's power over land distribution by ordering that "all grants
formerly granted and recorded although they be not signed by the
Townsmen, nevertheless the s[aid] grants and possessions shall be of
force, and the present Townsmen shall have power to confirm what shall
be proved to be grants."[44] This restriction must have frustrated the new

selectmen as they sought closer ties with Massachusetts but had to accept earlier recorded land grants given to men who had led a rebellion against Massachusetts' authority. That they could no longer abide such circumstances became clear when, on January 13, 1652/53, they deliberately took matters into their own hands and destroyed many of the earlier town records: "This night the selectmen examined the old Town Book and what was not approved was crossed out, and what was approved was left to be recorded in this Book and to be confirmed by the present Selectmen."[45] Thus, they either eliminated or reduced both the anti-Massachusetts language and the holdings of some anti-Massachusetts settlers.[46]

Having decided to accept Massachusetts' jurisdiction and influence, the selectmen that same night gave forty-six new grants of land, varying from ten to fifty acres, to the inhabitants. In this division they ignored at least four and perhaps as many as fourteen of the inhabitants.[47] Subsequently, the selectmen copied all pre-1652 entries they wished to preserve into the new town book and began issuing new grants of marshes, meadows, and "planting lands" to the inhabitants. The variety of acreages granted indicates that these grants were given on the basis of each individual's economic and social status in the town.[48]

The treatment given to new inhabitants sheds some light on both economic and social values at Portsmouth. In 1654, the selectmen had decided to issue eight-acre home lots to "such as the town shall accept of to habitation" in an attempt to attract new settlers.[49] But by 1658, land scarcity had changed this approach: "There shall be no more 8 acre lots granted to any strangers in this town, but only lots for tradesmen according to the discretion of the Selectmen . . . also no tradesman that shall desire any lots shall have any privileges to any commonage that belongs to this town."[50] Thus, by 1658, the town leaders had recognized the main direction the town's economy would take—toward development of trade and commerce. Between 1658 and 1672 new inhabitants received minimal town grants of one or two acres of either commonage or town lots, depending entirely upon their occupations.[51]

Given such land scarcity it was only natural that the existing inhabitants should advance themselves rather than newcomers with land grants. By 1660, four of the settlers had obtained over one hundred acres each through individual town grants. Captain Francis Champernoun's 300-acre farm was the largest single grant.[52] In 1656, the long controversy with the Squamscot patentees over town bounds ended with the placing of legal control over some 5,000 acres of common lands in the hands of the town selectmen.[53] Pressure began increasing for a division of the commons. In early 1661, the selectmen surrendered, and after granting some 550 acres to twenty-three of the "old planters" and those "that stand in need," they parcelled out 4,139 acres to ninety-one people. This 4,139-acre grant went to three elements in the population: those who were inhabitants by 1657, their married sons and sons over twenty-one years of age, and their married and unmarried daughters of eighteen years and over. This land dowry must have helped many an ugly maiden capture a husband in later years. The method utilized in determining what proportion of land each should receive in this division of 1661 was based generally upon each individual's social and economic status: "The proportions abovesaid are made to every inhabitant as if no land had been given at all, and all such as have received above the proportion aforesaid by former town grant, such are to possess the same still, and must not expect further encouragement."[54] The grants varied from 13 acres to 410 acres: over 60 percent were under 50 acres, while about 85 percent were under 100 acres. Each inhabitant received at least 13 acres—enough commons to supply the necessary hay for animals and lumber for building and firewood, but not enough for a farm. From 1661 on Portsmouth had a large group of privileged land proprietors, those who received commons rights and grants in this division; later, such privileges could be obtained only through purchase, inheritance, or marriage. But under such circumstances of land scarcity, the 1661 grant attempted to reward every inhabitant of eighteen years or more and in the process illustrated the strong community feelings of the settlers.

The pressure of new settlers coming from England and Massachusetts into Portsmouth during the 1660's brought new demands for land divisions and enlargements of the town boundaries and placed a strain on the commons acreage still undivided. Finally, in 1672 the selectmen ordered that all the commons not yet "granted, given, nor laid out" shall remain as they "now are . . . and not be given unto any particular person."[55] Although this order held back new land grants for the next twenty-seven years, gradually such strong pressures arose for new grants that in 1699 the selectmen unconditionally surrendered their hold over the commons by ordering that "all the common lands be divided amongst the inhabitants in equal proportion according to their respective rates."[56] Economic status as reflected in property tax thus became the basis for the last division of the commons. Of necessity, after 1699 Portsmouth's more ambitious men would turn outward for economic expansion—toward the sea and trade and toward the provincial government for new land grants westward.

In these varied ways the four towns in their first century disposed of their most valuable physical possession—the land—and in doing so, each reflected its dominant needs and values. Community service was a very significant consideration in all the towns. Hampton and Dover placed special emphasis upon freemanship and religious leadership, which in effect meant that the largest portions of land went to those interested in service and responsibility. Exeter rewarded its ministers and lumberers, Hampton and Exeter their farmers, Portsmouth its earliest inhabitants. Undoubtedly, high social status in the community was a paramount consideration in the awarding of land, for all the towns rewarded those who held important political, religious, or social positions. But at the same time, by relying primarily upon either commonage ownership or the community property tax as the basis for land distribution after the first grants, each community indirectly used economic status as a basis and favored the early comers and already wealthier inhabitants over newcomers. Nevertheless, before about 1700, nothing hindered a man of ability, wealth, or initiative from entering a town, accumulating wealth as a laborer, buying property, and thus becoming a recipient of new town grants.[57] By the eighteenth century, however, new settlers needed some prior wealth in order to establish themselves as inhabitants in most of the older New Hampshire towns. Free land no longer served as a source of new economic opportunity for the propertyless in three of the four towns (Exeter, of course, was an exception).

Thus, during the seventeenth century the New Hampshire settlers, in their preoccupation with establishing and organizing permanent communities, aggressively sought the exploitation of the land through town-meeting land grants to each individual on the basis of his economic and social status or his physical and social needs. While the relatively inferior quality of land in the coastal region precluded large-scale production of such a necessary staple crop as wheat, by the 1660's the best available lands—meadows, marshes, and "upland planting lands"—had provided the foundation for some agricultural expansion in each of the four towns. Hampton, the most prosperous agricultural community among the towns during the seventeenth century, specialized in raising cattle and grain crops. By the 1640's there were over 450 head of cattle in the town. When Samuel Maverick described Hampton in 1660, he saw a "large town . . . the inhabitants living well by corn and cattle of which they have great store."[58] Maize, rye, and wheat were the main crops, while the cattle fed on salt hay from the meadows and marshes.

Estate inventories and the customs records for New Hampshire reveal that in all the towns the settlers produced their own fruit and vegetables. Almost everyone who owned land had a vegetable garden (even in Portsmouth where the land was least favorable), and vegetables were seldom imported. Most of the farmers possessed an orchard as well. Nor did the Piscataqua settlers lack meat. Their lands provided fairly adequate fodder for cattle, sheep, goats, and pigs. The sale of farm animals and of meat at town fairs and in Boston provided the farmers with one of their chief sources of profit in what generally remained a subsistence agricultural economy throughout the colonial period. Another source of agricultural profit lay in the sale of horses. In fact, farm animals constituted New Hampshire's chief agricultural export.[59]

Regulation of Timber Use

The greatest promise of the land in New Hampshire's first century lay not in its agricultural advantages but in its dense forests. The trees had to be cleared away before one could efficiently work the land, build a house, or establish a community. More important, lumber was in great demand for building, transportation, and firewood within the community, in nearby towns, at Boston, in the West Indies, and even to some extent in England. Then, too, the towering white pines could provide masts for local and Boston ships and for the Royal Navy. Pine and oak could serve for pipe, barrel, and hogshead staves used in trade and storage. It was only natural that the trees would be utilized, for they blocked agricultural progress within the community while commanding both local and distant markets.

From the first, the settlers adhered to manorial tradition in allowing all inhabitants to utilize the timber on the commons for their own needs. But it was not long before various individuals in each of the towns envisioned the profits awaiting their exploitation of the free lumber on the commons and began taking what they wanted rather than what they needed. These actions forced each town government to seek to reconcile community needs with individual interests. Their success in doing so depended chiefly upon the availability of timber in each community.

The agricultural community of Hampton faced this problem first, worked out some partial solutions, but never eliminated it until most of the commons had been granted out to individuals. Within a year of its establishment, the town government ordered anyone seeking to cut timber from the commons without payment to obtain a license from the "woodwards," who would then assign trees to them on condition that they be felled within one month or be forfeited to the town.[60] When Richard Knight sought a grant for a sawmill and gristmill in 1640, the town gave him accommodations provided he build a meetinghouse forty feet long, twenty-two feet wide, and thirteen feet high for the town.[61] In continuing attempts to encourage both individual ambition and community progress, the town in 1646 allowed every inhabitant to produce 500 staves from the commons timber for each share of cow commons he possessed.[62] This rule was intermittently enforced until 1658, but it evidently aroused discontent, for in December 1658, the town adopted the more restrictive, yet more equalitarian policy of allowing all inhabitants to make staves enough for an eighty-shilling profit so long as they obtained a license from the selectmen and did not fell any trees within five miles of any houses.[63]

By 1665, so much timber had been lost that the freemen issued a special order to the town selectmen to preserve the commons timber. When this did not achieve its purpose, the freemen assumed complete control over all land exchanges and timber grants.[64] Four years later, the freemen launched an investigation into the great waste of trees on the commons and ordered that no more trees be felled there until further notice. A final clarification of timber policy followed this investigation. The town leaders decided to return to the policy of 1646, ordering that no inhabitant could make more than 500 staves per share of cow commons and that no commons timber could be felled for any other use outside the town.[65] This restrictive measure and appropriate fines slowed violations but did not stop them.[66]

Hampton's inhabitants, then, followed similar directions in both land and timber policies—limiting land and timber grants to cow commons owners, gradually adopting restrictive policies in their use, yet insuring that all inhabitants would obtain some share for their own needs and profit.

Portsmouth, with its limited commonage, faced similar problems when, in 1651, Ambrose Lane built a sawmill on Sagamore Creek and asked the town for use of the commons timber. The town granted him this privilege provided he give all town inhabitants a one-shilling discount per hundred feet of lumber off the market price if they sought the lumber only for their personal needs. But if they desired it for building "ships, and barks, or boats," they had to pay the full market price.[67] Another community service approach was initiated in 1658. John Cutt received a sawmill grant from the town including use of the commons timber provided he build a grist mill and grind all the town corn at no cost to the inhabitants.[68] Although a few individuals received special grants of timber for their own profit from the town commons, more often people stole the lumber they wanted to sell elsewhere.[69] Undoubtedly, these pressures helped force the decision of 1661 to grant out most of the commons among the inhabitants.

In this timber-scarce community the selectmen and the town granted rights to commons timber on the basis of each individual's needs, not his profit; and this principle was followed through 1699, when the last of the commons lands were distributed.

Dover's inhabitants, blessed with plentiful supplies of timber, at first placed no limits on its exploitation. But when felled trees, left underfoot to rot on the commons, became a hindrance and an eyesore, the selectmen placed a small limitation on free usage in 1642 by ordering that anyone who felled more than ten trees for clapboards or pipestaves from the commons before "making them up" would be fined ten shillings per tree.[70] Between 1647 and 1652 the town gave at least six sawmill grants of timberland to individuals in return for a community payment. The first such grant went to two church elders, Hatevil Nutter and Edward Starbuck.[71] These grants must have made considerable inroads into the available timber, for in 1648 the selectmen forbade the felling of any trees on the commons without their permission.[72]

During the same years the selectmen gave ten choice trees to various individuals from timber already granted to the mill-owners. These gifts fanned discontent among the millmen and spurred significant changes in Dover's timber policies. In 1652, the townspeople chose selectmen "to order all the timber and towne . . . and the order of ten trees granted to particular men shall stand till the townsmen shall order other ways."[73] The five selectmen (two of whom owned large mills) then established what emerged as the permanent solution to Dover's timber problems by giving all town inhabitants permission to fell timber on all sawmill grants for use as staves, bolts, canoes, buildings, fencing, and firewood without interference from the owners so long as no more than five trees were felled at any one time to make staves or bolts. In return for this sacrifice on the part of the mill-owners, the selectmen voided all "grants of ten trees to particular men both of mast trees and clapboard trees and pipestave trees." Thus, the millmen kept control of the valuable mast trees while allowing considerable opportunities for profit to the townspeople. The town gained profit from the masts as well, for it was also ordered that for each mast over twenty-four inches in diameter cut on their property, the mill-owners must pay the town ten shillings.[74] This last act was broadened in 1657 when it came to the town's attention that some mill-owners were avoiding payment of the duty on masts by using trees smaller than twenty-four inches in diameter. To ensure community profit the town placed a six-shilling duty on masts fourteen to eighteen inches in diameter and an eight-shillings duty on masts eighteen to twenty-four inches in diameter.[75] The entire community, then, both individually and collectively, profited from Dover's timber resources until the commons disappeared.

Exeter even more than Dover abounded in timber resources. Throughout the town's first century, lumbering in one way or another provided the main source of profit for its inhabitants. From the first settlement, its woodlands lay open to all inhabitants freely. Until 1647 the only limitations placed on the commons timber were that it not be wasted but utilized within six months of its felling; that all lumber used for anything except fencing or building be cut at least one-half mile from the town or on private property; that trees offensive to neighbors be felled; that sawpits be filled; and that "none but settled inhabitants shall make use of wood or common, nor that no inhabitant shall employ any about wood work but of the settled inhabitants."[76]

But the demand for sawmills after 1648 changed this open approach. Between 1647 and 1652 some twenty-four people successfully established eight sawmills in Exeter, receiving land appropriations from the town. The grant to Edward Gilman, Jr., in 1647, the first and perhaps most important in the town's early history, allowed him to set up mills anywhere in Exeter and utilize the commons timber in whatever ways he saw fit. In return he promised to become a town inhabitant, allow other inhabitants all the lumber they needed for their own use at three shillings per hundred feet, and give the town one-third of all masts he cut.[77] Within three months of this grant the town, as encouragement to Gilman, ordered the inhabitants to stop cutting commons timber except in fulfillment of earlier grants and purchases. Three new mill grants in the next two years followed the same principles as Gilman's.[78] Because of widespread discontent among the inhabitants over these restrictions, the town voted in 1650 that settled inhabitants could use commons timber but that only one person per house lot could exercise that privilege. The town gave generous land grants to each inhabitant in the 1650's, however, so that the partial deprivation of commons timber created no serious discontent.

That lumbering had become a primary concern of most Exeter inhabitants by the 1650's is manifested in the town order of April 1650 requiring that town taxes be paid in proportion to the number of pipestaves, hogshead staves, and bolts sold by each individual.[79] In continuing attempts to encourage lumberers, the town selectmen granted privileges for five new mills in 1652. At this time, however, some changes had to be made in the use of the commons timber. Each miller (including all earlier grantees) was limited to using only the commons timber near his mill. Also, instead of providing the town with a fixed proportion of all masts cut, town officials now required an annual money payment of £5 or £10, depending upon the size of the mill grant.[80]

While the mill-owners received generous timber grants throughout the 1650's, the other townspeople faced continuing limitations on their use of commons timber. In 1652, the town forbade selling any commons timber for pipestaves; in 1657, it ordered "that all the pines upon the commons from this time forward shall be reserved for the use of the sawmills already set up, or that have been granted and shall be set up, except that there is liberty for masts, fence-building, and canoes; and if at any time there shall be any particular grants made to any, yet the owners of sawmills shall have liberty to carry off the pine timber, except before excepted."[81] A final limitation of the 1650's allowed but one member per family to be employed in taking white oak from the commons for staves or bolts unless it served the family's local needs of fencing, housebuilding, or milling.[82]

By 1660, then, the commons timber in Exeter had become chiefly a profit preserve of the mill-owners while remaining available to meet the actual needs of each town inhabitant. Yet by allowing each inhabitant "liberty for masts," the town encouraged individual initiative and offered opportunities to all to share in the commons timber profit.

In the 1660's, though large quantities of timberland remained ungranted, the lumberers could see dangers ahead because of the arrival of new settlers coupled with the gradual depletion of the choicest timber lands. In 1668, they persuaded the town to petition the Massachusetts General Court for "an enlargement of the bounds of the town." The town received its enlargement with the limitation that mast trees twenty-four inches or more in diameter within three feet of the ground were reserved to the town.[83] This grant attracted new settlers and brought what turned out to be Exeter's final rules governing use of commons timber. The first rule allowed all new inhabitants to reap a profit from the commons by granting to every single person admitted to the town the privilege of making 1,000 white oak pipestaves or their equivalent value in barrel staves or hogshead staves from the commons within a year, provided that this privilege not be sold to someone else. Three thousand pipestaves were granted to every new family of fewer than four people on the same conditions. The second rule provided that "those who have felled any pine trees have liberty to take them away within a year; after which any of those to whom mills appertain, may take them away for the use of their mills; but hereafter, when those who fell pine trees shall not carry them away within three months, they shall be forfeited to anyone who takes them away for the use of the owner of one of the mills." The final rule ordered that "whoever shall fell any pine tree (except for canoes, masts, [or] building), and shall not improve it and bring it to the use of mills to which the privilege of the timber is granted, for every tree so felled shall forfeit two shillings to the town."[84] Thus, because of its plentiful timber resources, Exeter could balance community and individual interests, offering all new inhabitants a share of the commons timber profits and use of the timber for their own needs while maintaining both the opportunities for profit possessed by the earlier inhabitants and the special privileges of the millmen.[85]

Eighteenth-Century Continuities

The land and timber use policies of the seventeenth-century New Hampshire towns continued through the early eighteenth century and were adopted by the towns that incorporated between 1679 and 1741. The extension of these policies to new settlements occurred primarily because eleven of the fourteen newly incorporated towns within this period were simply parishes of the original four; but the remaining three—Londonderry, Chester, and Rochester—followed similar patterns.[86] In Londonderry, for example, each of the original settlers obtained a proprietary share of the land which could be sold or regranted if the original proprietor neither settled in the town nor paid town taxes. Similarly, all new land grants within the town were based upon one's proprietary holdings or his property.[87] Londonderry's commons timber had originally been available to all inhabitants according to their needs, but within two years of its incorporation the townspeople limited commons timber to town proprietors, forbade the use of commons timber for private profit outside the town, and placed penalties upon those who abandoned any trees or staves they had cut on the commons.[88]

While the various town governments were the primary sources of land and timber grants, there were other sources. Before 1679 one could seek such favors either from the Crown or from Massachusetts. Since most of the Piscataqua settlers accepted the jurisdiction of Massachusetts between 1641 and 1679, it was only natural that individuals and the towns looked to Massachusetts for new land grants. But there were a few individuals, primarily those who expected to gain from recognition of the Masonian proprietorship claims, who looked to the Crown or to Robert Mason for such grants.[89] Largely through Mason's efforts, the four towns found themselves part of a royal colony after 1679. From that time forward the governor and council became the prime target for petitioners who sought land grants beyond town jurisdiction.

Massachusetts' main contribution to New Hampshire land problems during its years of authority in the Piscataqua region lay in solving the plethora of boundary controversies among the towns. In 1672, however, the Massachusetts General Court did issue one land grant to Portsmouth (probably because of that town's generous donation to Harvard University) on condition that the area be settled within five years, that its settlers pay taxes and maintain an approved minister, and that a 300-acre area of upland and meadow be set aside for the entire county.[90] Such stipulations were normal in Massachusetts land grants, and when New Hampshire became a royal colony, it used similar principles.[91] In the thirteen new township grants between 1679 and 1740 the governor and council generally required the granting of equal shares to each proprietor, certain minimum land improvements such as building a "dwelling house," the planting of at least three acres of land within three to five years, and the obtaining of a minister, whose salary would come from town taxes.[92] Inhabitants who failed to meet the requirements for individuals within the specified time limits forfeited their rights to the other proprietors and settlers unless an Indian war hindered the settlement of the town.[93] Once a town was granted, however, all power over internal land grants passed into the hands of the town proprietors.

Despite the basic similarities between the Massachusetts and New Hampshire principles in the granting of townships, there existed one important difference. The New Hampshire government required the payment of a nominal quitrent from each new township: an ear of Indian corn, a pound of hemp, a pint of turpentine, a pound of flax, or a peck of potatoes served this function. Although these quitrents were payable only if demanded by the government, an action which seldom if ever occurred; nevertheless, the inclusion of quitrents in New Hampshire land grants originated from the colony's royal status and from the uncertain legality of the Masonian proprietary claims to the land of the colony.

By these generally similar principles, then, the New Hampshire people dispensed their most valuable physical resources throughout their first century of settlement. The techniques and direction of each local government in developing its land resources emerged from three intermingled factors: the ideals and values of the local community, the quantity and quality of land available, and the external pressures and internal economic problems affecting the Piscataqua environment. These external pressures and internal economic problems now merit consideration.

CHAPTER **III**

THREATS TO UTILIZATION OF LAND: THE PROPRIETARY CONTROVERSY

Captain John Mason's Claim

The Mason proprietary claim was one of the greatest threats before 1713 to the security of New Hampshire settlers. As the primary political issue until at least 1708, it embraced fundamental questions of economic and political jurisdiction, and its outcome would determine the settlers' basic rights to exploit the land and its resources.

This controversy had its origins in the land grants Captain John Mason received from the Council for New England in the 1620's and 1630's.[1] Mason, a naval captain and adventurer, had had his first contact with New England as a governor of Newfoundland from 1615 to 1621. During these years he had befriended Sir Ferdinando Gorges, who was highly interested in New England's resources and was the leading organizer of the Council for New England. Through Gorges' influence, in 1620 the council gave Mason a grant of the seashore from the Naumkeag River to the Merrimack River. In August 1622, after Mason's return to England, he and Gorges obtained a joint patent from the council for all the lands between the Merrimack and Kennebec Rivers to their sources. Between 1622 and 1629, however, the council also granted some individual patents and the New England Company patent (the basis of Massachusetts Bay Colony's claims) to lands within the same areas already given to Mason and Gorges.

Mason, busy with service at Cadiz and as treasurer and paymaster of the navy during these years, had never attempted a settlement in New England. Fearful of losing his claims, he obtained a grant from the council in November 1629 to the land between the Merrimack and

Piscataqua Rivers and extending back into the country for sixty miles. He named this grant New Hampshire. But having little capital, he decided to join with Gorges and some London merchants in establishing a colony under the auspices of a joint stock company. On November 17, 1629, this Laconia Company received from the council a rather vague grant of lands "bordering upon the great lake or rivers and lakes . . . upwards from the rivers of Sagadahok and Merrimack." It was this joint stock organization that sent out the only settlers ever associated with John Mason, and these colonizers settled outside the Laconia Company grant but within the earlier grants of Mason and Gorges, on both sides of the Piscataqua River. Accordingly, in November 1631, Mason and Gorges along with the other members of the joint stock company obtained a new grant to correspond to their actual settlements, plus land extending thirty miles inland and the fishing grounds at the Isles of Shoals.[2] In a real sense this patent of 1631 canceled out all earlier grants in this area to both Mason and Gorges as individuals, for, as Judge Elwin Page explains, "Captain Mason, by accepting as owner in common this grant of title, the only grant under which he ever had any part in the settlement of New Hampshire, could no longer claim title in severalty to the described premises under other grants."[3]

In December 1633, the Laconia Company decided to award part of its holdings to the various stockholders; and though Mason received a small tract in Maine along the Newichewannock River, the land south and west of the Piscataqua (New Hampshire) remained undivided.[4] With the Laconia Company on the verge of bankruptcy and Puritan elements threatening Mason's and Gorges' plans for New England, the two men decided to attack and destroy the Massachusetts Bay Company charter. One of the actions they took in this endeavor was to scrap the Council for New England so they could work directly through the Crown. But since they did not want to lose control of the New England lands they coveted, in 1634 and 1635 they divided the lands among the council members on the assumption that each member would obtain the king's approval for his grant. Gorges received what became the province of Maine; while Mason received land between the Naumkeag and Piscataqua Rivers and inland for sixty miles, part of the Isles of Shoals, and 10,000 acres along the Kennebec River, called New Hampshire, in a grant dated April 22, 1635. This grant was in direct conflict with the Massachusetts Bay Company charter, which granted land southward of a line three miles north of the Merrimack River, and also in conflict with the grant given the Laconia Company in 1631, under which all Mason's earlier efforts had been carried on and which already covered all areas settled by Mason, Gorges, and the other enterprisers of the Laconia Company. It also conflicted with the Hilton patent. By December 1635, however, Mason had died, and the Crown never confirmed the 1635 patent.[5] The Laconia Company dissolved shortly afterwards.

Thus, after being a party to six different New England grants within fifteen years, Mason at his death could legally prove sole ownership only of the lands northeast of the Newichewannock River (in an area soon obtained by Gorges as part of his Maine patent) and common ownership (along with the other Laconia Company stockholders) in some lands south of the Piscataqua River. The latter claims were never pressed as such after the Laconia Company dissolved.[6] John Mason's heirs could have no legal claim in severalty to any land south of the Piscataqua River in what came to be called New Hampshire. But Mason's will unintentionally disguised this fact by awarding 7,000 acres of land "in my County of Newhampshire or Mason Hall in New England" and 10,000 acres of land along the "South East side of the Sagadahock" River to his various relatives, paving the way for the entire Masonian land title controversy in the colony.[7]

No doubt John Mason deserves credit as one of the founders of New Hampshire but less than he has traditionally been given. He was the most enthusiastic and far-sighted of the Laconia Company enterprisers in his establishment of two sawmills and a fur-trading center at the falls of the Newichewannock River in Maine. By 1634 only Mason and Gorges were actively encouraging the Laconia Company settlements, of which Mason owned three-eighths; and after all, the colony received its name from Mason's grants. But he was not the only founder, nor the most important. In the final analysis, Mason was but one of many English imperialist-adventurers searching for land, profits, and prestige in the New World—and a relatively unsuccessful one at that. Yet his vision of New Hampshire's future—a colony which would establish its prosperity upon the exportation of lumber and fish—rang true.

Robert Mason's Assertion of Title

After John Mason's death his widow, Ann, refused assistance to the Laconia Company servants in New Hampshire and leased out the property at Newichewannock Falls. The leaseholder, however, allowed the lands to pass out of his hands, so in 1651 Mrs. Mason sent an agent, Joseph Mason, to recover her losses. Joseph Mason brought three suits in Massachusetts courts for recovery of these lands and lost them all, but these actions dealt only with lands in Maine (at Newichewannock Falls): no land titles in New Hampshire were challenged.[8] Nevertheless, Mason's appearance encouraged discord at Portsmouth, and his complaints against some leading Portsmouth settlers who had exploited the resources at Newichewannock Falls helped persuade the town to accept Massachusetts' authority and protection.[9]

Upon Richard Cromwell's death in 1659, Robert Tufton Mason, a grandson of John Mason, petitioned Parliament as one of the patentees of Maine and Laconia seeking redress for their losses, a recognition of the fact that he did not have individual ownership in New Hampshire.[10] Parliament ignored this petition. After the Stuarts regained the throne, the Masons changed their tactics. At first Joseph Mason and Edward Godfrey, an agent of Gorges' son, petitioned the Crown for a "General Governor" over the Piscataqua River and lands eastward; but by April 1661, both Robert Mason and Ferdinand Gorges were claiming full proprietary rights in New Hampshire and Maine, respectively.[11] In February 1661/62 Robert Mason reported to the king that he was sole proprietor of New Hampshire because his grandfather, John Mason, had received and occupied several patents and had spent £15,000 in New Hampshire. From this point on, the Masons ignored the complex facts of the past in favor of a simplified tissue of half-truths or, at worst, outright falsehoods in pressing their claims.[12] Their new claims argued that the patents of 1629 and 1635 were valid legal grants of both soil and government in New Hampshire which had been usurped by Massachusetts in 1652 through fraud and violence. Having royal influence and working in an atmosphere of strong suspicion against Massachusetts, the Masons developed four main tactics to obtain their goal: attacking Massachusetts as a colony of usurpers, traitors, independence-seekers, and violators of English law; encouraging a small coterie of Anglicans, Quakers, and agents and relatives of Mason and Gorges to foment local demands for either proprietary or royal government in Maine and New Hampshire; exaggerating the economic and political potential of the Piscataqua region; and, finally, seeking the revocation of the Massachusetts charter.[13]

The events of the 1660's and 1670's both aided and thwarted them in their quest. When the Crown sent a commission composed of Richard Nichols, Samuel Maverick, Robert Carr, and George Cartwright to investigate New England conditions in 1664, Robert Mason obtained their support for his New Hampshire claims by granting power of attorney to Nicols to settle his "Province grant" and by offering Carr a chance at the governor's post in the new proprietorship.[14] With Masonian support, the commission held a highly controversial meeting at Portsmouth in July 1665 in which it sponsored the presentation of two petitions: one from Portsmouth with thirty-two signatures attacking the economic, pro-Massachusetts, political, and Congregational biases of the town leaders and asking for royal protection and government; the other

containing sixty-one signatures from all four towns pleading to be united
with Maine as a new royal colony. After the commissioners left, a second
town meeting at Portsmouth completely disavowed the earlier proceedings, but the petitions reached the Crown.[15] The second and third Anglo-
Dutch wars postponed until the mid-1670's all further attempts in
London to deal with the Mason claims, however.

In 1660 Mason had obtained a favorable opinion of his claims from the
attorney general, and by the late 1660's he was sending New Hampshire
masts to the Royal Navy; but in 1671 he became so discouraged that he
offered to sell his patent for New Hampshire to the Crown in return for
the privilege of importing "300 tons of French wine free of all customs" in
three ships.[16] The Crown ignored his offer. After the new Lords of Trade
were appointed in early 1675, Mason and Gorges presented their cases
before them, and Mason, especially, pressed them for action. He even
brought before them a naval captain who had visited Boston in 1673 and
had been roughly treated.[17] His report convinced the Lords of Trade that
both sides of the Mason-Gorges claims should be heard and that Massachusetts should send agents to London for that purpose (as well as for
other purposes). Probably at Mason's suggestion, his cousin Edward
Randolph was chosen to deliver the king's order. Conditions were
improving for Mason. Once more the attorney and solicitor general
reported that on the basis of the patents of 1629 and 1635 Mason held "a
good and legal Title to the lands above conveyed by the name of the
province of New Hampshire."[18] When Edward Randolph returned, he
brought more evidence of Massachusetts' foul play and added his support
to Mason's claims in New Hampshire; and with the arrival of the
Massachusetts agents, the case went before the Lords Chief Justices.[19]

In July 1677, the judges handed down an impartial decision. They
asked the right questions: Who owned the land? Who should govern?
They correctly awarded Gorges the proprietorship of Maine on the basis
of his 1639 Charter for the Province of Maine, signed by King Charles I.
They correctly rejected Robert Mason's claim to the government of New
Hampshire on the grounds that the Council for New England had never
possessed the power to grant governing authority with its land titles and
that therefore the power of government still remained with the Crown.
Then, instead of examining Mason's claims to land ownership in New
Hampshire, they rebuffed him for the moment by explaining that the
initial determination of ownership must be made in the presence of the
"pertinents or some other persons on their behalf" and in the courts
"upon the place having jurisdiction"—in other words, among the New
Hampshire people in Massachusetts-oriented courts.[20]

Given the existing dominance of Massachusetts in northern New
England, Mason knew he had no chance of winning his suits there. So he

joined Randolph in attacking Massachusetts before the Lords of Trade, demanding that its charter be revoked. Since the king still held governing rights over New Hampshire, in January 1677/78 Mason persuaded Gorges to join in a petition asking that a royal governor (hopefully Mason himself or one of his friends) be sent to rule over a united Maine and New Hampshire. In support of this request they pointed out that Massachusetts had no jurisdiction there and was oppressing the people, that the "best and most wealthy" people there in 1665 had asked for royal government, and that all masts and most timber and fish came from there. They concluded by offering to surrender all claims of government in the two colonies if the new royal government's jurisdiction would extend "over all your petitioners lands according to their grants"—a backhanded method of recognizing the Masonian claims to the land.[21] Two months later Mason lost an ally as the Massachusetts agents purchased Maine from Gorges; but actually he gained considerably, for his petition to the Lords of Trade informing them of the sale brought consternation and a reconsideration of New England affairs. Cousin Edward Randolph was called before the Lords of Trade to present the latest news of New England. Supported by Mason, he launched an attack against both the Massachusetts agents and the Massachusetts government for failing to comply with the Lords' proposals of 1677. By the time they had finished, the Lords of Trade had reversed their views toward Massachusetts and were favoring both the revocation of the Massachusetts charter and the appointment of a royal governor to New Hampshire.[22]

In February 1679, the Lords of Trade called for the creation of a royal governor and council in New Hampshire and referred Mason's claims to the Privy Council. In July the Privy Council reported to the king recommending a royal government in New Hampshire which would protect Robert Mason's claims if he compromised with the New Hampshire settlers. Mason then agreed with both the Lords of Trade and the Crown that he would charge the inhabitants no more than six pence per acre for their improved land; that he would seek a peaceful settlement of his claims with the help of the New Hampshire Council; that he would forfeit all quitrents due before June 12, 1678, and "make out titles" to the possessors of the land in return for their future quitrents; and finally, that all the unimproved lands except woodlands would belong to him. These provisions were written into the Cutt Commission, the first royal commission and government for New Hampshire.[23] Meanwhile, Randolph was appointed collector of customs for New England and instructed to carry the Cutt Commission to New Hampshire and establish the new government there.

So after some thirty years of protestations, Robert Mason achieved the Crown's support for his claims, even though they had not been tested in the courts. Three important factors had aided his weak case: Mason's family had served the Stuarts long and well, Mason did not hesitate to exaggerate grossly his claims in pressing his case, and the Massachusetts Bay Colony's independent and illicit actions after 1660 had earned the wrath of the king, who saw the creation of a royal government in New Hampshire as one means of reducing Massachusetts' influence in New England. In the final analysis, English officialdom prejudged the Masonian claims in Mason's favor; and, as a result, the New Hampshire colonists found themselves face to face with either payment of quitrents or loss of their land titles.

Mason had already received some local New Hampshire reactions to his claims. In 1665, he had empowered commissioner Richard Nicolls and, in 1667, Nicholas Shapleigh to grant out land in his name. But most of the grants had ended up in the Massachusetts-oriented courts, where his claims were thrown out.[24] When the Massachusetts agents sent word to New Hampshire of Mason's efforts toward establishing a royal government, the leading men of each of the four towns sent petitions to the king begging that they might remain under the benign jurisdiction of Massachusetts, "unto which we at first voluntarily subjected ourselves and have never yet had any cause to repent of our so doing."[25] Having received news of the Cutt Commission in January 1679/80, the members of the new New Hampshire Council hesitated to accept their own appointments because they disagreed with the support for Mason in the commission and desired to remain under Massachusetts. But they finally accepted their new offices, feeling that it was better to accept than to have other persons in their place. Within two months the president, council, and House of Representatives succinctly expressed their opposition to the Masonian claim by enacting two very pointed laws: "To prevent contention that may arise amongst us by reason of the late change of government, it is ordered by this Assembly and the authority thereof that all land, townships, town grants, with all other grants lying within the limits of this Province, and all other rights and properties, shall stand good, and are hereby confirmed to the towns and persons concerned, in the same state and conditions as they did before this late alteration"; and "that if any difference or controversy shall hereafter rise amongst us about the titles of land within this Province, it shall not be finally determined but by a Jury of 12 able men, chosen by the freemen of each town according to law and custom."[26] Thus the Cutt government gave notice to both Mason and the Crown that it would not accept those clauses in the king's commission that recognized the Masonian claim.

As if this challenge were not enough, the new government proceeded to enact a system of legislation almost identical to that of Massachusetts. It sent the Massachusetts government a letter warmly thanking it for its past protection and interest, explaining that New Hampshire had neither sought nor desired the separation. It also sent a letter to the Crown in which it revealed that it disapproved of the change because this would increase the number of "small and weak governments, unfit either for offence or defence," and labeled Mason a "pretended claimer to our soil."[27]

Upon Mason's arrival in New Hampshire, he announced that the Cutt Commission recognized his title to New Hampshire as lord proprietor and began granting land and collecting quitrents from whoever would accept his authority.[28] The New Hampshire Council, however, refused to accept either his title or his land claims, indicated its willingness to hear individual cases involving the claims, and called upon Mason to accept his council seat and bring his cases forward. When Mason refused to do so and went so far as to publish under his own name a summons to the president and council to appear before the king within three months, the council issued a warrant for his arrest on the grounds that he had misused royal authority.[29]

Realizing that under this government all the cards were stacked against him (since the council, judges, and any juries would be personally interested and probably anti-Masonian in any court cases), Mason fled to England and petitioned the Crown for a change in government to one that would effectively reinforce "royal authority" in New Hampshire.[30] In this petition he attacked the pro-Massachusetts orientation of the council and the new land law which had usurped his authority; he asked that all land grants based upon Massachusetts' authority be declared void and that the "evil-minded men" who "refused or delay" agreement with him and continued to fell trees on his lands be summoned before the Privy Council in England for trial. With strong support from letters of Edward Randolph and Richard Chamberlain,[31] Mason persuaded the English government to strike down all legislation passed under the Cutt Commission and send a new royal governor to New Hampshire.

Meanwhile, in May 1681 the New Hampshire Council sent the king a letter which clearly and briefly put forth the views of New Hampshire leaders on the Masonian case. This petition, probably the work of Dover's Richard Waldron, declared that Robert Mason's claims were based on falsehoods.[32] His patents were not authentic; his talk of John Mason's expenses were "mostly . . . a pretense." Waldron pointed out that John Mason had never individually planted a colony in New England and that though he had, as a partner in the Laconia Company, built a house in New Hampshire, most of his "disbursements" had been in Maine—yet Robert Mason "would appear amongst us as sole proprietor." Waldron also declared that while Mason asserted that the people of New Hampshire claimed title only from Massachusetts, in truth "we were possessed of this soil long before Massachusetts meddled with us," and the Masons had deserted the area several years before Massachusetts extended its jurisdiction. Aside from all this, Waldron wrote, Robert Mason's behavior in New Hampshire was "very unbecoming to his place and pretensions": he threatened and cajoled the poor, giving them "fair promise and ungrounded intimations" and "imperiously commanded them as Proprietor . . . to attend his pleasure"; he obtained the signatures of children, servants, and apprentices to use in England which "made a great confusion here" and disrupted society, "the dangerous consequences whereof we dread." Waldron's petition concluded that the "generality of whole Province that are householders and men of principle, parts or estate" could not live under such a proprietor and that the only way to resolve the case was to bring it into the New Hampshire courts, an action which Mason "utterly declines, though we have often offered it."

The council's letter notwithstanding, a new royal official for New Hampshire was appointed; and at this point, Robert Mason lost all sense of discretion and embarked upon one of the more opportunistic ventures in all colonial history. His first step was to obtain the support of this new lieutenant governor, Edward Cranfield. Mason persuaded Cranfield to accept a mortgage for all New Hampshire in return for a payment to Mason of £150 per year for seven years (to come from projected New Hampshire quitrents).[33] Mason and Cranfield arrived in New Hampshire together. According to his commission Cranfield was to assume the responsibility that had earlier fallen to the New Hampshire Council. Mason was to negotiate quitrent agreements with the people; if that failed, Cranfield was to reconcile the parties. If the reconciliation failed, then Cranfield was to send each case, impartially stated but with his opinion included, to the Privy Council. This process deprived the colonists of trial by jury.[34] But Cranfield proved balky. After two months in the colony he found that Mason had "misrepresented the whole matter": the province was inconsiderable and "much impoverished," loyal to the king, and willing to pay taxes; but "few or none" except for some Quakers were willing to accept Mason's claims.[35]

By January 1682/83, however, events had played into Mason's hands. Cranfield became involved in a customs case which so frustrated him that with Randolph's persuasion he completely changed his views on the colonists' motivations. When the New Hampshire Assembly refused to raise any taxes for his salary, he became further embittered and dissolved the assembly. At this point, Edward Gove, one of the members of the House of Representatives, decided that the dissolution was illegal and that Cranfield was a traitor and tyrant who should be overthrown. He traveled from town to town seeking support for this revolution but could find only twelve supporters. Gove and his followers were quickly arrested.

Within a month after their arrest and Gove's conviction for treason, Cranfield gave his wholehearted support to Mason and fled the colony for four months.[36]

Before he dissolved the assembly, however, Cranfield had created a tool sufficient for Mason's purposes. After complaining to the General Assembly that the method of electing jurors by the freemen was repugnant to the laws of England, Cranfield persuaded it to place the choice of jurymen in the hands of the sheriff (appointed by the governor).[37] After Cranfield's return from Boston, he aided the Masonians by removing their enemies from the council and appointing their friends as sheriff, judges, and justices of the peace. With this official support, Mason began suits against the inhabitants in September 1683. Through the next nine months some 160 land cases were heard; and with the aid of friendly judges, bribed juries issuing decisions "twelve at a clap," and Cranfield's refusal to allow defendants to give proof of their title to the courts, Mason probably won every case. Historians will never know for certain exactly how many cases were heard and won by Mason because after his death in 1688 one of the New Hampshire officials deliberately destroyed twenty-four pages of the court judgment book and a number of other court papers relating to these cases.[38]

These disruptive land suits were only half the situation confronting New Hampshire inhabitants. Cranfield harassed anyone who spoke out against his tactics. He ordered the Portsmouth Congregational minister to administer Anglican rites to him and, upon his refusal, had him thrown in jail. Several others who opposed him also found themselves in jail.[39]

The New Hampshire leadership responded to these actions of Mason and Cranfield in two directions. Those who lost lawsuits refused to give up their homes and property, so that Mason could not take possession. Meanwhile, Nathaniel Weare journeyed to England with a complaint against Cranfield and a brief against Mason's claims. The Weare complaint against Cranfield charged him with violating his commission and instructions regarding the Mason claims and with tyrannizing the New Hampshire people. Upon hearing Weare's complaint the Lords of Trade decided to launch an investigation into the activities of Cranfield and Mason. Even Edward Randolph turned against Cranfield, suggesting that he had "quite ruined" New Hampshire.[40] Cranfield then suspended all executions in Mason's land suits and prepared a brief in defense of his actions. Cranfield's concluding words represent well both his point of view and some of the issues at stake during his administration: "I call God to witness that I have done nothing but for the King's service and for the maintenance of justice; but to gratify the people in matters prejudicial to the King respecting trade and to deny Mr. Mason his trials is not according to my conscience, though had I done so, I should not now be called upon to write this defense."[41]

By January 1684/85 Cranfield was ready to leave New Hampshire for greener pastures. In March, the Lords of Trade found him guilty of ignoring his instructions regarding Mason and of exacting excessive court fees. They also attempted a final solution to the Masonian controversy by ordering William Vaughan, a New Hampshire merchant, to appeal his case before the king within two weeks and by ordering Mason to stop all suits concerning his title until a final decision was made on Vaughan's appeal.[42] By May 1685, Cranfield had departed, leaving Mason's son-in-law, Deputy Governor Walter Barefoote, in charge.

Barefoote and Mason ignored the order of the Lords of Trade and continued to collect quitrents based upon past court decisions. Their actions brought about another episode that revealed the contempt many New Hampshire colonists felt for the king's law under such administrators. In December 1685, two men—Thomas Wiggin, one of the richest men in the colony, and Anthony Nutter—visited Barefoote and Mason at Barefoote's house. Wiggin told Mason that his claims were invalid. Mason argued heatedly with him, ordered him to leave, and tried to shove him out the door. Wiggin then threw Mason into the fireplace, burning his clothes and legs. Barefoote entered the fray and found himself lying in the fireplace with two broken ribs and a missing tooth. Though Wiggin was tried and found guilty of assault in March 1686, the Barefoote administration had become the laughingstock of the colony.[43] In May 1686, the Barefoote administration ended as New Hampshire came under the temporary jurisdiction of the Dudley Council in Massachusetts—a prelude to the Dominion of New England. Control of the New Hampshire courts slipped from Mason's hands.

Although Mason won his case against Vaughan in November 1686 on a technicality[44] and had influence enough to obtain a place on both the Dudley Council and the Andros Council, he still had little success in executing his earlier suits. He returned to New Hampshire in 1687 but died in August 1688 without trying any new cases.

Mason's death and the Glorious Revolution brought an end to the most active and ominous era of the proprietary controversy. Proprietary suits were never again successful in New Hampshire, though the cards continued to be stacked against New Hampshire inhabitants as individuals. In the course of the 1680's the New Hampshire settlers had been forced to take sides over this issue. Factions had developed, but the vast majority of the settlers were antiproprietary. Nor did the pro-Mason faction emerge from any single element in the population. It attracted a few rich landowners and merchants (John Hinckes and Robert Elliott, for example) but also some of the landless and newcomers to the province. Despite the political and economic unrest engendered by this controversy, it is difficult to assess its overall impact in New Hampshire, for the colony's population expanded more rapidly than ever before during this decade. Its primary effects appear to have been political and psychological: the breeding of suspicion of royal officials and royal authority,[45] political factionalism, and disrespect for the law. Yet none of these factors were entirely absent from the region before the Masonian controversy occurred.

Robert Mason had known that his claims were highly misleading if not completely invalid—as evidenced by his petition of 1659 and the later changes in his claims—but he was probably the last of the English proprietary claimants to possess this knowledge. The later claimants —Samuel Allen, Thomas Allen, and John Mason—appeared to believe sincerely in the validity of their claims.

Samuel Allen's Claim

After Robert Mason's death and the Glorious Revolution, Mason's heirs sold their claims to a London merchant, Samuel Allen, for a sum of £2,750. Allen immediately petitioned the Lords of Trade for the governorship of New Hampshire on the grounds that his purchase of New Hampshire made it his colony and that he had just signed a contract to supply the Royal Navy with masts and timber from New Hampshire for seven years. Though the Massachusetts agents opposed his petition and petitioned for a permanent annexation of New Hampshire to Massachusetts, Allen's numerous appearances before the Lords of Trade and his attacks on Massachusetts finally paid off, for he was awarded the governorship of the separate royal colony of New Hampshire with a promise that he could try his suits in its local courts.[46] Once again the royal government had supported Mason's proprietary claim to New Hampshire, but this time the governor's commission contained no special instructions concerning the claim.[47]

Lieutenant Governor John Usher, a Massachusetts merchant and the agent of Allen, arrived in the midst of King William's War. Fearful that lawsuits over land titles might induce the settlers to abandon the colony ("to quitt all to their Majesties' enemies"), he agreed to postpone any land suits involving land worth £20 or more for the duration of the war.[48] In October 1692, he called an assembly and suggested to its members that they continue the laws of the Cranfield period, but the assembly answered that the many revolutions had erased all earlier laws.[49] At this point Usher faced two problems. The court system that had aided Mason so well in the 1680's was gone and so were the court records of those cases. Somehow he would have to reconstruct a favorable legal system and find those court records. This time, however, the New Hampshire antiproprietary leaders were alert to the dangers.

Usher first attempted to gain control of court records and other province records. He ordered John Pickering, the recorder of deeds for the past three years, to turn the records over to Thomas Newton, the newly appointed secretary of the colony. But Pickering ignored the order and did not even acknowledge that he had the records until he was threatened with imprisonment. He did not surrender the records until late in 1695, at which time Usher discovered that the twenty-four pages of Robert Mason's cases had been torn out of the court judgment book.

Meanwhile, in 1692, Usher and the council had introduced a law establishing courts for New Hampshire which empowered justices of the peace (appointed by the governor) to hear land cases under forty shillings' value (which would allow favorable precedents supporting the proprietary claim to be established). The antiproprietary leaders countered by inserting a clause in the law which stated that "no person's right of property shall be by any of the aforesaid courts determined, except where matters of fact are either acknowledged by the parties, or judgment be acknowledged or passed by the defendant's fault for want of plea or answer, unless the fault be found by the verdict of twelve men of the neighborhood, as it ought of right to be by the law." But Usher had the last word when the General Assembly accepted the creation of a special Court of Chancery—a court appointed by the governor with the responsibility of determining all matters of equity in the colony—because all land cases could be brought before this court.[50]

Thus, Usher was partially successful in rigging the courts to favor the proprietary claims. In 1695, he appointed Robert Tufton Mason attorney general of New Hampshire, continuing to prepare the way for action once peace was restored.[51] But without those lost pages of evidence that the proprietor had obtained the right to possession in the colony and in the face of continued warfare, nothing more was done toward a final settlement of the controversy in the courts.

Instead, Usher decided to reward the proprietor's friends and woo some of his land-hungry enemies by granting a new township from the western commons of Hampton. Since his actions were of questionable legality, Usher protected himself by granting the charter of Kingstown only "as far as in us lyes." Confronted with this usurpation of their town lands, all the Hampton settlers could do was grant land at Kingstown to themselves and join the royal grantees in developing the new township.[52] Usher also gradually displaced those members of the council who outspokenly opposed the proprietary claims—especially Richard Waldron, John Hinckes, and William Vaughan—and sought the support of anti-Massachusetts elements in New Hampshire.

But the antiproprietary elements in the colony were not idly observing Usher's antics. Besides petitioning various officers in England and the agent for New England, Sir William Ashurst, that New Hampshire be annexed to Massachusetts, they worked through the council by calling special sessions and carrying out the colony's political activities while Usher was out of the colony. By 1696, they were petitioning for Usher's removal from office. Usher became so angry and frustrated as he described these activities to the Lords of Trade that the Board finally reprimanded him for his unintelligible and "ill-digested" writing.[53]

Meanwhile, William Partridge, a shipwright and merchant whom Usher dismissed from the office of treasurer for New Hampshire, was in England attacking Usher and seeking the lieutenant governorship for himself. He persuaded the proprietary claimant, Allen, to accept him in Usher's place; and upon his return to New Hampshire in 1697 he supported the antiproprietary elements in the colony, allowing them to remove Usher's main supporters from office.[54] But on the pretext that no one in New Hampshire was qualified to administer his oath of office to him, Partridge did not officially publish his commission for almost a year. This placed the onus of responsibility for antiproprietary activities upon the president and council.[55] Their actions provided Usher with material for charges that New Hampshire was in a state of revolution, operating in defiance of his (Usher's) commission.[56] The Board of Trade and Privy Council assured Usher that his commission remained in force until Partridge published his own and then notified him that the Treaty of Ryswick had ended the war. Armed with this information and official support, Usher journeyed to New Hampshire to reestablish his authority and friends and to begin land suits. But within two days of Usher's arrival and much to his chagrin, Partridge dropped all pretexts and published his own commission.[57] Since a new governor, the Earl of Bellomont, had just been chosen for Massachusetts, New Hampshire, and New York, both Usher and Partridge sought to win him to their position. Usher, fearful of what Bellomont might do as governor, persuaded Governor Allen to assume his New Hampshire office and exercise authority himself if he wanted to try his cases. After Allen's arrival, Partridge's supporters refused to sit in the council with Usher, and some trials were commenced. Two of these cases reached the Supreme Court of Judicature (where judges and juries could be controlled by the governor) in the spring of 1699.[58] But time ran out for Usher and Allen as the antiproprietary leaders contacted the Earl of Bellomont in July 1699 and persuaded him to publish his commission in New Hampshire so that they might be protected from Allen's attempts to take away their lands through corrupting the courts.[59]

Within a few weeks of his arrival Bellomont recognized the impact of the proprietary controversy upon New Hampshire growth. He wrote the Board of Trade that Allen's claim, "hovering over the country as it does, gives great disturbance to the present proprietors and hinders others from going to inhabit there." He added that a fair trial in New Hampshire would be impossible, "for all are parties against him except those that have no substance and are not qualified to be jurors." He concluded: "Let his title be what it will, I am sure the people here will never submit to part with their lands to him, and he must bring an army if he means to get possession of them." Bellomont, antagonized by Allen's actions and personality, immediately supported the antiproprietary group by removing the officers under Allen's administration, dismissing Usher's complaints as "not well grounded," and refusing Allen's proferred bribe of £10,000 sterling to divide the colony between the two of them.[60]

The first General Assembly under Bellomont quickly reorganized the court system and selection of juries in a manner favorable to the antiproprietary elements. Jurors could no longer be chosen arbitrarily by the sheriff. The sheriff must choose men who possessed a forty-shilling freehold or personal property worth £50 sterling, and they had to be selected proportionally from each town according to its population. Justices of the peace lost the power to hear land cases. The special Court of Chancery was abolished. The governor and council could hear appeals only on cases of over £100 sterling value, rather than the previous £50, while cases appealed to the king and Privy Council must value over £300 sterling, rather than the £100 sterling or more provided by the law of 1692. These changes revealed the suspicion of executive authority that had been fostered among New Hampshire politicians by the proprietary controversy.[61]

As a result of these changes and Governor Bellomont's attitude toward Allen's claim ("an abomination and mystery of iniquity" and a hindrance to New Hampshire prosperity), Allen was forced to sue in courts unfavorable to proprietary claims.[62] He brought at least four suits before the courts (one for each town) in the summer of 1700, lost each of them, and asked to appeal the cases to the Privy Council; but the Superior Courts of Judicature ruled that since the value of each case was under £300 sterling, the cases did not deserve an appeal. This did not stop Allen. Using his influence in England, he appealed anyway; and though the Privy Council affirmed the original ruling, it also declared that this judgment was not final and gave Allen permission to start a new ejectment suit. This time the jurors were to be instructed that if either party in the case asked for a special verdict to reserve all questions of law concerning the land title to the Queen in Council, then the jury must comply with the request.[63]

Thus, even though antiproprietary elements controlled the New Hampshire courts, they could not stop Allen from bringing his case before the Queen in Council. The English government still favored the proprietary claim.

Before this decision was handed down, however, and with the knowledge that Allen had obtained a hearing for his appeal in England, the New Hampshire General Assembly in 1701 sought greater protection for the colony's land titles. Three new laws pursued this objective, all of which asserted that the New Hampshire settlers held legal title to their property. The first law declared all past deeds valid. The second stated that all land grants in each town were "good and legal," and the third described the boundaries of each town and confirmed the property ownership within them.[64] But the deaths of the Earl of Bellomont and of King William brought New Hampshire to the Board of Trade's attention. After reading Bellomont's correspondence, its members concluded that William Partridge should be removed as lieutenant governor and John Usher be reappointed in his place.[65] Since his earlier removal, Usher had cemented his relationship with Samuel Allen by marrying his daughter Elizabeth (March 1699) and by accepting a mortgage from Allen (who badly needed money) of £1,500 for half the province of New Hampshire. In 1702, Usher traveled to England to aid Allen in his case and keep him abreast of New Hampshire politics. With Usher's information Allen petitioned the Privy Council to repeal these three New Hampshire laws because they ignored his proprietary claim, and the Privy Council responded by repealing the last two acts in 1703 and the first act in 1706.[66]

Usher also persuaded Allen to claim immediately all "unoccupied" and "uninclosed" lands in the colony and petition the Crown for approval of his entering into possession of them. The Queen, after consulting the attorney general on the validity of this claim, granted the petition and sent orders to the new governor of Massachusetts and New Hampshire, Joseph Dudley, that in case Allen was hindered in possessing these "wastelands," Dudley should order the New Hampshire juries to give a special verdict, reserving the final decision on all "matters of fact" to the Privy Council.[67] Once again the proprietary claimant, with help from the English government, had checkmated New Hampshire desires for secure land titles; and now he confronted them with claims to the common ("uninclosed") lands of each town. But the colonials still could control their local courts if they could persuade Governor Dudley to maintain the political status quo in the colony.

When Dudley first met with the New Hampshire General Assembly, he was granted a £250 gift; and in October 1703, he received a salary grant of £160 per year for the length of his administration—the first permanent salary ever given to a royal governor by the New Hampshire General Assembly. Dudley responded by maintaining the existing political officialdom in the colony over Usher's many objections.[68]

Allen lost his appeal before the Privy Council in 1702 because he could not prove that Mason had ever possessed land in New Hampshire. One of his first actions after returning to New Hampshire in 1703 was to take possession "by turf and twig" of the common lands in each of the five towns as well as the land beyond town boundaries. After Governor Dudley announced that Allen had taken title to the wastelands of the colony, the New Hampshire Council and House asked Dudley to tell the Queen that the New Hampshire people had no objection to Allen's title to the two-thirds of the province that was unoccupied. In fact, they would be glad to see him establish settlers there, for it would bring greater security to the entire colony. But they also told him that Allen's claim to each town's common lands was a grievance which they would contest in the courts.[69] Here was Allen's opportunity to obtain uncontested ownership of the western two-thirds of the colony, but he wanted it all and brought a suit against Richard Waldron into the New Hampshire Superior Court in 1704. When Governor Dudley failed to appear at the trial and did not order the jury to issue a special verdict, the case was decided against Allen. Allen then appealed his suit to the governor and council to be heard in May 1705.[70]

In the meantime, however, many New Hampshire settlers had rallied behind Waldron, organizing subscription committees from each town to raise money for his appeal. Aware of the strong sentiment in favor of Waldron and aware also of his own debts, Allen decided to compromise with these New Hampshire leaders. First, he offered to sell his claims to Waldron and other leading New Hampshire settlers but was refused. Then he asked Governor Dudley to advise the New Hampshire House of Representatives of his willingness to compromise. As a result, the House called for a meeting of its membership plus two elected "principal freeholders" of each town "to discourse, debate, and determine what may be most advantageous for the benefit of this province relating to Mr. Allen's claim."[71] On May 3, 1705, ignoring the legal problems of Allen's claims, this assemblage offered Allen a compromise settlement which would recognize his claim to 800 square miles of wasteland; give him 500 acres from Portsmouth and New Castle and 1,500 acres each from Hampton, Dover, Exeter, and Kingston; and pay him £2,000 in New England paper currency in return for Allen's quitclaim of all land lying within the existing town boundaries and his cessation of all lawsuits concerning proprietary claims. It even offered to recognize any contracts or leases that Allen had previously issued in the colony.[72] Why Allen did not immediately accept this highly favorable offer is unclear—perhaps severe illness prevented his doing so—but his hesitation proved fatal to his claim. He died of a "malignant fever" the next day, and his heirs never again came so near to possession of his New Hampshire claims because greedy John Usher, acting upon his belief that "one foot of land by the seaside is of more value than 100 feet up in the country," persuaded

Allen's son, Thomas, to reject the compromise offer and bring a new suit into the New Hampshire courts.[73]

This last and most famous case of *Allen* v. *Waldron* taxed the resources of both sides. Young Thomas Allen was so short of money that he mortgaged one-fourth of New Hampshire to Charles Hobby for £750, while Richard Waldron accepted subscriptions (over £2,000 worth, according to the unreliable John Usher) from his New Hampshire friends.[74]

During the trial in the Superior Court, Allen based his case primarily upon Mason's grants of 1629 and 1635 and his will of 1635 (ignoring the Laconia grants); the various attorney generals' opinions of 1660, 1675, and 1703; the depositions of six aged New Hampshire inhabitants who testified that Mason had sent some servants and built a house along the Piscataqua River and at Newichewannock Falls; King Charles II's inferential recognition of Mason's claim in the Cutt and Cranfield commissions; the Privy Council decision against Vaughan in 1686; the deed of sale to Allen in 1691; and Allen's "turf and twig" possession of the wastelands in 1703. Allen claimed title to all the lands of New Hampshire as deriving from the title of John Mason, and he requested that the jury be ordered to bring in a special verdict.

Waldron's defense centered upon attacking the legality of Mason's grants of 1629 and 1635. He argued that Mason himself must have been suspicious of his grant of 1629 because he sought a new grant to the same lands in 1635, that this grant was technically invalid because it did not follow the normal legal forms of the time, that the grant included some lands already given to Massachusetts Bay Colony in 1628, that the 1635 grant was invalid because it had not been signed by the members of the Council for New England nor by the Crown nor had "livery and seizin" been taken of the lands, and that Allen could not legally claim title under two separate grants. Moreover, he contended, Mason had never actually taken possession of the lands of either Waldron or New Hampshire. Waldron's brief stated that the only settlement established by Mason's servants was under the auspices of the Laconia Company, which had then deserted New Hampshire within a few years, and that Mason himself had never visited New Hampshire; therefore, if he had ever possessed a legal title, it was invalidated because he had never taken legal possession. Waldron also for the first time introduced a deed dated May 17, 1629, purporting to have been signed by John Wheelwright and the Indians of the Piscataqua region, granting Wheelwright all the lands between the Piscataqua and Merrimack Rivers (since John Wheelwright did not enter the Piscataqua region until 1638, the deed was a forgery). Waldron claimed that because this deed predated Mason's grant and because both he and his father had peacefully possessed the land for over sixty years (bringing several statutes of limitation into effect), the Masonian claim was invalid.[75] Neither party mentioned the crucial Laconia Patent of 1631; Waldron probably would have if he had known of its existence since it would have bolstered his defense. Allen probably had no knowledge of the grant either. Waldron concluded his case by arguing that the jury had no obligation to return a special verdict unless it doubted either the facts of the case or the laws involved.

The jury, following Waldron's contentions, brought in a verdict for the defendant in July 1707. Lieutenant Governor Usher then ordered the jury to return a special verdict, but it again returned a verdict for the defendant.[76] Hence the case went before the Privy Council without the special verdict; the Crown's influence had not materially aided Allen in the New Hampshire courts.[77]

The New Hampshire General Assembly sent an agent, George Vaughan, to England to support Waldron's case before the Privy Council and incidentally to obtain military aid from the Crown. Vaughan carried a petition to Queen Anne attacking Allen's claims as "unreasonable" and "unjust" because the first settlers had peaceably inhabited "a miserable desert" which was "vacuum domicilium" and yet through hard work and heavy expense had created a "fruitful field." In the process the inhabitants had fought two "long and distressing wars" and developed a trade "of great importance and advantage" to Great Britain, "without the least aid or assistance imaginable" from either Mason or Allen. Besides, the inhabitants had peacefully possessed the lands for almost seventy years. The petition concluded by promising the Crown that if Allen's claims were rejected, England would "reap the benefit" because New Hampshire's overall trade and its supplies for the Royal Navy would increase.[78]

This petition, strong evidence of popular New Hampshire support for Waldron's position, must have properly influenced the Privy Council, for in December 1708, it dismissed Allen's appeal, this time with no special permission to bring a new case forward in the New Hampshire courts, ending all attempts by Allen to obtain a favorable legal decision.[79]

When the good news reached New England, the New Hampshire General Assembly sent a petition of praise and thanksgiving to the Queen, while Usher, stunned and dejected, urged the Crown to purchase the Allen claim. Even Governor Dudley supported Usher's purchase plan, as it would bring a final resolution of the controversy and allow the immediate settlement of the "wastelands," which would, in turn, aid in establishing a militarily "defensible" and secure New Hampshire.[80] But such a purchase settlement was not to be obtained for another forty years—and not through the Crown, but, ironically enough, through a clique of New Hampshire merchants so interested in land speculation that they accepted the legitimacy of the proprietary claim as a means to that end.[81]

Never again did the Masonian controversy threaten the New Hampshire colonists so forcefully as it had before 1708, though it continued as an unresolved issue. Governor Dudley stressed its pre-1708 significance when he wrote the Board of Trade: "This Province is very small and poor, and a frontier to the enemy gives it a great check, but above all the controversy between Mr. Allen and tertenants keeps the Province at a great uncertainty, and it would dispose all things to a perfect settlement, if that were determined."[82] Its impact had been as much political as economic.

Nor did the Crown or English officialdom ever again take sides in the controversy. For a period of almost fifty years the New Hampshire settlers, confronted with direct Crown support for the proprietary claimant, had effectively thwarted this powerful combination. Chance, skill, determination, and the good will of local royal officials all played a part in this success. In the 1660's and 1670's the Crown's preoccupation with foreign policy had delayed the reckoning. In the 1680's the determination of the settlers in the face of lieutenant governor Cranfield's tactics and the opportune death of Robert Mason again deferred the problem. The Indian wars of the 1690's brought more postponements, and after 1699 the New Hampshire governors favored the antiproprietary elements, so that when the reckoning came, the determination of New Hampshire politicians and juries to remain firm against even royal orders emerged as the crucial factor. Yet chance again had played its part, for had Samuel Allen lived on in 1705, undoubtedly the controversy would have been settled by compromise.

A Pragmatic Solution

After 1708, the heirs to the New Hampshire proprietorship kept the issue alive by seeking various compromise agreements. When Charles Hobby died in 1716, for example, his estate executors offered to sell his title to the New Hampshire government; but the government refused his offer and supported the judge of probate, Richard Waldron, who refused to grant letters of administration to the heirs.[83] Again, in 1726 John Hobby sought a peaceful compromise that would render the New Hampshire colonists "entirely contented" while not "utterly disinherit[ing]" himself, but the House of Representatives ruled that any controversy over land titles should be determined in the common law courts according to provincial law, and Hobby dropped the matter.[84]

Yet the continued existence of this controversy caused minor difficulties for those settlers who sought new township grants from the New Hampshire government in the "wastelands" of the colony. By the 1720's all the older towns had experienced serious shortages of arable land; this fact coupled with new immigration, the need for timber resources, and a growing interest in land speculation persuaded the governor and council to resort to the tactics Usher had utilized in 1694 in the Kingston charter—granting new townships only "as far as in us lyes."[85] Another continuing problem arising from the proprietary controversy lay in the establishment of permanent town boundaries within the colony. Attempts had been made from time to time ever since the 1640's to solve this problem, but not until 1719 did the General Assembly establish permanent boundaries for the towns. Even then there was still a persistent aura of impermanence both in the older towns and in the new township grants. In some of the towns such disputes were tied in with the larger controversy over the location of the boundary line between Massachusetts and New Hampshire.[86] In comparison with the years before 1708, however, the proprietary controversy remained in a relatively quiescent state and had little effect upon New Hampshire growth or land utilization between 1713 and 1740.

It was no accident that when John Tufton Mason reopened the proprietorship issue in 1738, a group of New Hampshire merchant–land speculator–politicians interested themselves in his claims. Mason claimed that because Allen had docked the entail to his New Hampshire lands in England but not in New Hampshire, Allen's title to the land reverted to the original proprietary heirs after his death; therefore, Mason was now the sole heir. In June 1738, he presented his claim to the Massachusetts General Court and asked that he be allowed to be present at the hearings of the Boundary Line Commission (dealing with the Massachusetts-New Hampshire line) to protect his interests. The Massachusetts government purchased his claims in Massachusetts for £500 and considered buying his claims in New Hampshire as well, but some royal officials thought it would confuse the boundary commissioners and put Massachusetts in a bad light, so the project was dropped. But the New Hampshire agent in London, John Thomlinson, heard about the claim, consulted with his anti-Massachusetts friends in New Hampshire, and then persuaded Mason to sign a tripartite agreement relinquishing his claims to New Hampshire for £1,000 of New England currency payable within a year after New Hampshire became totally separated from Massachusetts' government, provided that Mason share proportionately in all future land grants from his claims.[87] From the viewpoint of the five New Hampshire signers, this tripartite agreement of 1739 would guarantee and stabilize all land titles within the colony while thwarting Massachusetts' attempts to expand into areas coveted by land- and timber-hungry New Hampshire colonists, perhaps ushering in an era of economic stability and prosperity.[88] In 1746, five years after the New Hampshire government had become entirely separate from that of Massachusetts, this tripartite agreement was fulfilled (though not exactly in the way the five New Hampshire signers had originally envisioned), and land titles east of the Merrimac River obtained security.[89]

Thus a controversy which had disrupted New Hampshire for almost a hundred years, and had been a major political and economic issue for its first seventy years, was resolved opportunistically through a compromise that grew out of a separate political and economic issue involving contested boundaries between New Hampshire and Massachusetts. A new group of New Hampshire leaders had solved this problem pragmatically by accepting the old Masonian claim (as an earlier group had been willing to do in 1705) once it no longer threatened the lands they occupied and offered them new and secure economic opportunities for westward expansion.

CHAPTER IV

THREATS TO UTILIZATION OF LAND: INDIAN WARS AND LESSER IRRITANTS

The New Hampshire colonists faced a variety of threats other than the Masonian controversy as they sought to attain the promise of the land in the seventeenth and early eighteenth centuries. Indian wars, boundary disputes, and land speculation each significantly affected their efforts. But evaluating the import of these factors is complicated by the presence of other threats, some of which—shortages of capital, labor, and cash—were prevalent in all the colonies, while others were more peculiar to New Hampshire.

The factors most specific to New Hampshire stemmed from its comparatively unattractive physical environment: a rugged, rocky, forested terrain relatively near the coastline, a cold climate, and a short growing season.[1] Undoubtedly this environment itself contributed greatly to the relatively slow growth of the province before 1740. A cursory glance at population statistics for the thirteen original colonies reveals that by 1740 only Delaware and Georgia had fewer people than New Hampshire.[2] A closer look shows that between 1640 and 1680 the population of Massachusetts increased fourfold (from 8,932 to 39,752), Connecticut's increased twelvefold (from 1,472 to 17,246), Rhode Island's tenfold (from 300 to 3,017), and Plymouth's sixfold (from 1,020 to 6,400); however, the population of New Hampshire only doubled (from 1,055 to 2,047). In the entire century from 1640 to 1740, New Hampshire's population increased from 1,000 to only 23,000, while the populations of Massachusetts grew from 9,000 to 152,000, of Connecticut from 1,500 to 90,000, and of Rhode Island from 300 to 25,000. The many attempts by New Hampshire towns to enlarge their boundaries so as to obtain valuable farm lands from another local town, or from Massachusetts, or from the Indians may be taken as further evidence of the stultifying effect of the environment upon the colony's growth.[3] In 1681 the New Hampshire Council confessed to the king that "our soil is so barren, and the winters so extreme, cold, and long that there is not provision enough raised to supply the inhabitants."[4] It is difficult, however, to give an accurate assessment of the role of this factor upon New Hampshire's growth, and this difficulty renders it almost impossible to isolate the relative impact of such other factors as the Indian wars, the New Hampshire boundary dispute, and the land-speculating, nonresident proprietors.

Wars with the Indians and French

Aside from the physical environment, the Indian wars were probably the most important factor limiting New Hampshire's growth during its first century. They created an atmosphere of anxiety and chronic insecurity and brought periods of depressed agricultural conditions and relative poverty. Before 1713 and as late as 1725 they retarded and at times halted the settlement of New Hampshire lands. In the later period from 1713 to 1740, the New Hampshire boundary dispute and such other minor irritants as land speculation and absentee landholders in the new towns limited to some extent the settlement of the land. But the impact of these factors was far less than that of the Indian wars.

Population statistics provide revealing evidence of the effect of the Indian wars. New Hampshire colonists fought three major and one minor war with the Indians before 1740: King Philip's War, 1675–78; King William's War, 1689–97; Queen Anne's War, 1702–13; and Dummer's War, 1722–25. In the decades in which Indian wars occurred, population increased at a rate of about 15 percent (see Table 1), while in the peaceful decades following each war, the population almost doubled. In the twenty years of intermittent war from 1690 to 1710, the population increased by about one-third (4,164 to 5,681), but in the thirty years of relative peace between 1710 and 1740, it increased fourfold (from roughly 5,700 to 23,300).

New Hampshire's geographical location as a northern frontier colony subject to attack from French Canada and from hostile Indians profoundly affected its people. For fifty years the Piscataqua settlers had lived in peace with their Algonquian Indian neighbors, the Pennacook and the Abnaki.[5] They had bargained with them for land and furs, sometimes ruthlessly so, as they gradually advanced westward and northward. These

Indians had generally reacted by accepting English cultural supremacy, retreating farther north and west, or by resorting to guerrilla tactics—attacking frontiersmen's homes. In the 1640's each of the New Hampshire towns had organized militias from the males between sixteen and sixty years of age to cope with marauding Indians. But it was King Philip's War that brought the first significant setbacks to New Hampshire's growth.

Though the war broke out in southern New England in June of 1675, by September the Abnaki, or "Eastern Indians," of Maine decided to join the fray. They raided the Oyster River lumber settlement on the edge of

TABLE 1

ESTIMATED POPULATION OF NEW HAMPSHIRE: 1630-1780

Year	Number[1]	Negroes
1630	500	0
1640	1,055	30
1650	1,305	40
1660	1,555	50
1670	1,805	65
1680	2,047	75
1690	4,164	100
1700	4,968	130
1710	5,681	150
1720	9,375	170
1730	10,755	200
1740	23,256	500
1750	27,505	550
1760	39,093	600
1770	62,396	654
1780	87,802	541

[1]These estimates combine Negro and white population.

Source--Historical Statistics of the United States, Colonial Times to 1957 (Washington: 1960), p. 756.

Dover and attacked settlers near Exeter and Hampton and across the Piscataqua River in Maine.[6] Dover's most eminent citizen, Major Richard Waldron, scoured the frontier with 120 men in search of the Indians but was so unsuccessful that he ordered the frontier settlers to live in garrisons for protection. He wrote the Massachusetts government that "the distractions of those places by reasons of persons being forced to forsake their plantation and leave their corn and cattle to the enemy doth portend inevitable want, etc., to ensue, unless God by his extraordinary providence prevent."[7] In response, the Massachusetts General Court sent him forty more men and ordered the collection of seven "single country rates" from Hampton and Exeter and nine "rates" from Portsmouth and Dover for the war effort.[8] But the Indian raids continued through the fall, bringing the harvesting to a halt and filling the frontiersmen with fear and insecurity.

The heavy snowfall in December brought an end to the Indian raids, and in the spring of 1676, Waldron and two others negotiated a peace treaty with the Pennacook and the Abnaki tribes which became effective in July.[9] With Indian defeats in southern New England and King Philip dead, it appeared by the middle of August that the war was over, but the fleeing southern Indians, seeking refuge among the Abnaki, persuaded them to continue harassing the settlements in the Piscataqua region. Major Waldron also played a part in the continuance of the war when, in September 1676, he tricked some 200 Indians into surrendering and in the process lost the confidence of his Pennacook Indian friends, who now had proof of the white man's treachery.[10]

In the wake of renewed raids in lower Maine, six of the leading men of Portsmouth and Dover advised the governor of Massachusetts that it would be better to secure "what is left" rather than "attempting to regain what is lost." In simple, straightforward language they explained their insecurity:

Sure we are that ourselves (that is the County of Norfolk with Dover and Portsmouth) are so far from being capable of sparing any forces for that expedition that we find ourselves so thinned and weakened by those that are out already that there is nothing but the singular Providence of God hath prevented our being so utterly run down. The enemy observes our Motions and knows our strength (weakness rather) better than we are willing he should and probably had been with ere this had not the Highest Power ruled him. . . . Our own men are not enough to maintain our own places, if any Assault be made and yet many of ours are now on the other side of the Piscataqua River. We expect an onset in one place or other every day and can expect no relief from those that are so far from home. . . . We design not a lessening or discouragement of the Army who rather need strengthening and encouragement for we verily think that if . . . the Army had not been there, all the parts on the other side of the River had been possessed by the Enemy perhaps ourselves too ere this time. But what we aim at is that ourselves also may be put into a capacity to defend ourselves.[11]

In this difficult situation the Piscataqua settlers returned to the garrison houses, where they endured shortages of wheat and bread as well as hit and run Indian raids.[12] Not until April 1678 did peace come to the Piscataqua area.[13]

King Philip's War settled nothing in northern New England, for the treaty allowed the Abnaki to remain on their lands while paying a token quitrent to proprietary claimants. But the war's effects were calamitous. There were economic dislocations both in agriculture and in trade; money was scarce; Dover and Portsmouth were behind in taxes some thirty-two "country rates"; and unemployment was so rampant that the Massachusetts General Court ordered "the sundry men and single persons . . . that are out of employment" to be impressed into the town militias at York, Dover, and Portsmouth.[14] The war also stopped westward and northward expansion. Ten years later Dover's Oyster River precinct would still be the edge of the New Hampshire frontier, and Dover itself would suffer the first ravages of King William's War.

Those ten years (1679–89) brought extraordinary changes in New Hampshire politics, placing the towns in a far more insecure position than ever before. In 1679, through the influence of the proprietary claimant, Robert Mason, New Hampshire became a royal colony. In 1686 it became part of the Dominion of New England, which was destroyed with the Glorious Revolution in Massachusetts in 1689. The New Hampshire towns emerged from these changes as four independent republics—for the moment left to themselves. The English government ignored them until 1691; while, with the overthrow of Andros, the new Massachusetts government recalled all troops in frontier areas, leaving the Piscataqua frontier invitingly open to the French and Indians.[15] At this inauspicious time the Pennacook Indians decided to obtain revenge against Major Waldron for his treachery of 1676.

The Indians raided the Cochecho area of Dover June 27, 1689, killing Waldron and twenty-two others and taking twenty-nine prisoners.[16] A second raid in August, this time at the Oyster River precinct, brought eighteen more deaths.[17] Once again the Piscataqua settlers fled to the garrison houses for security.

Confronted with an Indian war and having no organized government to protect them, the New Hampshire leaders attempted the creation of a new central government to persevere until they received further word from the Crown, but this effort proved unsuccessful. Then, after a private petition was sent to the Crown for troops, weapons, and a new royal governor, the four towns petitioned the Massachusetts government, asking that they be taken under its jurisdiction: "And we, who were under your government, having been for some time destitute of power sufficient to put ourselves into a capacity for defence against the common enemy; and having, with great expectation, awaited their Majesties' order for a settlement amongst us, which not yet arriving, considering how liable we are to destruction by the enemy, which of ourselves we cannot prevent, we are therefore necessitated at present to supplicate your Honors for government and protection, as formerly, until their Majesties' pleasure shall be known concerning us."[18] In March 1689/90 the Massachusetts government extended its "protection and care" to New Hampshire and sent 400 troops to the frontier towns (Dover, Exeter, and Portsmouth were described as such), with sixty of them to be stationed at Portsmouth's fort.[19] But this action had little immediate effect, for later in the month the Indians attacked the Salmon Falls settlement (above Dover on the Piscataqua River), killing some thirty people and carrying away about fifty more; then, in May they destroyed the fort and town at Casco Bay in lower Maine.[20] After these attacks the frontiersmen fled either to the garrisons or to the larger eastern towns. Wells (in Maine) and Portsmouth became refugee centers by the end of the summer and faced both housing and food shortages in the wake of trade dislocations and the loss of the fall harvests.[21]

For the next four years the Piscataqua region suffered from desultory raids and ambushes, but it lost much of its military protection when Massachusetts withdrew most of its troops after the Crown reestablished a royal government in New Hampshire in 1692. In the wake of Massachusetts' refusal of troops, the new lieutenant governor, John Usher (the agent of the proprietary claimant), sent a request for soldiers to the Connecticut government in which he pointed out that New Hampshire had been left "wholly to defend itself, which it is not able to do, unless aided and assisted by some other of the neighboring provinces; for that the Indian and French enemies are frequently making incursions and desolations, cutting off our frontier places and the inhabitants thereof."[22] Just a few months earlier some members of the New Hampshire Council had petitioned the Crown "that we may be annexed to the Government of . . . Massachusetts." Their petition stated that the war had generated "great Poverty" in New Hampshire and that without the assistance of Massachusetts "we must quit the province to the enemy and be exposed to ruin and destruction."[23] Neither petition achieved its goal.

In July 1694, in a well-planned offensive, some 250 French and Indians attacked the Oyster River precinct, destroying five of its twelve garrisons, killing or carrying off about 100 people, and burning some twenty homes. A French priest occupied the town meetinghouse and defaced the pulpit with chalk during these actions.[24] This attack was the single most devastating Indian raid in New Hampshire's history—well calculated to force the settlers to "quit the province." With most of the Dover and

Exeter inhabitants evacuating their homes for the garrison houses or safer towns eastward, the New Hampshire government petitioned Massachusetts for sixty troops to be stationed in the garrisons and the fort at New Castle. This time Massachusetts sent troops, but only on condition that the New Hampshire government pay one-third of their wages.[25] Lieutenant Governor Usher, dissatisfied by the reluctance of Massachusetts to aid a proprietary-claimed colony, wrote the Lords of Trade in September 1694, asking that a general governor be appointed for New England to facilitate the creation of a unified military strategy.[26]

Although there were no more major raids in New Hampshire during the remainder of King William's War, the settlers maintained a state of military preparedness, continued to live in the garrison houses, and neglected their crops. By March 1696, the colony faced such famine conditions that the government had to purchase corn and pork from Boston to feed the soldiers in its employ.[27] Moreover, poverty had increased, and the New Hampshire Assembly used this as an excuse for denying the lieutenant governor a salary. In a message to him the assembly spoke of "our extreme poverty and scarcity of bread for the year," the "danger of an invasion both by sea and land from the French and Indian enemy," and the need for a petition to the Crown "that it will be much better defense of this Province to be annexed to Boston."[28]

The general insecurity confronting the Piscataqua settlers is illuminated in the New Hampshire Council's letter to Massachusetts requesting sixty troops as protection for the New Hampshire towns. After describing the exposed conditions of the five towns, the letter pointed out their peculiar predicament: "Indeed the whole Province are so much frontiers to the enemy by sea or land, that one place is not able to give relief to another."[29] The Massachusetts government responded by sending forty soldiers.

When the Abnaki Indians finally signed a treaty of submission in 1698, ending King William's War, the people of New Hampshire had suffered some 400 deaths and contributed as much as £2,500 in war taxes.[30] The respite from war was brief. By the winter of 1699, rumors of Indian "mischief" were rife, and the New Hampshire government ordered the towns to appoint a "watch and ward" in each precinct, repair all garrisons, and send out scouts. Although the Indians did not attack until after the War of the Spanish Succession had begun, the Piscataqua frontiersmen maintained a state of military alert during the five years of uneasy peace.[31] During these same years the General Assembly, endangered by both Indians and the proprietary claimant, appointed an agent, William Vaughan, to present the settlers' grievances to the Crown. Vaughan requested a grant of powder and stores from the treasury for Fort William and Mary at New Castle because "the country by reason of their poverty are not able to repair [it] . . . and . . . are not in a condition to make any defence."[32] But even a coincidental request from the new governor of Massachusetts and New Hampshire, Joseph Dudley, had no effect on the queen.[33]

During Queen Anne's War the brunt of the French and Indian attacks fell once again on Maine and Massachusetts. New Hampshire escaped with relatively light Indian raids on the outlying towns. Nevertheless, the settlers lived in constant fear of a full-fledged invasion and alternated between living in garrisons and at home.[34] The worst Indian raids came in 1703-4, 1706-7, and 1710-11; only the year 1705 was relatively tension free in the colony.

Probably the main reason why the New Hampshire settlers had relatively fewer casualties during this war than in King William's War lay in the fact that Massachusetts and New Hampshire had the same governor, who planned military strategy in terms of all the territory under his jurisdiction. Large numbers of Massachusetts troops guarded the Piscataqua frontier from time to time; frontier scouts were encouraged to go scalp-hunting during the winters; the governor aided in repairing and restoring the fort at New Castle and in describing New Hampshire's military needs to the queen—all of which gave greater security to the colony, partially at Massachusetts' expense.[35] In a petition to Queen Anne in July 1706, the New Hampshire General Assembly recognized Governor Joseph Dudley's contributions: "Notwithstanding the very great troubles this little Province lies so immediately exposed unto by the barbarous savages and French, our neighbors: yet by the good Providence of almighty God, the courage, care, and prudence of Colonel Dudly, your Majesty's Captain-General and Governor, we have been exceedingly preserved beyond what has been in former wars."[36]

Nevertheless, New Hampshire inhabitants experienced unpleasant hardships during Queen Anne's War, especially through taxation. Between 1704 and 1712, their government collected over £15,000 in taxes, of which at least £12,000 was directly related to the war (compare this with £2,500 raised during King William's War).[37] These taxes came at a time of great scarcity of money. In 1703, the New Hampshire government required all able-bodied men to give ten days service to the militia and all other men to hire substitutes because the government itself could not afford to pay the militia.[38] In early 1705 the General Assembly petitioned the Crown for powder, ammunition, and forty soldiers because the New Hampshire people, "being burdened with the Indian wars," had become "miserable poor."[39] By 1706 gunpowder was so scarce in the province that, given rumors of a French invasion, the council forbade the export of powder and ordered a search of all houses and warehouses so that an accurate inventory of powder could be obtained.[40] In October 1707, the mounting costs of the war drove the government to authorize the sending of an agent with a new petition for arms and supplies to the queen. This petition was an expressive portrayal of the difficulties of a frontier province:

The great expense of rebuilding [the] fort and constant keeping men in pay for the better defense of this . . . Province towards the sea, together with the extraordinary charge of defending the frontiers by land against the Indian rebels, assisted by the French . . . has reduced your Majesty's poor subjects to a great distress; many of whom have been necessitated to remove, by which our number and strength are lessened; others cannot provide their families but with hazard of their lives, many fields lying untilled, unless such as are under cover of the garrisons; at present we labor under a great want of good small arms and ammunition, which are daily wasted and lost in the wilderness in pursuit of the enemy, and by reason of our poverty cannot be supplied.[41]

In the wake of her decision to support Samuel Vetch's idea of an expedition against Canada, the queen in early 1709 gave New Hampshire a generous supply of powder, muskets, and miscellaneous military supplies.[42] But now the New Hampshire government was confronted with the necessity of raising money in support of the Canada Expedition. After pointing out "that our poverty is such that one-third of the inhabitants have not bread to eat nor wherewithal to procure it,"[43] the New Hampshire General Assembly issued the first paper currency in its history by authorizing £4,000 in "bills of credit."[44] Between 1709 and 1713, a total of £11,000 in bills of credit was issued, most of it for support of the various expeditions against Canada and Port Royal.[45]

The war's effect on land settlement can be seen in the attempts to establish the new town of Kingston. Chartered and granted in 1694, Kingston was first settled in the lull between 1700 and 1703, only to be abandoned when the war was renewed. In 1705, during another lull in the war, the Kingston grantees asked the General Assembly if they could resettle the town. The General Assembly renewed the grant provided that thirty or more families settle there, build a fort, and establish a minister within three years. For the next eight years these settlers eked out a precarious living on the edge of the frontier. Harassed by the Indians, they spent most of their time in garrison houses. Some of the settlers abandoned the town, weakening the defenses of those who remained. In 1708, the General Assembly allowed the town a representative to the House of Representatives, which meant that the town would have to pay its proportion of province taxes as well. Kingston ignored this privilege for three years, until it was ordered to send a representative. Then, the townspeople petitioned that they might "yet stand on the establishment wee did before" because "the enemy now insults us as much as ever and . . . our circumstances [are] in a very low condition." The General Assembly granted their request for the duration of the war.[46] The other harassed frontier settlement, Oyster River (part of Dover), was set back so far by the two wars that it was not incorporated as the town of Durham until 1732. Nonetheless, neither of these frontier settlements was completely abandoned during Queen Anne's War, attesting to the courage of the settlers under great duress and to the aid received from the eastern towns and the Massachusetts government.

When peace was concluded with the Indians in July of 1713, New Hampshire's frontier was still more or less what it had been in 1676. Dover, Exeter, and Kingston (originally part of Hampton), along with the Maine settlements, constituted the frontier of the Piscataqua region.[47] The main difference was that there were no longer any Indians living within New Hampshire. The nearest Indians now lived at Penobscot and Norridgewock in Maine, some 150 miles away.[48] Governor Dudley correctly understood the significance of these wars to the development of New Hampshire when he wrote the Board of Trade: "This Province is very small and poor, and a frontier to the enemy, gives it a great check."[49] Perhaps one of the main topics of conversation at the unprecedented dinner for the civil and military officers and the "gentlemen of the Town of Portsmouth," held at Treasurer Samuel Penhallow's home (at public expense) to celebrate the war's end, was how best to exploit New Hampshire backcountry land and timber resources now that the war was over.[50]

In the ten years of relative peace following Queen Anne's War, the New Hampshire government chartered five new townships beyond the older towns. Nevertheless, when Dummer's War broke out in 1722, most of the older towns were still part of the frontier; for example, Indian skirmishes plagued Dover, Oyster River, and Kingston during the war.[51] Only Portsmouth, New Castle, and Hampton could no longer be considered part of the New Hampshire frontier in the 1720's.

The Abnaki, or Eastern Indians, had not settled back into peaceful ways after Queen Anne's War. Instead, spurred on by a French Jesuit, Father Rale, who had a missionary post at Norridgewock on the Kennebec River,[52] the Indians resorted to violence as the best method to redress their grievances against the colonial land speculators and sharp traders in Maine.[53] In 1722, the Massachusetts government authorized an expedition to capture Father Rale. The expedition missed Rale but captured his incriminating letters to the Quebec governor, and the Indians retaliated by attacking the Maine settlements and destroying the town of Brunswick. These actions brought Massachusetts to a declaration of war.[54]

Dummer's War had relatively little effect on land development in New Hampshire, since there were no major invasions of New Hampshire by French or Indians and no serious threats to New Hampshire towns during the three-year war. Most of the fighting took place in Maine. The New Hampshire government did send out some scouts to guard the frontiers, promising them £100 for each Indian scalp they brought back; it also sent some ninety men into Maine to help Massachusetts expeditions against the Indians.[55] The war stimulated some economic expansion, for the government used it as a pretext for issuing over £14,000 in bills of credit badly needed for an adequate medium of exchange within the colony.[56] None of the frontier towns were abandoned during this war; and although Kingston once again petitioned for relief from the "Province tax" because of its "exposed" conditions, the General Assembly ignored the petition.[57] Nonetheless, the war undoubtedly stifled potential westward expansion among the colonists, who waited for a more psychologically propitious moment. Within a year after the war's end, six more new townships were chartered by the governor and council.[58]

The treaty signed with the Eastern Indians at Casco Bay in the spring of 1726 ushered in an eighteen-year era of uneasy peace with the French and Indians. By the time King George's War broke out in New England, the New Hampshire frontier had moved west of the Merrimack River, leaving all of the older towns (those established before 1727) in a new and secure status. After 1725 the French and Indians no longer threatened the utilization of land resources by eastern New Hampshire settlers. The Piscataqua colonists owed this new security primarily to the efforts of their neighbors in Massachusetts, and their military dependence upon Massachusetts continued through the remainder of the colonial period.

A Boundary Dispute with Massachusetts

Another factor affecting the New Hampshire colonists' utilization of the land, particularly after 1713, was the dispute over the exact location of the Massachusetts-New Hampshire boundary line. Though the actual economic impact of this dispute was negligible while the controversy raged, both its political impact and its long-range economic benefits for New Hampshire were crucial in determining future directions within the colony. The dispute brought the political ascendancy of the Wentworth family, and its resolution increased New Hampshire's land area threefold.

The origins of the boundary controversy lay in the jurisdictional separation of Massachusetts and New Hampshire in 1679, which placed the two colonies in competition with each other. The northern boundary of Massachusetts had been established in its original charter and was restated by English judges in 1677 as "all those lands . . . which lie and be within the space of three English miles to the northward of the . . . Merrimack River, or to the northward of any and every part thereof." But when Massachusetts received its new charter in 1691, the phrase "of any and every part thereof" was omitted from the boundary description, although the commissions of the various New Hampshire governors from Allen in 1692 through Burnett in 1728 continued the former phrasing when describing the borders of New Hampshire.[59]

Both legal and practical problems were present in the dispute. The main legal question, arising from the change in the Massachusetts charter, was whether the boundary should follow a westward course from a point three miles north of the mouth of the Merrimack River, or whether it should be a crooked parallel line three miles above or north of the river, following its meandering course. This problem was complicated by the fact that the course of the river westward from the coast turns northward after some sixty miles into the interior and continues a northerly and at times northeasterly direction to its source near Lake Winnepesaukee (see Map 2). In other words, the river flows southwest, south, southeast, and then east from its source to the Atlantic Ocean. If one literally interpreted the phrasing of the charter, the line would cross and recross the Merrimack River innumerable times.[60] Until about 1720 the general assumption in both Massachusetts and New Hampshire was that the Merrimack River in both its westward and northward course established the boundary between the two colonies. Massachusetts' leaders considered its title to the lands west of the Merrimack River's northerly course secure and unchallenged. To them the whole dispute was how to determine the exact point from which the three miles north should be computed—whether from the center of the Merrimack River, from the north side of the river, or at the "black rocks" which marked an older and more northerly mouth. The practical aspects of the issue lay in the fact that a few of the Massachusetts border towns (Salisbury and Haverhill, for example) had expanded beyond the three-mile limit north of the river at the time when New Hampshire had accepted Massachusetts' jurisdiction. The Indian wars had brought tax increases in both colonies, so some of the people in this area took advantage of its unresolved jurisdictional status to claim residence in the other colony whenever either colony attempted to tax them. Others experienced double taxation as zealous local officials in both colonies worked for the elimination of tax evasion among the "borderers."[61]

The whole issue first arose in 1693 when Lieutenant Governor Usher, seeking a determination of the bounds of Allen's claim, used the existence of tax evasion along the boundary near Hampton and Salisbury as a basis for sending surveyors out to run the line. The Massachusetts government postponed the issue, however, by refusing to participate in a survey until any conflicts of interpretation were settled.[62] After Kingston received a charter and Hampton's townspeople complained again, Usher in 1695 pushed once more for a settlement of the boundary, this time instructing surveyors to work out the boundaries without Massachusetts' assistance if

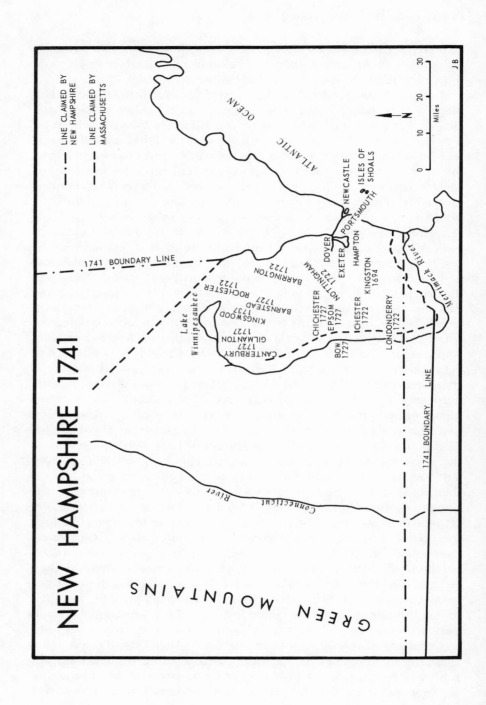

NEW HAMPSHIRE 1741

LINE CLAIMED BY NEW HAMPSHIRE

LINE CLAIMED BY MASSACHUSETTS

ATLANTIC OCEAN

NEWCASTLE
PORTSMOUTH
ISLES OF SHOALS

DOVER
EXETER
HAMPTON
KINGSTON 1694

NOTTINGHAM 1722
BARRINGTON 1722
ROCHESTER 1722

CHICHESTER 1727
EPSOM 1727
BARNSTEAD 1727
ICHESTER 1722

KINGSWOOD 1737

GILMANTON 1727

CANTERBURY 1727

BOW 1727

LONDONDERRY 1722

1741 BOUNDARY LINE

Lake Winnipesaukee

Merrimack River

Connecticut River

GREEN MOUNTAINS

1741 BOUNDARY LINE

N

0   10   20   30
Miles

J B

necessary.[63] After Usher's removal from office, the issue died. But he revived it again upon his return, and it continued unresolved.[64]

Until 1713 the determination of the boundary, though a minor problem, received little attention in New Hampshire, primarily because its people had been too preoccupied with the wars and the proprietary controversy but also because its foremost advocate was the unpopular Usher. By 1713, however, the external threats had almost disappeared while a number of internal social and economic motivations urged many settlers to look outward and westward for satisfaction. Outlying areas of the older towns, for example, began demanding separate parish status and ultimately complete independence from their parent towns, and the governor and council received numerous petitions requesting new township grants above the older towns.[65]

Upon Queen Anne's death, George Vaughan, the New Hampshire agent in London, replaced Usher as lieutenant governor; and within two months of his arrival, he appointed a new committee which met with some Massachusetts commissioners to draw the "partition line." But this group had no more success than the others in resolving their differences.[66]

Nevertheless, a turning point was at hand. In 1718, some 500 Scotch-Irish immigrants arrived in Boston and sought a township grant, but the Massachusetts government could not satisfy their needs. In April 1719, a number of them (without legal authority from any source) established a settlement at Nutfield, partially within the area contested by Massachusetts and New Hampshire, north of the Merrimack River. Seeking legal support for their claim, they first purchased the invalid Wheelwright deed, having no knowledge of its real status, and then petitioned Massachusetts for legal recognition or a township grant. The Massachusetts government refused either alternative on the grounds that their town was out of its jurisdiction.

This refusal indicated that the Massachusetts government was not aggressively pushing its boundary claims against its smaller neighbor, for the Nutfield petition offered it a strong opportunity to do so. Instead, throughout the controversy Massachusetts aimed at settling only those areas which its people assumed were not legally questionable—particularly the land west of the Merrimack's northerly course—while cautiously awaiting an equitable solution to the thorny problem of the exact location of the west line above the river.

The Nutfield settlers next approached the New Hampshire government for a township grant, but the continuing proprietary claim and the boundary issue caused the petition to be dismissed. Nevertheless, Nutfield's presence triggered a turning point in the boundary controversy, for sometime between April 1719 and April 1720, the New Hampshire governor and council decided to change their legal contentions. In April

1719, after the Nutfield settlers' arrival, the New Hampshire government had appointed a new committee to survey and map the Merrimack and "run the line" according to the Massachusetts charter. The Nutfield petition was presented in September; in December, the New Hampshire General Assembly instructed its commissioners to run the line westward from the coast "till you meet the great river which runs out of Winnepesaukee Pond," discriminating for the first time between the Merrimack River in its east-west course and in its north-south course and contesting the traditional view that the Merrimack River represented the western boundary of the colony as well as the southern boundary. When, in April 1720, the General Assembly chose a new agent for New Hampshire, it pointedly explained to him the conflict of interest between the two colonies and instructed him to place the dispute before the Board of Trade along with the proper maps. He was instructed that "the extent of this province is all the lands between Massachusetts and Province of Maine, our south bounds is three miles north of the Merrimack River at the Atlantic Ocean . . . and from thence a west line into the main land so far as the Massachusetts extends"—a direct challenge to Massachusetts' claims west of the Merrimack.[67] Moreover, for the first time the northern boundary of New Hampshire was challenged. Traditionally, as defined by Massachusetts, this boundary was a line running due northwest from Lovell's Pond, the source of the Newichewannock River. But the New Hampshire agent was now instructed to seek a line running from "the head of the Newichewannock River . . . a very few degrees westward of the North up into the mainland."

John Wentworth—the lieutenant governor of New Hampshire and a prominent local sea captain, mast trader, and merchant—led this challenge. He wrote the Board of Trade in December 1720 that Massachusetts was both unneighborly and "strangers to all Kingly power"; that the people of New Hampshire hoped for an early settlement of the boundary line; and that it was a "pity" that a west line drawn from the mouth of the Merrimack and north line drawn from the mouth of the Piscataqua into the country were not the actual boundaries, for then New Hampshire would no longer be a "little" province.[68] From 1721 until the final decision on the boundary line in 1740, Wentworth and an ever-widening circle of interested "friends" and relatives used the minor discontent along the southern border as the "whipping boy" for an all-out, aggressive attack on Massachusetts' relationships with New Hampshire in an attempt to obtain a favorable boundary decision and, after 1731, a separate governor.[69]

Massachusetts land grants constituted a major object of their attack. In 1726 the Massachusetts government granted the township of Penacook to some settlers. This grant was located just west of the Merrimack River near present-day Concord, New Hampshire. The New Hampshire government responded by granting the township of Bow in the same area. In the 1730's Massachusetts granted a line of townships between the Merrimack and Connecticut Rivers in the area the Wentworth group contended should be part of New Hampshire.[70] These grants and many other relationships—trade, religion, timber policy, the governor's home colony —were exploited by this group, who portrayed the Massachusetts government as tyrannical, unjust, conspiratorial, and disloyal toward the "poor little distressed loyal Province" of New Hampshire. In actuality, the Wentworth group resorted to opportunism and conspiracy more frequently than Massachusetts politicians did in this intracolonial controversy.

Until 1730 the Wentworth faction (some lumberers, merchants, and local royal officials) had its way in New Hampshire politics, but the appointment of Jonathan Belcher—a relative of the Waldrons, Cutts, and Vaughans, who held anti-Wentworth attitudes—to the governorship of Massachusetts and New Hampshire forced the Wentworth supporters into the background as Belcher appointees displaced them from positions of power and influence in the colony. From this point on, the Wentworth faction—portraying Belcher as unsympathetic, prejudiced, and tyrannical—sought a separate governor for the colony; and the outspoken stands of the group brought about the development of strong anti- and pro-Massachusetts parties in New Hampshire.[71] With goals such as new western lands, a separate governor, and domination of New Hampshire politics guiding them, this faction sought to force the boundary dispute before the Privy Council, displaying an unwillingness to compromise at any other level. Their determined opportunism brought success, for in 1740 the Privy Council awarded them wider bounds than they had sought, opening the western lands between the Merrimack and Connecticut Rivers to the New Hampshire settlers.[72] According to Francis Wilks, the Massachusetts agent in London, the Privy Council awarded New Hampshire the victory because it looked upon the dispute as between Massachusetts and the Crown, and therefore, "whatever was not granted to us [Massachusetts] belonged to the Crown."[73] To Wilks the key factor in this loss was official bias against Massachusetts in England.

But this was only the first step. With the boundary dispute no longer available as a cause célèbre, the Wentworth faction turned to the London mast contractors for support. Benning Wentworth and John Thomlinson[74] persuaded Ralph Gulston, the mast contractor for the Royal Navy, to join them and other London merchants in a petition for the appointment of a separate governor for New Hampshire as the only way "to keep that province from sinking and to make it a useful and flourishing colony."[75] This petition and agent Thomlinson's varied connections and skills made the difference. In August 1741, Benning Wentworth was commissioned governor of New Hampshire. He returned home to establish a new political order in the colony—a monopolization of political power never before seen in New Hampshire but nevertheless acceptable to the inhabitants.[76]

Thus, New Hampshire emerged from the boundary dispute with more land than even the Wentworths had expected. Just as Crown influence had ultimately aided the New Hampshire colonists against the proprietor, so it aided them against Massachusetts. Never again in the colonial period did a shortage of western lands exist in New Hampshire. After 1740, promising new lands across the Merrimack River beckoned New Hampshire colonists; and with a century's experience behind them, they stood ready to realize the promise of this new land.

Land Speculation and Nonresident Proprietors

In their first hundred years in the Piscataqua environment the settlers of New Hampshire had confronted various obstacles as they developed the land and its resources. The topography, climate, Indian wars, proprietary claimants, and disputed boundaries had all conjoined with many other less tangible factors to limit their agricultural, geographical, and numerical expansion. Until 1713, New Hampshire's growth in these realms had been minimal; its condition had remained that of a frontier in arrested development. After 1713, however, with some of these obstacles at least partially overcome, the New Hampshire people began to make substantial progress in several directions.

The return of peace had brought steady increases in agricultural production, as farmers returned to their lands and worked them in relative security. It also had brought new immigration and some pressure for the development of new western lands. At first some of the older towns absorbed these pressures, but in 1722 the New Hampshire government succumbed to various demands and granted five new townships in the wastelands of the colony, including a grant to the Nutfield petitioners (Londonderry). Since a few of these grants challenged Massachusetts claims along the Merrimack River (Chester and Londonderry), in 1726 the Massachusetts government granted the township of Penacook along the Merrimack as well. The next year the New Hampshire government granted six new townships, encompassing almost all the ungranted land east of the Merrimack River along its entire course.[77] In 1737, Governor Belcher and the council granted out the last unchartered land east of the Merrimack as the township of Kingswood.[78]

These land grants of the 1720's initiated a new era in New Hampshire land customs, for while actual usage of timber and commons in the new towns tended to remain similar to the practices of the older towns, other important changes appeared. In the first place Lieutenant Governor Wentworth used these grants for political and speculative purposes. This is not to suggest that there had never been any land speculation in the colony before 1722; it was the quantity that changed. For instance, the governor and lieutenant governor each received 500 acres and a home lot in all township charters of the 1720's, while each member of the council (which, with the governor, granted the charters) and many other leading men of the colony received proprietary shares. In each township grant of 1727 almost every member of the House of Representatives received a share as well. It is no wonder that John Wentworth was a popular executive, for if one were searching for a crude list of the most prominent men of New Hampshire in the 1720's, he would have to look no further than the various proprietary lists of 1727. Then, too, many if not most of these people had no intention of residing in the new towns, but only of profiting as town land values increased—selling their share for a good profit at the right time. The result was an increase of tenancy in new towns and large numbers of nonresident proprietors, and this situation sometimes created social and economic tensions which affected the development of the new towns.

The impact of nonresident proprietorship varied from town to town, with fewer conflicts generally in those towns which grew rapidly or which contained far more resident than nonresident proprietors: Chester and Londonderry are examples of each.[79] In most of the conflicts that did occur between resident proprietors and inhabitants on the one hand and nonresident proprietors on the other, the town inhabitants won their points, discriminating against nonresidents in town land divisions and commons and timber usage, for example; but when taxation of nonresident proprietors appeared desirable, some of the towns faced difficulties. Most of the town charters (Barrington and Epsom excepted) stipulated that each proprietor had to pay any town charges or forfeit his share in the town, but this stipulation did not contain provisions for town enforcement. Thus, neither the resident proprietors nor the inhabitants could legally force nonresident proprietors to pay their fair share of taxes. As a result, there were a number of complaints to the New Hampshire government about this problem in the 1730's and 1740's. Six of the new towns separately petitioned for redress. The Rochester petition of 1736 was typical:

We, the inhabitants of Rochester, being persuaded that the gospel and means of grace is a rich and invaluable privilege, for which reason we can't but much lament our sad state while we live without said means; and seeing no rational

prospect of obtaining them for some considerable time to come without the help
and assistance of the non-resident proprietors . . . and hoping it may not be
deemed unreasonable to desire some assistance from them . . . since tis too evident
to need any proof that their temporal interest is greatly advanced by us . . . by our
settling in said town . . . do once more humbly request the legislative power to
pass an act whereby to oblige the proprietors of said Rochester to assist . . . in
supporting the gospel in . . . Rochester for the space of six or seven years.[80]

That this problem continued in the later towns established after 1740 is
illustrated by the Chichester petition of 1760:

That for want of a proper general law for enabling proprietors of unsettled
townships to transact their affairs relating to making said settlements (the said
proprietors not having obtained a particular act in their favor) the business of said
settlement is very backward. . . . That such a situation of affairs is not only a
prejudice to particular proprieties and townships but to the province in general by
retarding many settlements which long since would have been made and much
more land cultivated than there is at present in this province had there been a
general law by which such backward selfish proprietors who would gladly raise
estates at other people's expense might have been compelled to have done their
duty towards making the settlements in a summary way as the affairs of the town
are transacted, especially respecting the payment of taxes.[81]

This petition not only illuminates a continuing realm of conflict between
new towns and their nonresident proprietors but also reveals that before
1760 each town with such conflicts had to petition the government for a
"particular act in their favor." In the period before 1740, at least, the New
Hampshire General Assembly supported such petitions, upholding the
power of town residents over nonresident proprietors and reducing the
potency of this threat in towns which actually contained resident proprietors.[82]

Land speculation was almost as prevalent in the 1720's and 1730's
under Lieutenant Governor John Wentworth as it would be in the 1750's
under his son, Governor Benning Wentworth. Of the eleven new towns
granted between 1722 and 1728 only three (Londonderry, Chester, and
Rochester) had any extensive growth before 1740. Among the other eight,
four had fewer than thirty families and four had no settlers at all by 1740.
The Kingswood grant of 1737 was abolished in 1746 because no settlement had been established there. A survey of the probate inventories of
estate in the 1720's, 1730's, and 1740's indicates that many nonresidents of
the new towns (not the original proprietors) were acquiring shares in
these towns, but so were the residents themselves. For that matter, some
leading men—George Vaughan, William Partridge, and William Vaughan, for example—had been speculating in Maine lands as early as
1716.[83] John Wentworth, himself a nonresident proprietor, was actively
procuring settlers for his grants in the new towns, which totaled at least

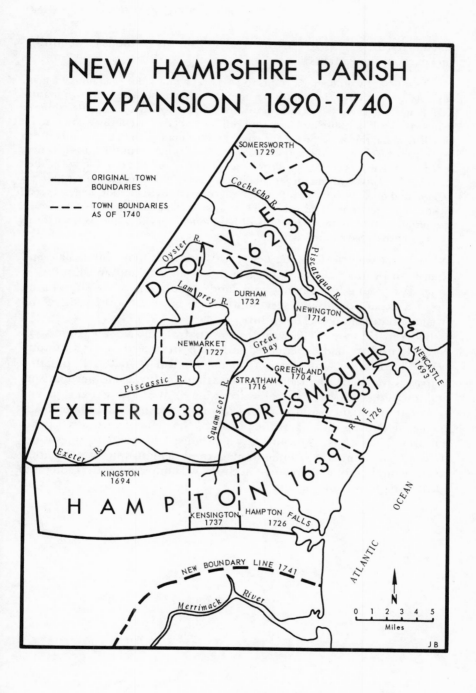

NEW HAMPSHIRE PARISH
EXPANSION 1690-1740

SOMERSWORTH
1729

ORIGINAL TOWN
BOUNDARIES

TOWN BOUNDARIES
AS OF 1740

Cochecho R.

D O V E R
1 6 2 3

Piscataqua R.

Oyster R.

Lamprey R.

DURHAM
1732

NEWINGTON
1714

NEWMARKET
1727

Great Bay

GREENLAND
1704

PORTSMOUTH
1631

NEWCASTLE
1693

Piscassic R.

STRATHAM
1716

Squamscot R.

EXETER 1638

RYE
1726

Exeter R.

KINGSTON
1694

1639

H A M P T O N

KENSINGTON
1737

HAMPTON FALLS
1726

ATLANTIC OCEAN

NEW BOUNDARY LINE 1741

Merrimack River

N

0 1 2 3 4 5
Miles

J B

5,500 acres. In a letter to a friend he described his methods of obtaining profits from these grants:

Now Sir, what I would advise you is to send over a family for each house: a man, his wife, and children; but be sure to bind them fast, otherwise some insinuating people may endeavor to stock them in your service the way I have settled some of mine in. I build a house and barn and put on a yoke of oxen, three cows, and a breeding mare; the oxen, two of the cows, and the mare with half their increase to be delivered [to] me at the end of seven years for which term the lot is [in] lieu. When the home lot is in 20, 30, 40, or 50 acres, then its on the home lot; if less, then on the second division and the tenant obliges himself to enclose ten or twelve acres of land and make it fit for the plough. . . . I conclude twill be your interest to send people from Europe. The other five towns, viz. Barnstead, Bow, Chichester, Canterbury, and Gilmantown you will have longer time to settle. As these towns settle, you shall have timely advice.[84]

What better way to stock the new towns and gain both immediate and long-term profits than to solicit servants from England and Europe—a practice encouraging tenancy and land speculation while stimulating frontier expansion. Land speculation thus brought both positive and negative results in New Hampshire.

Between 1713 and 1740, with the threat of war abated, the colonists of New Hampshire had experienced growth both in territory and in numbers. The frontier was extended to the Merrimack River. Population increased fourfold. The land was increasingly cultivated as new parishes and townships appeared and grew (see Map 3). With this expansion land speculation, tenancy, and nonresident proprietorships had dramatically increased. During these years the people of New Hampshire, less dependent upon Massachusetts for military assistance, had gradually questioned its political dominance. Time alone would demonstrate whether these trends would become permanent as the New Hampshire settlers sought to fulfill the promise of the land.

PART III

THE ASCENDANCY OF TRADE

CHAPTER V

OPPORTUNITIES AND DIRECTIONS

Despite their previous motivations and occupational experiences, the earliest New Hampshire settlers had had to turn to agriculture to ensure their survival. Each town had provided its settlers with the necessary land, which enabled them to attain at least a subsistence level of existence and whetted their appetites for profits. But the character of the land made impossible the production of profitable staple crops. This fact and the original material goals of many of the settlers led them, within a decade of their arrival, to pursue multiple occupations. These included farming-fur trading, farming-lumbering, farming-lumbering-merchandising, farming-merchandising, farming-fishing, farming-carpentering, and the like. Later settlers of the 1650's and 1660's began immediately to trade in lumber or fish for profit. By the late seventeenth century the greatest opportunities for profit lay in trade, particularly the lumber trade; and the wealthiest and most influential people in the colony usually were merchants, traders, and mariners. This trend continued and became more marked through the early eighteenth century, so that by the 1730's and 1740's most of the economic, social, and political leaders of New Hampshire earned their profits through trade and commerce.

Furs

One of the first but relatively minor mercantile opportunities to be exploited by the early New Hampshire colonizers was the fur trade. In the

1620's and 1630's Plymouth and Massachusetts dominated the fur trade of the northern New England frontier, but the absence of law and order in this area aided the more venturesome of the Piscataqua settlers—particularly those in Dover and Exeter, who had close contacts with the Indians—in exploiting this competitive and profitable enterprise. Edward Hilton of Dover, for example, was well known to Plymouth and Massachusetts traders because he usually sold the Indians a better quality of goods at lower prices than did his competitors to the south; and by the 1640's, Richard Waldron, another Dover settler, was also involved in the fur trade.[1] Exeter, whose land had been purchased from the Indians but was still available to them for hunting, attempted to regulate this wide-open trade in early 1640 by allowing every inhabitant the opportunity to trade with the Indians but forbidding the sale of arms, ammunition, or "strong waters" and establishing a ceiling on grain prices charged to them.[2]

The most famous early venture to tap the inland fur trade of the Piscataqua was organized by the Laconia Company in 1629. These London merchants, including Captain John Mason and Sir Ferdinando Gorges, using the Piscataqua River as an entrepôt, had hoped to profit by the furs reputedly abounding at the "Lake of the Iroquois"; but their exploration revealed that the Piscataqua had no connection with this famous lake. Nevertheless, a small trade in beaver skins was established at the Newichewannock Falls settlement. But after three years and the collection of less than 500 pounds of furs, the company began to collapse. By 1635, its investors had withdrawn, leaving whatever profits that might arise from the fur trade to the company servants. Ambrose Gibbons, the company factor at the Newichewannock trading post, moved to Oyster River and continued exploiting the fur trade.[3]

This open and unruly trade with the Indians in the Piscataqua region was a primary consideration behind the Massachusetts' extension of its jurisdiction over the area in 1641. Undoubtedly, its action brought a degree of stability to the fur-trading activities in the region, but the surviving evidence is so sparse that all conclusions must be tentative. In 1644 Valentine Hill, a Boston merchant and one of a "free company of adventurers," received as part of that "company" a twenty-one-year monopoly over all fur outlets he and they could establish. In 1643, Hill had appeared in the Oyster River area of Dover and obtained a 120-acre grant along the river. By 1652 he had a 500-acre farm grant and sawmill grant on the Lamprey River and had become one of Dover's leading men while remaining an active Boston trader. From 1641 to 1679 any Piscataqua settlers engaged in the fur trade had to secure a license either from the group of Massachusetts merchants who had received a monopoly of the trade from the General Court or, after 1645, from a committee of the

General Court.[4] Richard Waldron must have held one of these licenses (probably obtained from Hill), for he had a truckhouse (trading post) at his Cochecho mills by the late 1640's and by 1660 had another truckhouse at Penacook on the Merrimack River (the site of Concord, New Hampshire). In 1668, after a murder at Penacook, Waldron, his son John, and Peter Coffin appeared before the Massachusetts General Court to answer Indian accusations that they had sold liquor to the Indians. Both Waldrons swore an oath before God and the General Court that they were innocent, but Coffin, who had earlier claimed innocence, confessed his guilt when confronted with the oath.[5] This case reveals both the Massachusetts government's desire for an equitable and wholesome Indian trade and the difficulties of maintaining such a policy.

The fur trade continued as a minor source of profit for a favored few in New Hampshire for the remainder of the seventeenth century; however, it all but disappeared after 1700. Robert Mason claimed in 1671 that New Hampshire exported several thousand beaver and otter skins a year, but this was a gross overstatement.[6] The first surviving New Hampshire customs records of the seventeenth century, those of 1692, provide evidence of the fur trade's insignificance. One ship handled the entire trade for that year, carrying eighty-four pounds of beaver and 130 small "furskins" to London. By 1695, fur exportation had dwindled to one hogshead of "skins," and there is no record of any fur exportation in the extant customs records of New Hampshire between 1695 and 1742.[7] The trade had become so inconsequential that when the towns merged into a separate royal colony after 1679, the royal governor made no attempt either to regulate or to tax it. When the Massachusetts government established its truckhouse system after 1700, Governor Samuel Shute projected a truckhouse at the Oyster River precinct of Dover in 1713 and offered Captain John Wentworth the privilege of supplying it; but Wentworth declined the offer, and the truckhouse was never established.[8]

Not surprisingly, the fur trade had little impact upon New Hampshire's economy. It provided a few men with quick profits and capital for other endeavors. It probably aided Richard Waldron's expansion in lumbering, shipbuilding, and general commerce by the 1650's, for example. But the fur-bearing animals had disappeared from the eastern Piscataqua region by the late 1650's, moving the sources westward to the Merrimack River and Lake Winnipesaukee and northeastward to Casco Bay and the Kennebec River in central Maine. After 1679, these areas were controlled by Massachusetts. This fact together with the severe decline in the New Hampshire Indian population by 1700 meant that New Hampshire people could no longer exploit this economic opportunity unless they ventured into areas outside the jurisdiction of Massachusetts.[9] The favorable boundary line decision of 1740 brought the colony into contact with Indians once again; but after a short-lived attempt to establish its own truckhouse system, the New Hampshire government ignored the trade.[10] In sum, the fur trade contributed an early and significant but minor stimulation to the emergence of a mercantile community in New Hampshire.

Fish

From the time of the earliest settlers, fisheries provided a substantial but frustrating source of profit to seafaring New Hampshire colonists. David Thomson, Edward Hilton, and such Laconia Company servants as Edward Godfrey fished profitably during the 1620's and 1630's off the Piscataqua coast, sending their catches to London or West England markets. For instance, by 1632 Godfrey was operating a fishing fleet containing six shallops, five smaller fishing boats, and thirteen skiffs, using Strawbery Banke as his home base. Within a few years of the establishment of Dover and Exeter, certain individuals had received exclusive fishing privileges in nearby rivers in return for fulfilling specific obligations to their town. These fishing monopolies applied particularly to the use of weirs (a wood fence or net used to catch fish); and while they did not usually prohibit individual line fishing, such monopolies brought special commercial opportunities to the recipient.[11]

The most important Piscataqua fishery in the years before 1680 lay among the seven barren islands off the northeastern coast of New Hampshire known as the Isles of Shoals. West Country fishermen had been involved in occasional expeditions to upper New England since the beginning of the seventeenth century, and by the 1620's the Isles had become a yearly target. Upper New England had first attracted these fishermen because it provided two fishing seasons each year (spring and fall), compared to the one season at Newfoundland; however, the Isles of Shoals had more unusual conditions—a generally sunnier and drier climate than most of New England, which allowed the fishermen to obtain higher quality codfish through a distinctive curing process.[12]

In the course of the 1630's and 1640's the Isles became one of the more important fishing stations in New England. The Laconia Company had placed some laborers and fishermen there to secure quick profits from the Piscataqua region, but its fishing ventures had proved unsatisfactory. But with resident laborers on the Isles, other New England and English fishermen soon brought their catches there for curing. After the dissolution of the Laconia Company and the decline of the Council for New England's authority, both Massachusetts and New Hampshire settlers were attracted to the Isles for part-time fishing activities: they farmed in the summer and fished in the late fall and early spring.[13] The English Civil War, which broke the ties between West Country fishermen and their home markets, brought more change to the New England fisheries. Some of the West Country fishermen settled on the Isles of Shoals as permanent residents, while others became full-time suppliers of New England fish markets; however, the majority returned to England.[14] This decline of West Country dominance in New England encouraged New Englanders to take up the slack both in fishing and trading. By the late 1640's the Isles of Shoals had become a major entrepôt for trade in the Piscataqua region, attracting investments from such New Hampshire farmer-fisherman-traders as Richard Waldron, Edward Hilton, and Henry Sherburne, particularly in cod and mackerel.

In the 1650's and 1660's the ready profits from the Isles fisheries plus the uncertain situation in England persuaded a significant number of the West Country fishermen on the Isles to seek higher economic and social status by relocating in New Hampshire and obtaining larger estates while maintaining fishing businesses on the Isles. Such leading New Hampshire mercantile families as the Cutts, Hunkings, Odiornes, and Langdons and many other lesser families established themselves at Portsmouth in this way.[15] And within thirty years of their relocation, a number of other ambitious New Hampshire men and families had established economic and social ties with these newcomers or with such earlier prominent fishing families as the Hiltons and Waldrons to constitute a large portion of the wealthier people of New Hampshire society in the late seventeenth century.[16] By 1681, for example, eight out of the richest ten taxpayers in Portsmouth and the wealthiest thirteen taxpayers in Dover were directly involved in the fisheries of the Isles of Shoals. These fisheries, then, significantly aided the development of a mercantile class in New Hampshire, particularly by providing a source of capital for other economic endeavors, such as establishing a lumber trade and shipbuilding, and by attracting new merchants.[17]

The heyday of the Isles of Shoals fisheries occurred during the 1660's and early 1670's. In the height of the fishing seasons as many as 1,500 men may have been working there. Interested English observers, such as Robert Mason and Edward Randolph, described an extensive Piscataqua fishery, exporting 10,000 to 12,000 quintals of fish per year.[18] But King Philip's War and continuing conflicts with the Abnaki Indians brought an abrupt decline in the Piscataqua fisheries. In 1681, for example, the New Hampshire Council, in a letter to the Lords of Trade, did not mention fish as an article exported and stated that all fish were imported, "there being none in our Province." Lieutenant Governor Cranfield, on his arrival in October 1682, sent off letters to the Lords of Trade and Secretary of State deploring the situation in New Hampshire: "It will be impossible for the King's government to be supported however it has been represented by Mr. Mason at Whitehall, [for] the condition of the people in his Province is very mean and not likely to improve having no fishery nor timber considerable left to carry on trade."[19] Of course, New Hampshire leaders grossly overstated the decline of their trade as part of their antagonism toward Robert Mason and his political adherents. Nevertheless, the Anglo-French wars after 1689 effected a permanent decline in the Shoals fisheries, and by 1692, there were only about one hundred men on the Isles of Shoals.[20] As a result of the Indian wars some New Hampshire fish merchants in the 1680's and early 1690's sought safer fisheries and, following the example of Massachusetts, began trading and fishing off Nova Scotia and Newfoundland.[21]

The earliest extant and relatively complete customs returns for New Hampshire reveal that between August 1694 and September 1, 1695, the colony's traders imported 160 quintals of fish and exported 2,197 quintals. Thirteen outgoing vessels out of twenty-seven carried fish, and eleven of those thirteen vessels were bound for Barbados. The other fish markets of the 1680's and 1690's included Bilbao, Madeira, the Canary Islands, Virginia, and Boston.[22] Cod and mackerel were the only fish exported in this year, with cod most prevalent and sorted generally into three categories: "merchantable" cod, a good quality table-fish usually sent to Bilbao and from there to Catholic Europe; "middling" or "Jamaica" cod, a relatively inferior quality fish usually exported to Jamaica or Madeira; and "refuse" cod, or "scale fish," an extremely poor quality fish usually sent to Barbados or other plantation areas for use in feeding slaves.

These trade patterns were similar to the general patterns of the New England fishing trade but on a surprisingly small scale in comparison to Massachusetts. Though New Hampshire had the advantage of a comparative geographical proximity to the North Atlantic fisheries, the Massachusetts ports were exporting about 100,000 quintals of fish to New Hampshire's 1,300 quintals about 1700. Boston alone exported 50,000 quintals.[23] Governor Bellomont attributed New Hampshire's poor showing to its preoccupation with lumber exportation. His anger over what he considered the New Hampshire merchants' violations of the Navigation Acts in their exports of ship timbers caused him to suggest to the Board of Trade, first, that a total prohibition on lumber and ship timber exportation be placed upon New Hampshire and, second, that such a prohibition would not hurt the New Hampshire economy, since its superior geographical location would soon have the colony surpassing Boston in fish exportation.[24] Bellomont's explanation for New Hampshire's declining fishery was unrealistic, however. More significant were two other factors which made fishing a relatively risky and insecure venture: the almost continuous warfare between 1692 and 1713, which deeply and personally involved the people of this frontier colony; and the French attempt to seize all foreign interlopers in the Nova Scotia fisheries after the Treaty of Ryswick in 1697. Neither of these factors lost importance until the Treaty of Utrecht in 1713. George Vaughan, a New Hampshire fish merchant and agent in London in 1708, succinctly explained the problem to the Board of Trade: "Were it not for the *enemy* . . . the fittest place of all the present settlements of New England for fishing for the supply of foreign markets" is New Hampshire.[25]

In the years after 1713 the New Hampshire fishing trade experienced significant expansion and specialization. Whereas in the seventeenth century most traders and merchants owned and operated their own fishing vessels, by the 1720's some individuals—including William Pepperrell, Joshua Peirce, Sampson Sheafe, William Vaughan, Mark Hunking, John Penhallow, Samuel Deering, and Richard Wibird—had emerged as fish suppliers for both wholesale and local retail trade in the Piscataqua region.[26] Also, relatively fewer vessels were carrying fish exports. Where in 1695 thirteen vessels out of twenty-seven clearances carried fish, only eleven out of fifty-one in 1723, eighteen out of fifty-two in 1725, twenty out of fifty-two in 1727, and twenty-five out of seventy-eight in 1742 carried fish—a drop from about one-half to one-third in a forty-five-year span.[27]

Basic to the expansion of the New Hampshire fishing trade after 1713 was the exploitation of the Canso fisheries by such men as William Pepperrell, William Vaughan, Joshua Peirce, Jacob Sheafe, Hugh Reed, and Hunking Wentworth. In a letter of June 1, 1720, to the Board of Trade, Governor Samuel Shute commented upon New Hampshire's "much increased" fishing trade, which involved some 400 "seafaring men and fishermen" and 100 fishing vessels.[28] Unfortunately, it is impossible to assess the exact extent of expansion because many of the vessels involved in the Canso (and to a lesser extent the Newfoundland) fisheries sailed directly from these areas, leaving no record of their cargo. But the increase must have been enormous, for the New Hampshire customs returns alone reveal almost a fourfold increase in fish exportation by 1718 over the 1695 exportation: whereas 2,197 quintals were exported through customs in 1695, the clearances for 1718, 1723, 1725, and 1727 respectively were 8,816 quintals, 7,738 quintals, 8,810 quintals, and 8,165 quintals. Joshua Peirce alone was probably exporting between 3,000 and 4,000 quintals of fish per year directly from Canso, as he sent his fishing fleet there four times a year—not to mention the exports of other Canso-based New Hampshire fish traders. In 1727, at a time of uncertain diplomatic relations between Spain and England, Lieutenant Governor Wentworth wrote the Board of Trade that some 200,000 quintals of fish sat useless in

New Hampshire for want of vessels to export them.[29] Undoubtedly, Wentworth exaggerated his estimate, but even one-fourth that amount would show the significant expansion of the New Hampshire fishing trade.

This increase of the fishery encouraged some general expansion of trade by the 1720's, as it had in the seventeenth century, though not so extensively as before.[30] Portsmouth and New Castle particularly enjoyed prosperity. In fact, New Castle, located at the mouth of the Piscataqua River, became a fisherman's town. Fish was so important in the New Hampshire economy during the 1720's that it was used as currency (at its June price).[31]

In the 1720's Piscataqua fish merchants plied many of the same markets as they had in the late seventeenth century—the West Indies, Bilbao, Madeira, and England—but the bulk of the trade probably went to Catholic southern Europe, particularly to Lisbon, Cadiz, Gibraltar, and Bilbao. For example, in 1725, though eleven out of the eighteen fish-carrying vessels cleared for the Caribbean islands, they carried only about 5 percent of the total fish export. Over 70 percent of the fish went to Catholic Europe, and 25 percent went to Marblehead in Massachusetts. In 1727, a time of undeclared war with Spain, the fifteen of the twenty-two fish-exporting vessels bound for the Caribbean islands carried only about 12.5 percent of the fish export, while 43 percent went to Catholic Europe and another 43 percent to England.[32] Spain and Portugal had emerged as important markets for New Hampshire's fish trade and remained so until the outbreak of war between Spain and England in 1739. Writing in 1737 to the Board of Trade, Governor Belcher described the New Hampshire fishing trade as exporting "casked dry codfish to the British West Indies" and "merchantable codfish to Spain, Portugal and the Mediterranean."[33]

After 1739 the war with Spain brought a significant decline in Piscataqua fish exportation. Though the New Hampshire Shipping Returns are missing for most of the years from 1728 through 1741, the records for 1742 partially reveal the war's effect upon the fishing trade. Only 2,045 quintals of fish cleared the port of Piscataqua—at least a fourfold decline in terms of exports in the 1720's and more similar to the exportation rate of the 1690's. In addition, only 350 quintals, or about 17 percent of the exportation, went to southern Europe, normally New Hampshire's primary fish market. In this year the Caribbean islands received the bulk of Piscataqua fish (1,592 quintals, or 78 percent), and Virginia appeared as a fish market for the first time, receiving 90 quintals, or 4.5 percent of the trade.[34] Another important reason for the declining fishing trade between 1739 and 1745 lay in the erection of a new French military fortress at Louisbourg, which directly threatened the Canso fishery and ultimately led to a successful New England expedition against Louisbourg in 1744–45.[35]

The exploitation of fish significantly affected the development of New Hampshire's society from the 1640's through 1740. By providing an easily accessible source of fluid capital, the fishing trade aided the expansion of New Hampshire's economy into shipbuilding and a far-flung lumber trade. At the same time, as the more ambitious fishermen expanded their enterprises, they became both mariners and merchants, adding to a growing mercantile element in New Hampshire society. Although the fishing trade became more specialized in the eighteenth century and proportionately fewer vessels carried fish, nevertheless, about half the Piscataqua traders continued to export fish through 1742.[36] And yet, comparatively speaking, the New Hampshire experience with fisheries was disappointing. Although the Piscataqua region enjoyed a favorable proximity to the Northern New England and Newfoundland fisheries, although fish was usually one of its most consistent and profitable exports, and although a significant number of prominent Piscataqua families gained their wealth in the fisheries, nevertheless, throughout its first century New Hampshire never emerged as one of the really important fish-exporting areas. Its insecure frontier location and its plentiful lumber resources, coupled with the aggressive fishing activities of the Massachusetts seafarers, probably explain this situation. In the final analysis, the Massachusetts seaports dominated the entire New England fishing trade.[37]

Lumber and Allied Products

New Hampshire's most significant mercantile opportunities, profits, and economic expansion came from its forest resources. Its towering white pines provided masts, yards, spars, boards, planks, joists, clapboards, and shingles—and represented the most important single lumber resource in the colony. Red and white oak trees were utilized for staves, planks, ship timber, and rafters; while cedar shingles, ash rafters, hemlock planks, and spruce spars also served as exports.[38]

The earliest settlers gave little attention at first to the potential opportunities provided by the forests, but by the late 1630's some individuals were exporting sawn boards and various types of staves along with their fish. As early as 1635 the Laconia Company servants had erected a sawmill, probably the first one accessible to New Hampshire's settlers and a harbinger of the future.[39] By the 1650's, many Piscataqua colonists were giving their full attention to forest opportunities. In Exeter some twenty-eight men had pooled their resources to build six sawmills between 1648 and 1660. In Dover ten sawmills were erected between 1642 and 1660 through the combined resources of fifteen men. Portsmouth and Hampton each had at least two sawmills before 1660, owned by John Cutt, John

Pickering, Ambrose Lane, Richard Knight, and Robert Page respectively.[40] The lumber trade was so lucrative in the 1650's that the town government of Dover sold lumber products as the most expedient method of obtaining revenue, after accepting lumber in payment of town taxes. When the king's commissioners described conditions in upper New England in 1665, they reported finding "above twenty sawmills" on the Piscataqua River, producing "excellent masts" and a "great store of pipestaves." The New Hampshire court records of 1640–53 disclose at least twenty-six lumber traders busily exporting clapboards and pipestaves to Boston.[41]

In fact, Massachusetts merchants played an important role in the early development of the New Hampshire lumber trade. Many sought New Hampshire contracts, sent in their own agents and capital, or moved in themselves. For example, Valentine Hill, a thriving Boston merchant, had moved to the Oyster River lumber camp by 1648 to exploit more effectively his 500 acres of timber there; and Bryan Pendleton, another Massachusetts merchant, arrived in Portsmouth in 1651 as an agent for William Paine, a Boston merchant who sought investments in New Hampshire sawmills.[42] By the 1670's Pendleton had acquired at least 1,640 acres of timberland and several islands, including "Timber Island." In *The New England Merchants in the Seventeenth Century* Bernard Bailyn suggested that the Boston merchants actually "developed the New Hampshire lumber industry."[43] Undoubtedly, the demands by these merchants for timber products encouraged many New Hampshire people—especially in Dover, Exeter, and Hampton—to make up staves, bolts, and clapboards for export.[44] But the New Hampshire town records reveal the presence of local millers and lumber traders as well—the Cutts of Portsmouth and Kittery, the Waldrons of Dover, and the Gilmans of Exeter, for example—each of whom was building a few ships and trading lumber and masts to Barbados and England by the mid-1650's.[45] Thus, although Boston served as the main market for New Hampshire lumber and although Boston merchants played the most significant role in the emerging lumber trade, it was the confluent effort of Boston merchants and local New Hampshire lumberers that explains the development of New Hampshire's timber trade before 1660.

The last forty years of the seventeenth century witnessed a gradual expansion of the Piscataqua lumber trade, until, by the 1680's, it had become the primary determinant of New Hampshire's commercial prosperity. In a period of local depression in 1681 the New Hampshire Council spelled out this dependence: "The trade of this province exported by the inhabitants of its own produce is in masts, planks and boards, staves, and all other lumber which at present is of little value in other plantations to which they are transported so that we see no other way for the advantage of the trade, unless His Majesty please to make our rivers of Piscataqua a free port."[46] This expansion and dependence was reflected in the increasing number of sawmills and in the expansion of the coastal trade in lumber. Between 1665 and 1705, some fifty new sawmills appeared, so that by 1705 there were a total of seventy.[47] In 1644 Samuel Maverick had noted that "above twenty ships yearly" were loaded at Piscataqua for export; by 1681 as many as fifty-one vessels were carrying lumber from New Hampshire to Boston, with at least twenty-six of them (380 tons) owned by nineteen New Hampshire traders.[48] The customs returns of 1695, the first systematic record of New Hampshire's shipping in the seventeenth century, reveal that there were at least 134 vessels, averaging ten tons' capacity, plying the coastal trade in lumber between New Hampshire and Massachusetts and that these carried 1,679,300 feet of boards and 156,300 staves. Twenty-nine larger vessels, eighteen of which were Piscataqua-based, exported lumber products from New Hampshire to England, the West Indies, Madeira, Fayal, Newfoundland, Pennsylvania, and Rhode Island.[49] Pine boards, staves, shingles, and ranging timber bound for Boston, the Caribbean, and the Wine Islands constituted the bulk of Piscataqua's lumber export in this period (see Table 2).

As early as the 1650's, however, in response to England's desperate wartime need for naval masts, New Hampshire traders had begun exporting large white pine masts to the mother country. With New England masts commanding a consistent price in England of about £100 each, the mast trade became the lodestar of the Piscataqua region, attracting local lumberers, new capital, and settlers from England and Massachusetts.[50]

The mast trade was organized around contracts issued by the Navy Board to English merchants, who then worked out arrangements with the colonial merchants who actually provided the masts. As Bernard Bailyn has shown, the colonial merchants chosen by the English contractors were those who had the best contacts, family connections, or reputations among English merchants. The English contractors involved in this trade between 1650 and 1700 included Sir William Warren, Samuel Allen, William Wood, Josiah Child, Edward Deering, Captain John Taylor, and Sir John Shorter, who competed both for contracts from the Navy Board and masts from New England and the Baltic.[51] Also, the New Hampshire mast traders were competitive and felt no obligation to trade only with the naval contractors.[52] Thus, the New Hampshire mast business provided bountiful opportunities in the seventeenth century. Between 1650 and 1700 a number of New Hampshire enterprisers took advantage of these opportunities—including Thomas Wiggin, Richard Waldron and Richard Waldron, Jr., Phillip and Thomas Chesley, Peter Coffin, and Joseph Hall of Dover; Robert Wadleigh, Moses, John, and Edward Gilman,

TABLE 2

PISCATAQUA LUMBER EXPORTATION, 1695-1752

LUMBER PRODUCTS:	1695	1718[a]	1727	1742	1752
1. Pine boards	260,000 ft	915,331 ft	1,701,653 ft	1,843,269 ft	6,249,400 ft
2. Staves[b]	235,000	252,710	17,500	452,844	898,200
3. Shingles	129,000	614,950	24,000	1,032,100	2,051,050
4. Hoops	1,700	6,000	6,000	31,550	26,400
5. Clapboards	----	11,000	10,000	----	3,000
6. Oak plank	----	1,022 tons	----	3,889 ft	107 tons
		26,880 ft		14 pieces	7,600 ft
		483 pieces			10 pieces
7. Ranging timber[c]	73 tons	5,515 ft	355 tons	32 tons	2,000 ft
			18 pieces	41,400 ft	4,010 pieces
8. Pine plank	----	644 pieces	----	----	----
9. Oak, ash rafters	----	13,905 ft	----	26,532 ft	3,132
10. Joists	10,000	55,472 ft	----	9 ft	----
11. Dyewoods[d]	----	----	----	4 cords	5,963 lb
				40 pieces	
12. Firewood	----	----	----	----	2 tons
					17 cord
13. Walnutwood	----	----	----	----	100 ft
14. Lathewood	----	----	----	----	20 cord
15. Masts	56	199	123	524	570
16. Spars	13	520	64	1,106	2,815
	1,500 ft				
17. Bowsprits	16	151	82	171	42
18. Yardarms	4	----	30	102	51
19. Standards	74	----	----	----	----
20. Knees	50	73	----	----	----
21. Booms	----	----	----	2	2
22. Anchor stocks	----	17	----	----	----
23. Houseframes	----	----	6	4	10
24. Boatframes	----	----	----	3	----
25. Axes	----	----	----	596 ft	----
26. Oars	----	----	----	7,030	----
				701 ft	
27. Desks	----	----	----	59	9
28. Tables	----	----	10	51	4
29. Chairs	----	----	----	311	156
30. Wheelbarrows	----	----	----	----	16
31. Oxbows	----	----	----	24	----
32. Drainspouts	----	----	----	----	5,000 ft
33. Handspikes	----	----	----	3,740	420
34. Pails	----	----	----	72	----
35. Pumps	----	----	----	19	----

[a]These figures were copied by Malone, 153-154, from CO5/867.
[b]This includes hogshead staves, barrel staves, and pipestaves.
[c]This includes such indiscriminate classifications as "timber," "square timber," and
"ranging timber."
[d]The exported dyewoods included "fustic," "logwood," and "sashwood."

Ralph Hall and Edward, Richard, and William Hilton of Exeter; Henry Roby, Andrew Wiggin and Joseph Chase of Hampton; and Sampson Lane, John Cutt, Bryan Pendleton, Walter Abbot, Francis Champernowne, Thomas Seavey, Samuel Haines, and Samuel and John Wentworth of Portsmouth.[53] Moreover, many immigrants from Massachusetts after 1660 became involved in the mast industry. Among these were John Gerrish and John Wingate, who moved to Dover; Nathaniel

Weare and Henry Green in Hampton; Samuel Leavitt in Exeter; and William Partridge, Samuel Penhallow, Reuben Hull, and John Plaisted in Portsmouth.

The mother country served as another source of immigrants seeking profits in masting. These immigrants fell into one of three somewhat overlapping categories. The first group were those people who because of kinship or potential economic benefit worked for recognition of Robert Mason's proprietary claims; these included Mason himself, John Hinckes, Walter Barefoote, Samuel Allen, and even Edward Randolph.[54] The second group included individuals who had special connections with London mast contractors—William Vaughan, for example—while the third element was made up of immigrants with capital to invest in trade: Thomas Daniel, Thomas Graffort, Robert Elliott, and William Pepperrell of Kittery were examples of this type. It is evident that these mast and lumber traders found economic and social success in the Piscataqua region, both by their high places in town tax lists and by their appointments to the New Hampshire Council and/or election to the New Hampshire House of Representatives after 1679.[55]

Unfortunately, the only relatively complete seventeenth-century shipping records for New Hampshire are for 1695, a time of war and trade dislocation in New England. Nevertheless, these records indicate the growing importance of the mast trade and other allied naval products, because 56 masts, 16 bowsprits, 4 yardarms, 74 standards, 50 knees, and over 1,300 feet of lumber for spars cleared customs at Piscataqua for exportation in that year, with most of the spars bound for the Caribbean islands and the remainder of the lumber goods bound for England.[56] Before 1700 William Partridge, lieutenant governor and one of the richest lumber merchants and shipbuilders in New Hampshire, had begun sending masts and ship timber to Spain and Portugal, establishing a pattern of trade that would provide another source of profit for New Hampshire lumberers during the next forty years (see Table 3).[57] Partridge claimed that one shipload of timber that had cost him less than £300 had cleared a £1,600 profit at Lisbon.

This expansion of both the lumber trade and the fisheries after 1650 encouraged the growth of another industry which utilized lumber products, namely shipbuilding. And naturally enough, the lumber traders and fish merchants took the lead in this industry. By the 1650's Richard Waldron, Hatevil Nutter, Thomas Wiggin, John Hall, Thomas Trickett (or Trickey), Valentine Hill, Edward Gilman, John Cutt, Samson Lane, and Edward Colcord were building a few vessels for use in local trade.[58] In the next forty years other mariners and merchants—John and Nathaniel Jackson, John and Mark Hunking, William and Howard Henderson, Thomas Daniel, Nathaniel Weare, John Tuttle, and William Partridge,

TABLE 3

NEW HAMPSHIRE LUMBER EXPORTS TO SPAIN AND PORTUGAL

	1712-1718[a]	1723[b]	1725[c]	1727[d]	1742
No. of vessels	28	0	8	4	0
Oak timber	90,776 ft		252 pieces 576 tons		
Oak plank	98,925		75 tons & an un- determined no. of pieces		
Joists	59,070 ft				
Pine plank	43,880 ft		30 pieces	1,000 pieces 39,500 ft	
Pipestaves	93,250		8,000 & 5 vessels carrying an unde- termined amount	2,500	
Hogshead staves	42,360				
Bolts	5,470				
Standards	168		an undetermined amount		
Knees	12				
Bowsprits	8				
Spars	1,511				
Pine timber				305 tons	
Small masts				11	

[a]These statistics are quoted from CO5/867, No. 2 in Malone, Appendix E, 154.
[b]These statistics are culled from the New Hampshire Customs Returns from June, 1723–June, 1724, in CO5/968, pp. 1 ff.
[c]Ibid., 27 ff. for September 25, 1724– September 25, 1725.
[d]Ibid., 42, for December 25, 1726– December 25, 1727.

for example—turned to shipbuilding. In fact, William Partridge, acting as agent for John Taylor, the mast contractor, helped build two warships in the 1690's for the Royal Navy, the *Falkland* and the *Bedford Galley*.[59]

Most of the vessels built by the early 1680's were small ketches, ships, and sloops. For example, in the August customs returns of 1681 there were seventeen New Hampshire–owned (and probably New Hampshire–built) ketches averaging 9.3 tons, seven ships averaging 30.3 tons, and two sloops of 5 tons each—a total of twenty-six vessels averaging 14.6 tons each.[60] By the mid-nineties, however, New Hampshire entrepreneurs were building and using vessels over double the average size of those of 1681.

Between 1687 and 1695, they built and used at least seven ketches averaging 24.3 tons, five sloops averaging 18.4 tons, two ships averaging 75 tons, eight barks averaging 30.6 tons, one pink of 25 tons, and eleven brigs averaging 27.3 tons—a total of thirty-four vessels averaging 28.9 tons per vessel.[61] Not only was there a marked increase in average size but the vessels of the 1690's were barks and brigs, as compared to the ketches and ships of 1681. One must be cautious in using these figures, however, because they apply only to overseas trade of the 1680's and 1690's, excluding the coastal Piscataqua trade. Of the 134 vessels plying the Massachusetts–New Hampshire coastal trade in 1695, 131 vessels were sloops and 3 were brigs.[62] It can be safely concluded that in the 1690's there was a trend at Piscataqua toward building brigs and barks of about thirty tons' capacity, particularly for use outside the New England coastal trade, and that between 1678 and 1700 New Hampshire enterprisers had expanded their shipping by at least 78 new vessels—an average of 3.5 per year.[63]

Thus, the late seventeenth century saw the Piscataqua lumber trade mature, as lumber traders developed the major markets they would continue to tap through the 1740's—Boston, the Caribbean islands, England, Catholic Europe, and Newfoundland. The coastal trade with Boston, their single most important market in the 1690's, reached a level by 1695 that would remain relatively constant for the next three decades.[64] Moreover, the mast trade and shipbuilding, two specialized aspects of the lumber business, were becoming increasingly important to the Piscataqua economy.

The extensive timber resources had provided wide-open opportunities for acquisitive, ambitious newcomers and settled residents alike, but it was the presence of Massachusetts and English capital along with local capital accumulation that spurred this expansion and development. These developments had enormous consequences in New Hampshire society: they established on a sound basis the more profitable occupations, such as sawyer, cooper, carpenter, lumberer, cordwainer, blockmaker, joiner, shipwright, sailmaker, mariner, and merchant; and more important, they provided the foundations for the increasing dominance after 1650 of lumberers and lumber merchants in the economy, society, and politics of New Hampshire towns.

The early eighteenth century witnessed continued expansion in the Piscataqua trade of lumber products, but the unfettered opportunities of the late seventeenth century declined, as both the timber resources near the coast and the amount of good timber land throughout New Hampshire gradually decreased. As a partial consequence, comparatively few immigrants achieved affluence through the lumber trade in the early eighteenth century; and those who did—Archibald MacPhaedris and

Richard Wibird from England and John Frost, Daniel Warner, and
Joshua Peirce from southern New England—married into lumber-
trading families and/or utilized capital obtained through other enterprises.[65]

While the lumber trade became relatively inaccessible to immigrants,
three general developments transpired during the early eighteenth century. In the first place a number of established mariners or retail
merchants who had hitherto dealt in wine, fish, or other products outside
the lumber trade now began wholesaling lumber as well. The Jaffreys,
Odiornes, and Sherburnes exemplify this trend.

George Jaffrey (1638–1707) was a Scot who came first to Boston and
then, in 1676, to the Isles of Shoals as an agent of Patrick Crawford, a
Scotch merchant. After purchasing land on Star Island and engaging in
the fish trade, he moved to New Castle and by 1677 was licensed to sell
liquor to his fishermen. Within a few years he opened a shop and became
a general retail merchant. By 1707 he had amassed an estate worth almost
£3,000, had served on the New Hampshire Council for five years, and had
seen his son, George Jaffrey, Jr. (1682–1749), graduate from Harvard.
George, Jr., married a daughter of David Jeffries, a wealthy Boston
merchant, and by the 1720's was both a wholesaler and a retailer
exporting lumber, fish, soap, and candles and importing sugar, molasses,
rum, wine, and at least twelve Negro slaves from the West Indies. By 1742
he was exporting lumber products almost exclusively and importing
sugar, rum, and cotton wool, and was among the top 25 percent of New
Hampshire traders in terms of total volume of trade (excluding the coastal
trade, which is unknown). At his death in 1749, his estate was valued at
over £10,000.[66]

The Sherburnes' experience exhibits a somewhat different pattern
within the same general trend. The first generation (John, 1617–1693, and
Henry, 1612–1681) had settled in New Hampshire as yeomen farmers by
the 1650's. Henry soon became an innkeeper at Hampton. The younger
sons in the second generation went to sea and became mariners, while the
older sons worked the farms. Henry's oldest son, Samuel Sherburne
(1638–91), for example, was a farmer and innholder at Hampton. His son,
Henry (1674–1757), became a mariner, moved to Portsmouth, and married
Dorothy, the daughter of Samuel Wentworth and sister of Lieutenant
Governor John Wentworth. With these connections and a father and
cousin (of the same name) who were innkeepers, Henry eventually
became a wholesale merchant as well as a mariner, built what was
probably the first brick house in Portsmouth, became relatively wealthy
(the fifth highest taxpayer in the town by 1727), and may have been the
top New Hampshire local trader in volume of trade as well.[67] By 1742 he
and his son, Henry Sherburne, Jr. (1709–67), owned vessels totaling at

least 820 tons and were second only to Mark H. Wentworth in total volume of Piscataqua trade.[68] The bulk of the Sherburnes' trade was lumber to the French and British West Indies, but they also exported some fish and miscellaneous products to Virginia and North Carolina, returning to New Hampshire with provisions, sugar, cotton wool, and rum. Thus, capital acquired elsewhere helped some older families break into the lumber trade of the early eighteenth century.

A second development affecting the lumber trade was the gradual monopolization of the lucrative mast trade by a relatively few lumberers and merchants. This trend developed partially as a result of the mother country's attempts after 1691 to enjoy the full benefits of New Hampshire masts. First, the navy began limiting the number of mast suppliers with whom it contracted, so that in the eighteenth century there were seldom more than two at a time.[69] These English merchants then usually selected one or two colonial agents to procure the masts on a commission basis, which meant that relatively few people could legitimately become involved in this aspect of masting. Finally, the mother country sent over a Surveyor General of the Woods with the responsibility (among other duties) of supervising masting procedures in the colonies under the newly established "Broad Arrow" policy; this policy forbade the cutting of white pines above certain specified dimensions, except on private property, thereby limiting a hitherto relatively free access to masts.[70] As time went on, these Crown restrictions became more severe, until by 1729 no white pine of any description could be cut without a special license from the surveyor general; and violations were prosecuted in the vice-admiralty courts. Under such circumstances lumberers became ruthlessly competitive for mast agencies from English merchants and for posts as surveyor general or deputy to the surveyor general—positions that could provide security for one's family and friends in the lumber business. At the same time, the losers in such competition grumbled at the laws and flagrantly violated them from time to time. In this economic and political environment, then, masting—and, to a lesser extent, lumbering itself—was gradually limited to fewer people. The colonial agents who supplied the mast contractors from 1690 to 1742 were William Partridge, John Mico, Ichabod Plaisted, John Plaisted, David Jeffries, Thomas Westbrook, George Craddock, Samuel Waldo, and Mark H. Wentworth. These colonial agents in turn relied upon their "kin" and friends for the masts, rewarding the Vaughans, Waldrons, Plaisteds, Pepperrells, Huskes, Weares, Gilmans, Hiltons, Chesleys, Gerrishes, and Wentworths in their lumbering activities. By the 1720's the only vessels with masts for England that cleared New Hampshire customs belonged to the mast agents.

A third development among lumber traders in the early eighteenth century was their growing interest in obtaining new land grants in the back country of New Hampshire and in Maine. This land hunger increased rapidly after 1713, as desirable timber disappeared along the coast while the demand for timber increased. By 1718 lumber exports outside of the coastal trade with Boston had increased fourfold over the exportation of 1695, with the export of pine boards, shingles, hoops, masts, spars, and bowsprits most prominent in that expansion (see Table 2). Between 1712 and 1718 New Hampshire had exported 637 masts, 176 yardarms, and 226 bowsprits to England, providing more evidence of an expanding timber trade. At the same time, leading traders like the Waldrons, the Wentworths, the Vaughans, and Thomas Westbrook were speculating in Maine timberland; and the Berwick, Falmouth, and Casco Bay areas of Maine were expanding in population and timber exportation. Other leading New Hampshire lumberers were petitioning for new townships grants, fearful that the surveyor general might persuade the Crown to enforce the New England White Pine laws effectively.

Contrary to the inferences drawn by Joseph Malone in *Pine Trees and Politics*, the New Hampshire White Pine Law of 1708, which attempted to preserve masts, actually had no real effect on lumbering operations in the colony because it contained a clause exempting all pine trees on private property and then specifically defined a township's common lands as private property. Because of the Masonian controversy and the Massachusetts–New Hampshire boundary dispute, this clause in effect nullified the stated purpose of the act.[71] When population pressure in 1722 persuaded the New Hamphire government to establish one township, Londonderry, the lumber interests and their merchant allies easily convinced the government of the need for nine more grants between 1722 and 1727. Since the lieutenant governor and every member of the council had important private lumber interests, it is not difficult to understand their prompt acquiescence. Nevertheless, in order to obtain the support of the New Hampshire House of Representatives and of public opinion, they gave proprietary rights in most of the grants to each assemblyman and to almost every important lumberer and socially prominent family in the colony. Though each township charter contained a clause reserving all mast trees in the township to the Crown "according to the Acts of Parliament," this very phrase in the clause nullified the Crown's reservation because Parliament's White Pine Act of 1722 reserved only those white pines growing outside the bounds of townships.[72] Nor can one fully understand either the Massachusetts–New Hampshire boundary controversy or the proprietary controversy without checking the economic and political connections of the lumber traders supporting each side in both disputes.[73]

That the trade in lumber products expanded significantly in the early eighteenth century is evident from a cursory inspection of Table 2, lumber exportation from 1695 to 1752, which is based only upon the Piscataqua trade carried on with ports outside Massachusetts.[74] Other evidences of this expansion can be found in the increased number of sawmills in New Hampshire. Where there were perhaps 90 mills by 1700 in the whole of the Piscataqua region, fifty years later the four older towns and their new parishes (within the old town boundaries) accommodated some 75 mills, while the townships granted between 1700 and 1740 contained some 133 more, totaling more than 200 mills. The location of these mills reveals that the center of New Hampshire lumbering had shifted inland: Londonderry, Kingston, Exeter, Nottingham, and Chester averaged eighteen mills each, while Portsmouth had none, and Dover, fewer than ten.[75]

The mast trade expanded as well. In 1695, some 56 masts were exported, but by 1718 almost 200 were sent to England. Although Dummer's War affected mast exportation to England (only seventy-five were exported from New Hampshire in 1725), by 1727 recovery was under way. In 1742, an excellent year for Piscataqua trade, the Piscataqua region exported over 500 masts, a 150 percent increase over the exportation of 1718. These figures do not take into consideration the illicit trade in masts with Spain and Portugal, a trade that had proved lucrative, though masts had been enumerated in the Naval Stores Act of 1705.[76] A sampling of Piscataqua mast exportation between 1742 and 1775 suggests that by 1742 the New Hampshire mast trade with the mother country reached its highest general level of expansion. The records also reveal that in the periods of Anglo-French war, when overseas trade was endangered, the Piscataqua settlers relied more upon West Indian markets for their mast trade (see Table 4).[77]

The shipbuilding industry also reflected the general expansion of lumbering in the early eighteenth century, as New Hampshire–built vessels increased in both size and quantity. Using the vessels built in 1687–95 as a base—thirty-four New Hampshire-built vessels at 982 tons for an average of 28.9 tons per vessel—one can perceive a gradual expansion occurring through 1729, followed by a rapid expansion in the next fifteen years. Thus, for example, in the year 1727 alone, forty New Hampshire–built vessels totaling 2,900 tons in carrying capacity were involved in the Piscataqua overseas trade, as compared to twenty vessels for 1695 alone, or thirty-four for the period 1687–95. In a little over thirty years the number of New Hampshire–built vessels in the Piscataqua trade had doubled; but, far more important, the total carrying capacity of such vessels had increased threefold, and the average capacity of each vessel built in 1727 was 72.5 tons or about 2.5 times the average capacity of the 1687–95 vessels. This increased size and carrying capacity came primarily from the increase in the size and number of ships utilized in 1727, but all

TABLE 4

MAST EXPORTATION FROM PISCATAQUA 1742-1768

YEAR	TOTAL	TO ENGLAND	TO CARIBBEAN OR OTHER NORTH AMERICAN COLONIES
1742	524	427	97
1743	366	294	72
1744	350	318	32
1745	202	160	42
1746[a]	0	0	0
1747	263	189	74
1752	570	554	16
1753	441	414	27
1754	391	374	17
1755[b]	266	252	14
1756	124	93	31
1757	50	0	50
1758	302	218	84
1759	285	189	96
1762	279	124	155
1764	392	377	15
1767	260	258	2
1768[c]	61	59	2

[a]Last quarter missing
[b]Incomplete
[c]Incomplete

the vessels in use in 1727 had a larger average capacity than their counterparts of the 1690's (see Table 5).

The most important shipbuilding expansion, however, took place between 1727 and 1742. By 1742 there were eighty-two New Hampshire-built vessels totaling 6,822 tons capacity engaged in the Piscataqua overseas trade—a twofold increase in carrying capacity over the vessels of 1727 in only fifteen years. Governor Belcher fleetingly referred to the

TABLE 5

SHIPBUILDING EXPANSION: NEW HAMPSHIRE BUILT VESSELS
IN PISCATAQUA OVERSEAS TRADE

VESSEL TYPES	1687-1695			1727			1742		
	NO.	TONNAGE	AVERAGE TONNAGE	NO.	TONNAGE	AVERAGE TONNAGE	NO.	TONNAGE	AVERAGE TONNAGE
Ketches	7	170	24.3	0	0	0.0	0	0	0.0
Sloops	5	92	18.4	13	435	33.5	17	615	36.2
Brigs	11	300	27.3	8	390	48.8	13	685	52.7
Ships	2	150	75.0	10	1750	175.0	19	4160	218.9
Schooners	0	0	0.0	6	155	25.8	27	797	29.5
Pinks	1	25	25.0	2	130	65.0	0	0	0.0
Snows	0	0	0.0	1	40	40.0	6	565	94.2
Barks	8	245	30.6	0	0	0.0	0	0	0.0
TOTAL VESSELS 1687-1695	34	982	28.9	40	2900	72.5	82	6822	83.2
TOTAL VESSELS 1695 only	20	675	33.8						

NHPP, 2: 77-84; Shipping Returns, 1695-1742, CO5 967, 968;

Mass. Shipping Records, 1686-88, CO5 848.

increase in a 1737 letter to the Board of Trade when he wrote that "the trade of building ships and loading them with oak has increased something of late" and observed that New Hampshire's trade probably increased "near one-fourth" within the preceding four years.[78] In comparison with the statistics of 1695, New Hampshire–built vessels used for the overseas carrying trade in 1742 had quadrupled in number and increased tenfold in total carrying capacity. As the Shipping Returns make clear, most of this increase was in the number of ships, brigs, snows, and, after 1727, schooners.

The Shipping Returns, which contain the registration date and the year each vessel was built, provide more evidence of this expanding industry. They reveal that between 1722 and 1727 at least ninety-four vessels, averaging about 60 tons each, emerged from New Hampshire shipyards. The vast majority of these new vessels were sloops and brigs, but a significant number were 200–400-ton mast ships.[79] The most prominent shipbuilders of the 1720's included Sampson Sheafe of New Castle; Joshua Peirce, Daniel Jackson, John Harvey, and Thomas Phipps of Portsmouth; Thomas Trickey of Newington; and Thomas Millet of

Dover.[80] At least 142 vessels were built between 1740 and 1745, averaging about 90 tons each, a 50 percent increase over the number produced from 1722 to 1727, and an equal increase in the carrying capacity of each vessel.[81] The men leading this expansion of ship construction in the 1730's and 1740's included John Moffatt, Nathaniel Meserve, Ebenezer Wentworth, Thomas Cotton, John Shackford, John Seward, Abraham Senter, and Thomas Hammett of Portsmouth; Samuel Bickford and the Trickeys of Newington; members of the Folsom and Gilman families, Charles Rundlett, and Zebulon Gidding of Exeter; and the Milletts of Dover. Each of the New Hampshire towns along the Piscataqua River and its tributaries harbored important shipbuilders, in fact; and these builders were turning out between twenty-five and thirty vessels a year in the 1740's. Undoubtedly, the Piscataqua area ranked second or third in ship production in all of New England by the 1740's. The increased number of shipbuilders in the 1730's and 1740's reflects not only an expanding industry but its accelerating attractiveness as a field of economic opportunity.

Sometime in the mid-1720's New Hampshire craftsmen began exporting finished wooden tools and furniture such as desks and tables—another dimension of the lumber trade's overall expansion. The first record of such exportation appeared in the customs returns of 1727, when Daniel Warner, a Portsmouth mariner-merchant, exported ten tables to Barbados. The production and exportation of such products increased during the 1730's, so that by 1742 New Hampshire merchant-shippers exported at least 25 tables, 53 desks, 32 desk tables, one chest of drawers, 459 chairs, over 7,000 oars, 596 axes, 24 oxbows, 3,740 handspikes, 72 pails, and miscellaneous woodenware.[82] The primary markets for these products were Newfoundland, Maryland, Virginia, North Carolina, and the West Indies. The development of this trade reveals both the continuing expansion of economic opportunities with lumber resources and the growing diversity and specialization within the New Hampshire economy.

The lumber trade had an immense impact upon the individual lives and the expanding economy of the New Hampshire people. Frontiersmen, farmers, craftsmen, merchants, seamen, and unskilled laborers—almost every walk of life in the colony—gained a measure of profit from some aspect of its exploitation. Those individuals who engaged in trade and commerce found lumber products their primary export. As late as 1742 there were probably over 200 vessels carrying lumber to Boston yearly, and of the 78 vessels that cleared Piscataqua for overseas ports in 1742, only 5 vessels (6.4 percent of the total number of vessels clearing) carried no lumber products.[83] Of all the resources available to New Hampshire settlers, lumber held by far the most significant role in the colony's first century of economic development.

CHAPTER VI

INTERNAL THREATS TO MERCANTILE ENTERPRISE

By the early 1640's a few economic leaders in the Piscataqua region had acquired enough experience to recognize the internal economic problems that had been confronting both themselves and the people of Massachusetts since the end of the Great Migration. These problems—a general scarcity of both capital and cash, a chronic shortage of cheap labor, and a dependence on English manufactured goods without an adequate medium of exchange within the English mercantile system to pay for them—would continue to plague New England throughout the colonial period. This lack of money was due to the unfavorable balance of trade with the mother country and aggravated financial problems within the colonies. To a lesser extent, inflation threatened economic opportunities, particularly in the eighteenth century. In attempting to solve these problems, New Hampshire colonists followed general approaches already instituted by Massachusetts, but their specific methods were conditioned by the particular values and needs of their own society.[1]

Capital Scarcity

It is impossible to assess accurately the effects of capital scarcity on the New Hampshire economy in the seventeenth and early eighteenth centuries. Undoubtedly, the relative lack of capital slowed the development of every significant economic endeavor in the colony to some extent and eliminated the possibility of attempting a few enterprises. The Piscataqua settlers were very aware of this threat, however, and the methods they developed to alleviate its effects had significant social and economic consequences.

Since land was the most abundant resource on the Piscataqua frontier, the Piscataqua settlers of the 1640's and 1650's used it to lure craftsmen and enterprising men with capital into their communities. In this way Edward Gilman, Jr., founder of the most important lumbering family in Exeter and builder of its first sawmill, was attracted to that community.[2] The New Hampshire provincial government also used this technique as late as 1720 to encourage the exploitation of iron deposits along the Lamperell River. In that year, the General Assembly granted two miles of land to a company of Portsmouth merchants, who used the land to lure Scotch-Irish laborers into the area.[3] A further extension of the use of land as a source of capital can be found in the intensifying land speculation of the 1720's and 1730's. John Peagrum, the new Surveyor General for North America, noted it in 1736: "What I have observed of the New England people is [that] . . . their chief aim is to procure tracts of land, tho there is no advantage arises from their possession than to sell them at high rates to persons that come over to settle."[4] Profits from land provided capital for other endeavors.

Perhaps the easiest method of obtaining capital lay in finding staple products for export that would return quick profits. Thus, New Hampshire enterprisers sought to develop the fur trade, fisheries, and lumber trade. But generally these activities required both a preliminary investment of some capital and the establishment of mercantile connections in the marketing locations. Frequently, the new settlers who brought capital into New Hampshire between 1645 and 1689 were acting as agents or suppliers of London or Boston merchants. These mercantile newcomers held an advantage over the earlier settlers in their trading and credit connections and their knowledge.[5] But within a few years of their arrival, these mercantile immigrants had developed numerous alliances—economic, political, and in many cases, marital—with the earlier settlers.[6] Such alliances brought outside connections, capital, and credit facilities to the original settlers while strengthening internal mercantile ties in the Piscataqua region. For example, in the 1690's William Partridge had accounts with Thomas Hutchinson, Elisha Cooke, and David Jeffries of Boston; and John Taylor, Sir Henry Ashurst, Samuel Allen, William Crouch, Joseph Tatum, and Henry Phillips of London. At the same time Partridge also dealt with such New Hampshire merchants and lumber suppliers as George Jaffrey, Samuel Penhallow, Robert Tufton, Edward Ayers, Charles Story, Samuel Hilton, Thomas and Samuel Chesley, Thomas Packer, Richard and John Gerrish, Joshua Moodey (the Congregational minister), Obadiah Morse, and John Knight. Such pooling of capital resources among friends and relatives was common, particularly in seventeenth-century trading ventures. Fifteen of the 28 vessels trading at Piscataqua in the summer of 1681 (53.6 percent) were owned by between two and six New Hampshire people; in contrast, only 12 out of 85 vessels in the Piscataqua trade in 1727 (14.1 percent) and 31 out of 139 in the Piscataqua trade in 1742 (22.3 percent) had more than one owner.[7]

Thus, from the 1640's onward New Hampshire's frontier economy attracted capitalist investment and exploitation from Boston and London, while its economic needs forced its expanding population to seek outside capital and credit connections. Alliances soon appeared among individuals and groups from all these questing interests, but the presence of a wide-open economy and the prevailing capitalist values encouraged the development of ruthless competition and antagonisms among these groups and alliances and influenced the political and social development of New Hampshire.

As it became clear that New Hampshire's mid-seventeenth-century exports were not adequately profitable in England, New Hampshire enterprisers embraced two general courses of action. They sought markets for their products from which they could obtain either cash or products that could be marketed in the mother country. In other words, as Bernard Bailyn puts it, "exchanges were to be made in places outside of England and profits translated into credit in England." Secondly, they attempted to develop New Hampshire products that were attractive to the English economy. In both cases, the prior experiences of Massachusetts merchants along these lines proved instructive to New Hampshire entrepreneurs. In addition, the futile mid-seventeenth-century experience of Massachusetts capitalists in attempting economic self-sufficiency through the local development of manufactured woolen and iron goods precluded such efforts in New Hampshire during the seventeenth century.[8] After 1715, however, the New Hampshire government embarked on policies encouraging local manufacture of both these raw materials—policies that were notable for their relative failure.[9]

The scarcity of capital particularly affected New Hampshire's production of commodities demanded by the English economy in the seventeenth century. In general, only those people who had acquired capital from some other source (either furs, fish, lumber, or outside connections) were able to provide these goods. Thus, Richard Waldron was probably the first New Hampshire man involved in the mast trade and undoubtedly the first to experiment in tar production.[10] A friendly town government proved to be the best ally of original settlers seeking capital. Through free land and timber grants, or even through the grant of a liquor license, many early settlers and, for that matter, newcomers acquired the means for diversification. In fact, most of the people involved in the three major new economic developments of the later seventeenth century—the rise of the mast trade, shipbuilding, and attempts at naval stores production —either held or quickly obtained liquor licenses.[11] Liquor retailing was probably the most lucrative business within the seventeenth-century Piscataqua economy, as New Hampshire lumberers and fishermen were notorious for their heavy drinking. This enterprise served as one of the few important internal sources of New Hampshire capital.[12]

The attempts of New Hampshire enterprisers to develop exportation of naval stores in the late seventeenth and early eighteenth centuries reveal their prevalent beliefs about the effects of capital scarcity in the Piscataqua region—namely, that capital scarcity was one of the key factors restricting its economic expansion. Because of the fear on the part of English merchants and mercantilists that New England would seek self-sufficiency through the manufacture of woolen goods, English imperial officials supported the development of naval stores production in New Hampshire. Thus, the Board of Trade encouraged William Partridge and Jonathan Bridger in their efforts to establish pitch, tar, and turpentine production after 1696.[13] Both these men recommended establishing imperial bounties on the major naval stores. On the other hand Lieutenant Governor John Usher, Partridge's bitter political enemy, recommended that a chartered monopoly be granted to a company of New England and English merchants.[14] These proposals indicated that the lack of sufficient capital was an important consideration in the production of New England naval stores; and upon the urging of the Board of Trade, the English government enacted a series of premiums or bounties in New England naval stores in 1705.[15] This assumption can also be seen in the various actions of the New Hampshire government in support of naval stores production. Governor Bellomont wrote the Board in 1699 that the basic problem was its "extravagant cost," and the New Hampshire General Assembly acted from this premise when, in 1719, it placed a bounty of one shilling per pound on all "good bright sound and merchantable hemp, being the growth of this Province."[16]

But the primary problem in achieving satisfactory profits from the naval stores trade was not so much the scarcity of capital as the shortage, high cost, and unskilled nature of the labor force and the fact that higher profits could be found in shipbuilding. William Partridge had told Governor Bellomont in 1699 that in the last two years he had obtained £22,000 through the sale of vessels in England. Earlier in the year Partridge had suggested the encouragement of naval stores to the Board of Trade. Partridge's personal interest, however, was in the encouragement of colonial masts, ships, and ship timber, rather than the other naval stores. He later told the Board that the Baltic area would ultimately provide a closer and better source of tar and pitch, and that, therefore, the colonies would never develop a satisfactory staple in those items. As Governor Bellomont put it: "I see plainly that he [Partridge] has so found the sweet of building ships that he will not be broke of it."[17] Eight years later Governor Dudley recommended that New Hampshire would "particularly increase, grow rich, and strong if they were put upon building great ships for Her Majesty's Navy."[18] Not all New Hampshire traders saw the difficulties in tar and pitch production as clearly as Partridge; for as late as 1723 Lieutenant Governor John Wentworth, assuming that capital scarcity was a major aspect of the problem, proposed a New England company, composed of New Hampshire and Connecticut investors, that would tackle (with the Board of Trade's "encouragement") the development of a significant trade in naval stores.[19] Capital scarcity, regardless of contemporary beliefs, played but a minor role in deterring New Hampshire naval stores production before 1740. Labor scarcity and the lack of a strong demand in England for colonial pitch and tar—in spite of the Board of Trade's advocacy of these items—were the real culprits.[20] By 1742, however, the Piscataqua region emerged as a net exporter of naval stores (see Table 6), primarily because mast contractors and their agents now dominated the production of Piscataqua naval stores.[21]

Labor Shortages

The scarcity and high cost of labor had an immense impact upon economic and social behavior in New Hampshire during its first century.[22] That it hindered the economic growth of the colony may be seen in the testimony of William Partridge, Governor Bellomont, George Vaughan, and Governor Jonathan Belcher. In 1699 Partridge and Bellomont argued that the main reason naval stores—particularly pitch and tar—could not be produced in large quantities at Piscataqua lay in "the scarcity of hands and dearness of labor," and both suggested the use of royal troops as potentially the most effective labor force for naval store production.[23] Sixteen years later George Vaughan—another New Hampshire shipwright, mast trader, and merchant—wrote in the same vein and suggested that each vessel importing masts, lumber, and naval stores into England should bring back at least ten "begging vagrants from the City of London" to New England.[24] In 1735 Governor Belcher blamed New Hampshire's dilatory production of hemp on the fact that the colony was "small and thin of people which makes labor dear and the farmers poor."[25] Confronted continuously by this labor problem and working within the framework of traditionally accepted values, New Hampshire enterprisers evolved substantial yet imperfect solutions.

Perhaps the earliest solution they adopted was the utilization of Indian laborers, whom they paid in corn and other agricultural produce. Both Exeter and Dover had resident Indians employed in this manner.[26] After

TABLE 6

PISCATAQUA NAVAL STORES IMPORTATION AND EXPORTATION, 1695-1752

Commodities	1695 Import	1695 Export	1718[a] Import	1718[a] Export	1723 Import	1723 Export
Pitch	0	0	0	0	170 bbl.	0
Tar	0	28 bbl.	0	149 bbl.	0	0
Turpentine	0	0	0	74 bbl.	0	10 bbl.
Resin	0	46½ bbl.	0	0	0	0
Pitch and Tar	0	0	0	0	0	0

Commodities	1725 Import	1725 Export	1727 Import	1727 Export	1742 Import	1742 Export	1752 Import	1752 Export
Pitch	?[b]	37 bbl.	0	42 bbl.	33½ bbl.	581 bbl.	285 bbl.	61 bbl.
Tar	40 bbl.	60 bbl.	0	54 bbl.	22 bbl.	222 bbl.	380 bbl.	817 bbl.
Turpentine	0	0	0	18 bbl.	6 bbl.	140 bbl.	15 bbl.	637 bbl.
Resin	0	0	0	0	0	0	0	77 bbl.
Pitch and Tar	0	0	260 bbl.	0	0	122 bbl.	0	0

[a]No record of importation for 1718.
[b]? denotes an extant but unspecified amount.

the Pequot War in southern New England, captured Indians were sold as slaves throughout New England. By the 1660's there were at least four and probably many more such slaves in New Hampshire. Many of the Indians captured at Cochecho in 1676 during King Philip's War were sold into slavery outside New England.[27] The New Hampshire colonists, then, were not averse to the practice of Indian enslavement. Nevertheless, by the 1690's the New Hampshire government found itself compelled to protect Indian servants and slaves from "inhuman severities" committed by their masters and overseers—fragmentary evidence of white discontent with Indian labor.[28] A number of laws enacted between 1702 and 1714 reveal the problems engendered by Indians and other labor elements. The Indians commonly escaped their masters, committed burglary and other crimes, started riots, and wandered about the towns in a drunken state.[29] As a consequence, the New Hampshire General Assembly passed a law "Prohibiting the Importation or Bringing into this Province any Indian Servant or Slave," which did not actually prohibit such importation but merely placed a £10 head tax on each imported Indian.[30] The preamble to this law provides insight into the apprehensions concerning and general discontent with the Indians: "Diverse conspiracies, outrages, barbarities, murders, burglaries, thefts, and other notorious crimes and enormities at sundry times have of late been perpetrated and committed by Indians and other slaves within several of Her Majesty's plantations in America; being of a malitious [sic], surly, and revengeful spirit, and very ungovernable; the overgreat number and increase whereof within this province is likely to prove of fatal and pernicious consequence . . . here unless speedily remedied, and is a discouragement to the importation of white Christian servants." These general prejudices and difficulties with the Indians, as well as their growing scarcity, brought a gradual decline in the use of Indian labor in New Hampshire after 1715.[31]

Negro slaves provided another source of labor at least as early as the 1660's. Perhaps the first slave owner was Bryan Pendleton, but several of Portsmouth's leading families had imported blacks from the West Indies to work as servants by the 1670's and 1680's. By 1713 perhaps one hundred Negro slaves were living in New Hampshire, most of whom worked for Portsmouth mariners, merchants, and wealthy widows as domestic servants.[32] Though the relatively small number of Negro slaves and the nature of their occupations might suggest that these blacks were generally well treated and perhaps even contented in New Hampshire, the evidence reveals a more complex reality.

As early as 1694 the General Assembly felt compelled to pass a law providing the death penalty for anyone who willfully killed his Negro servant; and when the Crown disallowed this law as not protecting the master in cases of provocation or self-defense, the New Hampshire government responded by reenacting exactly the same law.[33] In 1714 new legislation, the first slave code in New Hampshire, was directed against what must have been an increasingly grave problem: "Whereas great disorders, insolencies, burglaries are oftimes raised and committed in the night time by Indians, negro, and mulatto servants and slaves . . . for prevention whereof . . . that no Indian, negro or mulatto or slave may presume to [be] absent from the families where they respectively belong or be found abroad in the night time after nine o'clock, unless it be on errand for their respective masters and owners." Another law punished anyone who received stolen property from any "Indian, mulatto, negro servant or slave, or other lewd, disorderly person" under penalty of whipping or payment of double the value of the stolen items to the owner. As part of a general law encouraging temperance in the next year, the government forbade servants or Negroes to drink without their master's consent.[34] In evaluating the significance of this legislation, one should note that these were the only laws relating to Negroes enacted before the 1760's. They became law at a time of economic depression, following the Treaty of Utrecht; and though Negro slave importation was relatively insignificant until 1730, yet no new regulative legislation was forthcoming in the 30's and 40's, when slave importation increased considerably.[35] Probably, the depressed conditions following Queen Anne's War led New Hampshire legislators into an exaggerated expression of their fears and prejudices. Nevertheless, these laws reveal some of the bases for their actions and indicate a widespread low opinion of Negro slaves.

Despite the fact that Negro slaves were not considered a very satisfactory source of labor, when Indian slaves and white indentured servants declined in numbers after 1713, Negroes gradually took their place as permanent servants in the homes of New Hampshire's wealthier inhabitants. By the 1730's over two hundred slaves were scattered throughout the older towns, with Portsmouth possessing more than one-third of them. At least forty families in Portsmouth, fifteen families in Exeter, five families in Hampton Falls, and four families each in Hampton and Dover owned three or four slaves.[36] But in the final analysis this labor source did little to alleviate New Hampshire's continuing scarcity of cheap labor, because only the wealthier could afford Negro slaves and, at least before 1740, they were not used to supply the crucial demand for skilled craftsmen or unskilled town and farm laborers.

In the mid-seventeenth century, the New Hampshire colonists began utilizing another source of cheap labor—the indentured servant. Before 1650 relatively few, if any, indentured servants came into New Hampshire unless they were runaways from Massachusetts seeking a fresh start on the frontier. If such newcomers showed a willingness to work and live a settled life, the New Hampshire townspeople, eager for new settlers, urged them to remain by granting them land and admitting them as inhabitants. In the early 1650's, however, perhaps as many as thirty Scotch servants were brought into Dover, Exeter, and Portsmouth from Boston by such lumberers as Valentine Hill, Richard Waldron, Edward Gilman, and Bryan Pendleton. These Scots had been prisoners of war captured by Cromwell's troops in the battles of Dunbar and Worcester and had been exported to Boston, where they were sold as servants or apprentices for six to eight years to pay off their costs of passage across the Atlantic. Many of them became permanent inhabitants of the New Hampshire towns in the 1650's and 1660's, and they probably attracted more Scotch servants into the colony in the 1660's and 1670's.[37]

Another form of indentured servitude was the use of apprentices. Traditional apprenticeships as established by Elizabethan law required seven years of service to a merchant or craftsman, but in New Hampshire, as elsewhere in the colonies, both the terms of service and the occupations of masters varied considerably. Many settlers apprenticed their children to mariners, lumberers, and successful farmers as well as to merchants and craftsmen, particularly before 1713. Probably the majority of those who apprenticed their sons were farmers seeking to better their sons' economic status by establishing them in "good trades," while the "good traders" found apprentices a satisfactory form of cheap labor.[38]

In fact, informal apprenticeships were common whereby children, after their father's death, chose a guardian who was relatively wealthy, who desired young workers, and who could advance their individual prospects. These informal apprenticeships were probably the most common form of indentured servitude after 1713.[39] The New Hampshire government encouraged this type of labor through such an expedient as allowing thieves to pay for their crimes through service to their victim until they had provided labor worth twice the value of the stolen items. It also allowed debtors to work off their debt through indentured service, allowed each minister a free servant, and in 1712 authorized the town selectmen to examine all "youth of ten years of age" and "binde out" to good masters all those who could not read. The masters would keep them until they were twenty-one, teaching them to read and write. As early as 1692 the government ordered that all men between sixteen and sixty who were unable to pay the cost of outfitting themselves with the proper weapons must "be put to service" and the master would then pay these costs during their service to him.[40]

The wars with the French and Indians between 1689 and 1713 were probably the most significant factor in the gradual decline of indentured servitude in New Hampshire by the early eighteenth century. In the first place, the wars interrupted immigration into New Hampshire, cutting off most outside sources of indentured servants. In addition, servants usually substituted for their masters in watches, garrison duty, and road improvement labor—none of which were popular activities.[41] These conditions, plus the generally depressed economic situation throughout the wars, so encouraged underage sons, apprentices, and "covenant servants" to abandon their contracts and families for opportunities at sea that the New Hampshire government described the problem as follows: "Sundry of the inhabitants of this province have sustained great damage by their sons and servants deserting their service without consent of their parents or masters, being encouraged to enter themselves on board private Men of War or merchant ships."[42] It punished such offenders by fining ship captains £5 for every week they "detained" the runaway. The runaway himself received up to a year's further service to his master for his offense. Aside from the greater economic opportunities in trade, there were numerous other enticing opportunities for the servant: witness Peter Greeley's Scotch-Irish servant who ran off to Maine in quest of more rapid gain from the bounties on Indian scalps.[43]

Finally, what immigrant after 1713 would choose New Hampshire over New York, Pennsylvania, Virginia, or even Massachusetts unless he received highly favorable advantages?[44] It is not accidental, then, that relatively few indentured servants settled in New Hampshire between 1713 and 1740. But, Lieutenant Governor John Wentworth may have been attempting to establish an attractive system for new indentured servant immigration along agricultural rather than trade or craft lines by 1730, when he brought servants in from Ireland as tenant laborers on his land grants in the new townships of the 1720's for a seven-year term. If the tenant improved ten to twelve acres and satisfactorily increased the number of livestock within the seven years, Wentworth gave him the home lot and improvements.[45]

Despite these varied attempts to secure an adequate source of cheap labor, both positive and negative evidence suggests that New Hampshire settlers did not solve this problem to their satisfaction before 1740. As early as 1642 the town of Exeter sought to establish a system which actually ran contrary to its traditional distrust of outsiders, as it provided that different types of laborers play competitive rather than complementary roles: "No foreigners shall work within the limits of our town to be paid out of timber or pipestaves for their work, nor to hinder any of the inhabitants from employment, provided that the inhabitants can or will do that work as cheap and sufficient as the foreigner; but if they will not, then are the inhabitants free to bring in foreigners."[46] This attempt, however, was unsuccessful either in gaining an adequate labor supply or in driving down the high costs of labor. The continuing shortage of labor forced the various towns to put all males between sixteen and sixty to work on whatever projects were necessary—the building of roads, bridges, and garrison houses, or serving in the militia—and these adjustments continued throughout the period before 1740.[47]

The labor shortage placed a premium upon large families working as economic units, and by the 1650's New Hampshire people were rewarding younger sons and even the daughters in their wills for their contribution to the family's economic efforts. Though it was the Massachusetts government that established this practice in law in 1649 in relation to the administration of intestate estates, early New Hampshire wills reveal that the common practice in private wills, as well as in the distribution of intestate estates, was to divide the estate into equal portions, giving the eldest son a double portion and the younger sons and daughters property or money roughly equivalent to a single portion.[48] After New Hampshire received its government in 1692, it enacted these principles into law; and when the Crown vetoed this bill in 1706, the New Hampshire courts ignored the veto and the government reinstated the law. The justification given for this action was that anyone could distribute his estate as he pleased in his will so long as each member of the family received a bequest of some sort; however, since the younger sons usually contributed effective and plentiful labor on the land, all children should obtain an equal share, or "portion," of intestate estates with the eldest son receiving a "double portion."[49] Thus, family solidarity in economic matters received due encouragement, not only from the shortage of labor, but also from other factors.

Furthermore, abundant economic opportunities for skilled and unskilled laborers contributed to the continuing labor shortage. Attempts by the New Hampshire government to regulate the laborer's activities provide ample evidence of this abundance. Though neither the New Hampshire towns nor the New Hampshire government enacted legislation regulating labor wages or prices between 1641 and 1741, they did take steps toward eliminating the most common abuses arising from the extraordinary economic situation.[50] For instance, in the 1660's the towns of Dover and Portsmouth appointed a "sealer of leather" to check the quality of goods the tanners were producing. Portsmouth also chose "cullers of staves" and "packers and gagers" in the 1660's, who served as a check on the hasty efforts of laborers striving to meet the heavy demands for their products.[51] In 1701 the provincial government forbade tanners to make shoes and shoemakers to "exercise the . . . mystery of a tanner," authorized the creation of "searchers and sealers of leather" in every town that needed them, and placed heavy fines on anyone who either sold or used leather or hides that had not received the proper "seal." These actions sought to control the quality of craftsmanship and avert the danger of vertical monopolization.[52]

Another type of labor legislation was passed during the trade dislocation and population expansion after Queen Anne's War. The New Hampshire government sought to protect the town craftsmen and the quality of their goods by punishing those "hawkers, pedlars, and petty chapmen" who sold inferior goods from house to house in the country towns. The preamble to this act reveals the prevalent shortage of skilled labor in relation to market demand for quality products, one effect of the scarcity of goods upon established skilled laborers, and the appearance of new enterprisers in the New Hampshire economy: "Complaint is made of great hurt to, and the decay of trade occasioned by the hawker, pedlar, and petty chapmen passing to and fro through the country to vend goods, wares, and merchandizes, so that diverse men of trades, handy crafts-men and others, none of the best fame having left off the exercise of their trades and business turn hawkers, pedlars, and petty chapmen."[53] This migration of the less qualified skilled laborers to the countryside illustrates the prevailing shortage of products and skilled laborers in a period of population growth. In 1718, after its expiration, the act was renewed on the grounds that the hawkers and peddlers were destroying the trade of the towns and luring more and more tradesmen into their practices.[54] Thus the New Hampshire government, guided in part by its concern for the quality of locally manufactured products, enacted legislation that also served the interests of the established craftsmen and shopkeepers of Portsmouth.

A final series of New Hampshire labor enactments fell into the realm of maritime relations, and as might be expected, the primary consideration was to assure the shipmasters of an adequate supply of labor. In 1694, for example, the New Hampshire government exacted a £2 fine from any seaman who deserted his ship to sail with another master and even fined anyone who entertained a contracted seaman aboard another vessel the sum of £3. If the seaman "ran away," the justices of the peace could arrest and jail him until his ship was ready for departure, taking any expenses out of his wages. This act was strengthened in 1701, when the government forbade the imprisonment of seamen debtors by their creditors (usually innkeepers) and postponed any seizures or claims until the end of the seaman's voyage.[55] In 1718, the government applied the same general principles to the fishing industry by decreeing that no fisherman could abandon his employer and take a new job until his contract with the original employer had expired. The shipowners, in return, were required to supply adequate provisions for their fishermen and never to sign on a fisherman who was under contract to another master.[56]

Such legislation provides a crude indication of the opportunities for laborers and of the types of economic problems arising from the continuing labor shortages. Although the colony's legislation incidentally favored employers over employees and skilled labor over unskilled, its guiding principles centered upon the sanctity of contracts and honesty and fair play in economic relationships. In the wake of the continuous labor shortages and the generally imperfect solutions attempted, the New Hampshire colonists' most common adjustment was the jack-of-all-trades or the economically cooperative, self-reliant family.[57]

An Inadequate Medium of Exchange

A third general threat to economic growth in New Hampshire was the lack of an adequate medium of exchange, both within the local economy and in the wider imperial economy. The most significant single cause of this problem was the difficulty of finding money to pay for English manufactured products purchased from either England or Massachusetts.[58] This lack of currency and the necessity of adjustment to it permanently influenced New Hampshire's colonial society, affecting the development of religious, political, military, and economic customs from the 1630's onward.[59]

In the seventeenth century New Hampshire settlers adjusted as best they could to this economic reality by following the lead of Massachusetts. The barter system—using lumber and fish and to a lesser extent Indian corn, furs, beef, pork, wheat, and peas as "commodity money" —became the most common form of economic exchange. Since the various towns and provincial governments specified these commodities and a few others as acceptable in payment of taxes and public debts, they were in wide demand in local private business agreements as well.[60]

But the use of commodity money had a number of disadvantages. One might "spend" his most inferior products in the local economy, saving those of better quality for export. Passage of legislation governing minimum quality of lumber, fish, meat, and leather and the creation of such supervisory local officials as cullers of staves, Gagers and Packers, and cullers of fish represented in part attempts to halt the circulation of inferior commodity money. Then, there was always the possibility that meat or grain might spoil or deteriorate while in the creditor's hands; however, spoilage was never much of a problem in New Hampshire because lumber was the most common commodity and all the other products were in strong local demand.[61]

A more serious problem lay in establishing an equitable market price reflecting the true worth of each commodity. The New Hampshire government, in response to this problem, allowed private creditors to accept commodity money at either the price set by the government or the actual market price; and when the money was turned in for taxes, if the market price of the commodity involved was below the set price, the government would pay the difference to the treasurer. If the market value was above the set price, the treasurer would make an adjustment with the taxpayer. Thus, in New Hampshire the actual market price governed over legislatively established commodity prices.[62]

Probably the greatest disadvantage to commodity money as a medium of exchange was that the most common commodities could not be used in direct trade with England as returns for manufactured goods. The most valuable lumber products—those falling under the category of naval stores (masts, ship timber, tar, pitch)—were either too valuable or too uncommon to serve as effective commodity money, although the New Hampshire government encouraged tar, hemp, and flax production, hoping that these products would become plentiful enough to alleviate this problem.[63]

The use of a barter system and the prevailing framework of values caused the New Hampshire colonists to develop other social practices that reflected the continuing lack of an adequate medium of exchange. Thus, the land grants of the early towns did not require money payments or quitrents, nor did the township grants of the New Hampshire General Assembly in the 1720's and 1730's. Religious and political leaders either received their due rewards in land or in exemption from military service.[64] The use of labor was deeply influenced by the lack of a medium, since most laborers (outside the family) usually were indentured servants, apprentices, or slaves who received their "wages" (if they received them at all) in room, board, education, and perhaps a grant of land—a system requiring very little money. Labor itself was often substituted for money, particularly through community work on roads and bridges. Even the military system reflected the absence of an adequate medium, as well as the general shortage and high cost of labor, since all males between sixteen and sixty were required to bear arms, supply their own military needs, and serve garrison duty without monetary compensation. The frank preamble to the militia act of 1703 reveals that New Hampshire politicians were not in principle opposed to paying military wages: "The present state of this Province, their poverty and want of trade disable them from paying soldiers wages."[65] In fact, New Hampshire's first issue of paper currency in 1709 was enacted primarily "to pay soldiers' wages" in the Canada Expedition. Two years later, however, the government changed its approach again by discarding wage payments and introducing scalp bounties in payment of military service as an inducement for volunteers. In 1718 the traditional pre-1709 approach was restored in regard to liability for service, but by 1721 soldiers were receiving low wage payments in paper currency as well as the bounties on Indian scalps.[66]

The New Hampshire government also tried to attract foreign gold and silver into New Hampshire's economy in order to obtain an adequate medium of exchange. Borrowing a technique from the Massachusetts government, it passed legislation raising the legal value of Spanish pieces of eight above its sterling value. The assumption was that if the value of the foreign coin were inflated, it would be attracted from areas outside the colony; and once it was lured in, the inflated value would keep it there. In the 1680's the sterling value of a Spanish piece of eight was four shillings and six pence; in Massachusetts the piece of eight value had been set at six shillings. In November 1682, the New Hampshire government set the legal value of a Spanish piece of eight at eight shillings "in the hopes of bringing plenty of money into this Province," even from Massachusetts. But within a year the New Hampshire government reduced the legal value to six shillings (on a par with Massachusetts) because the first act had not succeeded in "the ends it was intended for."[67] This failure ended New Hampshire's experiments in the regulation of foreign coin values. From 1683 on, it followed the law and practices of Massachusetts, practices which continually inflated the value of foreign currency.[68] It is difficult to assess the success of this policy. The Indian wars after 1689, by disrupting New Hampshire's trade and agriculture, without doubt limited its effectiveness. In 1708 John Usher wrote that whatever cash flowed into New Hampshire flowed right out again. The adoption of paper currency after 1709 suggests the ineffectiveness of foreign coin inflation in obtaining an adequate medium of exchange.[69]

The journals of the New Hampshire General Assembly between October 1707 and December 5, 1709 (the day the House authorized the use of paper currency), reveal the New Hampshire government's reluctance to adopt this new policy. In fact, the enabling act proposed that, if possible, Massachusetts should lend New Hampshire the bills of credit, showing how temporary the General Assembly expected this policy to be.[70] But as the bills of credit became dispersed within New Hampshire's economy and as the war demanded new revenue, New Hampshire politicians and traders began to recognize the benefits that paper currency could bring the colony, especially in alleviating the shortage of cash and establishing an adequate medium of exchange both in internal and external transactions.[71] Thus, every year the war continued, new bills of credit were issued in payment of government debts to be retired by property taxes three to five years later. But when the bills of credit were turned in as taxes, they were reissued.

In 1714 the New Hampshire government, after receiving a full treasury of Massachusetts and Connecticut currency in taxes, decided to experiment with a "land bank," loaning out £1,500 of new currency for two years in return for land security. By 1715 some New Hampshire leaders were looking upon paper currency as the cure for all the province's monetary ills. The currency was holding its own in relation to sterling value and was widely used in the economy. George Vaughan even suggested to the Board of Trade that since the "want of a medium of exchange" was a crucial economic problem in New England, the Crown should allow the New England governments to emit £500,000 in bills of credit and "let them out to loan at 6% on land security."[72]

With Vaughan as lieutenant governor and with a General Assembly dominated by mercantile elements, the New Hampshire government in 1717 expanded its land bank business by authorizing a £15,000 paper emission to be loaned at 10 percent interest. The borrowers were required to submit land mortgages worth double the value of the currency they received. The preamble of the act described it as providing a medium of exchange that would encourage "husbandry, fishery, and other trade." The money was distributed among the towns according to their property tax proportions, and town committees were placed in charge of loaning out the money in quantities of not more than £300 nor less than £20 per person—evidence of a concerted effort to disperse paper currency as widely as possible within the limits of fiscal propriety, providing both capital for new endeavors and money for payment of debts.[73]

From 1718 to 1742 the New Hampshire General Assembly generally postponed retiring bills of credit in circulation and issued new currency at every opportunity. For example, from 1718 to 1721, although no new currency was emitted, neither were the old bills retired when they came due. With the danger of war and actual warfare between 1722 and 1726, the government issued and received over £14,600 in bills of credit for war purposes. After the war ended, some £3,557 in new bills appeared to "supply the empty Treasury" and defend the frontiers.[74] Since the conflicts of Dummer's War were almost all in Maine, it seems apparent that the New Hampshire General Assembly used the war as an excuse to further increase the volume of paper currency in its quest for an adequate medium of exchange.

In 1727 Lieutenant Governor Wentworth wrote the Board of Trade, attacking the Royal Instruction of September 1720 which forbade the emission of bills of credit without a clause suspending enactment until receipt of royal approval (except in acts "raising and settling a public revenue for defraying the necessary charge of the Government"). He asserted that paper currency increases had caused New Hampshire's trade to expand fivefold in the last ten years, that local wool manufacturing had declined, but that if England insisted upon "calling in the bills of credit, then the tradesmen nor countrymen can't have it so that they will be obliged to spin their own clothing or wear none and live within themselves." He suggested that the English government allow Massachusetts and New Hampshire to issue a total of £300,000 in paper currency.[75]

A year later, after receiving a disapproving letter from the Board of Trade, he renewed his proposals. This time he asked for £25,000 to £30,000 in bills of credit for New Hampshire and gave his reasons: "It would greatly encourage trade and also the settlement of our outlands, and the better enable us to defend ourselves against the Indians whenever they make a war upon us tho they are very quiet for the present; there seems to be a greater necessity for striking more paper credit now than for many years past . . . because some of our overgrown men have hoarded up the money to make an advantage thereof on the poor and middling sort of people when their mortgages are out which is with a year or less; now the making more would oblige those usurers to unlock their coffers by which the poor and middling people would be relieved."[76] These arguments from one of the richest creditors in the colony provide some insight into the varied economic groups involved in the pressure for paper currency, including farmers, small tradesmen, new enterprisers, and wealthy mercantile families. Wentworth himself was especially interested in advancing trade and land speculation. In the meantime the New Hampshire House had proposed an emission of £30,000 on loan, but the council and Wentworth cautiously rejected it.[77]

During the 1730's Governor Belcher found that he could not obtain either the payment of government expenses or his salary unless he consented to new emissions. Between 1730 and 1740 he reluctantly consented to the issuance of about £11,800 in bills of credit, and the currency problem became one of the most significant political conflicts in the colony.[78] Operating under the assumption that "the want of a medium" was the "greatest hindrance" to expansion of trade and commerce, a group of New Hampshire merchants made inquiries to John Thomlinson in London about the chances of obtaining royal permission for a £50,000 or £60,000 emission of paper currency to be loaned out at 5 percent interest based upon land security at double the value of the currency.[79] Thomlinson's reply must have discouraged them, for they soon decided to pool their local resources and create a private land bank, issuing £15,000 to £20,000 in "manufactory" notes based upon land values.[80] But Governor Belcher persuaded the Massachusetts government to issue a proclamation forbidding the acceptance of this currency and then asked the New Hampshire General Assembly to pass a similar order on the grounds that the emission was "unwarrantable"; if the Crown prohibited government currency emissions, "surely private persons ought not to presume upon it."[81] The House responded that there was nothing unwarrantable in the emission unless fraud was intended and argued that the Crown had not intended to stop private "negotiable notes among merchants and traders." Nevertheless, Belcher effectively destroyed the notes by undermining public confidence in them. In a speech to the House which was widely publicized he said that several people had complained that "the principal founders or undertakers in the scheme have refused to give credit to those their own notes" and asserted that the notes had become "a dead loss" and "a notorious fraud" to those who had accepted them.[82]

Nevertheless, the New Hampshire mercantile community continued its endeavors for an increased volume of paper currency as its best solution to the lack of an adequate medium of exchange, and in 1742, through the influence of London merchants (particularly John Thomlinson), the Crown permitted a £25,000 emission of New Tenor currency, at a 1 : 4 ratio with the existing local Old Tenor currency, to be lent throughout the colony at 6 percent interest for ten years on land security.[83] Thus, the political conflicts of the 1730's and the removal of Governor Belcher culminated in the largest single emission of paper currency in New Hampshire's first century of experience.

Inflation

The use of paper currency in New Hampshire after 1709 aggravated two problems—counterfeiting and inflation—neither of which was satisfactorily solved by the 1740's. Indications of the gradual increase in counterfeiting and altering the face value of bills of credit can be seen in the increasing strictness of legislation proposed to combat these crimes. Within two years of the first emission the New Hampshire General Assembly enacted legislation punishing offenders with fines of double the value of the forged currency and a jail sentence. By 1718 the government was offering a £50 reward to anyone providing information leading to the conviction of counterfeiters. In 1723 the House of Representatives sent a bill to the council requiring the death penalty for counterfeiting, but the council tabled the measure. Counterfeiting apparently was most common immediately after new emissions of currency, for each of the laws that increased the penalties followed new emissions. Thus, in 1738—after the emission of £7,100 in 1737, the first in seven years—the General Assembly found it necessary to penalize counterfeiters by "death without benefit of clergy." Governor Belcher did not proclaim this law publicly at the time, however. But after the emission of about £30,000 in bills of credit in 1742, the General Assembly ordered the law of 1738 to be widely circulated in the "public prints," so that the death penalty would be known by all.[84] Counterfeiting, then, was apparently assuming rather serious proportions by the 1740's.

Potentially more serious, however, was inflation, for it affected the entire economic system in the colony. That inflation occurred can be seen in the relationship between one ounce of silver and its equivalent in New Hampshire currency between 1709 and 1742. In 1709 one ounce of silver equaled 8 shillings of New Hampshire Old Tenor currency and "lawful, current money"; by 1721, it brought 13 shillings; in 1728, 17 shillings; in 1734, 27 shillings; and in 1742, 28 shillings—a 350 percent increase in thirty-three years.[85] In addition, by 1741 New Hampshire paper currency traded at a ratio of slightly more than 5:1 in terms of the English pound sterling on the exchange markets and 4:1 in terms of "lawful money" or "proclamation money," further evidence of extensive currency inflation.[86]

The reactions of New Hampshire settlers to inflation depended upon their values and interests. To those who sought to develop their lands or purchase new lands, enter a new trade or further develop an already existing one, the presence of "easy money" was a boon, as it allowed them flexibility in both borrowing and repaying the debts incurred. Inflated currency encouraged those willing to take economic risks in the hope of advancing themselves. It also gave the small man—the farmer and craftsman, especially—an opportunity to escape heavy indebtedness and the excesses of the barter system, particularly the situation of being forced by past indebtedness to deal every year with the same merchant, a merchant who juggled prices in his own interest because of his victim's economic dependence. The farmer could now seek out cash for his goods, pay his old debts, and henceforth seek the highest value for his goods and lowest prices on imported goods. In this sense, paper currency inflation encouraged a competitive, free enterprise economy and gave opportunities to new enterprisers. Moreover, it provided the already established mercantile community with a means of rapid expansion in trade and in land speculation.

On the other hand, currency inflation, as always, worked hardship upon those who depended upon fixed wages and income. Ministers, schoolmasters, officials dependent upon fees, laborers, and older, established agricultural or mercantile families who had chosen to rely upon income from loans or mortgages usually had misgivings about currency inflation. Similar apprehensions could be found among some of the older, wealthier agricultural and commercial men in the colony, who felt their economic and social status threatened by the newer entrepreneurs and who had already established some lucrative sources of capital and credit through political and social connections within New Hampshire and abroad.[87]

Yet even with these circumstances, there was surprisingly little complaint against inflation in New Hampshire before 1740. The colony's post-1716 executives—Shute, Belcher, and John Wentworth—all expressed anti-inflation attitudes to the Board of Trade at one time or another, but Shute and Wentworth usually accepted inflationary legislative proposals.[88] For example, Lieutenant Governor Wentworth pointed out to the House the sorry plight of New Hampshire ministers, whose salaries had been cut almost in half in ten years by inflation; yet two years later he advocated the printing of £25,000 in new paper currency. Governor Belcher consistently opposed inflation and sought the creation of more paper currency based upon gold and silver rather than land, but he received strong and consistent opposition from the New Hampshire House of Representatives, and it was probably because of this issue that he lost his post as governor of Massachusetts.[89] In 1729 Reverend Hugh Adams of Durham placed a petition before the New Hampshire House asking for a remedy against the "debasedness" of the currency. The House dismissed his petition without debating it.[90] Apparently, inflated currency provided so many advantages to rich and poor alike that the majority either supported it or were indifferent to it.

Debts

With the scarcity of capital and cash, the high cost of labor, and the subsistence agricultural economy in the seventeenth century, many New Hampshire people sought to advance themselves through borrowing. Short-term indebtedness was probably the common experience of the majority, particularly after the towns stopped granting free land.

That cases involving indebtedness constituted the majority of suits brought into the New Hampshire courts before 1660 reveals the general credit insecurity prevalent in this early period of groping. From this period a gradual stabilization of credit relationships emerged, as individuals acquired status in wealth and reputation. The heaviest borrowing was carried on by the more ambitious enterprisers, particularly farmer-lumberers seeking expansion into the coastal or overseas trade in lumber, fish, or shipbuilding.[91] New Hampshire wills between 1640 and 1690, although a relatively weak source because of the small number who wrote wills, reveal that 35.9 percent of those who wrote wills were debtors at their death, while only 8.3 percent were creditors.[92] Considering the fact that the more well-to-do generally wrote wills, it seems clear that indebtedness was widespread on the seventeenth-century Piscataqua frontier. The amounts of credit extended were usually relatively small, however, because of the scarcity of cash and the use of commodity money. Farmers generally did not take great risks; instead they borrowed only enough to see themselves through the next harvest.

By the end of the seventeenth century a general pattern of credit usage had developed in New Hampshire. The merchants and traders residing in Portsmouth, Dover, and Exeter who engaged in the overseas and coastal trade usually acted as the creditors for the colony though they themselves might be debtors to English or Massachusetts merchants. William Partridge's credit relationships reveal this pattern.[93] These merchants, as they brought in manufactured goods from England and Massachusetts, often extended credit to local shopkeepers and retailers until the retailers could collect enough commodity money from the farmers to repay them. The local retailers usually extended credit for the manufactured goods purchased by the townspeople (usually farmers) until the next harvest. In some cases relatively wealthy farmer-lumberers served as creditors in their local communities: Ichabod Plaisted of Portsmouth, Andrew Wiggin of Exeter, John Tuttle of Dover, and Joseph Chase of Hampton are examples. In some cases, the wholesale trader might also engage in retailing his imports locally and extending credit directly to the townspeople: Richard Martyn, Richard Cutt, Thomas Daniel, George Jaffrey, and John Cutt exemplify this pattern.[94] But whatever the variations, generally the pattern of indebtedness went from townspeople to shopkeepers and local retailers, from them to the wholesale merchants and traders, and from them to others among themselves, or to Massachusetts or London merchants.[95] Indebtedness was an accepted fact in New Hampshire's everyday life. It stemmed ultimately from the shortage of capital and cash and from the unfavorable balance of trade between country towns and port towns and between port towns and London or Boston.

In normal times debt did not threaten the health of New Hampshire's economy; in fact, under prevailing circumstances indebtedness was a sign of economic activity and expansion. There were two periods in New Hampshire's first century of development, however, when debts did pose a serious threat. The first era, from about 1640 to 1655, reflected attempts at adjustment to the economic conditions of a frontier colony, during which the inhabitants experimented with credit relationships until they found patterns which worked. The second era, between 1690 and 1718, saw a partial breakdown of the older patterns of credit relationships as the wars with the French and Indians disrupted agricultural activity and brought many frontier farmers and others into Portsmouth, where they sometimes went to sea as mariners or became local retailers, craftsmen, or laborers. With the war and the uncertainty of land titles, trade seemed to offer new enterprisers the best opportunities. Most of these traders-to-be needed credit advances; and since the war brought high risks to overseas trade investments, some of the established capitalists invested in the new traders. The times were not that auspicious for new local trading enterprises, however. Many of the new traders found themselves perennially short of cash to satisfy their creditors and borrowed further in the hopes of ultimate financial recovery. But the utilization of paper currency in New Hampshire after 1709 and the end of the fighting near New Hampshire encouraged these new traders. Some established themselves in the country towns, where they disrupted the old credit relationships by paying cash (paper currency) for agricultural and lumber products, thereby attracting many farmers away from their earlier creditors. The prospects of new markets and abundant currency emboldened such enterprisers.[96]

The end of Queen Anne's war brought large quantities of manufactured goods from England and Massachusetts, resulting in a scarcity of currency in New Hampshire at a time when creditors supported foreclosure on loans, in part because of better investment opportunities in shipbuilding and overseas trade. The resultant economic crisis in 1713–19 forced the General Assembly to pass a number of laws, at first protecting debtors, then creditors, and ultimately resorting to a massive paper currency expansion for the benefit of both in 1717.

The first such act (1714) pointed out that since there were so many debtors, and since houses and lands represented the chief wealth of the people, these could be used in payment of all debts provided that the debtor have seven years after such payment to repay the debt in cash and recover his lands—a remarkably lenient measure for debtors. In 1715, the New Hampshire General Assembly enacted its first bankruptcy law; and, unlike English practice, which applied bankruptcy only to traders, the New Hampshire law applied to both traders and freeholders. The preamble commented: "Often times . . . merchants, shopkeepers, traders, and others that deal on credit . . . have and may, either through adversity and losses, or through fraud and deceit, become bankrupt . . . to the great hurt or damage of trade and commerce in general."[97] In 1716 the House pressed for emission of £10,000 of paper currency and reissued £1,500, but another year passed before the General Assembly enacted its £15,000 loan to encourage "husbandry, fishery, and other trade." Soon afterwards the amount of time given for land redemption (after using it for payment of debts) was reduced to two years, and the bankruptcy law was repealed because it hurt creditors by allowing debtors to escape their debts.[98]

The emission of paper currency alleviated the crisis, for in 1718 the General Assembly fined hawkers and peddlers £20 per violation because an increasing number of tradesmen were following such pursuits, and it reduced the time for land redemption in case of debt to one year. The debt crisis did not immediately disappear, however. In 1719 the government enacted legislation against absconding debtors, prohibiting any shipmaster from carrying debtors out of the colony on penalty of a £100 fine. Each master had to post his passenger list and £1,000 security before leaving the colony—a stringent piece of legislation.[99] It is clear, then, that New Hampshire experienced a wave of bankruptcies and absconding debtors between 1713 and 1719; that the government experimented with a variety of economic solutions to this problem; and that it enacted the first peacetime emission of paper currency as its best response to the threat posed by indebtedness.

After 1720, indebtedness continued as a part of New Hampshire's experience, but before the 1740's there were no more crises between creditors and debtors similar to that of 1713–19. Generally, indebtedness served as a sign of economic growth and expansion, but in a society so dependent upon credit for its well-being, outside influences could always turn it into an economic threat.

CHAPTER VII

EXTERNAL THREATS AND TRADE DEVELOPMENTS

During its first century, the emerging New Hampshire mercantile community faced several threats to its economic well-being which originated from outside the Piscataqua region. These threats ranged from competition from English and Massachusetts merchants and attempts at economic imperialism by both, to the need for an adequate source of returns in payment for English manufactured goods, dislocations arising from devastating wars, and imperial restrictions on trade, to such infrequent irritants as impressment and piracy. The New Hampshire merchants used many approaches as they sought solutions to these problems, but their endeavors met with a mixture of success and failure. Nevertheless, their intermittent and sometimes continuous contention with these difficulties influenced the development of specific intellectual, economic, and political stances among New Hampshire's merchants and, to a lesser extent, among the whole of New Hampshire society.

Seventeenth-Century Trade Patterns

By the 1680's and 1690's a small but prosperous mercantile community, composed of about twenty-five merchants who owned perhaps twenty-five vessels engaged in overseas trade, had emerged in the Piscataqua region.[1] The exportation of lumber and fish to Boston had served as the most significant element in its prosperity, although the mast trade with England had also played an increasingly important role.

This interdependence between Piscataqua and Boston was fundamental to New Hampshire's economy, as New Hampshire traders found

Boston their best market and their primary source of English and European manufactured goods. For example, in 1695 New Hampshire traders exported 1,679,300 feet of lumber to Boston and only 260,000 feet elsewhere; and Governor Bellomont commented that nearly all lumber used in local building in Massachusetts and in Massachusetts exports to Spain, Portugal, and the West Indies originated in New Hampshire. Having sold their lumber and fish in Massachusetts, New Hampshire traders returned to Piscataqua with provisions, household goods, English clothing, and such miscellaneous items as tanned hides, wool, beer, rigging, and hay.[2]

Their dependence upon Massachusetts made seventeenth-century New Hampshire traders somewhat less conscious of the problem of returns for British manufactured goods, a problem that so plagued the neighboring colonies. The thriving mast trade with England also alleviated this problem, for the mast traders found ready English markets and returned with iron and brass manufactured goods; a large variety of clothing, linen, linsey-woolsey, various tools and weapons; and shipbuilding materials such as canvas, cordage, and rigging.[3]

Nevertheless, after 1670 some New Hampshire traders ventured into direct overseas trade, following some of the general patterns already established by Massachusetts merchants and most useful to Piscataqua requirements. By 1695, twenty-two of thirty-four vessels exported lumber and fish products to Atlantic and Caribbean islands (Barbados, Antigua, Bermuda, Fayal, and Madeira), carrying 55 percent of the overseas export volume; while seventeen out of twenty-three vessels returning from these areas (only 41 percent of the import volume) imported salt for the fishery; rum for the lumberers and fishermen; molasses, sugar, and cotton wool for the retail market; and wine for both local consumption and reexportation. This was the most common pattern for New Hampshire overseas traders in the late seventeenth century.[4]

Another common pattern saw merchants exporting lumber and any excess Caribbean products unsold in New Hampshire (particularly rum, salt, and wine) along the coast to colonies from Newfoundland to Virginia and returning with fish, provisions (wheat, pork, and corn), and tobacco. In 1695, for example, eight of the thirty-four vessels (about 13 percent of the export volume) followed this pattern of exportation, while four of twenty-three vessels (37 percent of the import volume) adhered to this pattern of importation. The mast trade—including the export of masts, spars, bowsprits, yards, and other naval stores—was carried on by only three vessels in 1695, but that comprised about 30 percent of Piscataqua's overseas export volume, while the return of English manufactured goods covered 22 percent of the importation volume.[5] Thus, New Hampshire enterprisers engaged in four patterns of overseas mercantile endeavor—the coastal trade with Boston, the mast trade with England, the Atlantic-Caribbean trade, and an extended coastal trade from Newfoundland to Virginia.

At the same time, however, a few Piscataqua traders ventured in different directions. George Jaffrey, for example, carried on a trade with Scotland. Mark Hunking traded tobacco to Ireland. William Partridge and a few others dealt directly with Spain and carried Virginia tobacco to Newfoundland for sale to the French or Dutch. Some traders were receiving goods indirectly from the French through a trade with Jersey or directly through Nova Scotia. The guiding philosophy behind most of these ventures was the capitalist ethic of finding "dear" markets and "bargain" returns, but the traders who engaged in these activities probably only followed patterns already established by the more mature mercantile community in Massachusetts.[6] Nevertheless, only through an understanding of these patterns and activities among the New Hampshire merchant-traders is it possible to perceive the significance of the first threat to New Hampshire's commercial advancement—the economic competition of English merchants.

Economic Competition and Regulation from England

The proprietary claimants—Robert Mason and, after 1689, Samuel Allen—posed a direct threat to the New Hampshire mercantile community before 1713. In fact, to the more discerning New Hampshire merchants it appeared that many of the imperial measures applied to New England in the late seventeenth century were direct results of the personal desires and economic interests of these people and their friends.

Both Mason and Allen were far more interested in the New Hampshire timber trade than in income from quitrents. For example, Edward Randolph, Mason's cousin and the man Mason suggested to the Lords of Trade to investigate New England conditions, had been supplying timber for the Royal Navy as early as 1661. All three—Mason, Randolph, and Allen—supplied masts to the Navy from the Piscataqua region in the late seventeenth century.[7]

Mason and Randolph's collaboration in obtaining the separation of New Hampshire from Massachusetts in 1679 and the destruction of the Massachusetts charter in 1684 has already been discussed.[8] New Hampshire merchants also gained early insights into this relationship when Randolph appeared as Collector of Customs for New England in December 1679, carrying the King's Commission for New Hampshire's new royal government, which supported Mason's claims to New Hampshire.

But the commission also benefited the local merchants, as it named local merchant John Cutt as president and several other merchants to serve on the New Hampshire Council, thereby giving them, from the new government's inception, an institution through which they could protect local needs and interests.[9]

The councillors proceeded almost immediately to exercise this function, doing everything possible to maintain the local economic and political status quo. They led in acknowledging New Hampshire's deep gratitude and obligations to Massachusetts, attacking the activity of "some pretended claimers to our soil," thanking the king for "not imposing strangers" on their government, and enacting the Cutt Code, a series of laws patterned after the Massachusetts legal experience.[10] When Randolph appointed a deputy customs collector in New Hampshire and attempted to enforce the Navigation Acts by seizing Mark Hunking's vessel, the *Providence*, for trading Virginia tobacco to Ireland, the New Hampshire Council dismissed the case, denying Randolph's authority in New Hampshire. The council fired and jailed Randolph's deputy for misusing royal authority and then appointed a naval officer to uphold the Navigation Acts.[11] The latter action directly undermined Randolph's authority in New Hampshire.

This incident with the *Providence* marked the first New Hampshire conflict over enforcement of the Navigation Acts. In general the Navigation Acts benefited New Hampshire traders by protecting their trade with the Caribbean colonies, the American coast, and the mother country. Two areas of conflict, however, became apparent in the seventeenth century. The "enumerated articles" clause in the Act of 1660, prohibiting the export of tobacco, sugar, and a few other items outside the British Empire, deprived the more energetic traders of lucrative tobacco markets in Europe and Scotland and provoked some smuggling in both products through Newfoundland and the Caribbean islands.[12] But this illicit activity was minor in seventeenth-century New Hampshire. A more important irritant was the Staple Act of 1663, which prohibited direct importations from European countries, Scotland, or the Channel Islands, except for such items as salt, servants, and wine. Although the exceptions made the Staple Act generally acceptable, there were a few merchants who carried on a direct trade with Europe, Scotland, and the Channel Islands in items not excepted.[13] George Jaffrey, a New Hampshire Scot, acted as a Portsmouth factor for Scotch merchants in violation of the Navigation Acts as well as engaging in a lucrative trade through legally sanctioned channels.[14] Philip Severett traded directly with Jersey, one of the Channel Islands, because he had emigrated from there and owned a large estate on the island; and as a consequence, he violated the law.[15] Despite these minor conflicts, however, New Hampshire traders generally operated within the imperial system because it both protected and enriched them as they pursued their major patterns of trade.

But in the 1680's the New Hampshire Council's distrust of imperial officials, particularly of officials who supported an unpopular proprietor, encouraged a policy of hostility and defiance. Between 1680 and 1682 Randolph suffered defeat after defeat in his attempts to assert his royal authority in New Hampshire, as his deputies were persecuted and each of his seizures was dismissed.[16] Robert Mason received similar treatment after he arrived in December of 1680 and worked to obtain a new governor for the colony.[17] The arrival of a "stranger," Lieutenant Governor Cranfield, in October 1682, with a commission that described Mason as "proprietor" brought immediate changes within the council. Waldron and Martyn, Randolph's leading antagonists, were dismissed; and Mason, Richard Chamberlain (another Anglican newcomer from England), and Walter Barefoote (Randolph's deputy) took their places. Chamberlain received appointments to the more important public offices in the colony—secretary; clerk of council; clerk of courts; recorder of sales, wills, and deeds; and deputy surveyor and auditor general of New Hampshire. Though he had been instructed not to give "open notice" of his support of the Masonian claim, when the case was first discussed in the council, Chamberlain declared that the council "had disabled themselves from being mediators" by "standing to gain" from the outcome. Then Randolph reappeared with a new customs case to prosecute, and Cranfield, who had begun to sympathize with the antiproprietary elements in New Hampshire, discovered the extensive latent hostility against English officials and opportunists.[18]

This customs seizure appears to have been a product of Randolph's prejudice against Scotchmen. Randolph seized George Jaffrey's ketch, the *George*, three months after it entered Piscataqua on the grounds that its owner and crew were Scotchmen and that they had not entered the vessel by certificate with the customs collector before unloading. Neither of these charges were valid because the owner and seamen were New Hampshire settlers of Scotch origin, and there was no necessity for a vessel engaged in normal trade patterns to enter with the collector unless the cargo included enumerated goods.[19] Randolph persuaded Cranfield to call a special court to hear the case. Cranfield must have acquiesced either because of prejudice against Scots or because of ignorance of the law, for he had just expressed disenchantment with both Mason and Randolph in letters to the Lords of Trade and other English officials. At any rate, news of the special trial persuaded Jaffrey to send his vessel into hiding, and the captain of the fort, a leading merchant, allowed its clearance in direct defiance of Cranfield's orders. When the trial was held, Randolph's case was dismissed; but Cranfield, angered by these untoward events, suspended Elias Stileman from his posts as councillor and as captain of the fort, investigated the duplicity of Jaffrey in hiding his vessel, called a new trial, and forced a condemnation of the vessel by threatening to prosecute the jury for perjury and "false verdicts." This event ended all local mercantile cooperation with Cranfield, as the House refused to vote taxes and demanded the power of nominating judges. Cranfield dissolved the assembly in disgust, frustrated in his efforts to obtain a revenue either from Mason or the New Hampshire people.[20]

The dissolving of the House, an action almost unknown in New England, stirred defiance among farmers as well as merchants. Edward Gove, one of the wealthier farmers of Hampton and a member of the dissolved assembly, declared that Cranfield was a Catholic leading a "Papist" conspiracy and a traitor whose commission had been signed in Scotland. He gathered about ten followers from Exeter and Hampton, seeking to establish legitimate authority and a restoration of New Hampshire "liberties." But the merchants refused any role in this affair and informed Cranfield of Gove's activities. Cranfield was so frightened that he declared New Hampshire in rebellion and called out the militia, whereupon Gove surrendered and was convicted of treason. The effect of this "rebellion" was to drive Cranfield back into the camp of Mason and Randolph. He dismissed the leading antiproprietary merchants from the council and appointed three non-Congregational merchants in their place. He then embarked on a series of dictatorial measures which brought so much opposition from the New Hampshire community, merchants and farmers alike, that the antiproprietary mercantile elements submitted a petition to the Crown which ultimately brought about Cranfield's dismissal and a temporary defeat for Mason's land suits.[21]

By 1684, the Cranfield government had challenged the entire framework of New Hampshire society by imprisoning the religious leaders, imposing taxation without the lower house's consent, upholding Mason's proprietary claims, giving Randolph the office of attorney general of New Hampshire, and imprisoning and harassing the merchants and others who opposed these actions. But it was the mercantile community (strongly encouraged by the Congregational ministers) that led the opposition and ultimately emerged victorious.

In the course of this conflict with imperial officials between 1680 and 1686, the New Hampshire mercantile community began to work out some of its basic interests. Having accidentally obtained domination of the council in 1680, the merchants used it to protect their interests against Randolph, Mason, and royal authority until 1682. They discovered, too, that the council served as a useful tool, not only against outsiders, but in advancing one's own political and economic prospects.[22] These lessons were reinforced by observation of the Cranfield-dominated council from 1683 to 1686 and of the Andros government from 1687 to 1689. The merchants also discovered that the lower house, though not as effective a tool because it represented a wider constituency and had a less permanent tenure and membership, could serve to establish advantageous legislation protecting mercantile interests and could limit the authority of an unpopular executive.[23] The merchants learned, finally, that they needed an effective voice in England to represent their needs and interests to the royal government. They found two solutions to this problem in the course of the 1680's, both of which would be utilized repeatedly between 1684 and 1741. First, they sent a local merchant to London to present their grievances and problems to highly placed officials and to the Crown.[24] Secondly, the merchants utilized London mercantile connections, particularly English merchants who would lose timber resources if the proprietor were to win in New Hampshire and merchants in high places seeking new opportunities; for it was becoming evident that English officialdom listened carefully to the merchants involved in the New England mast trade.[25]

The threat offered by Robert Mason and Edward Randolph to New Hampshire merchants and society in the 1680's provided the stimulus whereby most of the permanent economic interests of the New Hampshire mercantile community were established. But as the threat continued after 1689, another permanent economic interest became apparent, the need for a dominant role in the provincial government.

The Glorious Revolution, the overthrow of Andros, and the outbreak of an Indian war in 1689 revealed the political divisions current within the New Hampshire mercantile community and increased its realization of the need for local political dominance. A group of Portsmouth merchants suggested that the four towns choose commissioners to create an independent government until the king's pleasure might be known, and each of the towns sent their leading men to this "convention." Eighteen of the twenty-two commissioners chosen earned at least part of their income from trade. They created an unusually democratic representative government, in which a president, treasurer, secretary, and ten-man council would be elected by all the inhabitants of the towns; in addition, each town could elect three men to an assembly. Nevertheless, this three-branch government was rejected by the townspeople of Hampton, who claimed the other towns would dominate them.[26]

The Portsmouth merchants then drafted a petition to Massachusetts asking that New Hampshire be placed under its government until the Crown's pleasure could be known. They also submitted a list of officers for each of the towns, although Hampton's political leaders had not seen the list. This event suggests that the Piscataqua mercantile community feared that Hampton would separate itself from New Hampshire and become a part of Massachusetts—as it originally had been—and took steps to forestall such an eventuality. It also suggests a reluctance on the part of the mercantile community to become a permanent part of Massachusetts.[27]

Two months after Massachusetts accepted the New Hampshire towns, a group of New Castle inhabitants petitioned the Crown for a royal governor and the king's protection, alleging that conditions had become "deplorable" and the Massachusetts government "totally neglected" them. Most of the signers of this petition had found favor under Cranfield and Mason, particularly the three councillors—Fryer, Elliott, and Hinckes—and Mason's two sons, John and Robert Tufton. Most of them, too, were lumber and fish traders and their laborers.[28]

These differing petitions reveal divisions among the merchants over the proprietorship claims and the extension of either Massachusetts or royal government into the colony. But they also show that the mercantile elements had learned the lessons of the 1680's very well and were taking the initiative so that, no matter where the ultimate source of authority might rest, they would have local authority in the new government.

It was this emphasis on local economic and political authority that emerged as the final permanent economic interest arising out of the conflicts with English merchants and officials within the New Hampshire mercantile community. When Samuel Allen purchased the Masonian claim and persuaded the Crown to send his agent, Lieutenant Governor John Usher, to New Hampshire as its royal executive in 1692, the local merchants realized they would have to work for change within the imperial system rather than ignore it, as they had attempted to do with Randolph in 1680–82. Ideally, this meant dominating the mast trade locally and bringing the offices of governor, customs collector, judge of the Vice-Admiralty Court, and surveyor of the woods into local hands; but it took a period of conflict before these goals became a conscious quest. New Hampshire enterprisers achieved most of this ideal under Governor Benning Wentworth in the 1740's, but the period from 1692 to 1742 exhibited a continuous striving, at times unconscious, toward these goals on the part of various groups within the mercantile community.

The political methods utilized in this quest for local economic supremacy over English officials and merchants varied from time to time and from personality to personality. One might ignore the law and defy the official, fight him in the courts or strive to win him over, become a deputy under him, or replace him in his office. Each method was used at one time or another, but never for uniform ends or in a united way until the 1730's and 1740's.

For example, in the 1690's, Lieutenant Governor Usher was harassed by the council and assembly to such an extent that by 1695 even Allen was recommending his dismissal.[29] The council and assembly denied him a salary, held sessions of government when Usher was in Massachusetts, and sent agents to England to replace him. Their first success came in 1696, when one of their agents, William Partridge, replaced Usher as lieutenant governor. By not publishing his commission, Partridge allowed the council and assembly to govern alone, whereupon the councillors removed most of Usher's political appointees from office.[30]

When Governor Allen, the proprietary claimant, appeared, the councillors wrote to their governor-to-be, the Earl of Bellomont, for his protection against the "malproceedings" of Allen; and Bellomont supported them.[31] Governor Bellomont, however, had an aversion to colonials' holding imperial offices and a strong desire to enforce the Navigation Acts to their fullest intent. He appointed Robert Armstrong, newly arrived from England, as the new naval officer, brushing aside Partridge's local man, and attacked Partridge's timber trade with Portugal.[32] As a result of this attack Partridge was dismissed as lieutenant governor in 1703; and in 1705 Parliament placed naval stores on the enumerated list.[33] All these actions threatened the interests of New Hampshire's merchants. With the reappointment of Usher the proprietorship controversy again became the central issue in New Hampshire.

Not until 1715 and the appointment of Lieutenant Governor George Vaughan did the local mercantile community recapture the executive, and they never let it escape them during the remainder of the colonial period, as John Wentworth in the 1720's, Richard Waldron, Jr., in the 1730's, and the Wentworths after 1741 controlled New Hampshire's executive branch.

The latter period of Usher's government, particularly after Allen's death in 1705, further divided the New Hampshire mercantile community against itself. Usher rewarded the newer merchants in Portsmouth both politically and economically, creating a small faction interested in maintaining its new position of authority in opposition to an older faction that had lost some authority during Usher's years as lieutenant governor.[34] Though these factions and most neutral merchants had the same general economic interests, during the 1720's and 1730's they found themselves competing with each other for the positions of authority through which they could more easily attain these interests. As Governor Belcher put it when the officers he replaced petitioned against him: "It's impossible to be a Governor and not have enemies; malice, hatred, and envy will work." Or, as he explained it bluntly in his letters to his brother-in-law, the New Hampshire secretary, Richard Waldron, Jr., after nine years of political difficulties in New Hampshire:

The conflict is more with you (and my friends) than with me. Governor Belcher would be an angel if he would be with the Clan, and all the enemies I have in New Hampshire became so upon my settling of my Friends, yet I don't repent it, but will support them and myself to the last extremity. . . . You say if I had had other Friends, I must have had other enemies, very well, let a Governor do right or wrong, the case must be so, without any regard to truth, reason, or justice; but I would have you observe by the by, that the Clan have already expended £1100 Sterling to maintain their points, and are in a fair way to spend as much more, but our Friends have never parted with six pence, tho' the Governor has with £100 Sterling in defence of them and himself; so perhaps my present Friends, had they been my enemies would not have been so powerful, since they hug their dear dust so close.[35]

During Belcher's administration in the 1730's, one mercantile faction, the Wentworth "clan," effectively used the lower house, the offices of lieutenant governor and surveyor general of the woods, and English mercantile connections against another mercantile faction, led by Waldrons, Vaughans, and Sherburnes, who dominated the governor and council, until the Wentworth faction succeeded in obtaining a separate governor for New Hampshire and the appointment of a local merchant, Benning Wentworth, to the new post. Lessons learned from experience with English officials and merchants in the 1680's were applied against such officials after 1690 and also against Massachusetts after 1715.

The same general approaches used against unpopular executives were applied against customs officials after 1690. In the 1680's the mercantile community, working through the New Hampshire Council, had created a rival official, the naval officer, and had harassed Randolph and his deputies. After 1692, there were two kinds of customs officials in New Hampshire, naval officers and customs collectors. The naval officer's function was to maintain records on the vessels using the port and hold bonded security on vessels exporting enumerated commodities. The customs collector held responsibility for collecting the "plantation duty" on enumerated items and enforcing the Navigation Acts.[36] The naval officer earned his livelihood through fees received for the issuance of approval passes to vessels entering and leaving the port; the collector received a small salary plus one-third of the value of vessels he successfully prosecuted for violation of the trade laws.

But when the leading merchants in the New Hampshire Council found that John Usher was their new executive in 1692 and that a local man, Pheasant Eastwick, had been appointed deputy customs collector, they made no effort to appoint a naval officer. In 1694 Usher himself took the initiative, assigning Thomas Cobbett, a Portsmouth mariner, to the post. Cobbett kept an account of Piscataqua shipping for one year, but after the council began holding meetings without Usher, he stopped doing so, probably at the behest of the mercantile community.[37]

In fact, Usher had appointed Cobbett for his own political and economic purposes. Usher, acting as mast procurer in New Hampshire

for Samuel Allen, had on July 17, 1694, petitioned the council to seize a
mast ship owned by a competitor, John Taylor, after Taylor had refused
Usher's demand to see his contract and commission. A week later, Taylor
responded to Usher's threats by allowing the captain of one of his vessels
to impress seamen from one of Usher's vessels. The following day Usher
appointed Cobbett as naval officer and two weeks later had him seize two
more of Taylor's vessels. At this point the council refused involvement in
the situation, so Usher postponed any prosecution of the seizures; and
finally, after Usher had returned to his home in Massachusetts, the
council authorized clearance to Taylor's vessels on the grounds that the
case was a private matter between Usher and Taylor which Usher had
failed to prosecute.[38]

Unfortunately, this use of the naval officer and, to a lesser extent, of the
customs collectors in private political and economic feuds emerged as the
primary motivation behind most customs seizures in New Hampshire, so
that control of both offices, and after 1696, of judge of the local vice-
admiralty court, became a political compulsion for whichever mercantile
faction dominated New Hampshire politics before 1741.[39] Thus, even after
the Navigation Act of 1696, which brought naval officers under partial
control of the Commissioners of Customs in London and vice-admiralty
judges to the colonies, there was a tendency to appoint a new naval
officer, vice-admiralty judge, and customs collector with every local
change of administration.[40]

Sampson Sheafe, customs collector from 1698 to 1700 and 1701 to 1710,
learned from experience the difficulties of enforcing the Navigation Acts
in New Hampshire. When he seized the *Hopewell* in 1699 for importing
"elephant teeth" (ivory tusks) from Fayal without going through English
customs, he was given the excuse that the vessel had stopped only to
receive provisions, since maritime law allowed a foreign vessel to enter an
alien port for provisions so long as it shipped out within twenty-four
hours. Because no New Hampshire lawyer would prosecute his case,
Sheafe obtained one from Boston, only to have the jury throw his case out
of court because the "Style or title" of the case as given to the court was
unacceptable. Sheafe asked permission to amend his "information," but
the court refused. He then amended his case and resubmitted it, but the
court dismissed the case without a hearing. Sheafe demanded an appeal to
the King in Council, whereupon the court asked for £1,500 security for the
vessel and cargo. Since Sheafe did not possess that much cash, he asked for
time in which to raise it. But the court declared his appeal void, gave a
judgment for unreasonable costs against him, ordered the return of the
vessel and goods, and imprisoned him until he fully complied with these
judgments.[41]

A second case in 1701 completed Sheafe's disillusionment. He had
seized four bags of imported cotton wool which had not been registered

with the port authorities, and the Inferior Court of Common Pleas had upheld the seizure. But when the case was appealed to the Superior Court, it was dismissed. Sheafe then appealed to the new governor, Joseph Dudley, who ordered the case tried in the Vice-Admiralty Court with Judge Thomas Newton presiding. In the course of the trial the defense attorney, George Jaffrey, argued that coastal vessels were not subject to the Navigation Acts. The judge (with the governor in attendance) postponed the case, at which time the New Hampshire Council decided that if the court did not reach a decision within three months, the cotton wool would return to its owner. In the interim Newton lost his vice-admiralty commission, and the case ended for lack of a judge.[42]

During the period 1699–1704, as these cases went before the New Hampshire courts, Governors Bellomont and Dudley commented on the problems of customs enforcement. Bellomont felt that honest men were difficult to find in the colonies, but a collector's post was even harder to fill than most because it was "liable to temptations." Also, "a Collector's is the most ungrateful Office in these plantations that can be; if he is just to his trust in looking into their [the merchants'] trade, they hate him mortally."[43] The courts provided another source of complaint. Dudley commented that the judges were ignorant and the juries stubborn, while Sheafe wrote that no matter how "plainly forfeited," it would be "a very rare thing" for a New Hampshire jury to convict a violator of the "Acts of Trade." He also attacked the low fees, finding them insufficient for his subsistence.[44] All in all, the New Hampshire customs officials had a difficult lot. It was not accidental that they did not prosecute another case until 1723, almost twenty years later (and that case was manifestly political in nature), although there were many complaints of trade violations during the interim.[45]

In fact, the evidence suggests that smuggling was not unusual in the Piscataqua during the early eighteenth century. Robert Armstrong was dismissed as collector in 1723 after the Board of Trade investigated evidence that he had taken bribes for clearing vessels carrying illegal goods.[46] In the winter of 1723 William Whipple clandestinely unloaded wine and oil from Spain at Piscataqua and then went on to Boston, where his vessel was seized for importing oil and leather into Boston in violation of the Navigation Acts. The case received wide publicity, as did his clandestine trade at Piscataqua, but Whipple was not prosecuted in his home port of Portsmouth.[47] Other indications of smuggling come from the Shipping Returns. While in 1727 all vessels trading with the West Indies gave an exact island destination, by 1742 almost one-third of the tonnage that traded with the Caribbean listed "West Indies" rather than a specific island—an indication of trade with the French West Indies in violation of the Molasses Act of 1733.[48] The Shipping Returns contain only four clearances for Spain between 1723 and 1725; however, three of the four vessels carried large quantities of squared oak timber. Although there were no clearances for Spain in 1727, by the 1730's Benning Wentworth, John Frost, John Rindge, Joshua Peirce, and John Moffatt, among others, were carrying on an illicit lumber trade with the Spanish. While Theodore Atkinson was deputy customs collector, members of the Wentworth clan, particularly Benning Wentworth and Joshua Peirce, smuggled oil, raisins, powder, and canvas in from Spain and Holland.[49] When Belcher removed Atkinson in 1730, he brought a temporary halt to such activities but in doing so helped persuade the Wentworth faction to petition for a separate governor in 1731. Lieutenant Governor Dunbar attacked Belcher's appointments in letters to the Board of Trade, the outcome of which was the appointment of a collector from England. Richard Waldron, Jr., upon hearing of this event, wrote Belcher: "The report of Mr. Reynold's return administers no little relief to the distressed, especially as 'tis said that he is appointed Naval Officer as well as Collector from whence possible some may hope for an indulgent and licentious trade as in days of yore."[50]

Lack of evidence renders it impossible to judge the amount of smuggling in eighteenth-century New Hampshire, but there was ample opportunity if one wished to carry on illicit trade. It was difficult for officials to watch all the coves along the coast, more difficult to obtain willing witnesses in the courts, and in most cases the officials themselves were local traders, willing either to accept a bribe or to look the other way. Even such trusted officials as William Shirley and Robert Auchmuty could indulge in such activities when politics were involved. When Ellis Huske seized the *Caesar* at Portsmouth in 1739, he lost the case through their actions. Belcher, who urged Huske on, commented angrily: "I don't at all scruple but that those whose duty it is to pursue the Acts of Trade in punishing illicit traders are stoutly fee'd the other way, nor have I the least expectation of justice to the Crown, yet it's best you should urge a final decree." He wrote Huske that he would use this case as a weapon against Auchmuty and asked for all the relevant papers, saying, "I don't believe there has been more villainy transacted for a long time than has been in this case."[51]

As long as the normal paths of trade brought profits, most merchants obeyed the laws; but when the British West Indian markets could not absorb New Hampshire lumber and fish, some traders turned to the French and Spanish markets, even though naval stores has been enumerated commodities since 1705 and lumber since 1722. Others used Newfoundland to carry on a profitable but illegal trade in enumerated commodities and European products. Moreover, as Thomas Barrow has shown, the general characteristics of the entire English colonial administrative system—particularly its "inefficiency in departmental organization, indifference to reform, and the misuse of the power of patronage"—provided an environment in which illicit activities could thrive if anyone sought to pursue them.[52]

Of the illicit trade activities studied by historians of New England, New Hampshire's conflicts with imperial officials over timber and naval stores policies have received more extensive treatment than any others. This is not surprising, for imperial timber policies touched upon the most lucrative element in New Hampshire's economy and posed the most tangible external threat to its welfare.[53] A brief survey of English mercantile and imperial measures relating to the New Hampshire timber trade and of the colonial response to these measures further reveals the more basic economic interests of the Piscataqua mercantile community.

Long before the Crown became interested in the supervision of New Hampshire's timber trade, two local towns had undertaken this task. In Dover a sliding scale of duties was placed on the use of masts in the 1660's, the amount of duty varying with the size of the mast; Exeter reserved to the town all pines twenty-four inches in diameter at a height of three feet which were "fit for masts."[54] Timber-stealing and trespasses were common offenses in the seventeenth century, and by the 1690's the New Hampshire government had enacted legislation heavily fining anyone who cut timber on private or common lands without the owner's permission.[55] Thus, local governments had confronted timber problems and worked out rather inadequate solutions before imperial officials became involved in regulation.[56]

After 1690 English mercantile policy in New England was guided by two fundamental considerations: securing a sufficient supply of white pine masts for the Royal Navy and encouraging production of naval stores as a means of adapting the New England economy to the needs of the mother country.[57] In pursuit of these policies English officialdom encouraged both English and colonial merchants to invest in naval stores production and passed a series of acts relegating white pines to the use of the Navy. New Hampshire enterprisers reacted variously to both of these general measures.

The question that bothered New Hampshire merchants regarding the development of Piscataqua naval stores was simple: Who would carry it on? Before 1715, when English merchants sought monopoly charters for development of naval stores in New England, New Hampshire merchants joined Massachusetts merchants in opposing such grants. Although there is no evidence that they opposed Sir Matthew Dudley's monopoly proposal of 1693, by 1695 the New Hampshire Council had allied with John Taylor, a mast contractor and an opponent of Dudley, who supported their attempts to be reunited with Massachusetts. By 1696, William Partridge was in England soliciting with Taylor, Ashurst, Allen, Evans, and others to obtain naval contracts to build vessels for the Navy. He was appointed one of four commissioners to promote the production of naval stores in New England. Partridge felt that New Hampshire would be an excellent supplier of timber, masts, and vessels for the Royal Navy, but that Maine could more easily supply pitch and tar because New Hampshire colonists would not easily be diverted from the lumber trade. Nevertheless, Jonathan Bridger, another commissioner, naïvely and enthusiastically supported the production of naval stores of every kind in New England through payment of bounties, and his arguments converted the Board of Trade.[58] After Bridger's recommendations were heard, a number of English merchants again petitioned for semimonopoly charters in return for their production of New England naval stores. But this time New Hampshire had an agent in England, William Vaughan, who petitioned against such charters, saying that they "would tend to the utter ruin" of New England and begging that the Board would not "suffer the country to be surprised in a matter of such great concern to them."[59] By 1704, Partridge was in London complaining that 10,000 barrels of turpentine he had shipped to England in 1702 remained unsold; he asked the Board of Trade for a "substantial premium" on pitch, tar, and probably turpentine as well. Turpentine was the easiest of these three items to produce in New England, but it was not a naval store. Nevertheless, the Act of 1705, the outcome of all the naval stores endeavors from 1691 on, placed bounties on turpentine as well as all naval stores.[60] This act was a victory for New Hampshire economic interests over English merchants: monopolies had been thwarted and a bounty system for naval stores, including turpentine, had been obtained.

The Board of Trade's continuing concern over naval stores production and colonial wool manufacture led to another important victory for New Hampshire economic interests, the White Pines Act of 1722, which removed all English customs duties on colonial lumber. New Hampshire merchants had petitioned from 1715 on for such action because the markets for lumber in Boston and the West Indies were glutted and prices low. Even Jonathan Bridger, the surveyor of the woods, had supported this action because he felt it would encourage naval stores production.[61] But this act, by stimulating a new direction for the lumber trade, encouraged illicit cutting of mast trees for the new English markets.[62] By 1727, over 10 percent of the New Hampshire export of pine boards went to England. On the other hand, the act stimulated exports of oak and a large variety of other lumber goods to the mother country, encouraging a trade beneficial to both England and New Hampshire.

The expansion of this lumber trade with the mother country can be seen in the Shipping Returns. In 1725, nine vessels (14.3 percent of the total vessels) exported about 18 percent of the trade tonnage to England.

In 1727, eight vessels (16.6 percent of the total vessels) carried almost 33 percent of the total trade tonnage to England. In 1735, sixteen vessels (33.3 percent of the total vessels) cleared for England; and in 1742, thirteen vessels (16.6 percent of the total) carried about 42 percent of New Hampshire trade to England. This expansion from 18 to 42 percent of trade tonnage in seventeen years owed a great deal to the Act of 1722.[63] In retrospect, then, the act was a significant diplomatic victory for the New Hampshire mercantile community, as it provided another important commodity returning profits that could be used to redress the unfavorable balance of trade with the mother country.

New Hampshire merchants met failure, however, when a group of them, led by Lieutenant Governor Wentworth (who had just become a deputy surveyor of the woods), used the Board of Trade's growing disillusionment with New England naval stores production to petition for a privileged chartered company of New Hampshire, Connecticut, and English merchants "for raising naval stores." Ironically, the petitioners used the same arguments the Board had heard from English enterprisers for years: a chartered company was "the only and surest way" to obtain naval stores in New England; it would divert colonials from wool manufacture; and New England timber was "as good as the whole world affords." Three more arguments were added to the list by these New England entrepreneurs. First, they argued that such production would provide returns for English manufactured goods. Second, they charged the "East Country" interest with bribing navy officials to disqualify New England naval stores; and, finally, they added the more bizarre argument that if the company were not approved, in a few years the New England people would starve.[64]

Though nothing came of this petition, it reveals clearly the fundamental concern of New Hampshire merchants: local participation in any exploitive naval stores adventure in the Piscataqua region. Thus, when New Hampshire's mercantile community lacked the financial resources to produce naval stores, they opposed the granting of privileged charters to outsiders; but with changing local circumstances and the promise of local participation, they welcomed such a course of action. As it turned out, however, the mast contractors and their agents developed the Piscataqua trade in pitch, tar, and turpentine in the 1740's, as they commanded sufficient capital and labor to do so.

The earliest imperial regulation of mast-cutting appeared in the Massachusetts charter of 1691, which was viewed by English officials as applicable to New Hampshire as well. The charter provided that all trees "of the diameter of twenty-four inches and upwards at twelve inches from the ground," growing on lands "not heretofore granted to any private persons," could not be felled without royal license. The responsibility of enforcing this clause was given to the surveyor of pines and timber in Maine and New Hampshire, Jahleel Brenton. In 1705, the British government extended this prohibition by forbidding the destruction of "Pitch, Pine, or Tar Trees" under twelve inches in diameter at three feet from the ground, growing on ungranted land. A new official, the surveyor general of the woods, was sent to New England to protect the forests and encourage production of naval stores.[65]

In 1708, at the request of Jonathan Bridger, who held this post from 1706 to 1718, the New Hampshire government enacted legislation somewhat similar to the Massachusetts Charter provision of 1691. The differences, however, were crucial. Where the Massachusetts Charter said "all trees," the New Hampshire law said "mast trees or white pine trees"; and the New Hampshire law specifically exempted private property and the common lands within townships from the prohibition, interpreting the commons as private property. Moreover, the New Hampshire law provided that half the fines go to the New Hampshire government, one-fourth to the surveyor, and one-fourth to the informant; The charter had divided the fines between the Crown and its official.[66] This law had three effects. It limited imperial authority to pine trees alone and to the areas beyond the New Hampshire towns (areas in controversy with proprietary claimants). Also, by the distribution of the fines, it made the combined office of surveyor and governor or lieutenant governor of New Hampshire an attractive post because with such a combination of offices an enterprising official could collect all three portions of the fine. Between 1708 and 1775 every New Hampshire executive and surveyor general—Bridger, Robert Armstrong, David Dunbar, John Usher, John Wentworth, Benning Wentworth, and John Wentworth—sought this combination of offices; and Lieutenant Governor John Wentworth, Dunbar, Benning Wentworth, and Governor John Wentworth were successful.[67] This combination had far more to recommend it than just the profit from fines, for with proper management the holder of these offices could dominate the entire lumber trade of New Hampshire (as the Wentworth clan did quite effectively after 1741).[68]

In 1711, Parliament passed an act modeled somewhat after the New Hampshire law of 1708, in that it limited royal jurisdiction only to pine trees over twenty-four inches in diameter at twelve inches from the ground and not on the property of private individuals. This White Pine Act was the basic forest regulation for New England until 1722, when Parliament reserved all white pines outside townships and not on private property to the Crown, placed the burden of proof on the defendent, and limited jurisdiction in such cases solely to the vice-admiralty courts.[69] Because of continued friction with New England lumber interests and their creation of a host of new townships as a means of bypassing the Act of 1722,

Parliament passed a new forest law, the White Pines Act of 1729, which abolished the township clause of 1722 and reserved all pine trees anywhere to the Crown, except for those on private property granted before 1690.[70]

New Hampshire lumberers and traders responded to these legislative encroachments on their timber resources in several different ways. In the era from 1690 to 1706 New Hampshire lumberers had little conflict with royal authorities, but nevertheless petitioned the Crown through the New Hampshire agent, William Vaughan, to raise the dimensions of trees reserved for masts to thirty-two inches in diameter rather than twenty-four inches because the latter encompassed most of the available timber, the majority of which was "fit only for deals and planks."[71] This petition probably represented a fundamental truth about the quality of timber along the Piscataqua frontier. But whether it did or not, the lumbermen usually acted from this belief, and it served as one of the more significant reasons for resentment of the royal timber policies.

A second response to British timber policies in this early era was the passage of New Hampshire legislation in 1697 exempting from seizure trees on private lands and in townships. In the face of continuing royal regulations, the colonists reiterated this principle four times between 1697 and 1740 in attempts to keep both timber thieves and royal mast suppliers off the common lands of the towns.[72] Though each of these laws exempted royal masts and the surveyor of the woods from its provisions, such clauses were legally unenforceable until the White Pines Act of 1729 brought all white pines in townships granted after 1690 under Crown jurisdiction; and even then, they remained unenforced. The sanctity of private property—the basic principle enunciated in these New Hampshire acts—became the principal rallying point against royal timber officials in New England; for generally wherever the surveyor made a seizure of masts, the defendent claimed they had been cut on private property.[73]

The Crown's problem in protecting mast trees in New Hampshire was compounded by the fact that all New Hampshire land titles were uncertain because of the proprietary controversy. Perhaps even the "wastelands" outside the town boundaries would ultimately be determined as private property granted before 1690. Before 1722, the lumberers had never urged a settlement of the dispute because it allowed them to obtain masts in these wastelands with little fear of successful prosecution.[74] But by exempting all lumber within townships from royal regulation, the Act of 1722 changed this attitude. Within ten days of the news of this act, the New Hampshire governor and council granted new townships in the wastelands, greatly increasing the amount of timber land exempted from royal control.[75] It was the increase of such "paper" townships that led to the passage of the White Pines Act of 1729, which brought the pines in these new townships clearly under royal jurisdiction. But when David Dunbar, the new surveyor, attempted to enforce this measure in New Hampshire, particularly in a series of heavy-handed actions at Exeter in 1734, he provoked the famous Exeter "riot."[76] This affair neutralized Dunbar's effectiveness in New Hampshire, for he became far more interested in a political feud with Governor Belcher and his friends than in New Hampshire forest policy.[77]

During the early eighteenth century, then, the lumbermen and some of the traders effectively opposed the Crown's timber policies by relying on property rights as a legal defense; if that failed, they used threats, harassment, and tortured interpretations of the laws in the favorably prejudiced local courts.

Finally, the local merchants used one other tactic against the royal timber policies in New Hampshire. This approach, appealing especially to the wealthier and more advantaged lumber merchants, was utilized from the 1690's through 1775, though not always with consistency or with a clear understanding of ultimate goals. It reached full fruition under Governor Benning Wentworth in the 1740's and was best described by Wentworth's inveterate foe, Richard Waldron:

> There is one thing which rightly represented would break the Don [Governor Benning Wentworth] in pieces, that is the waste of the King's Trees, but there is hardly a man in the Province would mention it either as a complaint or a witness, as most of the people make earnings out of the unrighteous indulgence. Diego [Benning Wentworth again] is Surveyor of the Woods, his brother Mark is Undertaker for the Contractor with the Navy Board for Masts; the Undertaker agrees with any and everybody that applies, for as many trees as they will get of any size without regard to the number or dimensions mentioned in the Contract; the Surveyor licenses all that the Undertaker agrees with, so a two-fold iniquity ensues; the Undertaker has a dock of a Master [mast ship] always ready to supply the wants of those who stand in need at his own price of which doubtless the Brother has his share; and the Countrymen cut what trees they please, making masts of the best for the King and which others as the Undertaker supplies, and converting the rest into mill logs for their own use; but this is an affair not easily detected but by a Commission of Inquiry, and moving in it would be one of the most unpopular things in the world.[78]

This concentration of both royal and local political authority in the hands of the local mast agents, or "undertakers," was partially in force as early as the 1690's, when Ichabod Plaisted was both deputy surveyor and a mast agent. Plaisted pursued a completely laissez-faire policy in the woods, purchasing timber from all, and cutting the lumber unqualified for masts in his own mills for sale in private trade.[79] But the appointment of Bridger as surveyor in 1706 brought an end to this situation.

From 1706 to 1742 the leading traders sought to restore the concentration of royal and local authority in the local mast agents by becoming deputy surveyors and agents for the mast contractors. From 1706 to 1718 they were relatively successful, for Bridger's many deputies also supplied the mast contractors, as Bridger proved to be an ineffective official.[80] But the dismissal of Lieutenant Governor Vaughan in 1717 touched off factional conflict among the lumberers, and Bridger began discriminating among them through the issuance of licenses. This discrimination provided the newer enterprisers, led by Lieutenant Governor John Wentworth, with an opportunity to obtain Bridger's dismissal and control over the surveyor's office. During and after Armstrong's tenure (throughout the 1720's), Wentworth dominated the surveyor's office in opposition to Thomas Westbrook, the mast contractor's agent; and in the 1730's Dunbar and the Wentworth clan worked together against Westbrook and his son-in-law, Richard Waldron, Jr. From 1717 until the 1740's, then, one loose faction dominated the mast agency and another the surveyorship, each using whatever weapons it could against the other.[81]

When the two offices were again combined in the 1740's, the Wentworths ensured the success of this alliance by winning support among the lumberers with their open acceptance of lumber goods from all suppliers. Thus, the quest of New Hampshire merchants to dominate those local and royal offices concerned with royal timber policies achieved such success that after 1741 it was no longer necessary to use harassment and the courts against royal forest policies.[82]

In the course of these struggles to maintain their economic interests against English interference, the New Hampshire merchants had sought control of local politics and local imperial offices. Once successful, they pretended to enforce the law while in fact ignoring it to allow smuggling and a free rein in the woods. Thus, by the 1740's they had mastered the threats posed by English imperialists and by imperial policies antagonistic toward their exploitation of the Piscataqua forests.

War and Trade

Just as the Indian wars had posed a threat to the New Hampshire farmer tilling his land, so they also threatened the New Hampshire trader, menacing particularly his source of raw materials and marring the attractiveness of the Piscataqua region as a market for outside traders. Also, because of the need for manpower to wage the wars, there was a corresponding shortage of labor in the normal pursuits of farming, lumbering, and fishing. Moreover, the costs of warfare brought economic hardship to an economy where cash and currency were scarce enough without the widespread unemployment that war created.[83] In reacting to this threat, the New Hampshire people looked in two general directions for aid—first to their neighboring colony, Massachusetts, and then to England.

The insecurity of New Hampshire's exposed wilderness frontier had been significant in goading the four New Hampshire towns into Massachusetts' jurisdiction in the 1640's. Once under Massachusetts' protection, the towns followed the Massachusetts system of enlisting all males between sixteen and sixty years of age in the militia. By 1668, Dover and Portsmouth had erected a fort at the mouth of the Piscataqua River, after petitioning Massachusetts for a grant of land and "great guns" in return for their efforts in building it. Though the Massachusetts government refused this plea, it did authorize Richard Martyn, the naval officer at Piscataqua, to collect a powder duty from all incoming vessels, allowing the money from local traders to remain at Piscataqua for new fortifications and ammunition.[84] When King Philip's War spread to the Eastern (Abnaki) Indians, Richard Waldron led an expedition into Maine against them; however, a year later Waldron was pleading to the Massachusetts government for a contingent of troops to aid the Piscataqua towns. During these three years of war, though the New Hampshire troops performed well, it was evident that the New Hampshire community leaned heavily upon Massachusetts for men, materiel, and moral support. This dependence was strengthened during the administrations of Cranfield and Andros in the 1680's and after the Glorious Revolution. When King William's War erupted, most New Hampshire settlers sought a return to the protective shelter of Massachusetts. The Massachusetts government accepted them and sent them troops and supplies. It also authorized the collection of property taxes, import and export duties, and powder duties; and issued the first paper currency to be used in the colonies—all primarily for defraying the costs of defense.[85] But when New Hampshire became a royal colony with a proprietary claimant in 1692, the Massachusetts government, finding no good reason to support an area under either royal or proprietary control, gradually withdrew its troops and support from New Hampshire and discriminated against New Hampshire traders. In the meantime, the new New Hampshire government imitated Massachusetts' policies by following similar revenue and military measures (except for paper currency issues) and continued to seek Massachusetts military aid. The council and House refused to raise money for the new executive, asserting that he should be supported by the Crown or proprietor or be willing to have New Hampshire annexed to Massachusetts. After the Oyster River "massacre" of 1694 and Usher's continuing failure to obtain help either from the Crown, Allen, or Massachusetts, the New Hampshire House petitioned Massachusetts to be annexed to it.[86] During the seventeenth century, then, New Hampshire politicians depended consistently upon Massachusetts for leadership and aid in military crises.

After 1696, their strategy became more sophisticated. Probably the primary reason for the gradual change grew out of William Partridge's success in obtaining the posts of lieutenant governor and naval stores commissioner. His successes revealed in a tangible way the mother country's concern for upper New England and provided opportunities for the antiproprietary elements in New Hampshire to regain political dominance. When Governor Bellomont decided to support this group against the proprietary claimant, New Hampshire's local leaders obtained important favors from a Crown official for the first time. It was Bellomont, the first royal executive in New Hampshire who had no connection with the proprietary claimant, who actually worked a change of direction in New Hampshire's responses to military threats. He persuaded a military engineer, Wolfgang Romer, to repair and rebuild the New Hampshire fort and probably talked both Partridge and the New Hampshire General Assembly into petitioning the Board of Trade for a grant of money and supplies for the fort.[87] Although the petition was unsuccessful, New Hampshire horizons had broadened. In fact, the appointment of Bellomont as governor of both Massachusetts and New Hampshire had also aided in the gradual reassessment by the New Hampshire mercantile community of the Crown's possible role in local military affairs and of its comprehension of New Hampshire's problems.

Between 1700 and 1740, although the New Hampshire government counted upon the support of Massachusetts and cooperated with it in times of military crisis, it also sought direct support from the British army, navy, and the Royal Treasury; and the importance of the Piscataqua mast trade gave New Hampshire politicians a significant bargaining lever. In 1708, for example, George Vaughan proposed that England should send 200 troops, a "fourth rate man of war," two packet boats, and numerous supplies for New Hampshire's fort.[88] He was successful in obtaining supplies for the fort, and the navy had already begun protecting the mast fleet.

The decision to use paper currency in New Hampshire was instigated by mercantile leaders when it became evident that the Crown would support and aid a New England expedition against Canada in 1709. At that point the New Hampshire government promised to contribute its "utmost endeavors" because it was convinced the expedition would "produce a lasting quiet and repose" in New England. Yet its utmost endeavors proved so small that the lieutenant governor dissolved the House. The new House, meeting in July 1709, was dominated by merchants, who, after being bombarded with threats from the executive of

losing the favor of the Crown and after petitioning the Crown for military
aid, finally (after five months of hesitation) resorted to the use of paper
currency to pay the military debts of the colony.[89] At the same time the
council and the House petitioned the Crown for a new expedition against
Canada projected for the spring of 1710, expressing the hope that it would
bring "a glorious success as in Europe" and a "lasting repose" to "this
continent." News that the Crown was sending another expedition
brought from the General Assembly an order for a day of "General
Thanksgiving" in the colony, a special petition of gratitude to the
Crown, and a new emission of paper currency to pay the military
expenses. The capture of Nova Scotia by this expedition brought another
petition from the New Hampshire General Assembly for royal support of
an expedition against Quebec and Montreal, which would make the
whole continent English and greatly aid trade, "the improvement of
ships, and breed of sailors." Although this new expedition was an
abysmal failure, the government petitioned in October 1711 for another
expedition, pointing out its peculiar frontier insecurity until the French
and Indian menace could be destroyed.[90] While some of these petitions
only followed the lead of Massachusetts in seeking royal military aid,
nevertheless, they represent a growing awareness among New Hampshire
leaders of the contributions the mother country could make toward
solving New Hampshire's military problems.

That some New Hampshire enterprisers were thinking seriously about
a new relationship between the colonies and the mother country as a
result of the war experience may be seen in the extraordinary petition
presented by George Vaughan to the Board of Trade in 1715. Though the
primary motives behind this petition were self-interest and promotion of
the needs of New Hampshire, Vaughan talked in terms of an ideal
defensive system for the colonies that would also benefit trade.[91] He
pointed out that it was very unfair for larger colonies like New York to
receive royal favors and remain neutral in wars, while smaller colonies
like New Hampshire, which could ill afford it, bore the brunt of them. He
suggested that the remedy lay in a general property tax on all estates in the
colonies, to be paid into a general treasury. This money could then be
given out according to each colony's defense requirements. In peacetime
this tax money could be used for the salaries of political officials in each
colony.

But a general colonial property tax was just the beginning. Vaughan
suggested that since "the Plantations are very pinched by want of a
medium of exchange in their traffic" and always lacked gold and silver,
the Crown should allow the colonies to issue bills of credit, "and let them
out to loan at 6% on land security, to the value of £500,000 in New
England [currency], and in proportion to the rest." The revenue from this

interest could be used for subsidizing naval stores production and "victualizing ships of war." His third general proposal asked "that a General Name be given to the Country of North America where the English settlements and plantations are," and that every three years a "general Congress" of all colonial Governors meet "to consult the general good of the whole," although the function of this congress would be limited to providing information to the Board of Trade.

Vaughan then turned to what he considered the specific economic and political interests of New Hampshire. He requested that the Crown aid in resettling the frontier towns destroyed by the Indians and in reclaiming the Indians "from idolatry"; that bounties continue on naval stores and that the English import duty on lumber be abolished with a bounty taking its place; that all vessels importing naval stores into England be allowed to bring back ten "begging vagrants of the City of London to New England for every hundred tons imported"; that the New Hampshire fort receive both troops and supplies from the Crown; that the New Hampshire wastelands be granted out in return for quitrents to the Crown; that the New Hampshire-Massachusetts boundary dispute be settled amicably; and that the New Hampshire lieutenant governor be a resident of New Hampshire since the governor was not. To curry favor with the Board of Trade, Vaughan proposed something that would have been generally opposed in New Hampshire: that all good timberlands in the colony be reserved to the Crown for masts and naval stores.

The proposals and attitudes in this petition show Vaughan thinking on four different levels—as an Englishman, an American, a New Englander, and a New Hampshire man—but taken as a whole the petition is a localistic document, proposing solutions for the military dependence and the economic and social insecurity of a frontier colony. During the early colonial period, no one else in New Hampshire presented such a comprehensive analysis and list of New Hampshire's economic and military interests, nor did anyone else seek to ally New Hampshire so closely to the mercantile policies of the mother country. This document represented the views and experience of an astute merchant-politician who lived in an insecure frontier colony and sought political promotion from the mother country.

Later New Hampshire merchants, having the same purposes but living in a more secure and mature society, would reject the broader aspects of Vaughan's program (particularly the emphasis upon imperial and intercolonial unity) while supporting some of his specific proposals. They would seek these interests through a narrower localism that brought the political separation of New Hampshire from Massachusetts by 1741. Yet this provincialism could not erase New Hampshire's underlying military dependence upon both Massachusetts and England, as the New Hampshire mercantile community discovered in the 1740's and 1750's, when it reverted to the earlier patterns of dependence followed during Queen Anne's War.

Minor War-related Threats

The New Hampshire trading community experienced four minor threats—piracy, embargoes, impressment of seamen, and trade prohibitions—that were directly related either to its military insecurity or to its being part of an empire at war. These problems existed sporadically throughout the entire period before 1741 and were not amenable to decisive solutions.

Though piracy was a problem at Piscataqua during the 1630's, during the Dutch wars of the 1660's and 1670's, during King William's and Queen Anne's Wars, and from 1717 to 1722, it also could be beneficial to the economy, since pirates spent their "booty" for local goods, bringing cash into New Hampshire.[92] In addition, during wartime privateers and pirates carried on such similar activities that the New Hampshire government usually made no distinction between them.[93] Nevertheless, the presence of pirates in New England and the general military insecurity probably influenced the New Hampshire colonists in their decisions to accept Massachusetts' jurisdiction in 1641 and to build a fort at New Castle in the 1660's.

The only legislative actions New Hampshire took against pirates were the passage in 1699 of a law providing the death penalty for piracy and, in 1717, the imposition of an embargo on all Piscataqua vessels in overseas trade.[94] This embargo sought to protect New Hampshire vessels from Caribbean pirates, but it was probably ignored by the Piscataqua traders. All in all, piracy was a problem that could upset New Hampshire trade momentarily, but its effect was never so deleterious that a rigid permanent policy was developed against it.

Embargoes could also momentarily endanger a local merchant's trade, particularly if the purpose of the embargo had little direct connection with the merchant's economic interests. Embargoes were enforced in New Hampshire for two reasons: either to keep foodstuffs and provisions in the colony during a critical food shortage, or to keep the seamen in the colony during a military crisis. For example, the embargo of 1697 had both purposes, as the New Hampshire Council stated: "We are in daily expectation of an attack from the French and Indian enemy both by sea and land, and [find] it necessary to prevent the export of provisions and to keep our Seamen at home, so necessary at such a time."[95] This embargo, as it forbade only overseas exportation, did not affect the coastal trade and was probably unenforceable. But the embargo of 1712 included local fishing vessels as well as overseas vessels, and its severity brought a repeal seven days later.[96] On the whole, the New Hampshire mercantile community opposed embargoes, supporting limited ones only as a last resort in moments of great fear.[97]

British impressment of New Hampshire seamen was effectively stifled by the New Hampshire mercantile community. Impressment was a sporadic issue in most of the British colonies; in New Hampshire the only period of conflict before 1740 occurred in the 1690's. It started in 1694, when John Taylor, as a result of an economic feud with John Usher, impressed twenty seamen from Usher's vessel and a few others. Usher complained to the Lords of Trade, but nothing came of it.[98] By 1696, however, after the sole power of impressment had been given to the colonial governors, the New Hampshire Council opposed Lieutenant Governor Usher's attempts at impressment of seamen for the Royal Navy. When, in 1697, a naval commander petitioned council president John Hinckes for seamen (Usher being in Massachusetts), Hinckes and the council offered every possible excuse in their refusal to allow impressment.[99] Actually, it appears that the New Hampshire Council opposed impressment only when the beneficiary was the Royal Navy: there was no opposition to impressing a crew for New Hampshire vessels.[100] There is no evidence that New Hampshire executives allowed impressment into the Royal Navy between 1696 and 1741; therefore, New Hampshire settlers must have almost completely escaped this threat.

The trade prohibitions proved the most irksome of these minor threats because they endangered lucrative patterns of New Hampshire commerce. They were one of the few penalties New Hampshire traders paid for being part of the British Empire, for the traders found themselves at the mercy of British diplomatic decisions in Europe. For example, when Charles II granted Nova Scotia to France in 1667 in return for some West Indian islands, his decision brought French competition in furs and fisheries closer to New Hampshire.[101] More importantly, Britain's antagonism toward Spain and her various wars with Spain in the early eighteenth century directly impinged upon New Hamphire's lumber trade with that country. The New Hampshire mercantile community, as a result, carried on an important but illicit trade in ship timber with the Spanish throughout the early eighteenth century. The Molasses Act of 1733, a diplomatic victory for the British West Indies, provoked some New Hampshire merchants into ignoring the law and trading lumber and provisions to the French West Indies for sugar and molasses without paying the required duties.[102]

Of all the minor threats to New Hampshire's economic prosperity, these trade prohibitions could have been the most destructive; but they proved relatively ineffective because of the weak imperial administrative system and the willingness of New Hampshire traders to disobey the laws. Nevertheless, the prohibitions, by their very existence, exerted a check of indefinite proportions upon New Hampshire trade with the proscribed areas.[103]

Economic Competition from Massachusetts

A final external economic threat to the New Hampshire mercantile community before 1741 was the economic imperialism of Massachusetts merchants. This confrontation was deeply affected by New Hampshire's past economic dependence upon and connections within the Massachusetts mercantile community. In the seventeenth century the Massachusetts merchants and markets had dominated the New Hampshire economy with salutary effects. The prosperous merchants of New Hampshire soon found, however, that the Massachusetts traders who brought their own vessels into the Piscataqua to load timber threatened local expansion in the coastal and overseas trade. This threat increased in importance as readily accessible local timber resources gradually declined. By the 1720's and 1730's, competition from Massachusetts, coupled with other factors, had produced fears which, when properly manipulated by a faction of politically discontented merchants, led to deep internal divisions within the New Hampshire mercantile community and, ultimately, to a declaration of political independence from Massachusetts.

New Hampshire merchants reacted in three major directions against the dominance of the Massachusetts mercantile community: they used customs duties either in a discriminatory fashion or in an attempt to attract trade away from Boston; they sought an enlargement of New Hampshire's boundaries for access to more timber; and they sought alliances with British merchants so that they could be less dependent upon Massachusetts capital and other resources.[104]

The earliest attempt to use customs duties against Massachusetts traders occurred in the 1680's. The problem had its origins in the establishment of a royal government for New Hampshire in 1679, which separated the two economically interdependent regions from one another. New Hampshire traders depended upon easy access to Massachusetts' markets, but once outside its jurisdiction, they found themselves classed as "foreigners" and subject to powder duties and an impost of one shilling per ton. At the same time they paid a powder duty in New Hampshire. When the Massachusetts government refused New Hampshire's pleas for reciprocity, the New Hampshire Council passed an act placing duties on most imports, on lumber exports, and a powder duty on ship tonnage, exempting New Hampshire vessels from the act.[105] Whether this act was ever enforced is unclear. The House did not pass it, but Cranfield may have enforced it anyway. In 1684, Cranfield, seeking revenue, prohibited Massachusetts vessels from engaging in the New Hampshire timber trade without a license from himself. His justification for this act was that the Massachusetts traders injured New Hampshire trade by attracting all the trade to Boston.[106] This economic discrimination ended, however, with the creation of the Dominion of New England in 1686.

But when New Hampshire was again separated from Massachusetts in 1692, the problem reappeared. This time Lieutenant Governor Usher aided in the passage of a New Hampshire act placing import duties on wine, liquor, and enumerated commodities and a powder duty on non–New Hampshire vessels. This act put a special burden on Maine traders who used the Piscataqua River because they had to pay these duties both in Massachusetts and New Hampshire; in effect, they had no home port. The Massachusetts government responded by creating a separate naval office at Kittery; but when William Pepperrell's vessel the *Mary* returned to Kittery after clearing through the new officer, the New Hampshire fort fired upon it and forced its master to pay powder duties in New Hampshire for both the outward and inward voyages. When the Massachusetts government asked Usher for an explanation, he claimed that the entire Piscataqua River was within New Hampshire's boundaries.[107] After the Privy Council abolished the Kittery Naval Office, Massachusetts dropped the issue; Pepperrell's vessel was released, and a new New Hampshire act exempted all coastal vessels north of Connecticut from the impost and the powder duty, freeing Massachusetts traders from this special burden and restoring tranquility for the moment. Three years later, however, these exceptions were removed.[108] This complex series of events set the pattern for later Massachusetts–New Hampshire customs controversies.

During Queen Anne's War the New Hampshire government increased the import duties to obtain defense revenue, and Massachusetts did not complain. But after the war, in 1714, the New Hampshire government placed a substantial export duty on lumber. This act, the proposal of a new generation of New Hampshire merchants, aimed at shifting New Hampshire's internal tax burdens away from the retail traders and discriminating against non-Piscataqua traders.[109] The Massachusetts government objected strenuously to this act, and the new governor of Massachusetts and New Hampshire suspended it in 1715. But Massachusetts retaliated anyway by raising its import duties and exempting all the New England colonies except New Hampshire.[110]

Frustrated in its efforts to tax lumber exports, the New Hampshire government followed another direction, one which it had attempted as early as 1680, when the council had asked the Crown for permission to remain a free port.[111] At that time the primary motive had been to attract overseas vessels into New Hampshire because its trade was languishing, but this effort was abandoned in 1682. From 1717 to 1721, however, New Hampshire maintained an open port again, having repealed all its customs duties. It is impossible to assess the impact of this act upon New Hampshire's trade; but in 1721, at the urging of Lieutenant Governor Wentworth, the General Assembly enacted a new series of duties on imports and an export duty on all lumber shipped to Boston. The Massachusetts government reacted quickly, sending a naval officer to Kittery and imposing prohibitive import tonnage duties on all New Hampshire–based vessels. In the wake of these actions, New Hampshire suspended its law on condition that Massachusetts do likewise. The outcome of this conflict was New Hampshire's return to a free port status.[112]

Twice after 1713, then, the New Hampshire government had passed legislation strongly discriminating against Massachusetts traders, only to surrender in the face of strong retaliation. After 1721, in its continuous effort to compete effectively within the New England mercantile community, New Hampshire relied primarily upon its second choice of customs control, the maintenance of an open port.[113] And it continued this policy for the remainder of the colonial period. Though the relative success of this free trade policy cannot be accurately judged, it seems to have been popular and probably influenced the expansion of trade at Piscataqua in the 1730's and 1740's.

The Massachusetts-New Hampshire boundary dispute and the role of New Hampshire merchants, particularly the Wentworths, in that controvery have been discussed in earlier chapters. It is significant, however, that this problem did not receive serious attention until the 1720's, when Massachusetts was engaging in large-scale grants of new townships and New Hampshire lumberers were moving farther westward and northward for timber resources—a time, in other words, of intensifying economic competition. Lieutenant Governor Wentworth wrote the Board of Trade in 1725 that the best mast timber was in Berwick, Maine; but if the boundary line was settled, "the greatest part of the choice timber" would be in New Hampshire.[114] David Dunbar, the new surveyor, wrote in 1730 that the head of the Piscataqua River, Casco Bay, and central Maine were the present sources of white pines. Thomas Westbrook, New Hampshire agent to the mast contractor, moved to Maine in the 1720's to better fulfill his contract obligations; Richard Waldron, Jr., Westbrook's son-in-law and Governor Belcher's brother-in-law, had sawmills and masting operations at Casco Bay.[115] While the older towns such as Dover and Exeter still had abundant timber resources, they existed on private property and were not so attractive to the mast traders;[116] and the Wentworth faction used these fears of timber and land scarcity, as well as the paper currency issue, as political weapons against the Belcher administration of the 1730's. Their victory on the boundary question brought excellent timberlands within New Hampshire's bounds, and the victory against Belcher ensured their exploitation of these resources. One of the basic factors in both these controversies, then, was the competitive economic conflict between Massachusetts-oriented mercantile elements and those who sought more independence from Massachusetts.

Both of these victories exemplified the successful use of English merchants and imperial connections, the third main direction of New Hampshire mercantile opposition to Massachusetts domination. Through the efforts and English connections of five merchants—Benning Wentworth, Mark H. Wentworth, Theodore Atkinson, John Rindge, and Joshua Peirce—the Wentworth clan achieved its goals.[117] Their most successful English ally was John Thomlinson, but they also made use of David Dunbar, Martin Bladen, William Shirley, Ferdinand John Paris, Ralph Gulston, Joseph Gulston, Richard Chapman, and ultimately, the Duke of Newcastle in their quest for victory.[118] In fact, it was John Thomlinson's loan of £1,000 to William Shirley on condition that he recommend Benning Wentworth as governor of New Hampshire that probably obtained this victory. As Thomlinson had predicted, the leaders of the New Hampshire mercantile community soon discovered who their best friends really were in their struggle with Massachusetts, and they used them accordingly.[119]

Thus, in the years after Queen Anne's War the New Hampshire mercantile community gradually asserted itself against Massachusetts' economic, military, and political dominance. This development was paralleled by experiments in iron and wood manufacturing and an extensive expansion of overseas trade.

Eighteenth-Century Trade Developments

The meager evidence that remains suggests that Queen Anne's War had an adverse effect upon Piscataqua trade until at least 1710. The constant threat of French or Indian attack by land or sea in this frontier area was probably the most important factor in this decline.[120] The coastal trade with Boston, the heart of Piscataqua's trade, declined significantly. Not until 1713 did it return to even the approximate volume of 1695.[121] The second area of decline was the Atlantic-Caribbean trade. In the early years of the war, lumber glutted the markets there; by the later years, pirates and enemy warships were so common that five New Hampshire traders outfitted privateers for the Caribbean.[122]

But this decline did not ruin New Hampshire trade. The majority of the mariner-merchants who had prospered before the war probably adjusted fairly well to these dislocations, and some even improved their economic position, incidentally providing their sons with an economic advantage over new enterprisers.[123] William Partridge, for example, opened a profitable timber trade with Spain; and the Board of Trade's enthusiasm for naval stores encouraged his sending pitch, tar, turpentine, ship timber, and the vessels themselves for sale in the mother country. With the new bounties on naval stores after the Act of 1705, a few of the New Hampshire vessels in the Caribbean trade probably began stopping at North Carolina on their homeward voyages to obtain naval stores.

Moreover, the later years of the war, after 1709, brought an upturn in Piscataqua trade, as the New Hamphire merchants helped supply the various military expeditions against the French. These expeditions and the utilization of paper currency stimulated the New Hampshire economy to such an extent that a large number of new traders and enterprisers appeared. Although many of these traders represented the second generation of already-established mercantile families,[124] a significant number were newcomers to the mercantile community.[125] It was this new group of traders (and some additions after 1713) that dominated Piscataqua trade and politics before 1742.[126]

When the war ended, there was a great surge of lumber exportation to Boston and the West Indies; but the competition from other New England merchants soon exhausted the demand, bringing a commercial depression to New Hampshire and forcing New Hampshire traders to reevaluate their mercantile policies.[127] Between 1713 and 1742 New Hampshire commercial leaders diversified their trading patterns, seeking to ensure a continuous prosperity. Their success in this effort depended enormously upon their ability to adapt to changes in both English foreign policy and the local fluctuations of their markets. Their enterprises followed two main directions: gaining new markets for their lumber resources and developing a wider variety of products for overseas markets. By 1742, as a result of such activities, New Hampshire merchants had established patterns of mercantile endeavor almost as mature as Boston's and had become far less dependent upon outsiders.

With the West Indian trade in decline, finding new timber markets became a prime necessity. From 1713 to 1718, Spain, Portugal, and Gibraltar received some of the surplus, while the Piscataqua merchants sought the abolition of England's import duty on colonial lumber. Newfoundland, too, emerged as a Piscataqua lumber market after 1713, as did Ireland, Amsterdam, Fayal, Bilbao, and the Cape Verde Islands. The traders also sent their fish and their inferior naval stores to these ports. The outbreak of the war with Spain in 1718 had an adverse effect, however, and the New Hampshire merchants looked more seriously at the possibilities of an English market for lumber (see Table 7).[128] They were already sending increased quantities of naval stores and vessels to English markets; but the quality of the naval stores, particularly pitch and tar, was unacceptable to the Naval officials in England as well as difficult to produce in New Hampshire because of lack of labor and capital. When England relented in 1719 and abolished the duty on lumber, the Piscataqua traders were gradually able to exploit this new market, especially after the grant of new townships and the end of Dummer's War in the 1720's.[129] Moreover, the traders began sending lumber to the French West Indies. William Pepperrell, for example, traded in Martinique and St. Pierre by the mid-1720's, as did Theodore Atkinson and Daniel Warner.[130]

The New Hampshire mercantile community expanded its other exports after 1713. Perhaps the most spectacular immediate increase occurred in the fisheries. With the opening of Nova Scotia to English exploitation, the fish traders expanded their activities to Canso and Newfoundland, sending the fish to Catholic Europe and the eastern Atlantic and Caribbean islands in return for salt and wine. The manufacture and export of fish oil also increased, with Joshua Peirce, William Pepperrell, Jotham Odiorne, and Samuel Black the leading exporters by 1742. The Piscataqua fish trade expanded rapidly until the Spanish war in 1718, declined, and then expanded again in the 1720's, only to be threatened by French actions above Canso in the mid-1730's. It abruptly regressed with the outbreak of war in 1739 and remained in the doldrums until the mid-1740's and the capture of Louisbourg. After 1745 it increased somewhat until the outbreak of the French and Indian War, when it suffered a permanent decline.[131]

As New Hampshire's population increased, as its internal and external market demands grew more complex, and as its desire for returns for British manufactured goods became more pronounced, the New Hampshire mercantile community sought diversification in its exports and imports and in its methods of obtaining adequate returns. Before 1713, almost all English manufactured goods were purchased through Boston, which placed New Hampshire merchants at the mercy of Massachusetts market conditions. When lumber prices dropped in Boston, as they did after 1713, some New Hampshire enterprisers sought the development of new staple commodities as well as new markets. Archibald MacPhaedris, John Wentworth, and a few other merchants obtained a large grant of land in 1719 so that they could exploit some iron deposits along the

TABLE 7

EXPORT TRADE OF PISCATAQUA 1695-1752

	1695			1723			1725		
Destination	Vessels	Tons	% of Tons	Vessels	Tons	% of Tons	Vessels	Tons	% of Tons
A. West Indies	16	615	41.2%	15	835	26.8%	21	1225	34.2%
1. Antigua	1	15	1.0%	3	85	2.7%	3	135	3.8%
2. Barbados	14	540	36.2%	7	300	9.6%	10	580	16.2%
3. St. Christophe				1	150	4.8%	3	275	7.7%
4. Jamaica				1	50	1.6%	3	90	2.5%
5. Bermuda	1	60	4.0%	1	50	1.6%			
6. West Indies				2	200	6.4%	2	145	4.0%
B. Other Islands	7	265	17.8%	4	150	4.8%	7	380	10.6%
1. Terceiras				1	60	1.9%	2	100	2.8%
2. Fayal	5	180	12.1%						
3. Madeira	1	25	1.7%	2	60	1.9%	1	20	0.6%
4. Jersey							1	30	0.8%
5. Cape Verde							1	50	1.4%
6. Bilbao	1	60	4.0%	1	30	1.0%	2	180	5.0%
C. Europe	0	0	0	6	390	12.5%	7	600	16.8%
1. Spain				1	50	1.6%	3	210	5.9%
2. Portugal				3	180	5.8%	4	390	10.9%
3. Gibraltar				2	160	5.1%			
D. Great Britain	3	440	29.5%	8	650	20.9%	9	640	17.8%
1. Scotland							1	60	1.7%
2. London	2	400	26.8%	4	365	11.7%	3	270	7.5%
3. Topsham and other naval ports	1	40	2.7%	3	125	4.0%	2	90	2.5%
4. Liverpool and other sea ports				1	160	5.1%	3	220	6.1%
E. American Colonies	8	172	11.5%	25	1091	35.0%	19	740	20.6%
1. Northern N. E.	2	55	3.7%	7	265	8.5%	8	230	6.4%
a. Newfoundland	2	55	3.7%	3	110	3.5%	2	50	1.4%
b. Canso				4	155	5.0%	6	180	5.0%
2. Southern N. E.	5	97	6.5%	9	565	18.1%	4	380	10.6%
a. Boston	1	30	2.0%	8	545	17.5%	4	380	10.6%
b. Other Mass. ports	2	27	1.8%						
c. R. I.	2	40	2.7%	1	20	0.6%			
3. Middle Colonies	1	20	1.3%	3	56	1.8%	4	80	2.2%
a. Pa.	1	20	1.3%						
b. Md.				3	56	1.8%	2	35	1.0%
c. Va.							2	45	1.2%
4. Southern Colonies	0	0	0	6	205	6.6%	3	50	1.4%
a. N. C.				5	115	3.7%	3	50	1.4%
b. S. C.				1	90	2.9%			
Total Tons	34	1492	100%	58	3116	100%	63	3585	100%

Lamprey River. They even persuaded the New Hampshire General Assembly to pass an act prohibiting the export of iron ore from New Hampshire. By the 1720's they may have produced enough iron to provide some tools and implements for local markets; but by 1727 they were exporting iron themselves, an admission of failure in their broader attempt at iron manufacturing.[132] Nevertheless, in the 1730's and 1740's New Hampshire workers increased production of iron tools and implements, probably from imported iron.[133] While this early attempt at iron manufacturing was not successful, it did stimulate the export of some iron products from the Piscataqua region (see Table 8).

TABLE 7

EXPORT TRADE OF PISCATAQUA 1695-1752
(continued)

Destination	Vessels (1727)	Tons (1727)	% of Tons (1727)	Vessels (1735)	Vessels (1742)	Tons (1742)	% of Tons (1742)	Vessels (1752)	Tons (1752)	% of Tons (1752)
A. West Indies	20	1105	31.3%	18	31	2620	34.2%	84	5392	52.7%
1. Antigua	7	390	11.0%	6	3	140	1.8%	7	357	3.5%
2. Barbados	9	590	16.7%	8	10	575	7.5%	4	215	2.1%
3. St. Christophe	1	20	0.6%	1				2	220	2.1%
4. Jamaica	2	70	2%	1	6	505	6.6%	1	50	0.5%
5. Bermuda	1	35	1%		2	200	2.6%	1	50	0.5%
6. West Indies				2	10	1200	15.7%	69	4500	44%
B. Other Islands	1	40	1.1%					7	480	4.7%
1. Fayal					1	45	0.6%	2	85	0.8%
2. Madeira	1	40	1.1%		1	45	0.6%	1	30	0.3%
3. Placentia								4	365	3.6%
4. Bilbao								1	60	0.6%
C. Europe	4	390	11%					1	60	0.6%
1. Spain				3	1	30	0.4%			
2. Portugal	3	300	8.5%	1						
3. Gibraltar	1	90	2.5%	1	1	30	0.4%			
D. Great Britain	8	1160	32.8%	16	13	3425	44.8%	12	1955	19.1%
1. Scotland								1	80	0.8%
2. Ireland	2	70	2%							
3. London	6	1090	30.8%	7	3	560	7.3%			
4. Topsham and other naval ports				4	6	2200	28.8%	9	1735	17%
5. Liverpool and other sea ports				5	4	665	8.7%	2	140	1.3%
E. American Colonies	19	840	23.6%	27	32	1513	19.8%	53	2344	22.9%
1. Northern N. E.	7	215	6.1%	11	14	472	6.2%	41	1769	17.3%
a. Newfoundland	5	160	4.5%	7	14	337	4.4%	22	1022	9.9%
b. Nova Scotia				1	10			19	747	7.3%
c. Canso	2	55	1.6%	3	4	135	1.8%			
2. Southern N. E.	2	140	3.9%		1	50	0.7%			
a. Boston	1	100	2.8%							
b. Other Mass. ports										
c. R. I.	1	40	1.1%		1	50	0.7%			
3. Middle Colonies	8	435	12.2%	12	14	896	11.7%	6	295	2.9%
a. Pa.	1	30	0.8%		2	150	2.0%			
b. Md.	4	305	8.6%	2	1	45	0.6%	5	255	2.5%
c. Va.	3	100	2.8%	10	11	701	9.1%	1	40	0.4%
4. Southern Colonies	2	50	1.4%	4	3	95	1.2%	6	280	2.8%
a. N. C.	2	50	1.4%	4	3	95	1.2%	4	160	1.6%
b. S. C.								2	120	1.2%
Total Tons	52	3535	99.8%	64	78	7633	99.8%	157	10,231	100%

With the arrival of Scotch-Irish immigrants after 1718, the New Hampshire government encouraged local wool manufacturing by exempting sheep from the property tax in an "Act to Encourage the Raising of Sheep Within This Province." By the 1720's linsey-woolsey had become the clothing mainstay among New Hampshire families, and some excellent linen was being sold in local markets by the Londonderry inhabitants. In 1742 the Piscataqua region was exporting limited quantities of hats, leather, and linen.[134] In fact, the sheep themselves became an important export commodity in the 1720's as New Hampshire traders strove to satisfy the needs of the Canso and Newfoundland markets.

The production and export of wooden furniture, tools, and woodenware in the 1720's and 1730's exemplified another attempt to satisfy

TABLE 8

PISCATAQUA EXPORTS OTHER THAN
LUMBER AND FISH PRODUCTS
1695-1752

Commodities	1695	1723	1725	1727	1742	1752
Provisions:						
Salt	4,000 lbs	?[a]	?	27,600 lbs	76,229 lbs	189,600 lbs
Sugar	200 lbs	100 lbs		100 lbs	2,250 lbs	12,200 lbs
Molasses	882 gal			315 gal	578 gal	819 gal
Rum	1,334 gal	882 gal	?	1,827 gal	1,497 gal	4,692 gal
Pork	6,000 lbs			40,400 lbs	6,600 lbs	6,000 lbs
Ham						9,760 lbs
Bread	24 bbl			18 bbl	160 bbl	75 bbl
Butter	200 lbs					2,000 lbs
Flour	784 lbs				16,800 lbs	10,800 lbs
Corn				60 bu	40 bu	
Oats						200 bu
Hay						4 loads
Onions					2,000 lbs	
Apples					20 bu	130 bu
Cider			?	1,223 gal	283 gal	2,720 gal
Wine	3,308 gal	662 gal	?	252 gal		756 gal
Beef					1,060 lbs	4,000 lbs
Soap				8 boxes	8 boxes	
Animals:						
Horses		6	10-20[b]	12	27	95
Oxen				2	24	18
Cows			10[b]		22	102
Hogs				12	8	
Sheep			40	194	305	376
Ironware:						
Wheelbarrows						16
Skillets					54 &; 5000 lbs; 1 chest	190 &; 1 bundle
Guns					12 tons	
Shot						1 bbl
Nails						4 casks (800 lbs)
Handspikes					3,740	420
Kettles					83	
Pails					72	
Pumps					19	

overseas markets. By the early 1740's, axes, handspikes, oars, desks, pails, chairs, tables, oxbows, houseframes, and boatframes had become common exports. The production of hoops, shingles, and oak and ash rafters also increased significantly during these years, an illustration of the trend away from exportation of raw lumber alone.

Other new products were appearing in local markets in these years and being exported by the 1740's, particularly candles and bricks. Although it is not clear who started the Piscataqua manufacture of bricks (it may have been the Roberts and Henderson families of Dover), by the 1740's bricks had become a significant New Hampshire export.[135] Candles were exported on a much smaller scale. In the 1720's Henry Sherburne, George

TABLE 8

PISCATAQUA EXPORTS OTHER THAN
LUMBER AND FISH PRODUCTS
1695–1752
(continued)

Commodities	1695	1723	1725	1727	1742	1752
Clothing, etc:						
Hides						
Skins					8	50
Leather					48	
Hats					3 bales	
European goods				6 boxes, 2 cases	36, 6 chests	
English goods	1 trunk, 1 chest	?		1 chest, 3 hhds	41 chests, 2 bbls & 2 bundles	2 bales, 2 cases, 2 trunks, 17 chests, 3 bundles
Furskins	1 hhd					
Shoes						
Cottonwool			2 bags			20 pair
Merchandise					1 box, 20 bundles	2 bags
Miscellaneous:						
Indigo			17 bbls			
Iron				1 ton, 24 hhd		
Gold					20 oz	
Silver					71 oz	
Bricks					37,600	24,500
Candles	1 box			1 box & 300 pieces	49 boxes	
Tallow	400 lbs					
Fustic						
Tobacco	1 hhd					5,963 lbs

[a] "?" denotes an extant but unspecified amount
[b] An estimate

Jaffrey, and William Pepperrell imported tallow and wax from Maryland and North Carolina, selling the finished candles on the Caribbean market. In 1742, the Moors of Londonderry brought tallow from Virginia and sent forty-nine boxes of candles to Jamaica. Perhaps this small exportation reflected the high local demand for candles.

Between 1718 and 1742 the Piscataqua trade patterns became far more complex, increasing from the four patterns of the 1690's to at least seven with numerous variations, as the merchants sought profitable markets and returns while contending with the varied economic threats already discussed.

The coastal trade with Boston continued to be the most important Piscataqua trade route overall. This trade had suffered during Queen Anne's War but increased after 1714 to the volume level achieved in the mid-1690's. It maintained that level until the 1720's, when it suffered somewhat with the outbreak of Dummer's War. But by 1724 the trade with Boston had jumped to a level more than 50 percent above that of the earlier period. Valued at £5,000 sterling in 1730, this trade consisted of exporting lumber, cordwood, fish, and small quantities of other products (cider and fruit, for example) to Boston and returning with English manufactured goods (cordage, canvas, clothing and the like). Perhaps one-third of these coasters were Piscataqua-based traders. The primary advantage of procuring English goods from Boston lay in the fact that New Hampshire traders usually carried desirable staples for a market that was easily accessible any time of the year. In 1739, Richard Waldron emphasized New Hampshire's dependence upon Boston when he called it the "Grand Mart of New England." Thirty-five years later, Governor John Wentworth reemphasized this fact when he wrote the Board of Trade that "the British Manufactures consumed in New Hampshire [are] chiefly purchased at Boston, Salem, Marblehead, Haverhill, and Newbury in the Massachusetts Bay."[136] The Shipping Returns of 1742 support this generalization, as four of the six vessels entering Piscataqua from England (accounting for 1,600 of the 1,820 tons imported from there) carried ballast only. In fact, the one New Hampshire mast agent stopped at Boston on the way home from England to pick up cordage, canvas, foil, and clothing for the Piscataqua market.[137] Nevertheless, Piscataqua's dependence on Massachusetts had declined. If the New Hampshire merchants continued to purchase the bulk of manufactured goods at Boston, it was by choice, not necessity.

In terms of overseas export volume, the direct export trade with England held the most important position in the early eighteenth century. Naval stores—particularly masts, yards, and bowsprits—constituted the bulk of this exportation before the 1730's. During the 1730's, however, oak timber, "ranging timber," boards, planks and other naval stores such as pitch, tar, and turpentine were sent to England. By the 1740's, though some pitch and tar importation continued, the Piscataqua emerged as a net exporter of these naval stores (see Table 6). Also by the 1730's and 1740's, a few merchants—including Henry Sherburne, Joshua Peirce, William Pepperrell, and John Rindge—were loading newly built vessels with oak timber or naval stores and sending them to England to sell both vessel and cargo. A variation of this approach, more common among Massachusetts traders, was to send lumber and fish to the West Indies for sugar and molasses, then take these products to England, selling vessel and cargo for cash. By the 1740's a few of the Piscataqua traders were stopping at North Carolina for pitch and tar before going on to the West Indies and England. Nevertheless, the sale of vessels in England did not become a common practice among New Hampshire merchants until the 1740's. In 1742, for example, perhaps nine vessels from Piscataqua were sold on the English market.

Seeking new British markets in the late 1720's, some New Hampshire traders carried lumber, fish, and naval stores to Ireland, Bristol, Newcastle, and other English seaports. During the 1730's there was an especially brisk trade with Ireland in these items, as the traders returned with passengers for the frontier townships. A few merchants used Newfoundland as a way station in a three-cornered trade with Ireland, while others used Spain and Portugal in a similar triangular pattern (see Tables 7 and 9).

In sum, the general export trade with England increased significantly between 1723 and 1742. In 1723, only 21 percent of Piscataqua's export volume went to Great Britain; by 1727, however, this volume had increased to 33 percent. It continued to increase in the 1730's, reaching perhaps 40 percent in 1735 and 45 percent in 1742.[138] With this increasing exploitation of English markets after 1723, one can perceive why some New Hampshire merchants might pursue a political course more independent of Massachusetts.

The economic livelihood of the people of the Piscataqua frontier depended upon the development and exportation of lumber and fish products. Because the West Indies, Eastern Atlantic islands, and Iberian countries provided materials considered necessary to these occupations (rum, wine, molasses, and salt), and because lumber and fish commanded markets in these areas, a two-way trade between the Piscataqua and these areas remained an important part of New Hampshire's trade in the eighteenth century. The volume of trade with these regions fluctuated greatly between 1713 and 1742, however. The basic difficulty with the West Indies was that too often these tiny markets were saturated by other traders' products. In the Iberian and East Atlantic areas war was the most important inhibiting factor. In both of these places there was also probably a considerable illicit trade which the Shipping Returns never recorded. It is difficult, therefore, to establish anything except very tentative conclusions about Piscataqua trading patterns with these areas.

Generally, the Piscataqua trade with the West Indies gradually declined from the late 1690's through about 1722, increased somewhat between 1723 and 1729, decreased from 1730 to 1739, and increased rapidly between 1739 and 1752. The primary pattern was a direct, year-round back and forth trade: New Hampshire exported lumber, fish, livestock, and, after 1725, tools, furniture, and ironware and imported sugar, molasses, rum, and cotton wool.[139] But some Piscataqua traders developed more complex patterns in the West Indian trade. One such, developed after 1705, involved sailing directly to the West Indies but stopping at North Carolina, Maryland, or Virginia on the way back for tobacco, naval stores,

TABLE 9

IMPORT TRADE OF PISCATAQUA 1695-1752

Location	Vessels	1695 Tons	% of Tons	Vessels	1723 Tons	% of Tons	Vessels	1725 Tons	% of Tons
A. West Indies	11	545	30.3%	11	535	24.9%	12	445	32.3%
1. Antigua	. .	. .	. .	4	125	5.8%	6	230	16.7%
2. Barbados	10	345	19.2%	5	210	9.8%	5	190	13.8%
3. St. Christophe	. .	. .	. .	1	150	7%	1	25	1.8%
4. Jamaica	1	200	11.1%	. .	. .	. .	. .	. .	. .
5. St. Martin	. .	. .	. .	. .	. .	. .	. .	. .	. .
6. Bermuda	. .	. .	. .	1	50	2.3%	. .	. .	. .
7. Anquilla	. .	. .	. .	. .	. .	. .	. .	. .	. .
8. West Indies	. .	. .	. .	. .	. .	. .	. .	. .	. .
B. Other Islands	6	185	10.3%	2	90	4.2%	1	50	3.6%
1. Terceiras	. .	. .	. .	. .	. .	. .	1	50	3.6%
2. Saltatude	1	50	2.8%	2	90	4.2%	. .	. .	. .
3. Fayal	3	90	5.0%	. .	. .	. .	. .	. .	. .
4. Madeira	1	25	1.4%	. .	. .	. .	. .	. .	. .
5. Tortuga	. .	. .	. .	. .	. .	. .	. .	. .	. .
6. Bay of Clendoras	1	20	1.1%	. .	. .	. .	. .	. .	. .
7. Seal Island	. .	. .	. .	. .	. .	. .	. .	. .	. .
8. Tortola	. .	. .	. .	. .	. .	. .	. .	. .	. .
9. Cape Verde	. .	. .	. .	. .	. .	. .	. .	. .	. .
10. Santa Cruz	. .	. .	. .	. .	. .	. .	. .	. .	. .
C. Europe	. .	. .	. .	2	160	7.4%	1	40	2.9%
1. Portugal	. .	. .	. .	2	160	7.4%	1	40	2.9%
2. Gibraltar	. .	. .	. .	. .	. .	. .	. .	. .	. .
D. Great Britain	2	400	22.3%	2	210	9.7%	3	160	11.5%
1. Scotland	. .	. .	. .	. .	. .	. .	1	60	4.3%
2. Ireland	. .	. .	. .	. .	. .	. .	1	50	3.6%
3. Swanzea	. .	. .	. .	. .	. .	. .	. .	. .	. .
4. London	2	400	22.3%	. .	. .	. .	. .	. .	. .
5. Bideford	. .	. .	. .	1	160	7.4%	. .	. .	. .
6. Topsham and other naval ports	. .	. .	. .	1	50	2.3%	1	50	3.6%
7. Bristol	. .	. .	. .	. .	. .	. .	. .	. .	. .
E. American Colonies	4	665	37.0%	19	1155	53.7%	12	685	49.6%
1. Northern N. E.	1	40	2.2%	5	325	15.1%	5	260	18.8%
a. Newfoundland	1	40	2.2%	1	25	1.2%	2	80	5.8%
b. Nova Scotia	. .	. .	. .	. .	. .	. .	. .	. .	. .
c. Canso	. .	. .	. .	4	300	13.9%	3	180	13%
d. Louisbourg	. .	. .	. .	. .	. .	. .	. .	. .	. .
2. Southern N. E.	2	600	33.4%	10	750	34.8%	5	350	25.4%
a. Boston	2	600	33.4%	8	540	25.1%	5	350	25.4%
b. R. I.	. .	. .	. .	1	50	2.3%	. .	. .	. .
c. Salem	. .	. .	. .	1	160	7.4%	. .	. .	. .
3. Middle Colonies	1	25	1.4%	3	60	2.8%	2	35	2.5%
a. N.Y.	. .	. .	. .	. .	. .	. .	. .	. .	. .
b. Pa.	1	25	1.4%	. .	. .	. .	. .	. .	. .
c. Md.	. .	. .	. .	3	60	2.8%	2	35	2.5 %
d. Va.	. .	. .	. .	. .	. .	. .	. .	. .	. .
4. Southern Colonies	. .	. .	. .	1	20	0.9%	2	40	2.9%
a. N.C.	. .	. .	. .	1	20	0.9%	2	40	2.9%
b. S.C.	. .	. .	. .	. .	. .	. .	. .	. .	. .
Total	23	1795	99.9%	36	2150	99.9%	31	1380	99.9%

and provisions (depending upon the food situation in New Hampshire). Another pattern, important by 1727, involved loading furniture, tools, and ironware along with the normal lumber and fish cargo; stopping at Maryland, Virginia, or North Carolina to sell the manufactured products in exchange for provisions or naval stores; and then proceeding to the West Indies, where the entire cargo and perhaps the vessel itself were sold.

TABLE 9

IMPORT TRADE OF PISCATAQUA 1695-1752
(continued)

Location	Vessels	1727 Tons	% of Tons	1735 Vessels	Vessels	1742 Tons	% of Tons	Vessels	1752 Tons	% of Tons
A. West Indies	12	490	36.6%	7	14	1014	24.6%	46	2852	36.1%
1. Antigua	4	130	9.7%	2	2	110	2.6%	12	780	9.9%
2. Barbados	5	260	19.4%	4	9	759	18.6%	17	920	11.6%
3. St. Christophe	1	20	1.5%	..	..	..	..	8	590	7.5%
4. Jamaica	..	..	..	..	1	75	1.8%	3	230	2.9%
5. St. Martin	..	..	..	..	2	70	1.6%	3	165	2.1%
6. Bermuda	1	40	3%	..	..	..	..	..	..	..
7. Anquilla	1	40	3%	..	..	..	..	..	..	..
8. West Indies	..	..	..	1	..	..	..	4	167	2.1%
B. Other Islands	..	..	..	2	5	285	6.4%	18	1110	14.1%
1. Placentia	..	..	..	..	..	..	..	2	130	1.6%
2. Saltatude	..	..	..	..	..	..	..	..	..	..
3. Fayal	..	..	..	..	..	..	..	2	85	1.1%
4. Madeira	..	..	..	..	1	45	1.1%	..	..	..
5. Tortuga	..	..	..	2	3	190	4.4%	3	180	2.3%
6. Bay of Clendoras	..	..	..	..	..	..	..	..	..	..
7. Seal Island	..	..	..	..	1	40	0.9%	..	..	..
8. Tortola	..	..	..	..	..	..	..	4	190	2.4%
9. Cape Verde	..	..	..	..	..	..	..	1	30	0.4%
10. Santa Cruz	..	..	..	..	..	..	..	8	495	6.3%
C. Europe	3	170	12.7%	4	2	110	2.6%	1	100	1.3%
1. Portugal	3	170	12.7%	3	2	110	2.6%	..	..	..
2. Gibraltar	..	..	..	..	..	..	..	1	100	1.3%
3. Spain	..	..	..	1	..	..	..	..	..	..
D. Great Britain	2	120	8.9%	11	6	1820	42.6%	9	2125	26.8%
1. Scotland	1	30	2.2%	..	..	..	..	1	.80	1.0%
2. Ireland	..	..	..	5	..	..	..	..	..	..
3. Swanzea, Wales	..	..	..	..	..	..	..	1	90	1.1%
4. London	..	..	..	1	2	580	13.6%	1	500	6.3%
5. Bideford	1	90	6.7%	..	1	40	0.9%	1	50	0.6%
6. Topsham and other naval ports	..	..	..	4	3	1200	28.1%	3	1250	15.8%
7. Bristol	..	..	..	1	..	..	..	2	155	2.0%
E. American Colonies	16	557	41.6%	24	34	1015	23.8%	41	1719	21.7%
1. Northern N. E.	8	300	22.4%	12	13	346	8.1%	27	1129	14.3%
a. Newfoundland	5	210	15.7%	2	4	67	1.6%	10	405	5.1%
b. Nova Scotia	..	..	..	..	..	..	..	15	669	8.5%
c. Canso	3	90	6.7%	10	9	279	6.5%	..	..	..
d. Louisbourg	..	..	..	..	..	..	..	2	55	0.7%
2. Southern N. E.	3	142	10.6%	..	3	130	3.1%	..	..	..
a. Boston	3	142	10.6%	..	2	80	1.9%	..	..	..
b. R. I.	..	..	..	..	..	..	..	..	..	..
c. Barnstable	..	..	..	..	1	50	1.2%	..	..	..
3. Middle Colonies	3	75	5.6%	8	16	454	10.6%	8	340	4.3%
a. N.Y.	..	..	..	..	..	..	..	..	..	..
b. Pa.	..	..	..	1	..	..	..	3	170	2.2%
c. Md.	3	75	5.6%	4	5	151	3.5%	2	80	1.0%
d. Va.	..	..	..	3	11	303	7.1%	3	90	1.1%
4. Southern Colonies	2	40	3%	4	2	85	2%	6	250	3.1%
a. N.C.	2	40	3%	4	2	85	2%	5	230	2.9%
b. S.C.	..	..	..	..	..	..	..	1	20	0.2%
Total	33	1337	99.8%	48	61	4270	100%	115	7906	100%

Then, of course, there was the profitable trade in which Piscataqua vessels carried West Indian sugar and molasses to England after 1730.[140] In the final analysis, the West Indian trade was a fluctuating but invaluable and mutually desirable trade which incidentally provided New Hampshire merchants with commodities they could sell in other markets.

TABLE 10

PISCATAQUA IMPORTS 1695-1752

Commodities	1695	1723	1725	1727	1742	1752
Provisions:						
Salt	100,000 lbs	260,000 lbs	?	320,000 lbs	344,000 lbs	940,000 lbs
Sugar	11,432 lbs	11,661 lbs	36,688 lbs	27,495 lbs	159,936 lbs	89,240 lbs
Molasses	19,814 gal	3,623 gal	8,684 gal	10,248 gal	21,284 gal	10,025 gal
Rum	17,073 gal	9,723 gal	5,051 gal	12,354 gal	18,270 gal	33,019 gal
Wine	20,459 gal	12,632 gal	7,560 gal	10,723 gal	3,424 gal	5,040 gal
Pork	. .	?a	?	38,000 lbs	464,800 lbs	30,400 lbs
Bacon	. .	. .	. .	. .	. .	100 lbs
Lard	. .	. .	. .	. .	3,350 lbs	400 lbs
Bread	. .	. .	. .	12 bbl	10 bbl	. .
Flour	. .	. .	. .	2,400 lbs	. .	90,160 lbs
Corn	. .	?	. .	4,949 bu	22,050 bu	11,050 bu
Wheat	30,000 lbs	. .	. .	. .	189 bu	420 bu
Peas	. .	. .	. .	. .	149 bu	50 bu
Beans	. .	. .	. .	. .	203 bu	20 bu
Beef	. .	. .	. .	1,000 lbs	. .	. .
Cheese	. .	. .	. .	600 lbs	. .	. .
Tobacco	. .	8 hhd	2½ hhd	450 lbs & 350 leaves	1 hhd & 4,000 lbs	. .
Rice	. .	. .	. .	. .	. .	3,000 lbs
Beer	. .	. .	. .	. .	. .	12 bbl, & 720 bottles
Hops	. .	. .	. .	. .	. .	6 bags
Clothing:						
Hides	. .	. .	?	1 parcel	6,000 lbs	. .
Deerskins	. .	. .	. .	100 pieces	220	4 bundles
Cottonwool	30 pieces 1 hhd	86 hhd, 25 bags, 18 packets	8 bags & 14 packets	9 packets, 1,050 lbs	9 bags 4,844 lbs	2,786 lbs, 2 bales, 1 bag, 4 pkgs
Stuff	. .	. .	. .	. .	. .	400 lbs, 6 parcels
Hose	44 doz	. .	. .	. .	. .	. .
Hats	. .	. .	. .	. .	. .	1 cask
Haberdashery wares	4 bales 7 boxes	. .	. .	. .	50 lbs	. .
European goods	5 casks,	. .	. .	6 chests	4 bales, 2 chests, 8 boxes	3 chests, 3 boxes
English goods	3 trunks	?	?	1 box	20 hersies, 40 scoges, 20 foils	4 hhd, 5 trusses, 15 casks, 6 bales
Stays	. .	. .	. .	. .	60	. .
Irish Linen	. .	. .	. .	. .	. .	2 trunks
Silk	. .	. .	124 lbs	. .	. .	. .

The same conditions held for the trade with Spain; Portugal; the eastern Atlantic islands of Madeira, Fayal, and Cape Verde; and the Caribbean island of Tortuga. New Hampshire traders exported fish and staves to these locations, returning directly with salt for the fishery and wine for local and coastal markets. When lumber was a "dead" commodity in the West Indies, however, some merchants shipped small masts and other naval stores to the Iberian countries. A few of these merchants (Archibald MacPhaedris, Benning Wentworth, and Joshua Peirce, for example) exported naval stores and brought back illicit items such as

TABLE 10

PISCATAQUA IMPORTS 1695–1752
(continued)

Commodities	1695	1723	1725	1727	1742	1752
Miscellaneous:						
Tallow	..	..	?	190 lbs	500 lbs	200 lbs
English horses	..	..	..	..	5	..
Junk	..	..	..	..	48 tons	..
Iron pots	..	..	..	..	120	..
Negroes	..	..	..	33	2	..
Canvas	..	..	..	..	43 bales	..
Anchors	..	..	..	..	4	..
Coal	..	432 bu	864 bu	20 tons, 1,116 bu	..	9
Coke						7,632 bu, 40 tons
Grindstones	..	..	..	..	..	4 kill
Glass	..	..	..	..	..	80
Bottles	..	..	..	..	..	16 chests, 500 lbs
Bar iron	253 bars	..	..	..	..	25 gross
Nails	2,300 lbs	..	..	2 tons	..	16 tons
Hemp	..	..	..	..	..	1,220 lbs
Shoes	..	..	..	..	..	1,000 lbs
Lead	..	..	..	..	..	1 cask
Cordage	..	..	..	2 tons, 3 coils	100 lbs	40 bars
Chairs	9 bundles	..	..	..	..	..
Ginger	2 bags	..	4 bags	..	..	..
Anvils	3	..	..	..	..	..
Bricks	..	15,000	..	..	..	..
Pewter	8 bbls	..	..	..	..	..
Whiting	..	..	..	..	10 parcels	..

[a]"?" denotes an extant but unspecified amount

raisins, brandy, silk, fruit, canvas, and iron. The MacPhaedris Letterbook indicates that MacPhaedris, especially, carried on an illicit trade in an unorthodox pattern. He exported naval stores to Spain; then took Spanish paper, fruit, and wine to England and Ireland; went back to Cadiz with beer, provisions, and candles; and returned to New Hampshire with salt, wine, and illegal products. His agents corresponded with him from Ireland, Cadiz, Amsterdam, Madrid, Lisbon, Barbados, London, Bristol, and Fayal. With such widespread mercantile connections, Macphaedris had become one of the leading merchants by 1717, less than ten years after his arrival in New Hampshire.[141]

This trade with the salt and wine islands and Iberian countries fluctuated in response to changing conditions, especially in Anglo-Spanish diplomacy and warfare. The Iberian trade started briskly in 1699 but declined from 1702 to 1713, increased rapidly from 1713 to 1718, declined from 1718 to 1721, increased gradually in the 1720's and 1730's, and declined to almost nothing between 1739 and 1752. Meanwhile, the export trade to the Atlantic islands experienced a gradual decline from 18 percent of the total export volume to 1 percent between 1695 and 1742, then a minor increase to about 5 percent by 1752. The import trade from these areas paralleled the export trade, decreasing from 10 percent in 1695 to nothing by 1727, then gradually increasing in the 1730's and 1740's until it reached 14 percent in 1752. The Atlantic island import pattern tended to vary inversely with the trade to the Iberian areas. As trade with Spain and Portugal increased, trade with the Atlantic islands decreased, and a decreasing Iberian trade usually meant an increasing Atlantic island trade. The key to this pattern lay in the general availability of salt, for wine imports consistently declined in the early eighteenth century, while salt imports consistently increased, reflecting the expanding demand for salt in the Piscataqua region (see Tables 7, 9, and 10).

In the early eighteenth century the Piscataqua merchants developed two new general patterns of trade. The first of these—the trade with Newfoundland and Canso—blended opportunism and an economic commitment to the fish trade. In the late seventeenth century a few traders had exported rum, salt, tobacco, and wine to Newfoundland, where they obtained fish and English or foreign clothing and manufactured goods. But the opening of Nova Scotia after 1713 encouraged an increased trade to northern New England. The bulk of this increased trade involved a direct trade with Canso, with Piscataqua traders exporting provisions, rum, salt, and livestock and returning with fish and fishing stores for reexport abroad. But some traders, after taking their load of salt and provisions to Canso, exported fish directly from there to Ireland, Spain, or Portugal. A few others—Daniel Warner and Joshua Peirce, for example—carried lumber, foodstuffs, livestock, tools, furniture, rum, and naval stores to Newfoundland, there picking up fish, coal, and English or foreign manufactured items which they sold at Canso or Falmouth before returning to Piscataqua with ballast or fishing stores. Thus, Newfoundland and Canso served as markets for the surplus rum, salt, wine, and provisions that had been imported into Piscataqua through other trade patterns and also as outlets for such New Hampshire exports as livestock, furniture, tools, and lumber.

The second pattern, also a mixture of necessity and opportunism, emerged in the 1720's, as merchants sought markets in the middle and southern colonies. The earliest trade with Maryland, Virginia, and North Carolina had involved short stop-offs for pitch, tar, or provisions on the way back to Piscataqua from the West Indies. But by the mid-1720's Piscataqua traders were carrying on a direct trade to and from these colonies. They exported fish, fish oil, cider, salt, rum, and English and European clothing at first, and then in the 1730's and 1740's added their locally produced furniture, tools, ironware, woodenware, and linen, while importing provisions (beef, pork, wheat, corn, beans, and the like), tobacco, hides, tallow, and naval stores. During the early spring, provisions were often badly needed in New Hampshire; and the naval stores, tobacco, and surplus provisions could always be shipped off to other markets farther north or overseas. In fact, by 1742, there was a general pattern in which New Hampshire vessels cleared for the middle and southern colonies in November, December, and January, returned directly to Piscataqua by March with the necessary provisions, etc., carried these goods on to Canso and Newfoundland between March and July, and returned in September or October with fish to be reexported along with lumber products to the West Indies during November and December.[142]

By the 1720's and 1730's Newfoundland, Canso, and the middle and southern colonies, along with Boston, had emerged as the true hinterland of the New Hampshire mercantile community. Deprived of a significant local hinterland by the geographical and military realities and by a boundary dispute, the Piscataqua merchants acted as middlemen for the colonies to the south and north while also finding certain products (provisions and fish) from these areas necessary to their own economy. On the one hand the Piscataqua merchants stood in relation to these areas as Boston did to its neighboring towns, since they sent them products (rum, wine, salt, molasses) obtained in overseas trade elsewhere. Piscataqua's trade, like Boston's, was also primarily an export trade: both exported far more overseas tonnage than they imported. On the other hand the Piscataqua merchants were just as dependent upon products from these areas as Boston was upon England.[143] Because of this prior dependence, the Piscataqua mercantile community had shrewdly developed these areas into a hinterland relationship, and in doing so, had taken a long stride toward economic maturity. By the 1740's these complex and interdependent patterns of trade with the Iberian countries, the Caribbean islands, and the far northern, middle, and southern colonies exemplified not only the growth and expansion of New Hampshire's overseas trade, but the major patterns its merchants would utilize before the American revolution.

In the course of its first one hundred years the New Hampshire economy experienced extensive growth, most of which occurred after 1713. The causative factors included the gradually increasing population and labor force, the exploitation of new land after 1720, the successful export of staple products, the augmentation and reinvestment of capital, the increasing number of entrepreneurs, and the increasing complexity of New Hampshire trading patterns in the Atlantic world.[144]

Mercantile activity, particularly overseas trade, presented the greatest opportunities for economic expansion in the Piscataqua region, and the Shipping Returns, incomplete as they are, provide ample evidence of this growth. Hence, in the 1690's, after almost sixty years of precarious existence, the Piscataqua region boasted only about twenty mariner-merchants owning twenty-one vessels (755 tons) and carrying on an overseas trade of 1,420 tons, only 35 percent of the total Piscataqua trade (see Tables 11 and 12). Frontier threats had limited and would continue to limit mercantile expansion. But in the period from 1713 to 1718, a new generation of Piscataqua enterprisers partook in a surge of mercantile expansion in overseas trade. This expansion was limited by the Spanish war in 1718 and again by Dummer's War in the early 1720's, so that the trade statistics of 1727 provide the most adequate measure of growth from 1713 to 1727.[145] While the number of New Hampshire traders increased only 40 percent over the number in 1695 (from approximately twenty to twenty-eight), the number of vessels they owned more than doubled, their vessel tonnage more than tripled, the New Hampshire volume of trade more than doubled, and the proportion of the total Piscataqua trade in which New Hampshire traders participated increased from 35 to 64 percent. Nevertheless, the total volume of Piscataqua trade had increased only 20 percent. In 1709, a war year, Governor Dudley estimated the value of New Hampshire export trade at £5,000 sterling; in 1720, it was estimated at £50,000 New England money and £40,000 sterling—an eightfold increase.[146]

By 1727, the foremost New Hampshire traders (small fry compared to Massachusetts merchants) were Henry Sherburne, Joshua Peirce, John Rindge, Daniel Bell, Richard Wibird, and John Harris (Table 13). They carried on about one-third of the total trade at Piscataqua. The two mast traders carried one-fifth of the trade, and William Pepperrell of Kittery carried almost 9 percent, which left the other 40 percent spread among

TABLE 11

PISCATAQUA SHIPPING STATISTICS 1695-1752*

Items	1695		1727		1742		1752	
Entries	23		33		61		118	
Clearances	34		52		78		157	
N. H. vessels	21	(64%)	47	(78%)	67	(79%)	118	(80%)
Total vessels	33		60		85		147	
N. H. based traders	. .		28	(70%)	44	(81%)	80	(81%)
Total traders	. ∘		40		54		99	
N. H. vessel tons	755	(33%)	2,390	(85%)	5,100	(70%)	7,531	(78%)
Total vessel tons	2,297		2,817		7,254		9,706	
N. H. volume tons	1,420	(35%)	3,140	(64%)	7,939	(67%)	13,312	(73%)
Total volume tons	4,087		4,872		11,903		18,137	

*Source--New Hampshire Shipping Returns, CO5, 967, 968, 969.

thirty-one traders. The top 10 percent of the traders carried more than one-third of the trade, while the top 25 percent carried more than three-fifths. Among the top local traders, Pepperrell had seven vessels in overseas trade in 1727, Peirce had five, Sherburne four, and Rindge two.[147]

But the most significant expansion in overseas mercantile activity occurred between 1727 and 1742, especially after 1733, as the number of New Hampshire traders increased from twenty-eight to forty-four and the number of vessels they owned from forty-seven to sixty-seven, while the total exportation doubled and importation tripled. By 1742, a peak year for trade which was not surpassed until the 1750's, New Hampshire-based

TABLE 12

PISCATAQUA ENTRIES AND CLEARANCES 1695–1754

YEAR	ENTRIES	TONNAGE	CLEARANCES	TONNAGE
Sept. 1694– Oct. 1695	23	1795	34	2292
June 25, 1723– June 25, 1724	36	2150	58	3116
Dec. 25, 1724– Dec. 25, 1725	31	1380	63	3585
Dec. 25, 1726– Dec. 25, 1727	33	1337	52	3535
May 22, 1735– April 23, 1736	48	..	64	..
Jan. 1, 1741– Jan. 1, 1742	34	..	62	..
Dec. 25, 1741– Dec. 25, 1742	61	4270	78	7233
Dec. 25, 1742– Dec. 25, 1743	65	5186	77	7625
Dec. 25, 1743– Dec. 25, 1744	43	5550	48	5246
Dec. 25, 1744– Dec. 25, 1745	28	2058	44	4250
Dec. 25, 1745– Dec. 25, 1746	37	2650	76	4028
Dec. 25, 1746– Dec. 25, 1747	69	4137	114	7786
Dec. 25, 1751– Dec. 25, 1752	118	7906	157	10,231
Dec. 25, 1753– Dec. 25, 1754	115	7704	139	9297

TABLE 13

THE TOP TEN PISCATAQUA TRADERS -- 1727

Men		Vessel Tonnage Owned	Trade Volume Tons	% of N.H. owned vessel tons	% of N.H. owned trade volume	% of total vessel tons	% of total trade volume
1.	Samuel Waldo	450	500	..	..	11.8%	10.3%
2.	Henry Sherburne	200	440	8.4%	14.0%	5.2%	9.0%
3.	William Pepperrell	230	420	..	..	6.0%	8.6%
4.	George Craddock	410	410	..	..	10.7%	8.4%
5.	Joshua Pierce	230	270	9.6%	8.6%	6.0%	5.5%
6.	John Rindge	250	250	10.5%	8.0%	6.5%	5.1%
7.	Richard Wibird	80	200	3.3%	6.4%	2.1%	4.1%
8.	Daniel Bell	200	200	3.3%	6.4%	5.2%	4.1%
9.	John Harris	200	200	3.3%	6.4%	5.2%	4.1%
10.	John Gilbert	180	180	..	..	4.7%	3.7%
	Totals	2430	3070	38.4%	49.8%	63.4%	62.9%

THE TOP TEN PISCATAQUA TRADERS -- 1742

Men		Vessel Tonnage Owned	Trade Volume Tons	% of N.H. owned vessel tons	% of N.H. owned trade volume	% of total vessel tons	% of total trade volume
1.	Ralph Gulston	1200	2400			16.5%	20.2%
2.	Mark H. Wentworth	1210	1970	23.7%	24.8%	16.7%	16.6%
3.	Henry Sherburne, Jr.	420	900	8.2%	11.3%	5.8%	7.6%
4.	Robert Rae	450	450	8.8%	5.7%	6.2%	3.8%
5.	Henry Sherburne, Sr.	400	400	7.9%	5.0%	5.5%	3.4%
6.	William Pepperrell	235	370	..	..	3.2%	3.1%
7.	Daniel Warner	142	308	2.8%	3.9%	2.0%	2.6%
8.	Jacob Wendell	300	300	5.9%	3.8%	4.1%	2.5%
9.	Joshua Peirce, Jr.	170	265	3.3%	3.3%	2.3%	2.2%
10.	Thomas Bell	110	255	2.2%	3.2%	1.5%	2.1%
	Totals	4637	7618	62.8%	61.0%	63.8%	64.1%

THE TOP TEN PISCATAQUA TRADERS -- 1752

Men		Vessel Tonnage Owned	Trade Volume Tons	% of N.H. owned vessel tons	% of N.H. owned trade volume	% of total vessel tons	% of total trade volume
1.	Mark H. Wentworth	1330	2470	17.7%	18.6%	13.7%	14.5%
2.	John Henniker	500	1500	..	..	5.2%	8.8%
3.	Samuel Cutt	300	540	7.2%	4.1%	3.1%	3.2%
4.	John Moffatt	205	485	6.4%	3.6%	2.1%	2.8%
5.	Thomas Wallingsford	100	440	5.9%	3.3%	1.0%	2.6%
6.	Ralph Gulston	350	350	..	..	3.6%	2.1%
7.	Jonathan Warner	165	345	4.6%	2.6%	1.7%	2.0%
8.	William Moor	165	330	4.4%	2.5%	1.7%	1.9%
9.	George Jaffrey	145	325	4.3%	2.4%	1.5%	1.9%
10.	John Salmon	250	320	4.3%	2.4%	2.6%	1.9%
	Totals	3,510	7,105	54.8%	39.5%	36.2%	41.7%

traders had increased their total volume of trade by more than 150 percent over that of 1727. In fact, aided by the doubling population[148] and the increase in land use, the Piscataqua region's total volume of trade increased from 4,872 tons to 11,903 tons (a 144 percent increase) between 1727 and 1742, the largest Piscataqua trade increase in both quantity and percentage during the entire colonial period.[149]

A glance at Table 11 reveals the rapid increase in the number of traders in the 1730's and 1740's. The number had almost tripled by 1752, with the largest increase in the 1740's. Not only were the number of entrepreneurs increasing, but some of them were augmenting their capital and reinvesting it in their trade. The Sherburnes, for example, owned 200 tons in 1727, but 820 tons by 1742. Mark H. Wentworth, the new agent for the mast contractors, realized the most rapid increase. In less than ten years of trade he had accumulated over 1,200 tons of shipping, and he maintained this level into the 1750's, while selling vessels in England. In fact, between 1740 and 1747 alone, he owned at least sixteen vessels averaging 300 tons each. In 1742, he carried on almost 25 percent of the New Hampshire-based trade and 17 percent of the total trade of the Piscataqua region, largely because of his domination of local mast procurement.[150] Nor was Wentworth alone in his prosperity. The Sherburnes owned at least seventeen vessels between 1740 and 1747, and so did the Odiornes; and Thomas Bell, John Moffatt, Daniel Warner, William Pepperrell, Nathaniel Sparhawk, and the Peirces accumulated between seven and eleven vessels each.[151]

That capital and mercantile property were accumulating within the New Hampshire mercantile community can be seen by the fact that most of the top Piscataqua traders lived in New Hampshire by the 1740's. Whereas New Hampshire traders had controlled only 35 percent of the trade in 1695, they now carried about 70 percent and owned about 80 percent of the vessels in the Piscataqua trade. If one eliminates Ralph Gulston, the London mast agent, from this trade, New Hampshire enterprisers controlled 87 percent of the total remaining trade.

By the 1740's, there was a tendency toward concentration of overseas trade in the hands of fewer traders. Whereas in 1727 the upper 10 percent of the traders engaged in 36.3 percent of the total trade, in 1742 the upper 10 percent controlled over half (53.2 percent) of the trade. At the same time, however, the rapid increase in the number of traders between 1742 and 1752 indicates that opportunities were present for all who could afford the initial investment. Nevertheless, the vast majority of the traders carried on only 1–2 percent of the trade, each one owning two or three vessels at the most. One might generalize from this (and from the fact that most traders tended to maintain the same volume of trade[152]) that the opportunities for becoming wealthy were not so great after all, but this would be a fallacious conclusion. In reality, the investment of capital and the spending of profits were guided by a value system that placed primary emphasis upon land accumulation and the "gentlemanly" style of life.

In the final analysis, the extensive economic expansion in New Hampshire trade during the early eighteenth century, a result of an era of relative peace and of the merchants' triumph over most of the internal and external threats facing them, provided New Hampshire merchants with the wherewithal to intensify the realization of their salient values. Unfortunately, this economic expansion proved fragile, as war conditions and other problems of the mid-1740's and late 1750's brought setbacks that would take at least a decade to overcome.

PART IV

THE TRANSFORMATION
OF SOCIETY

CHAPTER **VIII**

THE EMERGENCE OF A PROVINCIAL SOCIETY

The Englishmen who established themselves in the Piscataqua region during the early seventeenth century sought to sustain the social and cultural values they brought with them, while coping with the varied problems of a frontier environment. Confronted with diverse religious, social, and economic backgrounds among themselves and their neighbors, the Piscataqua settlers decided that an intimate community setting—the town—would provide the best medium for perpetuating their most salient values. Within this milieu they used various social instruments—the church, the family, the town meeting, and the law—to uphold these values. But by the 1690's the New Hampshire towns seemed unable to resolve effectively the divisive problems and conflicting values arising among their inhabitants. In consequence, during the early eighteenth century the inhabitants, perhaps subconsciously seeking to avoid direct confrontations, turned more and more to their provincial government both for solutions to their difficult problems and as a more satisfactory unit for value perpetuation in an increasingly diverse society. Between 1713 and 1741, the province supplanted the town as the more important sociopolitical institution, while its leaders developed a more complex system of values which could solve, for the time being, the problems disrupting their expanding society.

Societal Values and Emerging Forms of Social Organization

Any analysis of New Hampshire's emerging society must begin with the social instability and disunity of its four earliest settlements. The inhabitants of these settlements held such diverse values that their leaders at first pursued a policy of competitive isolationism in regard to the others.[1] Within such a situation the town seemed the most promising form of social organization, one that could maintain order while conserving each settlement's special beliefs. By 1640, each of the settlements had assumed, either through the signing of compacts or through township grants, the political status and institutional organization of a town.

In establishing these town governments the colonists revealed a goal they held in common: their impelling desire for a stable social order. The Dover Combination signers, for example, spoke of "sundry mischiefs and inconveniences" that had occurred because they lacked "civil government" and "order." They promised to combine themselves into a "body politic" so they could "enjoy the benefit of His Majesty's laws, together with all such laws as shall be concluded by a major part of the freemen of our Society."[2] The signers of the Exeter Combination justified their action as a natural consequence of God's will and the "necessity that we should not live without wholesome laws and government amongst us." They promised to obey "Godly and Christian laws" of England, as well as those enacted "amongst us according to God." They expressed their desire for order quite simply: "That we may live quietly and peaceably together, in all godliness and honesty."[3]

But in three of the towns a peaceful social order proved unattainable when religious differences and frenzied competition for good land became uncontrollable because of the absence of legal civil governments and a legal judicial system. This general situation led Dover by 1641, Exeter by 1643, and Portsmouth by 1651 to acknowledge openly the legal jurisdiction that Massachusetts had first asserted throughout the Piscataqua region in 1641. Uniform courts, additional land, and secure land titles were paramount considerations in each town's acceptance of Massachusetts' jurisdiction, while Massachusetts' guarantee of former economic and political privileges within each town promised the settlers an opportunity for permanent order and stability.[4]

During the subsequent forty years the inhabitants of the four towns encountered generally similar problems under a uniform legal system and gradually drew closer together in their overall societal values. For the most part, they accepted the general orientations of Massachusetts, although they maintained remnants of their original diversity. Hampton and Dover, for example, directly followed the patterns of Massachusetts in religion and politics, but Exeter and Portsmouth did not. Exeter did not discriminate between inhabitants and freemen in local politics; Portsmouth did not establish the Congregational Church until 1671. The idea of Christian stewardship had relatively little emphasis in any of the towns except Hampton.[5] The predominant values of the Piscataqua settlers can be found in their reactions to the varied problems confronting them between 1640 and 1680 and in their first law code, the Cutt Code, established in 1680.

In their search for order and stability before 1680, the four New Hampshire towns pursued somewhat variant directions. At least two general patterns of social organization emerged during this era; and while the two patterns were similar in goals and in other ways, they also had significant differences.

The first pattern, prevalent in Dover and Hampton throughout the seventeenth century and in Exeter before 1645, placed great emphasis upon Puritan religious values. These towns maintained a theologically centered community, with the religious congregation and its leaders assuming political, economic, and social responsibility for the society and enforcing economic and social values consonant with religious orthodoxy. Strong emphasis was placed upon community cohesiveness, Christian stewardship, diligent pursuit of a "calling," church membership, and freemanship.[6] The town meeting, the family, and local legislation tended more often to mirror the values of the Puritan church than was the case in the second pattern.

The second pattern, dominant from the 1650's in Portsmouth and Exeter, was characterized by relatively less social cohesiveness and less emphasis upon religious values and authority. Economic individualism was predominant. The town meeting played a greater role in maintaining social order than did the church.[7] Town leaders, elected by all male freeholders and inhabitants, sought to advance the "good community" through majority consensus among the townspeople, finding this approach most suitable for effective enforcement of their policies. Perhaps the most important single reason for the enhanced role of the town meeting in Portsmouth lay in the social disunity of its inhabitants, arising from the economic, social, and religious heterogeneity of the port town. In Exeter, Wheelwright's departure in 1643 brought a decline in the town's religious orientation, as fear of economic collapse influenced its inhabitants to abandon their isolationist aloofness and open the town to all who wanted to settle permanently, regardless of their backgrounds. The continuing absence of an active church in Exeter enhanced the role of the town meeting in the community almost by default.[8]

Under both these patterns of social organization the basic goals were similar—upholding the welfare of the town above the welfare of the individual and maintaining order, stability, obedience to the law, and respect for authority in a Christian society. Nevertheless, by 1680, in all the New Hampshire towns the focus of political authority had shifted from the town selectmen to the town inhabitants.[9] This shift had occurred almost imperceptibly in Exeter; but in Dover, Hampton, and Portsmouth it had resulted from crises over land, timber, and taxation policies. Dover's crisis of 1659 occurred over the selectmen's land grant policies and resulted in an extension of town suffrage to all inhabitants who had taken the "oath of fidelity" and the town's acceptance of the principle that no land grants could be given without the consent of the majority of the inhabitants.[10] In Hampton the shift resulted from a crisis in timber usage during the 1660's which saw the freemen of the town assume control of all timber grants and land exchanges. By 1680, the Hampton freemen (now practically every town inhabitant) exercised authority over all grants of land, highways, timber, and commonage.[11] Portsmouth's shift occurred in 1672, after a new slate of selectmen in 1671 had granted some land to their friends and persuaded the town to establish a permanent salary for the Congregational missionary, Joshua Moodey. The townspeople responded by voting the rascals out, assuming authority over all land grants, and voting "that those Selectmen, nor no other that shall hereafter come, shall have power to make any Rate but what the General Town Meeting shall first conclude on for what any Rate is to be made and how much."[12]

The urgent concern for order was also present in the persecution of Quaker immigrants and proprietary claimants during the 1650's and 1660's.[13] In fact, when New Hampshire became a royal colony in 1679 and its new president and council received authorization in the Cutt Commission to establish suffrage qualifications for the colony, their concern for order and stability in the face of economic and religious dangers persuaded them to list by name the qualified voters of each town rather than establish uniform suffrage requirements. Congregational orthodoxy and antiproprietary prejudices appear to have been the most important suffrage qualifications to a president and council facing proprietary claimants and Anglican imperial officials. The actions and legislation of the first New Hampshire General Assembly from 1680 to 1682 bear this out.[14]

The seventeenth-century Piscataqua settlers dedicated the family, the Christian church, the town political system, and the legal and judicial system to maintaining "due obedience" to rulers who would "discountenance vice and promote virtue and just living . . . in all godliness and honesty," while protecting the "just liberties and properties" of each citizen.[15] In fulfilling these goals civil and religious rulers exerted their authority in every sector of human experience. When Massachusetts law was withdrawn in 1679, New Hampshire's leaders established a law code which provided the death penalty for idolatry, blasphemy, witchcraft, burglary, rape, false witness, and rebellion against one's parents, as well as for murder, kidnap, arson, and treason. The laws also penalized fornication, adultery, swearing, sabbath-breaking, lying, gambling, drunkenness, and speaking contemptuously of a minister or of the Bible. Perhaps the most explicit example of the prevalent concern for order may be found in the law which punished "publique rebellion" with death and defined public rebellion so broadly that it included anyone seeking reformation of the government.[16] The Cutt Code not only proscribed evil behavior but maintained order by upholding the power of family, church, and town government within New Hampshire society.[17] It also provided protection of individual liberties by confirming the land titles in all the towns, establishing trial by jury for all civil and criminal cases (the juries to be elected by the freemen of each town), authorizing the continuance of the judicial customs of Massachusetts, and placing political power and town suffrage in the hands of the freemen. These freemen by definition encouraged social stability, for they had to be Protestant Englishmen, at least twenty-four years of age, "not vicious in life but of honest and good conversation," settled inhabitants, and freeholders who possessed a £20 taxable estate and had taken the oath of allegiance to the English Crown.[18] A society governed by such good men and good laws, it was hoped, would preserve order.

It is easy and accurate to portray the Cutt Code of 1680 as a direct but crude imitation of Massachusetts legislative and judicial practices.[19] Yet it also represented a local compromise between the two emergent patterns of social organization outlined above. While the code contained strong Puritan overtones and overtones of the Mosaic Code, it did not create an established church.[20] Moreover, although it defined suffrage qualifications in terms of freemanship and probably restricted somewhat the town franchise in Portsmouth and Exeter, the concept of freemanship was defined in such liberal economic terms that it enfranchised almost all taxpayers twenty-four years of age or older and increased the political power of the inhabitants in the provincial government.[21] Most significantly, the code upheld the power and authority of town meeting government, thus protecting existing modes of social organization in the towns and encouraging the traditional localistic values.[22]

During the subsequent fifty years, however, a number of factors weakened the varied local foundations of order and stability that had developed among the New Hampshire towns during the seventeenth century. By the 1730's the older values of community cohesiveness, stewardship, and piety had declined, displaced by the values of capitalistic materialism, individualism, and religious pluralism among Protestants. Political power and initiative had passed from the towns to the provincial government. In the wake of the unpopular Cranfield and Usher administrations of the 1680's and 1690's, New Hampshire inhabitants recognized that civil authorities were rather weak (if not ill-intentioned) instruments of divine will and that provincial officials tended to exercise power to advance their own interests rather than those of the community. Consequently, individuals now sought to obtain power in the provincial government themselves and use it for their own ends.[23] Factionalism emerged as a fundamental aspect of New Hampshire politics, and a new configuration of values emerged from the strife. The settlers became far more conscious and suspicious of the policies of provincial government leaders and increasingly protective of liberties and property.[24] Nevertheless, the older values did not disappear; instead, they served as intellectual justifications for those who sought to maintain the status quo in society during the early eighteenth century.

At least four factors promoted these gradual changes in New Hampshire: the expansion of trade and commerce, the impact of the war era of 1689–1713, the creation of new parishes and towns, and the presence of a royal government in the colony.

The desire for economic profit was never a stranger to the settlers of the Piscataqua region. Visions of prosperity from the exploitation of fish and furs had lured many of the earliest settlers to New Hampshire. Even that Puritan religious tenet which urged every Christian to pursue a useful and profitable calling that would serve both society and the individual promoted economic ambition. The Piscataqua frontier's paucity of good agricultural land and the absence of law and order during the early stages of its settlement encouraged land hunger, covetousness, and ruthless economic competition during the 1630's; but Massachusetts' assertion of authority in 1641 brought a semblance of order to the towns.

During the 1640's the rising demand for fish and lumber in Boston and the West Indies encouraged many New Hampshire colonists to become part-time traders. Continuing and expanding pressures for these commodities in the 1650's and 1660's promoted land hunger and covetousness once again, as the town leaders faced increasing pressures for new town land grants and found it impossible to halt lumber thefts from the town commons.[25] Increased trade attracted entrepreneurs and capital from both Massachusetts and England into New Hampshire and enhanced the economic power and diversification of the port town of Portsmouth in the 1670's and 1680's, at a time when its rivals, Dover and Exeter, were experiencing economic and social dislocations from King Philip's War. During the following decades, Portsmouth's economic leaders held off English mercantile competitors with help from Massachusetts while expanding their economy through shipbuilding and the lumber and fishing trade. By doing so, they attracted ambitious men from nearby towns, made their town a leading port in northern New England, and established the economic policies desired by most of the towns along the Piscataqua River and its tributaries.

The activities of Portsmouth's merchants helped create a more diverse and complex social order in the towns, while increasing the merchants' political and social role in that order. In addition, such activities stirred desires for more land and timber, desires which by 1715 could no longer be fulfilled by the local towns. In the early eighteenth century, competing lumberers and traders looked to the provincial government to satisfy what they considered their most basic needs and engaged in political intrigue and land speculation to obtain their goals. By the 1720's, as town cohesiveness declined, individual greed and economic ambition ("covetousness") became an increasingly dominant characteristic of New Hampshire society, undermining older communal values.[26]

The Indian wars that raged intermittently from 1689 to 1713 along the Piscataqua frontier played an important part in the decline of social order. They brought economic depression to farmers who could not harvest their crops. In some cases, military events forced partial abandonment of frontier towns.[27] The wars forced greater emphasis on economic and physical survival, as many frontier farmers fled to Portsmouth, to Massachusetts, or to sea in order to obtain economic, physical, and/or psychological security. These events augmented the labor force at Portsmouth and encouraged the rise of new merchants and traders, while having debilitating social and economic effects at Dover and Exeter.[28] During these insecure war years, the frontier townspeople recognized their dependence upon the provincial government, sought its aid and beneficence, and used it to appeal to England and Massachusetts for military support.[29]

Probably the most significant effect of the social, economic, and psychological changes of the war years lay in the new authority and power assumed by the provincial government during this crisis era. Between 1692 and 1713, the provincial government passed comprehensive legislation concerning military service, paper currency, education, religion, highways, town land grants and boundaries, and treatment of servants and slaves.[30] It also established a provincial prison and post office, carried on negotiations for the various towns with the proprietary claimant, and contracted supplies from individual traders and merchants for the war effort. Perhaps many of these activities would ultimately have been established war or no war, but the pressure of the war gave special urgency to most of these measures and focused the settlers' attention upon the provincial government.

In the seven years after the war (1714–20), the General Assembly asserted its authority in almost every imaginable realm of New Hampshire society, encroaching directly upon the earlier autonomy of the towns and standardizing the activities of the New Hampshire people.[31]

For the first time it dealt with such social problems as relief of the mentally retarded and the "distracted," poor relief for beggars and "sturdy rogues," control of pollution from slaughterhouses and stills, quarantine of those persons having communicable diseases, and the capture and punishment of runaway sons and servants. It asserted authority in economic affairs by regulating the use of ferries, labor conditions in the fishery, procedures between creditors and debtors, bankruptcy, and the presence of hawkers and peddlers in the colony. Perhaps most significantly, the government intervened actively in local town affairs, establishing legislation on local common land divisions, town meetings, the admission of new inhabitants, and town suffrage and elections, and also solving town social crises over ministers and new parishes.[32] Thus, the war years brought an expansion of the provincial government's role in society and a corresponding decline in the local autonomy of the town.[33]

The third factor abetting the decline of the old social order was the demand for and creation of new parishes and towns in the early eighteenth century.[34] During the seventeenth century the inhabitants' pressures for land and timber had persuaded the towns to grant out the common lands, but as people moved away from the town centers, they became increasingly less subject to the social discipline of the community. Attendance at town and church meetings, contacts with social and political leaders, educational opportunities for the children, and the watchful supervision of church and neighbors all declined considerably as newcomers, younger sons, and poorer settlers moved away from the central communities and found it geographically inconvenient to participate in community affairs.[35]

Controversies between the community centers and these "outlivers"[36] usually began over the issue of the best location for the town meetinghouse. Outlivers contended that since the center of town population had shifted, the meetinghouse site should reflect the change. When inhabitants of the town center opposed changes, the outlivers petitioned the provincial government for parish privileges, requesting their own minister, church, schools, selectmen, and constables, and control over local taxation policies.[37]

Far more than geographical convenience was at stake in these controversies because the locations of meetinghouses affected nearby land and property values. The area near the meetinghouse was usually the main thoroughfare of business and travel. Shifting the location of a meetinghouse meant depreciation of land values near the old one and increased values near the new one. Desires for improved property values and new roads as well as for more convenient worship facilities helped motivate the actions of those who sought independent parishes. Furthermore, the creation of a separate parish meant more freedom in a new social setting.

The outlivers themselves would determine their own patterns and choose their own rulers. Thus, the possibility of increased power over their own actions in society also motivated them. On the other hand, the inhabitants of town centers generally opposed the creation of new parishes because of the consequent depreciation of property values and the loss of a large portion of taxpayers. Usually, they attacked such proposals before the General Assembly by arguing that this action would bring disorder, confusion, and animosities that might destroy their community and the public peace of the colony. But the outlivers replied that refusal would be more evil and disastrous, as it would force them to disobey the law by depriving them of the opportunity to carry on the public worship of God and maintain schools for their children.[38]

The overall effects of these controversies were legion. First, they destroyed the relative social homogeneity that had come to exist in the seventeenth-century communities and brought bitter conflicts over ministers, taxes, land jurisdiction, and political power in each town. The increasing agitation for new parishes and their successful creation weakened the influence of the church, the town meeting, and the established social and political leaders in the older communities, as the new parishes provided opportunities for new leadership in economic, social, and political relationships. The presence of physical mobility created opportunities for social mobility for the outlivers. Significantly, as these changes occurred, the outlivers looked to the provincial government for aid against the established town centers and generally obtained their wishes, while, simultaneously, some of the established town leaders sought to maintain as much of the old status quo as possible by using the provincial government to standardize, extend, and perpetuate the older values throughout the colony.[39] The effect of both of these impulses was a more diverse and unfettered population that looked toward the provincial government for authority, unity, and material favors.

Finally, the presence of royal government, royal officials, and increased mercantile relationships between New Hampshire and England after 1679 gradually influenced the values and actions of the New Hampshire people, breaking down older procedures and arrangements. The administration of Edward Cranfield (1682–86), for example, affected the social order in at least four directions. Cranfield augmented the role of the provincial executive in the towns and weakened local authority through the appointment of justices of the peace, sheriffs, and juries. The extreme tactics he utilized in support of Robert Mason and against the Congregational church both disrupted the social organization of the colony and aroused a deep suspicion of executive authority among the New Hampshire people that lasted until the proprietary controversy became quiescent after 1708.[40]

Another gradual change partially effected by the presence of royal government was the growth of religious toleration among Protestants. The royal commissions from 1679 on contained clauses upholding "liberty of conscience . . . unto all protestants," and by 1693, New Hampshire legislation partially supported this ideal.[41] By the end of the seventeenth century there were small Quaker communities in Dover and Hampton,[42] but the more important tests of religious toleration came with the arrival of Scotch-Irish Presbyterians during the 1720's, the rise of an Anglican church in Portsmouth in the 1730's, and the growth of "New Light" churches during the 1740's. The general New Hampshire religious position was that every citizen should support some religion, with the church of the majority of town inhabitants being the established church of that town. Although Quakers had won exemption from church taxes in 1693, during the 1730's Congregational selectmen at Chester taxed the Presbyterians in the town on the premise that they did not qualify for exemption. When the Presbyterians petitioned the General Assembly for redress, the House of Representatives voted to dismiss the petition; but when the governor and council upheld it, the House then concurred. In 1740 the General Assembly passed a law legitimizing two separate denominations in one parish at Chester, which had the effect of exempting Presbyterians from the town's church taxes.[43]

The appearance of an Anglican church at Portsmouth during the 1730's, supported by many members of the mercantile community, was largely owing to changed values instilled through years of contact with English merchants and officials.[44] Both Lieutenant Governor David Dunbar and the London merchant John Thomlinson played important roles in its creation, and most of its early members were either merchants or sea captains.[45] With the Anglican minister's salary paid by the Society for the Propagation of the Gospel in Foreign Parts, the new Anglicans promised to continue supporting the Congregational ministers in their Portsmouth parishes until their deaths; however, Anglicans in other towns were exempted from support of their town church so long as they attended the Anglican church at Portsmouth.[46]

Hence, largely through English values and influence, the Quakers, Presbyterians, and Anglicans received a measure of toleration in New Hampshire society. The older Congregational authority was declining, and by 1740 precedents had been established that could uphold the "New Lights" in their quest for recognition as separate churches after 1741.[47] Perhaps most significantly, the increasing dependence upon the political, economic, and military power of England after 1689 and increased contacts with English mercantile leaders helped develop a provincial life style among the New Hampshire social elite that modified the earlier values and patterns of a neo-Puritan society.

Economic Expansion and the Economic Structure

During these one hundred years of social change New Hampshire expanded from four frontier villages of fewer than 1,000 total settlers to a diverse society of eighteen towns and 23,000 inhabitants. Portsmouth, located at the mouth of the Piscataqua River's water transportation system, with perhaps 3,500 inhabitants in 1740, had emerged as the largest and most prosperous of the towns.[48] Dover, Exeter, Hampton, and Hampton Falls supported approximately 1,500 people each, while the other towns each had 300 to 1,000 settlers. Almost all the New Hampshire towns served as Portsmouth's hinterland.[49] Probably 90 percent of New Hampshire's population lived within the seventeenth-century borders of the four original towns (which by 1740 consisted of fifteen separate towns and parishes), reflecting the significant urbanization that had occurred in eastern New Hampshire between 1710 and 1740.[50]

Portsmouth's hinterland towns supplied it with varied products. Nearby towns like Greenland, Rye, Newington, Hampton, Hampton Falls, Dover, Exeter, and Stratham—all relatively prosperous agricultural communities—marketed corn, meat, dairy products, fruit, and vegetables at Portsmouth and New Castle. Portsmouth itself, for that matter, had an important and prosperous agricultural population, for roughly 20 percent of its richest men between 1713 and 1741 earned their living from agriculture: its tax records reveal that such farmers as William Cotton, Sampson Babb, Edward Ayers, Edward Pendexter, John Bradford, and Joseph Caldwell were often among the top twenty taxpayers in the town. Nevertheless, approximately 70 percent of Portsmouth's richest taxpayers earned their living from trade and commerce, and roughly 75 percent of its taxpayers owned little or no land.[51]

As might be expected, Portsmouth contained the most diverse occupational structure and the most economically differentiated society of all the towns. Generally, the richest people in New Hampshire resided at Portsmouth and so did the majority of laborers. At the bottom of the town's occupational structure were the slaves (perhaps 10 percent of the population in 1740), indentured servants, free laborers, and skilled laborers, all of whom generally owned less than £50 of real and personal property. The middle occupations (owning £50–£1,000 in property) tended to be shopkeepers, retail merchants, craftsmen, farmers, fishermen, doctors, a few lawyers, and most mariners. The upper economic class (over £1,000 in wealth and property) consisted of wholesale/retail merchants who dealt in lumber and fish, some farmers, mariners, and a few lawyers. Of the 100 men among Portsmouth's economic elite between 1713 and 1741, about 20 percent were farmers, 25 percent were mariners, 5 percent were lawyers, 5 percent were craftsmen, and the other 45 percent

TABLE 14

NEW HAMPSHIRE TOWN REAL ESTATE AND ASSESSED TRADE INCOME PROFILE 1732

Town	Taxpayers	Houses	Acres of Land	Trade "Doomings"	Horses
Portsmouth	484	321	705	L 900	171
Greenland	104	73	507	L 50	62
New Castle	100	73	95	. .	12
Rye	94	66	483	L 50	67
Hampton	257	171	2379	. .	158
Hampton Falls	256	190	1965	. .	185
Kingstown	164	115	810	L 100	112
Dover	274	170	1960	L 800	232
Durham	260	126	1449	. .	193
Somersworth	107	81	601	. .	78
Newington	96	62	1159	. .	68
Exeter	327	182	1754	L 428	235
Stratham	165	99	1659	L 80	117
Newmarket	98	68	660	L 160	64
Londonderry	160	125	193	L 100	84
Totals	2,946	1,922	16,379	L 2,668	1,838

Town	Oxen	Cows	Calves	Pigs	Average Wealth Per Person	Total Valuation
Portsmouth	147	363	401	34	L 31.1	L 14,154.18
Greenland	78	195	263	40	L 36.3	L 3,723.13
New Castle	14	84	20	10	L 22.3	L 2,225.10
Rye	106	152	136	13	L 36.8	L 3,407.40
Hampton	241	486	676	44	L 38.8	L 9,974.14
Hampton Falls	165	389	750	42	L 37.4	L 9,575.00
Kingston	189	204	214	59	L 34.8	L 5,600.00
Dover	309	468	471	102	L 39.9	L 10,128.14
Durham	403	421	400	75	L 39.7	L 10,310.12
Somersworth	172	197	129	52	L 38.6	L 4,134.20
Newington	67	238	199	29	L 27.3	L 2,623.20
Exeter	389	439	468	94	L 36.8	L 11,607.00
Stratham	146	260	388	53	L 37.8	L 6,160.17
Newmarket	140	160	126	41	L 37.7	L 3,539.10
Londonderry	174	288	169	19	L 34.7	L 5,450.12
Totals	2,740	4,344	4,810	707	35.7	L102,611
						2,668
						L105,279

were retail/wholesale merchants.[52] The relative stability of the tax structure over time, as shown in Tables 20 and 21, suggests that while real property became more concentrated among fewer people in the mercantile towns of Portsmouth and New Castle, the varied opportunities for trade income encouraged a tendency toward more economic democracy and equalization of wealth in these towns.

In the other towns, however, these economic patterns were different because less than 20 percent of their inhabitants earned profits in trade or commerce[53] (Dover excepted), whereas 70 to 90 percent of their inhabitants owned enough real estate to be classified as farmers.[54] Dover, Exeter, Kingston, Durham, Somersworth, and Barrington, for example, supplied Portsmouth's merchants and mariners with masts and timber products, the mainstay of the Piscataqua export trade. Many people in these towns pursued profit as farmer-lumberers.

New Castle, strategically located at the mouth of the Piscataqua River, housed many of Portsmouth's fishermen, laborers, and mariners and was known as a fisherman's town. Over 80 percent of those whose names appeared in the probate records in wills or inventories of estates from New Castle earned their living from the sea and trade. Ten percent of these people were among the richest settlers in New Hampshire. By the 1730's more than 80 percent of the inhabitants of New Castle owned little or no real property, yet the economic structure of the town was not highly stratified. The richest 10 percent of its taxpayers in 1720 owned only 27 percent of the total taxable property and income, while the poorest 33.3 percent owned 17 percent of the taxable property. Even though New Castle had a larger percentage of poorer people than any other town in the colony,[55] every taxpayer in the town owned enough property to qualify for the town's suffrage requirements.[56]

Whereas the majority of Portsmouth and New Castle settlers looked to the sea and/or commerce for a livelihood and the majority of most hinterland townspeople looked to agriculture, Dover's inhabitants followed both avenues almost equally. Dover's location on the Piscataqua River fostered this course, particularly when opportunities for land in Dover declined after 1665. Until King Philip's War, Dover led the Piscataqua towns in masting, shipbuilding, and overseas trade. Though Portsmouth outstripped Dover in these areas during the late seventeenth century, Dover's leaders, economically crippled by the Indian wars, maintained their commercial interests and after 1713 gradually increased their mercantile activities, particularly in masting and shipbuilding. By 1732, for example, Dover's portion of assessed trade income was £800 out of a total of £2,600 for all New Hampshire, in comparison with Portsmouth's portion of £900. At the same time, however, Dover's 274 taxpayers owned more farm animals than did the 256 wholly agricultural taxpayers of Hampton Falls.[57] This prosperous balance of agriculture and

TABLE 15

NEW HAMPSHIRE TAXABLE REAL ESTATE OWNERSHIP 1732*

Total Taxable Real Estate	Portsmouth No.	%	Newcastle No.	%	Exeter No.	%	Hampton No.	%	Hampton Falls No.	%	Kingston No.	%
L0	145	30.0%	28	31.1%	28	11.5%	10	5.3%	6	3.1%	10	7.1%
L0-5	228	47.1%	45	50.0%	37	15.2%	14	7.4%	24	12.2%	26	18.6%
L5-10	32	6.6%	6	6.7%	41	16.9%	19	10.1%	42	21.3%	29	20.7%
L10-20	49	10.1%	4	4.4%	65	26.8%	58	30.7%	84	42.6%	52	37.2%
L20-40	24	5.0%	7	7.8%	64	26.3%	78	41.2%	37	18.8%	21	15.0%
L40-60	3	0.6%	. .	. .	8	3.3%	10	5.3%	4	2.0%	2	1.4%
L60-80	1	0.2%	. .	. .	. .	. .	. .	. .	. .	. .	. .	. .
L80-100	. .	. .	. .	. .	. .	. .	. .	. .	. .	. .	. .	. .
L100 & above	2	0.4%	. .	. .	. .	. .	. .	. .	. .	. .	. .	. .
Totals	484	100.0%	90	100.0%	243	100.0%	189	100.0%	197	100.0%	140	100.0%

Total Taxable Real Estate	Londonderry No.	%	Stratham No.	%	Rye No.	%	Newmarket No.	%	Durham No.	%	Newington No.	%
L0	2	1.4%	11	8.4%	2	2.8%	10	11.4%	17	14.4%	8	10.5%
L0-5	25	17.4%	21	16.0%	7	9.9%	15	17.0%	10	8.5%	6	7.9%
L5-10	28	19.4%	15	11.4%	13	18.3%	13	14.8%	17	14.4%	14	18.4%
L10-20	79	54.9%	51	38.9%	35	49.3%	24	27.3%	37	31.4%	19	25.0%
L20-40	10	6.9%	28	21.4%	14	19.7%	23	26.1%	26	22.0%	24	31.6%
L40-60	. .	. .	4	3.1%	. .	. .	3	3.4%	8	6.8%	4	5.3%
L60-80	. .	. .	1	0.8%	. .	. .	. .	. .	2	1.7%	1	1.3%
L80-100	. .	. .	. .	. .	. .	. .	. .	. .	1	0.8%	. .	. .
L100 & above	. .	. .	. .	. .	. .	. .	. .	. .	. .	. .	. .	. .
Totals	144	100.0%	131	100.0%	71	100.0%	88	100.0%	118	100.0%	76	100.0%

*This chart is based upon the inventory of taxable real estate turned in by each New Hampshire town in 1732 and collected in a manuscript volume deposited in the New Hampshire Historical Society entitled Inventories of the Polls and Estates in the Province of New Hampshire 1727-1773. The Exeter, Hampton, and Hampton Falls statistics are the only ones that include income or property related to trading activities.

commerce gave Dover the smallest number of poor people of all the towns in the colony and placed it highest among the towns in terms of average taxable wealth per person.[58]

Dover's extant tax records suggest that the town experienced an increasing economic stratification in the seventeenth century as the economically advantaged became richer and the economically disadvantaged grew poorer, but during the early eighteenth century the lower ranks raised their economic status (see Table 23).[59] These trends in Dover's economic structure largely paralleled the trends in the Piscataqua region; it experienced increased stratification during depressed years and decreased stratification during years of economic expansion and prosperity. While the causal connections between these two elements are not entirely clear, one can safely conclude that Dover's inhabitants (and perhaps most of New Hampshire's settlers as well) obtained more wealth

TABLE 16

NEW HAMPSHIRE TOWN REAL ESTATE OWNERSHIP PROFILE 1732*

Percent of Property Owners	Portsmouth			Newcastle			Exeter			Hampton		
	No.	Value	%	No.	Value	%	No.	Value	%	No.	Value	%
Upper 10%	48	L1477	57.6%	9	L 215	54.7%	24	L 920	27.0%	19	L 809	21.1%
Upper 33 1/3%	161	L2290	89.3%	30	L 321	81.7%	81	L2277	66.8%	63	L2068	53.8%
Middle 33 1/3%	162	L 254	10.0%	30	L 69	17.5%	81	L 930	27.3%	63	L1330	34.6%
Lower 33 1/3%	161	L 20	0.7%	30	L 3	0.8%	81	L 201	5.9%	63	L 445	11.6%
Lower 10%	48	L 0	0	9	L 0	0	24	L 0	0	19	L 27	0.7%
Totals	484	L2564		90	L 393		243	L3408		189	L3843	

Percent of Property Owners	Hampton Falls			Kingston			Londonderry			Stratham		
	No.	Value	%	No.	Value	%	No.	Value	%	No.	Value	%
Upper 10%	20	L 665	23.6%	14	L 436	25.4%	14	L 307	17.9%	13	L 534	29.5%
Upper 33 1/3%	66	L1594	56.7%	47	L1057	61.7%	48	L 870	50.7%	44	L1219	67.3%
Middle 33 1/3%	65	L 896	31.9%	46	L 506	29.5%	48	L 603	35.1%	43	L 454	25.1%
Lower 33 1/3%	66	L 322	11.4%	47	L 151	8.8%	48	L 244	14.2%	44	L 137	7.6%
Lower 10%	20	L 25	0.9%	14	L 4	0.2%	14	L 30	1.8%	44	L 2	0.1%
Totals	197	L2812		140	L1714		144	L1717		131	L1810	

Percent of Property Owners	Rye			Newmarket			Durham			Newington		
	No.	Value	%	No.	Value	%	No.	Value	%	No.	Value	%
Upper 10%	7	L 197	19.3%	9	L 333	27.1%	12	L 647	31.2%	8	L 352	27.2%
Upper 33 1/3%	23	L 539	52.8%	29	L 794	64.7%	39	L1428	69.0%	25	L 800	61.7%
Middle 33 1/3%	24	L 343	33.6%	30	L 360	29.4%	40	L 528	25.4%	26	L 400	30.9%
Lower 33 1/3%	23	L 139	13.6%	29	L 73	5.9%	39	L 115	5.6%	25	L 96	7.4%
Lower 10%	7	L 7	0.7%	9	L 0	0	12	L 0	0	8	L 0	0
Totals	71	L1021		88	L1227		118	L2071		76	L1296	

* This chart is drawn from the inventory of taxable real estate turned in by each New Hampshire town in 1732 and collected in a manuscript volume deposited in the New Hampshire Historical Society entitled Inventories of the Polls and Estates in the Province of New Hampshire 1727-1773. Taxable real estate included houses, improved lands, and most livestock. Each of the towns also assessed trade property and income, but these assessments were not available for any of the towns except Hampton, Hampton Falls, and Exeter where they were of relatively minor significance. The loss of these assessments limits the value of this profile to a comparative view of fundamentally agricultural estate values.

and an improved standard of living during the early eighteenth century and that Dover led the New Hampshire towns in these directions.

Further (though less reliable) evidence of New Hampshire's increasing wealth and improving standard of living in the early eighteenth century can be found in the probate records.[60] Of the 306 inventories recorded from 1640 to 1715 about 14 percent has less than £50 in real or personal property; and 63 percent had less than a £250 estate, 32 percent had between a £250 and £1,000 estate, and 5 percent had between a £1,000 and £3,000 estate. But of the 401 inventories recorded from 1715 to 1740, only about 7 percent had less than a £50 estate and 35 percent less than a £250

Table 17

NEW HAMPSHIRE OCCUPATIONAL STRUCTURE
FROM PROBATED ESTATES, 1640-1740

Occupation	No. of People	% of Total
Farmer	330	46.7%
Farmer lumberer	65	9.2%
Laborer	35	4.9%
Skilled laborer	38	5.4%
Craftsman	48	6.8%
Fisherman	31	4.4%
Mariner	46	6.5%
Merchant	37	5.2%
Shopkeeper	16	2.3%
Professional	24	3.4%
Widows	26	3.7%
Unknown	11	1.5%
TOTAL	707	100.0%

estate, while 45 percent had between a £250 and £1,000 estate and 19 percent between a £1,000 and £20,000 estate (see Table 25). These statistics suggest that both the poor and the rich became richer in the early eighteenth century. Whereas only four people had inventoried estates over £2,000 before 1715, twenty-six such estates were recorded between 1716 and 1740, seventeen of which ranked above the highest estate recorded before 1716.[61] Some caution must be exercised in evaluating these statistics, however, partially because of their relatively unrepresentative character and partially because of the excessive rate of inflation that occurred between 1709 and 1742.

In the late seventeenth century population pressures on the land supply of the older New Hampshire towns brought reduced town land grants, grants of marginal common lands, and rapidly rising land prices; and for a time (1700–1723) there was a resultant decline in local economic opportunities related to the land.[62] But the events of the 1720's and 1730's alleviated these problems for the time being, improving the socioeconomic situation to such an extent that little increased stratification of society developed among the New Hampshire towns before 1740.[63] One of

TABLE 18

PORTSMOUTH TAXABLE ESTATE PROFILE

Tax Value	1681 No.	%	1713 No.	%	1715 No.	%	1717 No.	%	1718 No.	%	1719 No.	%	1723 No.	%	1725 No.	%
0	1	0.8%	5	1.7%	3	1.0%	3	0.9%	1	0.3%	1	0.3%	15	3.8%	15	3.7%
L0-5	1	0.8%	..	..	..	..	..	..	1	0.3%	..	..	1	0.3%	2	0.5%
L5-10	1	0.8%	1	0.3%	1	0.4%	..	..	3	0.9%	..	..	46	11.6%	4	1.0%
L10-15	26	21.7%	9	3.1%	10	3.5%	3	0.9%	60	17.3%	7	2.1%	90	22.9%	32	7.9%
L15-20	17	14.2%	2	0.7%	3	1.0%	4	1.2%	35	10.1%	4	1.2%	31	7.9%	44	10.9%
L20-30	36	30.0%	5	1.7%	12	4.2%	4	1.2%	44	12.7%	16	4.7%	61	15.5%	60	14.9%
L30-40	8	6.7%	16	5.4%	27	9.4%	19	5.8%	85	24.6%	52	15.4%	56	14.2%	57	14.1%
L40-50	11	9.2%	16	5.4%	10	3.5%	7	2.2%	34	9.8%	50	14.8%	25	6.4%	29	7.2%
L50-60	3	2.5%	33	11.2%	55	19.3%	64	19.7%	23	6.6%	62	18.4%	23	5.8%	53	13.2%
L60-70	3	2.5%	37	12.6%	27	9.4%	19	5.8%	13	3.8%	21	6.2%	11	2.8%	23	5.7%
L70-80	3	2.5%	26	8.8%	33	11.6%	55	16.9%	18	5.2%	33	9.8%	9	2.3%	28	6.9%
L80-90	1	0.8%	9	3.1%	20	7.0%	10	3.1%	1	0.3%	9	2.7%	6	1.5%	8	2.0%
L90-100	..	..	25	8.5%	11	3.9%	21	6.5%	8	2.3%	15	4.4%	4	1.0%	19	4.7%
L100-120	1	0.8%	33	11.2%	21	7.4%	28	8.6%	10	2.9%	35	10.4%	5	1.3%	10	2.5%
L120-140	5	4.2%	15	5.1%	16	5.6%	23	7.1%	1	0.3%	7	2.1%	1	0.3%	5	1.2%
L140-160	1	0.8%	22	7.5%	7	2.5%	16	4.9%	1	0.3%	7	2.1%	..	..	5	1.2%
L160-180	..	..	6	2.0%	5	1.8%	9	2.8%	2	0.6%	3	0.9%	..	..	1	0.2%
L180-200	..	..	8	2.7%	7	2.5%	13	4.0%	..	..	5	1.5%	6	1.5%	4	1.0%
L200-250	1	0.8%	10	3.4%	8	2.8%	9	2.8%	3	0.9%	5	1.5%	1	0.3%	1	0.2%
L250-300	..	..	5	1.7%	2	0.7%	9	2.8%	..	..	3	0.9%	1	0.3%	4	1.0%
L300-350	..	..	3	1.0%	1	0.4%	..	..	3	0.9%	3	0.9%	1	0.3%	2	0.5%
L350-400	1	0.8%	3	1.0%	3	1.0%	2	0.6%	..	..	..	..	..	..	2	0.5%
L400-450	..	..	2	0.7%	2	0.7%	1	0.3%	..	..	1	0.3%	..	..	..	..
L450-500	..	..	2	0.7%	..	..	1	0.3%	..	..	..	..	..	..	..	..
L500-550	..	..	..	..	..	..	1	0.3%	..	..	1	0.3%	..	..	..	..
L550-600	..	..	..	..	..	..	2	0.6%	..	..	1	0.3%	..	..	..	..
L600-650	..	..	..	..	..	..	..	..	..	..	1	0.3%	..	..	..	..
L650-700	..	..	..	..	1	0.4%	1	0.3%	..	..	..	..	..	..	..	..
L700-750	..	..	..	..	..	..	..	..	..	..	..	..	..	..	..	..
L750-800	..	..	1	0.3%	..	..	..	..	..	..	..	..	..	..	..	..
L950-1000	..	..	..	..	..	..	1	0.3%	..	..	..	..	..	..	..	..
Totals	120	99.9%	294	99.8%	285	100.0%	325	99.9%	346	100.1%	337	100%	393	100%	403	99.8%

*Sources--N. H. P. P., I, 428; PTR, XIV, XV. To obtain the total taxable estates of each individual it would be necessary to multiply the tax values above by six.

the more important reasons why stratification did not increase was the presence of lucrative opportunities in seafaring and trade, which attracted people of all classes to Portsmouth after 1690 to work as laborers, craftsmen, mariners, fishermen, shopkeepers, and merchants. The expansion of overseas commerce and local merchandising from the 1690's to the 1740's helped forestall economic stratification. Also, increased urbanization in the eastern towns and better transportation facilities (more roads and river and ocean vessels) provided increased demand and a better local market for agricultural products, improving the economic situation for the farming community.[64] Moreover, perhaps the most significant step in breaking down the tensions of land scarcity among the older towns occurred when the New Hampshire General Assembly, responding to various town petitions for land after 1715, granted a series of new western townships in the 1720's and then obtained a highly favorable settlement

TABLE 18

PORTSMOUTH TAXABLE ESTATE PROFILE
(continued)

Tax Value	1729 No.	%	1731 No.	%	1732 No.	%	1735 No.	%	1738 No.	%	1740 No.	%	1741 No.	%
0	24	4.7%	17	3.3%	29	5.4%	19	3.6%	44	8.5%	16	2.8%	13	2.4%
L0-5	..	..	..	..	..	..	..	..	..	..	..	..	..	..
L5-10	..	..	..	..	..	..	..	..	..	..	..	..	..	..
L10-15	18	3.5%	46	8.8%	87	16.3%	32	6.1%	57	11.0%	11	1.9%	7	1.3%
L15-20	..	..	..	..	..	..	..	..	..	..	..	..	..	..
L20-30	30	5.9%	41	7.9%	67	12.6%	62	11.8%	141	27.2%	129	22.9%	10	1.8%
L30-40	50	9.8%	57	10.9%	62	11.6%	83	15.8%	74	14.2%	27	4.8%	51	9.3%
L40-50	77	15.1%	42	8.1%	64	12.0%	67	12.7%	43	8.3%	128	22.7%	83	15.1%
L50-60	58	11.4%	67	12.9%	32	6.0%	24	4.6%	33	6.3%	14	2.5%	30	5.4%
L60-70	..	..	..	..	..	..	..	..	..	..	..	..	..	..
L70-80	37	7.3%	40	7.7%	51	9.6%	69	13.1%	38	7.3%	71	12.6%	90	16.3%
L80-90	25	4.9%	42	8.1%	9	1.7%	12	2.3%	5	1.0%	3	0.5%	14	2.5%
L90-100	47	9.2%	32	6.1%	36	6.8%	49	9.3%	25	4.8%	72	12.8%	29	5.3%
L100-120	50	9.8%	31	6.0%	31	5.8%	39	7.4%	14	2.7%	32	5.7%	68	12.3%
L120-140	5	1.0%	5	1.0%	6	1.1%	4	0.8%	5	1.0%	2	0.4%	1	0.2%
L140-160	8	1.6%	21	4.0%	18	3.4%	21	4.0%	14	2.7%	21	3.7%	42	7.6%
L160-180	15	2.9%	22	4.2%	8	1.5%	8	1.5%	7	1.3%	7	1.2%	31	5.6%
L180-200	12	2.4%	13	2.5%	4	0.8%	3	0.6%	11	2.1%	2	0.4%	5	0.9%
L200-250	28	5.5%	23	4.4%	17	3.2%	16	3.0%	4	0.8%	17	3.0%	42	7.6%
L250-300	17	3.3%	10	1.9%	4	0.8%	9	1.7%	..	..	8	1.4%	17	3.1%
L300-350	3	0.6%	3	0.6%	4	0.8%	4	0.8%	4	0.8%	2	0.4%	1	0.2%
L350-400	1	0.2%	3	0.6%			1	0.2%	..	..	2	0.4%	11	2.0%
L400-450	..	..	..	..	..	..	..	..	..	..	..	..	..	..
L450-500	2	0.4%	..	..	4	0.8%	2	0.4%	..	..	..	..	4	0.7%
L500-550	..	..	..	..	..	..	1	0.2%	..	..	..	..	..	..
L550-600	2	0.4%	5	1.0%	..	..	1	0.2%	..	..	..	..	..	..
L600-650	..	..	..	..	..	..	..	..	..	..	..	..	2	0.4%
L650-700	1	0.2%	..	..	..	..	..	..	..	..	..	..	..	..
L700-750	..	..	..	..	..	..	..	..	..	..	..	..	..	..
L750-800	..	..	1	0.2%	..	..	..	..	..	..	..	..	..	..
L950-1000	..	..	..	..	..	..	..	..	..	..	..	..	..	..
Total	510	100.1%	521	100.2%	533	100.2%	526	100.1%	519	100.0%	564	100.1%	551	100.0%

TABLE 19

PORTSMOUTH TAXABLE ESTATES 1681-1741

	1681	1713	1715	1717	1718	1719	1723	1725
£0-15	24.1%	5.1%	4.9%	1.8%	18.8%	2.4%	38.6%	13.1%
£15-30	44.2%	2.4%	5.2%	2.4%	22.8%	5.9%	24.4%	25.8%
£30-40	6.7%	5.4%	9.4%	5.8%	24.6%	15.4%	14.2%	14.1%
£40-50	9.2%	5.4%	3.5%	2.2%	9.8%	14.8%	6.4%	7.2%
£50-80	7.5%	32.6%	40.3%	42.4%	15.6%	34.4%	10.9%	25.8%
£80-100	0.8%	11.6%	10.9%	9.6%	2.6%	7.1%	2.5%	6.7%
£100-160	5.8%	23.8%	15.5%	20.6%	3.5%	14.6%	1.6%	3.9%
£160-up	1.6%	13.8%	10.3%	14.8%	2.4%	5.4%	2.4%	3.2%

	1729	1731	1732	1735	1738	1740	1741
£0-15	8.2%	12.1%	21.7%	9.7%	19.5%	4.7%	3.7%
£15-30	5.9%	7.9%	12.6%	11.8%	27.2%	22.9%	1.8%
£30-40	9.8%	10.9%	11.6%	15.8%	14.2%	4.8%	9.3%
£40-50	15.1%	8.1%	12.0%	12.7%	8.3%	22.7%	15.1%
£50-80	18.7%	20.6%	15.6%	17.7%	13.6%	15.1%	21.7%
£80-100	14.1%	14.2%	8.5%	11.6%	5.8%	13.3%	7.8%
£100-160	12.4%	11.0%	10.3%	12.2%	6.4%	9.8%	20.1%
£160-up	15.9%	15.4%	7.9%	8.6%	5.0%	6.8%	20.5%

Sources--N.H.P.P., I, 428; P.T.R., XIV, XV

TABLE 20

PORTSMOUTH ECONOMIC PROFILES, 1660-1735*

Persons	Land Proportion 1660	Tax 1681	Tax 1715	Tax 1735
Upper 5%	34.4%	25.5%	17.7%	19.1%
Upper 10%	42.5%	39.0%	28.5%	31.7%
Upper 33 1/3%	82.4%	67.9%	59.6%	63.8%
Middle 33 1/3%	8.2%	20.1%	26.8%	26.5%
Lower 33 1/3%	9.4%	12.0%	13.6%	9.7%
Lower 10%	3.1%	2.7%	1.7%	1.0%

1732 and 1735

1732 Percent of Persons	Polls	L Value	Percent of Total Taxable Property
Upper 10%	53	L11,851	34.3%
Upper 33 1/3%	178	L23,978	69.4%
Middle 33 1/3%	177	L 8,175	23.7%
Lower 33 1/3%	178	L 2,383	6.9%
Bottom 10%	53	L 264	0.8%
Total	533	L34,536	. .

1735 Percent of Persons	Polls	L Value	Percent of Total Taxable Property
Upper 10%	53	L12,926	31.7%
Upper 33 1/3%	175	L26,016	63.8%
Middle 33 1/3%	176	L10,844	26.5%
Lower 33 1/3%	175	L 3,948	9.7%
Bottom 10%	53	L 398	1.0%
Total	526	L40,808	. .

*The land proportion of 1660 may be found in Brewster, I, 26-27; the tax of 1681 may be found in N.H.P.P., I, 428; and the taxes of 1715 and 1735 may be found in PTR, XIV, 75-82 and XV, 346-66. The percentages under each year above represent the per cent of the total taxable property that the various groups of taxpayers owned.

of the Massachusetts-New Hampshire boundary dispute in 1740. These developments postponed some of the problems of land scarcity in the colony for another forty years and forestalled further local economic stratification for a time.[65]

Ultimately, Dover's economic experience—increased economic stratification during the seventeenth century and decreased stratification during the early eighteenth century, with fluctuations paralleling economic crises—was probably the general pattern for most of the early New Hampshire towns before 1740. Exeter and Portsmouth were exceptions; Exeter retained a low stratification level, while Portsmouth gradually increased in stratification. While the New Hampshire economy expanded significantly between 1713 and 1740, bringing specific socioeconomic

TABLE 21

NEW CASTLE ECONOMIC PROFILES*

% Taxed	1677	1708	1720
Upper 10%	31.3%	28.1%	27.2%
Upper 33 1/3%	61.0%	63.8%	60.5%
Middle 33 1/3%	23.7%	23.9%	22.5%
Lower 33 1/3%	15.3%	12.3%	17.0%
Bottom 10%	3.5%	2.1%	3.7%

*The percentages under each year above represent the per cent of the total taxable property that the various classifications of taxpayers owned.

NEW CASTLE TAX PROFILE, 1720

Tax Valuation	No. of Polls	% of Taxpayers
£ 0–5	0	0.0%
£ 5–10	2	1.6%
£ 10–15	3	2.5%
£ 15–20	2	1.6%
£ 20–30	52	42.6%
£ 30–40	16	13.1%
£ 40–50	8	6.6%
£ 50–60	11	9.0%
£ 60–70	5	4.1%
£ 70–80	4	3.3%
£ 80–90	6	4.9%
£ 90–100	2	1.6%
£ 100–120	6	4.9%
£ 120–140	1	0.8%
£ 140–160	2	1.6%
£ 160–180	1	0.8%
£ 180–200	1	0.8%
TOTALS	122	99.8%

changes in various towns, the overall economic structure of New Hampshire's society remained relatively constant and open.

Preferred Roles and Values in the Dynamic Social Structure

Within the context of the physical and economic growth of New Hampshire society and the changing modes of social organization, certain specific social, economic, and political roles emerged as preferable to the New Hampshire settlers during their first century of experience.

In the period before 1660 most of the New Hampshire towns existed as relatively isolated religious and agricultural frontier communities. Within these communities religious piety, stewardship, social and economic service to the community (as represented in the concept of freeman-

TABLE 22

GREENLAND ECONOMIC PROFILE, 1720

Percent Taxed	Percent of Total Taxable Property
Upper 10%	27.3%
Upper 33 1/3%	58.2%
Middle 33 1/3%	27.5%
Lower 33 1/3%	14.3%
Bottom 10%	3.8%

Tax Valuation	No. of Polls	Percent of Taxpayers
£ 0	. .	. .
£ 0–5	. .	. .
£ 5–10	. .	. .
£ 10–15	. .	. .
£ 15–20	4	5.3%
£ 20–30	19	25.0%
£ 30–40	10	13.2%
£ 40–50	5	6.6%
£ 50–60	16	21.1%
£ 60–70	3	3.9%
£ 70–80	5	6.6%
£ 80–90	2	2.6%
£ 90–100	. .	. .
£ 100–120	6	7.9%
£ 120–140	2	2.6%
£ 140–160	2	2.6%
£ 160–180	2	2.6%
TOTALS	76	100.0%

ship), and economic achievement (through trade in Portsmouth and Dover and through agriculture in Exeter and Hampton) typified the settlers' most significant values. During these early years of settlement the various communities rewarded those able and aggressive men who willingly assumed leadership in projecting these dominant values with special land and timber grants, lucrative subsidies and monopolies, and election to positions of political authority in the town. Such positions included the offices of ruler, selectman, and deputy to the Massachusetts General Court, as well as local nomination for judicial and military posts (magistrates, assistants, and militia commanders appointed by the Massachusetts government).[66] Having attained high social, economic, and political status locally, the more aggressive and ambitious of such men found it relatively easy to augment their status so that they acquired high social prestige regionally as well. The lives of Thomas Wiggin, Bryan Pendleton, Edward Hilton, and Richard Waldron exemplify this trend.[67]

TABLE 23

DOVER ECONOMIC PROFILE 1648-1741*

Persons Taxed	1648	1663	1680	1741
Upper 10%	17.7%	31.1%	35.0%	27.2%
Upper 33 1/3%	41.0%	65.2%	72.6%	59.5%
Middle 33 1/3%	46.7%	23.0%	22.2%	26.2%
Lower 33 1/3%	12.3%	11.8%	5.2%	14.3%
Bottom 10%	1.5%	2.3%	0.1%	3.6%

1741

Percent of Persons	Polls	L Value	Percent of Total Taxable Property
Upper 10%	27	L10,751	27.2%
Upper 33 1/3%	88	L23,540	59.5%
Middle 33 1/3%	89	L10,360	26.2%
Lower 33 1/3%	88	L 5,655	14.3%
Bottom 10%	27	L 1,430	3.6%
Totals	265	L39,555	. .

TAX PROFILE, 1741

Tax Valuation	No. of Polls	Percent of Taxpayers
L0-10	1	0.4%
L10-20	. .	. .
L20-30	. .	. .
L30-40	. .	. .
L40-50	1	0.4%
L50-60	26	9.8%
L60-70	43	16.2%
L70-80	15	5.7%
L80-90	11	4.1%
L90-100	18	6.8%
L100-120	22	8.3%
L120-140	22	8.3%
L140-160	15	5.7%
L160-180	17	6.4%
L180-200	15	5.7%
L200-250	22	8.3%
L250-300	9	3.4%
L300-350	13	4.9%
L350-400	5	1.9%
L400-450	1	0.4%
L450-500	4	1.5%
L500-550	3	1.1%
L550-600	2	0.8%
Totals	265	100.1%

*The most accessible source for the Dover tax lists of 1648 and 1663 is Scales, I,
234-36, 244-46. The tax of 1680 is printed in N.H.P.P., I, 427, and the tax list
for 1741 is in Ibid., XXIV, 697-700. The percentages under each year above represent
the per cent of the total taxable property that the various groups of taxpayers owned.

TABLE 24

NEW HAMPSHIRE ECONOMIC PROFILE 1681[a]

Percentage Taxed	Portsmouth			Dover			Hampton			Exeter			New Hampshire[b]		
	Polls	L Value	%	Polls	L Value	%	Polls	L Value	%	Polls	L Value	%	Polls	L Value	%
Upper 10%	12	L1,681	39.0%	12	L 805	35.0%	12	L1,081	24.9%	6	L 637	30.2%	42	L4,204	32.2%
Upper 33 1/3%	40	L2,929	67.9%	39	L1,670	72.6%	40	L2,504	57.7%	21	L1,397	66.3%	140	L8,500	65.1%
Middle 33 1/3%	40	L 865	20.1%	40	L 511	22.2%	41	L1,314	30.3%	22	L 522	24.8%	143	L3,212	24.6%
Lower 33 1/3%	40	L 518	12.0%	39	L 119	5.2%	40	L 520	12.0%	21	L 188	8.9%	140	L1,345	10.3%
Lower 10%	12	L 117	2.7%	12	L 3	0.1%	12	L 70	1.6%	6	L 40	1.9%	42	L 230	1.8%
Total polls & estate values	120	L4,312	..	118	L2,300	..	121	L4,338	..	64	L2,107	..	423	L13,057	..

Taxable Estate Values	Portsmouth		Dover		Hampton		Exeter		New Hampshire[b]	
	Polls	%	Polls	%	Polls	%	Polls	%	Polls	%
0	1	0.8%	6	5.1%	0	0	0	0	7	1.7%
L0-5	1	0.8%	23	19.5%	1	0.8%	0	0	25	5.9%
L5-10	1	0.8%	25	21.1%	14	11.6%	13	20.3%	53	12.5%
L10-20	43	35.9%	20	17.0%	18	14.9%	15	23.4%	96	22.7%
L20-30	36	30.0%	20	17.0%	22	18.2%	15	23.4%	93	22.0%
L30-40	8	6.7%	5	4.2%	22	18.2%	2	3.1%	37	8.7%
L40-50	11	9.2%	7	5.9%	16	13.2%	5	7.8%	39	9.2%
L50-60	3	2.5%	4	3.4%	12	9.9%	5	7.8%	24	5.7%
L60-80	6	5.0%	5	4.2%	8	6.6%	5	7.8%	24	5.7%
L80-100	1	0.8%	3	2.5%	4	3.3%	2	3.1%	10	2.4%
L100-150	7	5.8%	0	0	4	3.3%	0	0	11	2.6%
L150-200	0	0	0	0	0	0	2	3.1%	2	0.5%
L200-300	1	0.8%	0	0	0	0	0	0	1	0.2%
L300-400	1	0.8%	0	0	0	0	0	0	1	0.2%
Totals	120	99.9%	118	99.9%	121	100.0%	64	99.8%	423	100.0%

[a]Based upon taxable estate ownership from N.H.P.P., I, 424-28.
[b]These figures represent the combined statistics of the four towns.

TABLE 25

PROFILE OF PROPERTY OWNERSHIP AS DETERMINED BY WILL INVENTORIES

	1640-1715		1716-1740	
Inventory Values	No. of Wills	% of Total Inventories	No. of Wills	% of Total Inventories
L0-50	42	13.7%	27	6.7%
L50-100	60	19.6%	29	7.2%
L100-150	45	14.7%	37	9.2%
L150-200	30	9.8%	28	7.0%
L200-250	16	5.2%	21	5.2%
L250-300	20	6.5%	23	5.7%
L300-350	11	3.6%	26	6.5%
L350-400	17	5.6%	13	3.2%
L400-450	12	3.9%	21	5.2%
L450-500	7	2.3%	19	4.7%
L500-600	9	2.9%	20	5.0%
L600-700	9	2.9%	23	5.7%
L700-800	3	1.0%	12	3.0%
L800-900	6	2.0%	13	3.2%
L900-1000	3	1.0%	12	3.0%
L1000-1250	7	2.3%	20	5.0%
L1250-1500	5	1.6%	14	3.5%
L1500-2000	0	0	17	4.2%
L2000-2500	3	1.0%	10	2.5%
L2500-3000	1	0.3%	4	1.0%
L3000-5000	0	0	6	1.5%
L5000-10,000	0	0	4	1.0%
L10,000-20,000	0	0	2	0.5%
Total	306	99.9%	401	99.7%

	1640-1740	
Inventory Values	No. of Wills	% of Total Inventories
L0-50	69	9.8%
L50-100	89	12.6%
L100-200	140	19.8%
L200-250	37	5.2%
L250-300	43	6.1%
L300-400	67	9.5%
L400-500	59	8.3%
L500-600	29	4.1%
L600-700	32	4.5%
L700-800	15	2.1%
L800-900	19	2.7%
L900-1000	15	2.1%
L1000-1500	46	6.5%
L1500-2000	17	2.4%
L2000-4000	24	3.4%
L4000-10,000	4	0.6%
L10,000-20,000	2	0.3%
Total	707	100%

Captain Thomas Wiggin (d. 1663) led a group of English Puritans to Dover in 1633 and, assuming leadership of the community, parceled out land and served as the town's political and judicial authority. His correspondence with Governor Winthrop and acceptance of Massachusetts freemanship encouraged the Massachusetts government to assert its

TABLE 26

PROFILE OF PROPERTY OWNERSHIP AS DETERMINED BY WILL INVENTORIES

Inventory Value	No. of Inventories	% of Total Inventories	% of Property Owned
1640-1715			
L0 - 50	42	13.7%	1.4%
L50 - 250	151	49.3%	21.1%
L250 - 500	67	21.9%	26.7%
L500 - 1000	30	9.8%	23.7%
L1000 - 2000	12	3.9%	16.7%
L2000 - 3000	4	1.3%	10.5%
Total	306	99.9%	100.1%

Total Value   L89,159.16s.2d.

1716-1740			
L0 - 50	27	6.7%	0.2%
L50 - 250	115	28.7%	5.6%
L250 - 500	102	25.4%	12.3%
L500 - 1000	80	20%	19.7%
L1000 - 2000	51	12.7%	24.3%
L2000 - 20,000	26	6.5%	39.3%
Total	401	100%	101.4%

Total Value L290,478.19s.

1640-1740			
L0 - 50	69	9.8%	0.5%
L50 - 250	266	37.6%	9.2%
L250 - 500	169	23.9%	15.7%
L500 - 1000	110	15.6%	20.7%
L1000 - 2000	63	8.9%	22.5%
L2000 - 30,000	30	4.2%	32.5%
Total	707	100%	101.1%

Total Value   L379,638.15s.2d.

TABLE 27

COMPARATIVE TOWN PROFILES TAKEN FROM ESTATE INVENTORIES 1640-1740

Amount of Inventory	Portsmouth No.	Portsmouth %	Hampton No.	Hampton %	Dover No.	Dover %	Exeter No.	Exeter %
L0-50	23	12.6%	4	2.9%	16	15.4%	12	17.1%
L50-100	21	11.5%	12	8.8%	9	8.7%	5	7.1%
L100-150	24	13.1%	16	11.7%	10	9.6%	4	5.7%
L150-200	11	6.0%	8	5.8%	8	7.7%	4	5.7%
L200-250	11	6.0%	7	5.1%	8	7.7%	4	5.7%
L250-500	41	22.4%	45	32.8%	27	26.0%	15	21.4%
L500-1000	22	12.0%	26	19.0%	16	15.4%	15	21.4%
L1000-2000	16	8.7%	14	10.2%	9	8.7%	8	11.4%
L2000-5000	10	5.5%	5	3.6%	1	1.0%	1	1.4%
L5000-20,000	4	2.2%	0	0	0	0	2	2.9%
Totals	183	100%	137	99.9%	104	100.2%	70	99.8%

Amount of Inventory	Newcastle No.	Newcastle %	Durham No.	Durham %	Stratham No.	Stratham %	Kingston No.	Kingston %	Isles of Shoals No.	Isles of Shoals %
L0-50	7	16.3%	7	20.6%	1	4.5%	1	3.6%	2	8.7%
L50-100	7	16.3%	8	23.5%	1	4.5%	3	10.7%	5	21.7%
L100-150	6	14.0%	9	26.5%	0	0	7	25.0%	1	4.3%
L150-200	1	2.3%	3	8.8%	5	22.7%	6	21.4%	2	8.7%
L200-250	2	4.7%	0	0	1	4.5%	0	0	0	0
L250-500	7	16.3%	2	5.9%	4	18.2%	3	10.7%	7	30.4%
L500-1000	4	9.3%	3	8.8%	4	18.2%	6	21.4%	4	17.4%
L1000-2000	5	11.6%	1	2.9%	2	9.1%	1	3.6%	2	8.7%
L2000-5000	3	7.0%	1	2.9%	3	13.6%	1	3.6%	0	0
L5000-20,000	1	2.3%	0	0	1	4.5%	0	0	0	0
Totals	43	100.1%	34	99.9%	22	99.9%	28	100%	23	99.9%

jurisdiction in the Piscataqua region. In 1643 Wiggin was appointed an associate judge for Norfolk County (which included all the New Hampshire towns), and from 1650 until his death he served as the presiding associate judge, enforcing Massachusetts judicial values from the most powerful judicial post in the Piscataqua region. During the 1640's and 1650's he acquired a large land grant in the Squamscott Patent, built some

TABLE 28

TOWN ECONOMIC STRUCTURE FROM PROBATED ESTATES

Town	Values	1640-1715		1716-1740		1640-1740	
		No. of People	% of Total	No. of People	% of Total	No. of People	% of Total
Hampton	£0-50	4	4.8%	0	0	4	2.9%
	£50-250	37	44.6%	6	11.1%	43	31.4%
	£250-500	25	30.1%	20	37.0%	45	32.8%
	£500-1000	14	16.9%	12	22.2%	26	19.0%
	£1000-2000	2	2.4%	12	22.2%	14	10.2%
	£2000-20,000	1	1.2%	4	7.4%	5	3.6%
	Total	83	100%	54	99.9%	137	99.9%
Portsmouth	£0-50	11	14.3%	12	11.3%	23	12.6%
	£50-250	32	41.6%	35	33.0%	67	36.6%
	£250-500	19	24.7%	22	20.8%	41	22.4%
	£500-1000	10	13.0%	12	11.3%	22	12.0%
	£1000-2000	4	5.2%	12	11.3%	16	8.7%
	£2000-20,000	1	1.3%	13	12.3%	14	7.7%
	Total	77	100.1%	106	100.0%	183	100%
Newcastle	£0-50	4	20%	3	13.0%	7	16.3%
	£50-250	9	45%	7	30.4%	16	37.2%
	£250-500	4	20%	3	13.0%	7	16.3%
	£500-1000	1	5%	3	13.0%	4	9.3%
	£1000-2000	0	0	5	21.7%	5	11.6%
	£2000-20,000	2	10%	2	8.7%	4	9.3%
	Total	20	100%	23	99.8%	43	100%
Kingston	£0-50	1	16.7%	0	0	1	3.6%
	£50-250	5	83.3%	11	50.0%	16	57.1%
	£250-500	0	0	3	13.6%	3	10.7%
	£500-1000	0	0	6	27.3%	6	21.4%
	£1000-2000	0	0	1	4.5%	1	3.6%
	£2000-20,000	0	0	1	4.5%	1	3.6%
	Total	6	100%	22	99.9%	28	100%
Exeter	£0-50	9	25.0%	3	8.8%	15	17.1%
	£50-250	10	27.8%	7	20.6%	17	24.3%
	£250-500	7	19.4%	8	23.5%	15	21.4%
	£500-1000	5	13.9%	10	29.4%	15	21.4%
	£1000-2000	5	13.9%	3	8.8%	8	11.4%
	£2000-20,000	0	0	3	8.8%	3	4.3%
	Total	36	100%	34	99.9%	70	99.9%
Dover	£0-50	11	24.4%	4	6.8%	11	14.4%
	£50-250	21	46.7%	14	23.7%	35	33.7%
	£250-500	10	22.2%	17	28.8%	27	26.0%
	£500-1000	2	4.4%	15	25.4%	17	16.3%
	£1000-2000	0	0	9	15.3%	9	8.7%
	£2000-20,000	1	2.2%	0	0	1	1.0%
	Total	45	99.9%	59	100.0%	104	100.1%
Durham	£0-50	7	28%	3	33.3%	10	29.4%
	£50-250	17	68%	1	11.1%	18	52.9%
	£250-500	1	4%	2	22.2%	3	8.8%
	£500-1000	0	0	2	22.2%	2	5.9%
	£1000-2000	0	0	1	11.1%	1	2.9%
	£2000-20,000	0	0	0	0	0	0
	Total	25	100%	9	99.9%	34	99.9%

TABLE 29

OCCUPATIONAL ECONOMIC STRUCTURE FROM PROBATED ESTATES

Occupation	Property Value	1640-1715		1716-1740		1640-1740	
		No. of People	% of Total	No. of People	% of Total	No. of People	% of Total
Farmer	L0-50	20	13.7%	7	3.8%	27	8.2%
	L50-250	78	53.4%	50	27.2%	128	38.8%
	L250-500	33	22.6%	53	28.8%	86	26.1%
	L500-1000	13	8.9%	40	21.7%	53	16.1%
	L1000-2000	2	1.4%	22	12.0%	24	7.3%
	L2000-20,000	0	0	12	6.5%	12	3.6%
	Total	146	100%	184	100%	330	100.1%
Farmer Lumberer	L0-50	0	0	1	2.1%	1	1.6%
	L50-250	4	22.2%	9	19.1%	13	17.5%
	L250-500	5	27.8%	14	29.8%	19	29.2%
	L500-1000	3	16.7%	16	34.0%	19	29.2%
	L1000-2000	4	22.2%	6	12.8%	10	16.9%
	L2000-20,000	2	11.1%	1	2.1%	3	4.6%
	Total	18	100%	47	99.9%	65	100%
Laborer	L0-50	8	61.5%	10	45.5%	18	51.4%
	L50-250	5	38.5%	11	50.0%	19	45.7%
	L250-500	0	0	0	0	0	0
	L500-1000	0	0	1	4.5%	1	2.9%
	L1000-2000	0	0	0	0	0	0
	L2000-20,000	0	0	0	0	0	0
	Total	13	100%	22	100%	35	100%
Skilled Laborer and Craftsman	L0-50	5	15.6%	3	5.6%	8	9.3%
	L50-250	20	62.5%	17	31.5%	37	43.0%
	L250-500	5	15.6%	16	29.6%	21	24.4%
	L500-1000	1	3.1%	9	16.7%	10	11.6%
	L1000-2000	1	3.1%	5	9.3%	6	7.0%
	L2000-20,000	0	0	4	7.4%	4	4.7%
	Total	32	99.9%	54	100.0%	86	100.0%
Fisherman	L0-50	1	5.9%	0	0	1	3.2%
	L50-250	10	58.8%	4	28.6%	14	45.2%
	L250-500	3	17.6%	5	35.7%	8	25.8%
	L500-1000	2	11.8%	2	14.3%	4	12.9%
	L1000-2000	1	5.9%	3	21.4%	4	12.9%
	L2000-20,000	0	0	0	0	0	0
	Total	17	100.0%	14	100%	31	100%
Mariner	L0-50	1	4%	1	4.8%	2	4.3%
	L50-250	12	48%	7	33.3%	19	41.3%
	L250-500	8	32%	8	38.1%	16	34 8%
	L500-1000	4	16%	1	4.8%	5	10.9%
	L1000-2000	0	0	3	14.3%	3	6.5%
	L2000-20,000	0	0	1	4.8	1	2.2%
	Total	25	100%	21	100.1%	46	100%
Merchant	L0-50	1	5%	0	0	1	2.7%
	L50-250	7	35%	1	5.9%	8	21.6%
	L250-500	4	20%	1	5.9%	5	13.5%
	L500-1000	4	20%	6	35.3%	10	27.0%
	L1000-2000	2	10%	3	17.6%	5	13.5%
	L2000-20,000	2	10%	6	35.3%	8	21.6%
	Total	20	100%	17	100%	37	100%
Professionals	L0-50	2	22.2%	2	13.3%	4	16.7%
	L50-250	0	0	5	33.3%	5	20.8%
	L250-500	4	44.4%	2	13.3%	6	25.0%
	L500-1000	3	33.3%	1	6.7%	4	16.7%
	L1000-2000	0	0	3	20.0%	3	12.5%
	L2000-20,000	0	0	2	13.3%	2	8.3%
	Total	9	99.9%	15	99.9%	24	100%

TABLE 30

EXETER TOWN LAND GRANT PROFILE, 1725

Acres Granted	No. of Persons	Percent of Total Persons
20	23	9.2%
30	54	21.7%
40	23	9.2%
50-100	69	27.7%
100-150	30	12.0%
150-200	18	7.2%
200-300	15	6.0%
300-400	9	3.6%
400-500	6	2.4%
550	1	0.4%
830	1	0.4%
TOTALS	249	99.8%

Source--Bell, 141-44.

sawmills, and became involved in the lumber trade. By 1660 the "Worshipful Captain Wiggin" owned one of the largest estates in the Piscataqua region and had established his family name as one of the leading names of New Hampshire.[68]

Bryan Pendleton (1602–81) had originally settled in Sudbury, Massachusetts, where he obtained land, became a freeman, and was elected selectman six times. A restless, enterprising man, he moved in 1651 to Strawbery Banke as an agent for William Paine, a Boston merchant, and was instrumental in carrying through the peaceful acceptance of Massachusetts patterns there during the 1650's. He obtained appointments from Massachusetts as associate justice and militia commander for Portsmouth by 1652. He was elected Portsmouth selectman and deputy to the General Court repeatedly from 1652 to 1664 and served as town treasurer from 1654 to 1663. During the 1650's he became involved in the timber trade and fisheries and acquired large quantities of land, owning approximately 2,000 acres (including Timber Island) at his death.[69]

TABLE 31

EXETER ECONOMIC PROFILE 1680-1732*

Persons Taxed	1680	1718	1725	1732
Upper 10%	30.2%	28.3%	39.0%	27.0%
Upper 33 1/3%	66.3%	60.3%	71.3%	66.8%
Middle 33 1/3%	24.8%	24.5%	18.5%	27.3%
Lower 33 1/3%	8.9%	15.2%	10.2%	5.9%
Lower 10%	1.9%	2.9%	2.2%	0.0%

1718 Percent of Persons	Polls	L Value	Percent of Total Taxable Property
Upper 10%	21	L 2,715	28.3%
Upper 33 1/3%	69	L 5,673	60.3%
Middle 33 1/3%	70	L 2,302	24.5%
Lower 33 1/3%	69	L 1,426	15.2%
Bottom 10%	21	L 270	2.9%
Totals	208	L 9,401	. .

1718 Tax Valuation	No. of Polls	Percent of Taxpayers
0	1	0.5%
L0-10	4	1.9%
L10-15	2	1.0%
L15-20	35	16.8%
L20-30	43	20.7%
L30-40	40	19.2%
L40-50	20	9.6%
L50-60	13	6.2%
L60-70	14	6.7%
L70-80	13	6.2%
L80-90	2	1.0%
L90-100	6	2.9%
L100-120	2	1.0%
L120-140	8	3.8%
L140-160	1	0.5%
L160-200	2	1.0%
L200-250	2	1.0%
Totals	208	100.0%

*N.H.P.P., I, 426 has the Province tax of 1680. For the tax of 1718 see ETR, I,
56-57. The figures for 1725 are derived from the town acreage distribution of
that year which was based upon the proportion of the Province tax each person
paid. The distribution may be most easily found in Bell, 141-44. The figures
for 1732 are in N.H. Inventories, 1727-1773. The percentages under each year
above represent the per cent of the total taxable property that the various
groups of taxpayers owned.

In contrast to Wiggin and Pendleton, Edward Hilton (1600–1671), the founder of Dover, was an Anglican fish trader who, after Wiggin's arrival, held himself aloof from Massachusetts during the 1630's by purchasing an estate between Dover and Exeter. Because of his widely known Anglican views, Hilton received an appointment as associate justice at Piscataqua in 1641 as a matter of diplomacy on the part of the Massachusetts government. During the 1640's and 1650's he expanded his holdings and went into the lumber business, amassing a small fortune of £2,204 by 1671, and establishing a family name of first rank in the lumber trade.[70]

The outstanding example, however, was Richard Waldron (1615–89). Waldron, a man of relatively high social status in England, came to New England in the late 1630's, lived in Boston for two years, and moved to Dover by 1640. He purchased a town lot from Thomas Wiggin and a large tract by Cochecho Falls, where he built a sawmill and an Indian trading post and engaged in the lumber and fur trade with Boston merchants. By the mid-1640's Waldron was a popular town freeman serving as a selectman. His willingness to serve the community brought him fishing monopolies and a series of land and timber grants for new mills. By the 1650's his business affairs included shipbuilding, masting, and a flourishing overseas trade with the West Indies and England. Waldron's enterprise stimulated Dover's economy, and the townspeople rewarded him by consistently electing him deputy to the Massachusetts General Court from 1654 through 1679. Waldron's abilities so impressed the Massachusetts deputies that they elected him Speaker of the House in seven different sessions. The General Court also appointed Waldron as associate justice and magistrate for Norfolk County (which included the Piscataqua region), as Dover militia commander, and ultimately, in 1675, as major in command of all troops north of the Merrimack River. In 1662 he received a special commission to prosecute Quaker "errors" at Dover and carried out his task with unwonted zeal. By the mid-1660's, Waldron had obtained perhaps 5,000 acres of land and was probably the richest man in the Piscataqua region. He was the primary target of the Masonian proprietors and the local moving spirit of the new New Hampshire government during the 1680's. More than any other individual, Richard Waldron exemplified the values of the aggressive, intelligent Puritan in a frontier society. His prestige and power in New Hampshire from 1650 to 1689 far surpassed that of any other Piscataqua settler. Throughout the entire colonial period his family continued among those of highest rank in New Hampshire.[71]

None of the four men discussed above were ordinary men—all had important social status before settling in the Piscataqua region. Yet all of them gradually found commercial pursuits the most effective means of increasing their economic status. Because ownership of land was the traditional symbol of status, each accumulated real property; but in their quest for economic expansion and prosperity they sought commercial success in markets at Boston and overseas. By doing so, they established Piscataqua patterns of economic activity that would remain dominant throughout the colonial period.

In the meantime, ambitious newcomers and many of the agricultural settlers already in the region began to emulate these social leaders by accepting whatever economic roles seemed personally applicable, becoming carpenters, fishermen, mariners, coopers, lumberers, liquor retailers, and mast traders as well as farmers. Hyphenated occupations became common as mercantile activities became more desirable. Newcomers and some of the earlier agricultural families who earned profits from trade and increased their economic status now sought increased social status by imitating the social patterns established by existing leaders. Thus, the nouveau riches of the late seventeenth and early eighteenth centuries—the Vaughans, Partridges, Wentworths, Peirces, Jaffreys, Wibirds, Sherburnes, Halls, Coffins, Penhallows, Weares, Folsoms, Gerrishes, Tuttles, Wingates, Wallingsfords, Westbrooks, Atkinsons, Plaisteds, Packers, Millets, Clarksons, Odiornes, Frosts, and Waltons—sought increased status by espousing accepted values and by obtaining political recognition through election as selectmen, representatives to the New Hampshire House of Representatives, or other prestigious town offices or through political appointment to such royal offices as judge, justice of the peace, treasurer, secretary, sheriff, or councillor.

The Piscataqua society of the mid-seventeenth century was a relatively open and undifferentiated society. Most people possessed farms and met town suffrage qualifications. Both the rich and the poor worked as farmers, lumberers, fishermen, laborers, craftsmen, and mariners. Those who obtained high status had usually brought some of it with them and then improved it through energetic economic and social behavior which benefited the community. Political and social authority was exercised by a relatively small number of town families, although participation in town officeholding was relatively egalitarian (see Tables 32 and 34).[72] In some cases, men with high social status, such as ministers and teachers, had received gifts of land to raise their economic status.

By the late seventeenth century, however, economic pressures in the open, expanding Piscataqua economy brought both greater emphasis upon success in overseas trade and increased social approval to those who prospered in trade. At the same time the extension in New Hampshire of a royal authority whose officials opposed both the values and the power of Massachusetts introduced alternative values which tended to undermine some older values in the colony. Where, originally, men of high social status had been given equivalently high economic and political status

through land grants and election or appointment to positions of authority, after 1660 men who desired higher social status used these economic
and political trappings as stepping stones and as ends in themselves. The
absence of any permanent symbol of status (such as a patent of nobility)
coupled with the presence of an open economy and competing values
provided ample opportunities for aggressive men in each generation to
contend effectively for the highest rank in the colony. And since economic
power emanated from trade, most of the pressure for increased political
and social stature came from those men who engaged in commerce.[73]

By the early eighteenth century the political positions most sought
after were at the province level, particularly the position of governor,
lieutenant governor, councillor, judge, secretary, treasurer, and justice of
the peace.[74] The main avenues to these positions lay in advantageous
trade connections in England and in New Hampshire, election to the
House of Representatives and good performance there,[75] marriage alliances or some other kind of economic or political alliance with the
leading families in the colony, a residence in Portsmouth at the center of
royal government in the colony, or some combination of these. Among
leading mercantile families, intermarriage was a particularly significant
method of achieving higher social status. The Cutts, Vaughans, Waldrons, Frosts, Gerrishes, Westbrooks, Plaisteds, Martyns, Joses, Huskes,
Coffins, Russells, Penhallows, Partridges, Belchers, Pepperrells, and
Sparhawks had established important family connections through marriage between 1670 and 1740. So did the Gilman, Folsom, and Thing
families of Exeter and the Wentworths, Hunkings, Wiggins, Sherburnes,
Langdons, Peirces, Ushers, Odiornes, Jaffreys, Jeffries, Atkinsons, Wibirds, and Packers at Portsmouth and Boston.[76] Almost all the prominent
men in New Hampshire's mercantile community had kinship relationships with each other by the 1730's.

During the late seventeenth and early eighteenth centuries, energetic
New Hampshire settlers pursued certain economic roles more aggressively than others. Domination of the mast trade, for example, became the
foremost goal of New Hampshire lumberers and merchants between 1690
and 1742. Those who were most successful in this quest obtained both
wealth and social status in a colony of lumber producers. Bernard Bailyn
assessed the situation for New Hampshire accurately when he portrayed
the mast trade as a "precipitant of the emerging social structure of New
England."[77] Almost every comparatively wealthy man in New Hampshire
had a hand in the mast trade, either as a lumber contractor or as a
merchant.

The basic avenue to wealth and increased social status in New
Hampshire society followed a general pattern: an enterprising farmer,
fisherman, craftsman, or mariner sells some lumber on the Boston

TABLE 32

COMPARATIVE OFFICEHOLDING AMONG NEW HAMPSHIRE SELECTMEN

Portsmouth

1652-1682

37 men held 130 offices (3.5 opm*)

No. of Men	No. of Offices	% of Total Offices
1 man	13	10.0%
top 10%	42	32.3%
top 20%	65	50.0%
top 33 1/3%	88	67.7%

1690-1740

83 men held 251 offices (3.0 opm)

No. of Men	No. of Offices	% of Total Offices
1 man	14	5.6%
top 10%	74	29.5%
top 20%	120	47.8%
top 33 1/3%	159	63.3%

Dover

1647-1677

32 men held 134 offices (4.2 opm)

No. of Men	No. of Offices	% of Total Offices
1 man	19	14.2%
top 10%	36	26.9%
top 20%	57	42.5%
top 33 1/3%	87	64.9%

1694-1744

61 men held 214 offices (3.5 opm)

No. of Men	No. of Offices	% of Total Offices
1 man	15	7.0%
top 10%	75	35.0%
top 20%	117	54.7%
top 33 1/3%	155	72.4%

Hampton

1650-1680

58 men held 183 offices (3.2 opm)

No. of Men	No. of Offices	% of Total Offices
1 man	12	6.6%
top 10%	51	27.9%
top 20%	86	47.0%
top 1/3%	114	62.3%

1692-1742

120 men held 252 offices (2.1 opm)

No. of Men	No. of Offices	% of Total Offices
1 man	9	3.6%
top 10%	74	29.4%
top 20%	112	44.4%
top 1/3%	152	60.3%

Exeter

1647-1677

22 men held 71 offices (3.2 opm)

No. of Men	No. of Offices	% of Total Offices
1 man	12	16.9%
top 10%	18	25.3%
top 20%	29	40.8%
top 33 1/3%	42	59.2%

1690-1740

67 men held 223 offices (3.3 opm)

No. of Men	No. of Offices	% of Total Offices
1 man	14	6.3%
top 10%	71	31.8%
top 20%	116	52.0%
top 1/3%	152	68.2%

Londonderry

1720-1760

69 men held 194 offices (2.8 opm)

No. of Men	No. of Offices	% of Total Offices
1 man	10	5.2%
top 10%	49	25.3%
top 20%	87	44.8%
top 33 1/3%	118	60.8%

20.0%

market, establishes a few connections there and enlarges his lumber trade; he imports liquor with his profits and sets up as an innkeeper or liquor retailer; opening up a direct trade with the West Indies, he begins building his own sailing vessels; after becoming a successful merchant shipper exporting masts, lumber, and fish, he establishes friendships among the ruling elites in both New Hampshire and England and obtains a political appointment to the New Hampshire Council or to another local royal post. From that position of authority he augments his economic and social position through land speculation and lucrative war contracts, leaving a tidy fortune in land and trade to his children.[78] Variations of this pattern, most prevalent in the country towns, saw farmers or craftsmen acquiring land, houses, mortgages, and varied credit roles, contracting lumber and agricultural products with Portsmouth or Boston merchants, and/or seeking election to such military and political offices as moderator, selectman, assessor, and town representative to the provincial House of Representatives. The Gilmans of Exeter and the Hiltons of Dover exemplify these patterns; they shipped lumber and masts to Portsmouth and Boston wholesalers and acquired town offices, military commissions, titles, and fame as Indian fighters. In a frontier society, possession of a military title brought special social significance.[79] Joseph Chase, probably the richest man in Hampton by 1717, possessed almost £1,700 in bonds, bills, mortgages, and book debts; had another £1,700 in land; owned £200 worth of sailing vessels; and held the title of gentleman.[80]

Although the most sought-after economic role in New Hampshire by the early eighteenth century was that of the landed, mast-trading merchant, another economic occupation, the law, increased in desirability. The leading Piscataqua men of the late seventeenth and early eighteenth centuries sent their sons to Harvard for an education in the law, rather than in religion, so that they could cope more effectively with the economic and political affairs of their families and of the colony.[81] Such aspiring sons as Benning Wentworth, Richard Waldron, Jr., Samuel Penhallow, Theodore Atkinson, George Jaffrey, Mesech Weare, Richard Wibird, Jr., William Vaughan, Thomas Wibird, Samuel Langdon, Samuel Sherburne, Matthew Livermore, Samuel Plaisted, Nathaniel Rogers, George Vaughan, Thomas Packer, Samuel Hinckes, Sampson Sheafe, Daniel Rindge, and Benjamin Gambling received the benefits of a Harvard education between 1700 and 1740. Seventeen of these twenty men later obtained significant political and legal posts in New Hampshire and enjoyed the status of gentlemen, attesting to the increased importance assigned to education and legal knowledge in the colony, particularly at Portsmouth.[82]

New Hampshire's social structure, like its economic structure, underwent some internal changes during the early eighteenth century but remained overall an open, fluid organization with blurred class lines because the changes for social advancement were so plentiful that avenues to the top continued to exist except at the lowest rung on the social ladder, which was occupied by slaves and indentured servants, who represented less than 5 percent of the total population.[83]

Within this generally open social structure, however, class consciousness, exclusiveness, and elitism were becoming increasingly visible among the higher social ranks, especially among those merchants who dominated the mast trade. Although traditional English values which emphasized the ideal of an hierarchical society and the need for deference toward one's social superiors remained dominant throughout New Hampshire's colonial experience, the settlers' concepts about who constituted their social betters changed considerably and continued in a state of flux. Traditionally, the Crown, the nobility, the clergy, and the country gentlemen in England received "due subordination" from the rest of society. But in late seventeenth-century New Hampshire the Crown and nobility had lost some status, while the clergy and country gentlemen held their own and the roles of merchant and military leader obtained new status. By the 1730's and 1740's the possession of the titles of "gentleman" or "Esquire," such occupations as merchant or lawyer, a college education, or high military or political office usually meant more in status than being a clergyman or owning a large agricultural estate.

As ambitious men strove for high social status, they impugned the motives and the social quality of their competitors. Richard Waldron and William Vaughan thought that it was indecent for members of the council to sign the royal oath of allegience with the "Rabble" or "among tag, rag, and bobtail." Lieutenant Governor Usher referred to his opponents as "commoners" and as disloyal leaders of the "mob"; Theodore Atkinson described Governor Belcher's supporters disparagingly as "the meaner sort."[84] Contemporary letters and documents contain many references to class. Nathaniel Weare of Hampton wrote of "the gentlemen of Piscataqua"; the New Hampshire councillors, almost all of whom were merchants, described themselves as "Gentlemen of the best quality and greatest ability to serve the Government . . . having as good and better Estate in lands and land securities than any in [the] said House [of Representatives]." Samuel Penhallow recommended Captain John Wentworth for the post of lieutenant governor of New Hampshire, describing him as "a deserved member of our Council and a gentleman in every way qualified as to estate, virtue, and loyalty, who studies the interest of the Country, and is an upholder of the Constitution of our churches; a true friend of the present Governor and universally beloved among us."[85]

Whereas in the seventeenth century men from exceedingly diverse economic and social backgrounds had obtained some social recognition, in the eighteenth century possession of certain relatively specific attributes commanded deference and social status. The most significant badges of distinction in New Hampshire were the possession of great wealth, a mercantile occupation, a landed estate, a college education, an important title, prestigious family connections, or appointment or consistent election to a respected political office. In every case this meant living a style of life above that of the ordinary man. Although no completely consistent relationship existed between a person's title and his exact social status, nevertheless such titles as "Esquire," "Gentleman," "Mr.," "Captain," and "Merchant" signified high prestige and were used by almost everyone who claimed high social status in New Hampshire during the early eighteenth century.[86] This increase in the use of titles was undoubtedly a product of closer connections with aristocratic England and heightened anxiety about status in the open, competitive New Hampshire social structure.

The rarest and probably most prestigious title, "Esquire," was held by men possessing great wealth, an extensive landed estate, and a prominent royal post in the New Hampshire government. Colonel Richard Waldron (1650–1730), Lieutenant Governor John Wentworth, Colonel George Vaughan, Lieutenant John Gilman, Colonel John Plaisted, Samuel Penhallow, Captain John Rindge, Thomas Packer, Thomas Phipps, John Frost, and Captain Richard Wibird, among others, held this title before 1740.[87] Right below "Esquire" came the "Gentleman," the rank claimed by most men of wealth and political ability, including wealthy landowners, merchants, ministers, lawyers, and mariners who held political office.[88] "Mister" usually denoted someone who had obtained a college degree or had professional standing as a doctor, lawyer, or minister but who did not use a title of higher rank. "Captain" and "Merchant" were occupational titles used extensively after 1690, particularly at Dover and Portsmouth. At least forty of the richest one hundred taxpayers in Portsmouth between 1713 and 1741 used the title of "Captain" at one time or another, including the "Esquires" John Wentworth, John Rindge, and Richard Wibird. The increasing usage of "Captain" and "Merchant" indicates the social prestige given to such occupations in New Hampshire's port towns. The designation "Yeoman," the most common title found in the probate records, generally denoted occupational rather than social status, since it symbolized a man who earned a profitable income from the soil—a middle-class farmer. The use of this title increased somewhat during the early eighteenth century as more individuals of average social status became concerned with possession of titles and the probate clerks became more efficient in classification.[89]

As New Hampshire society increased in complexity, individuals who desired social reputation often embraced the trappings of the English gentleman by obtaining the elegant appurtenances and imitating the cultured manners of the English upper strata. Possession of valuable land, fine mansions, slaves, mercantile property (vessels, wharves, and warehouses), carriages, English silk and lace clothing, silver plate, English furniture, silver buckles, patent leather shoes, felt hats, embroidered waistcoats, and the like provided concrete evidence to those who wore linsey-woolsey homespun and leather breeches and used homemade furniture and wooden tableware that they were observing a better sort. By the 1720's members of the House of Representatives could be arrested if they did not wear their swords, rather dangerous badges of distinction, in the House. Certain rituals—such as giving gifts of rings, scarves, gloves, wine, and even tobacco to the guests at a funeral—became common practice among those claiming high status.[90] Or consider the experience of traveler Robert Hale who, while journeying through New England to Nova Scotia in 1730, received exclusive entertainment among the Wentworth clan. He enjoyed five dinners among them but neither saw nor conversed with their women. He described the experience as follows: "Their manner of living here is very different from many other places. The Gentlemen treat at their own houses and seldom go to the Taverns. Their treats are splendid, they drink excessively all sorts of wine and punch—their women came not into company, no, not so much as at dinner."[91] These activities set apart the "gentlemen" in a society where there were few really wealthy people. (In 1751, Richard Waldron wrote that "there are not ten who can properly be called rich in the province."[92]) Under such circumstances, the pursuit of a gentlemanly life style by acquisitive-minded capitalists separated them effectively from others.

The political realm experienced the greatest degree of stratification in the early eighteenth century, as it gradually became the preserve, at the provincial level, of Portsmouth "gentlemen." In the late seventeenth century, members of the New Hampshire Council had dominated provincial politics and had represented all the towns in the colony. But as the province expanded in population and commerce and as Portsmouth came to dominate the colony in both areas, more and more Portsmouth merchants sought council appointments. The aggressive activities of these new merchants, coupled with population growth, brought a social crisis to Portsmouth between 1711 and 1716 over the location of the town's church. Should it be located on the north side with the Wentworths, Jaffreys, Gerrishes, and Wibirds, or on the south side with the Vaughans, Pickerings, Westbrooks, and Cottons? The major issues at stake were socioeconomic and psychological, as the older ruling elements of the town, led by John Pickering, sought to maintain the status quo against the new merchants who had gained prominence after 1700.[93] Coincidentally, George Vaughan obtained the post of lieutenant governor in 1715, after espousing a wider conception of New Hampshire's needs than most New Englanders could accept. Fresh from a victory in the Portsmouth church dispute, the new merchants replaced Vaughan with John Wentworth, who proceeded (with Governor Samuel Shute's aid) to replace most of the councillors from the other towns and the older Portsmouth parish with Wentworth's merchant allies.[94] By 1717, the council consisted of nine merchants, seven from Portsmouth and two from New Castle; and from 1717 on the council was completely dominated by merchants from these two port towns.

In the midst of these factional machinations the members of the House of Representatives objected strenuously to merchant domination, complaining that the country towns were for the first time unrepresented on the council, that "experienced, just and good men" had been dismissed, that both the courts and judges existed only in Portsmouth, that the merchants would raise land taxes while abolishing the impost, and that merchant domination of provincial politics brought "great discontent and uneasiness" to farmers and laborers. Their protests brought an elitist response from the council. The council pointed out that Portsmouth was the most prosperous town, "the metropolis of the Government," and "the seat of almost all the Gentlemen of the Province." Since Portsmouth possessed "Gentlemen of the best quality and greatest ability to serve the Government," the Crown was justified in its Portsmouth appointments.[95]

By 1720, provincial politics had become the preserve of those who called themselves "Gentlemen" and especially those "gentlemen" from the port towns. During the 1720's these men cemented their status in society by giving themselves substantial property in the various township grants and by establishing plural voting, creating a £300 real estate qualification for those desiring to stand for election into the House of Representatives, and raising the property qualification for suffrage somewhat by changing the base from possession of a 40s. freehold or £50 in personal estate to possession of £50 in real estate.[96] This last clause, if enforced, would have disfranchised 75 to 80 percent of the Portsmouth and New Castle taxpayers, but its enforcement was left in the hands of each town's moderator.[97] Each one of these clauses, however, encouraged an intensified political stratification at the province level. This act also tended to discriminate against newcomers in the older towns because property ownership and social status generally increased as years of town residency increased.[98]

But the increased provincial stratification did not produce a unified political elite in the colony. Portsmouth merchants competed with each other for control of the mast trade and formed opposing factions as they sought to obtain political power from whence they could manipulate the government to support their own values and interests. As Governor

Belcher put it in 1731: "I remember an observation of a great man, when I was at Whitehall, upon an opposition made in the House of Commons, that the pasture was strait and the cattle numerous. This . . . (comparing small things with great) is the case at New Hampshire. Men that are out of office would feign be in, and because they can't, the next thing is to murmur and grumble."[99] Or again: "If some people might enjoy all the places of profit and honor in the Province, as they have for many years past, they would be well content. But I think it time and very reasonable some other families should share in the advantages of the Government."[100]

In the course of the 1720's and 1730's various family and interest groups confronted each other on a variety of political and economic issues. These included the location of the provincial courts, the Triennial Act of 1728, the need to appoint council members from all the major towns, the power of a governor to veto the House of Representatives' choice for Speaker of the House, enforcement of the White Pine laws, limitation of the power of the governor and council in judicial appeals involving land titles, the Massachusetts–New Hampshire boundary dispute, the need for paper currency, the appointment of a London merchant as province agent, and the overall political relationship between New Hampshire and Massachusetts and New Hampshire and England.[101] Each of these "gentleman" factions appealed to the general populace for support, claiming that it would better protect liberty and property and that the other faction only served low, "mean" people or goals.

TABLE 33

COMPARATIVE TAXABLE PROPERTY OF PERMANENT RESIDENTS AND THE
GENERAL POPULACE OF PORTSMOUTH, NEW HAMPSHIRE, 1713-1743*

Taxable property value	Permanent Residents No.	%	General Populace No.	%
£ 0-20	6	2.6%	818	13.6%
£ 20-50	71	31.3%	2072	34.4%
£ 50-100	69	30.4%	1883	31.2%
£ 100 and up	81	35.7%	1254	20.8%
TOTAL	227	100.0%	6027	100.0%

*The figures under "General Populace" were drawn from a sampling of 14 years between 1713-1743, namely: 1713, 1715, 1717, 1718, 1719, 1723, 1725, 1729, 1731, 1732, 1735, 1738, 1740, 1741. "Permanent Residents" includes any person paying taxes for any twenty-year period between 1713 and 1743.

With the appointment of Governor Belcher in 1730, these factions coalesced into two shifting family alliances, the Wentworth and the Waldron "clans." Probably the most significant reason behind this sudden stabilization of factions lay in the contrasting values held by the leaders of each at a time when the religious and social foundations of the old order were weakening. New parishes, new social values, new religions, new immigrants, and relatively new economic problems buffeted New Hampshire society during the 1720's and 1730's, and the factional leaders took opposing positions on most of the major problems, positions in keeping with their contrasting values.

One faction, led by Richard Waldron, Jr., tended to think and act in terms of the traditional New England Congregationalist values, its leaders seeing themselves as a part of the country of New England with Boston as the capital and supporting the protection of Congregationalism, liberty, hard money, and property within a Massachusetts-oriented framework. Such men as John Pickering, Samuel Penhallow, the Waldrons, Vaughans, Gilmans, and Weares espoused these values.[102] The Wentworth faction, more openly materialistic and acquisitive, looked to England for its values, supporting a local Anglican church, the creation of an enlarged and separate political province, and more localistic conceptions of patriotism within New England. Its leaders promised protection and augmentation of liberty and property through a closer economic alliance with the mother country and its values. Such men as John Wentworth, John Rindge, Benning Wentworth, Theodore Atkinson, and Andrew Wiggin projected these goals. Both these factional alliances exhibited the amoral, acquisitive, elitist tendencies among the mercantile gentry that increasingly characterized New Hampshire's provincial politics after 1715.[103]

While political stratification increased at the province level, it tended to decrease at the town level. Town suffrage remained open to almost every male taxpayer throughout the period. In all the older towns except Exeter the proportion of men holding the office of selectman increased in the eighteenth century over the proportion in the seventeenth century. (Exeter's proportion remained the same.) In Portsmouth the percentage of offices held by the top one-third of the selectmen dropped from 67.7 percent in the seventeenth century to 63.3 percent in the eighteenth, an amazing statistic in view of the town's increased economic and social stratification.[104]

Nor was there any consistent correlation between socioeconomic achievement and political status in Portsmouth town politics during the early eighteenth century. During the 1730's Portsmouth chose selectmen with as low a tax valuation as £35 and as high as £575. The average valuation of selectmen was between £75 and £150; and this applied as well to the occupants of most of Portsmouth's town offices, including corders of wood, cullers of fish, sealers of leather, surveyors of highways, fence viewers, and lot layers. Only such offices as assessors and auditors (filled by merchants) averaged somewhat higher, while the office of hog constable averaged somewhat lower, with some people who held the latter office paying no taxes and one who paid £190 in taxes.[105] In general, then, the open economy and society of the town was mirrored in its local politics. If there was a local political hierarchy at all, it tended to ascend from hog constables toward assessors. Perhaps the most important reason for this diversified local political order lay in the fact that during the eighteenth century fewer spoils accrued to local officeholders; hence, comparatively speaking, competition for local office was not keen.

In fact, at the local level the emphasis upon consensus political decisions predominated. This was especially true in the country towns, some of which remained relatively homogeneous. After the Triennial Act, most of the towns still allowed every taxpayer to vote for assemblymen, as well as for all town officials, and projected consensus political values. Newmarket's freeholders, for example, all voted for assemblymen after 1728 and saw the right of free elections as "the foundation of the rights of the People and a fundamental Principle in the form of Government they are under." At Dover in 1745, the town clerk wrote that "people should agree and accord in love and unity" in town meetings.[106] In the new towns and parishes there were more political opportunities than in most of the older communities.[107] Ultimately, although the degree of political stratification varied from locality to locality, with more opportunities present in newer communities than in older ones, because of the need for consensus in more heterogeneous towns and the presence of an open socioeconomic environment, most people could vote and hold local political office.

Thus, stratification increased in provincial politics during the early eighteenth century, as aggressive, wealthy, Portsmouth merchant-gentlemen utilized their power and connections to dominate provincial offices and policies. This situation created tensions between some of the country townspeople and Portsmouth merchants, tensions which were manifested through factional political behavior, but deferential attitudes toward "betters" kept such conflicts at a relatively low level. In town politics, on the other hand, the presence of consensus values, an open economy, and an open society, and the breakdown of the older social order, all combined to decrease political stratification, even in Portsmouth.

The organization of New Hampshire's society by 1740 was a product of its open economic structure, the competitive political system, and a complex and shifting value system. Each of these factors was interrelated and constantly affecting the others. At the highest ranks of society there

TABLE 34

COMPARATIVE TOWN OFFICEHOLDING: PORTSMOUTH AND LONDONDERRY

Portsmouth

Selectmen 1690-1740

83 men held 251 offices (3.0 opm*)

No. of Men	No. of Offices	% of Total Offices
1 Man	14	5.6%
Top 10%	74	29.5%
Top 20%	120	47.8%
Top 33 1/3%	159	63.3%

All Offices 1713-1740

254 men held 1250 offices (4.9 opm)

No. of Men	No. of Offices	% of Total Offices
1 Man	55	4.4%
Top 10%	556	45.5%
Top 20%	800	64.0%
Top 33 1/3%	969	77.5%

Londonderry

Selectmen 1720-1760

69 men held 194 offices (2.8 opm)

No. of Men	No. of Offices	% of Total Offices
1 Man	10	5.2%
Top 10%	49	25.3%
Top 20%	87	44.8%
Top 33 1/3%	118	60.8%

All Offices 1720-1760

186 men held 708 offices (3.8 opm)

No. of Men	No. of Offices	% of Total Offices
1 Man	39	5.5%
Top 10%	346	48.9%
Top 20%	442	62.4%
Top 33 1/3%	526	74.3%

*opm means offices per man

was a significant correlation between economic status, political authority, and social status. The men with the highest-ranking titles generally held the greatest wealth and political power as well. Twenty-nine of the thirty-two men who held office as councillors or assemblymen from Portsmouth between 1704 and 1741 were also among the upper 5 percent of the town's taxpayers in those years. With the profusion of economic opportunities in trade and the high social value placed upon education and mercantile activity, it was not accidental that Portsmouth's richest merchants stood at the top of the social structure as well. The general tendency was to elect and appoint to provincial political office persons who had mercantile wealth, titles, ability, and a gentleman's style of life.

Below the highest stratum of the social structure, class lines were blurred. Farmers, shopkeepers, craftsmen, skilled laborers, and professional people earned their living in an open, fluid economy and society which provided opportunities both to rise and to fall. While an increasing number of such people in relatively urban areas owned no land, they possessed some mercantile wealth and were considered part of the broad middle class. Only the slave suffered a permanently low status.

During its first century New Hampshire witnessed the development of a more stratified, yet simultaneously more complex, diverse, and mobile society which contained a somewhat exclusive and wealthy mercantile elite nourished by the mast trade. Yet, because the social order had changed from a relatively cohesive system of social arrangements and values toward an order based upon economic, social, and religious individualism and capitalist ethics, and because economic and social opportunities remained so fluid and open, the chances for social advancement were so plentiful that avenues to the very top of the social structure remained open. Under these circumstances, no rigidly stratified social elite, nor any permanent proletarian class, emerged in New Hampshire before the 1740's.

In the course of a century New Hampshire's society had come a long way from those four small frontier communities that accepted Massachusetts' jurisdiction in 1641 because they could not cope satisfactorily with the Piscataqua environment. Taking advantage of every available economic opportunity, the Piscataqua settlers had gradually exploited the land and its attendant lumber resources, the fur trade, the fishing trade, ship and naval store production, and the all-important mast trade. By the 1740's New Hampshire's colonists had developed a thriving, complex coastal and overseas trade and a relatively mature mercantile economy based upon the exportation of lumber and fishing products. Coincidental with this extensive economic expansion, the early eighteenth century witnessed significant population growth and the acquisition and exploitation of new land by New Hampshire settlers. The colony's economic and social structure had experienced some stratification at the upper level over the years, and so had its political structure, as provincial politics became the preserve of the gentleman. Similarly, the older forms of social organization—the town and church—had lost much authority to the provincial government and a wider set of values. By the 1720's the wealthiest and most influential people in the colony were usually merchants, mariners, lumber traders, and a few farmers—a social elite which based its ascendancy on commercial profits and materialist values. By 1741, politicians from this social elite had gained a large measure of control over local enforcement of British imperial policies, excellent political and economic connections in London and Boston, and political independence from Massachusetts.

These changes occurred, ultimately, as a result of the perceived needs of the New Hampshire settlers in confrontation with various internal and external problems and opportunities, ranging from proprietary claimants, boundary disputes, wars, capital and labor scarcities, an inadequate medium of exchange, debt, inflation, and imperial trade regulations to economic competition from England and Massachusetts.

But one must also ask why New Hampshire did not experience more rapid geographical and population expansion and social and economic changes. When one addresses these questions, the limited success of the New Hampshire colonists in solving their problems becomes clear. The main reason for such limited expansion during this first century lay in the almost constant threat of Indian wars. In addition, the relatively unattractive agricultural environment and the proprietary controversy tended to keep prospective new settlers away before 1715. The wars, however, were a tremendous drain on New Hampshire's economic and physical development, as they drove settlers away from the colony and disrupted the social order. Ultimately, the New Hampshire people, whatever their successes, could not escape the consequences of their failure to solve this problem effectively. Although they acquired extensive new lands and larger bounds by 1740, the outbreak of new wars in the 1740's and 1750's forced them to postpone settling these lands, to reduce their commercial activity, and to recognize once again both their fundamental military dependence upon Massachusetts and England and their proximity to frontier status.

The Piscataqua settlers and villages of 1641 contrast sharply with the New Hampshire inhabitants and towns of 1741. The former lived in grossly dependent, immature, and relatively undifferentiated agricultural societies. The latter possessed a more heterogeneous and more rapidly expanding population, a more mature commercial economy, a dynamic economic and social structure with increased stratification at the top, a relatively cosmopolitan and materialist value system which looked more to the province government as the most important sociopolitical institution, and a social elite that had developed effective solutions to many of the varied threats confronting New Hampshire during its first century of experience. Yet the societies of 1641 and 1741 had at least two important situations in common. Both were in the process of experiencing a change in political leadership and authority that would usher in a period of relative political stability, and both also optimistically looked forward to utilizing the new lands opened to them by new political decisions. Time alone would reveal whether the maturer New Hampshire of 1741 would more effectively exploit these opportunities.

ABBREVIATIONS AND SHORT TITLES

Full bibliographical detail for the works listed below may be found in the list of Works Cited.

APC Col	*Acts of the Privy Council of England, Colonial Series*
CSP Col	*Calendar of State Papers, Colonial Series: America and West Indies, 1574–1736*
DTR	Dover Town Records
ETR	Exeter Town Records
HTR	Hampton Town Records
LTR	Londonderry Town Records
Mass. Records	*Records of the Governor and Company of the Massachusetts Bay in New England*
MHS	Massachusetts Historical Society
MHS Coll	*Collections of the Massachusetts Historical Society*
NHHS	New Hampshire Historical Society
NHHS Coll	*Collections of the New Hampshire Historical Society*
NH Laws	*Laws of New Hampshire*
NHPP	*Provincial Papers: Documents and Records Relating to the Province of New-Hampshire*
NH Probate Records	Probate Records of New Hampshire
Noyes	Sybil Noyes, Charles Libby, and Walter Davis, *Genealogical Dictionary of Maine and New Hampshire*

PTR   Portsmouth Town Records
Shipping Returns   Shipping Returns for the Port of Piscataqua

NOTES

Chapter I

1. The first royal commission is printed in *NHPP*, 1: 373–82. Strawbery Banke had its name changed to Portsmouth in 1653. The original town name had a variety of spellings, but "Strawbery Banke" has been preferred by those working on the historic restoration project in Portsmouth.

2. *NH Laws*, 1: 2, 49. The southern Isles of Shoals came under New Hampshire's jurisdiction in 1692 (ibid., p. 501).

3. *NHPP*, 1: 18–21; Jonathan Belcher to Board of Trade, April 4, 1737, in Colonial Office Papers, Class 5, vol. 880, Cc. 54, pp. 1–4. Hereafter cited as CO5. Even those seeking larger borders acknowledged these general bounds. In a petition to the King in Council, November 4, 1737, Andrew Wiggin complained that Governor Belcher by granting a town charter to Kingswood (just below Lake Winnipesaukee) had "granted the only tract of land unappropriated and out of controversy" (Weare MSS., New Hampshire Historical Society).

4. *APC Col*, vol. 3, no. 432; 19: 476–79.

5. Charles W. Brewster, *Rambles about Portsmouth* (Portsmouth, N.H., 1859–69), 1st ser., pp. 9–14; William G. Saltonstall, *Ports of Piscataqua* (Cambridge: Harvard University Press, 1941), p. 4; Bernard Bailyn, *The New England Merchants in the Seventeenth Century* (Cambridge: Harvard University Press, 1955), p. 5; John Smith, *The Generall Historie of Virginia, New-England, and the Summer Isles* (London, 1632), pp. 205, 214.

6. John S. Jenness, *The Isles of Shoals*, 2d ed. (Boston, 1915). For short, informative descriptions of the Isles, see Jeremy Belknap, *The History of New-Hampshire*, 2d ed. (Boston, 1813), 3:147; and Byron Fairchild, *Messrs. William Pepperrell: Merchants at Piscataqua* (Ithaca: Cornell University Press, 1954), pp. 4–5.

7. George Vaughan to Board of Trade, July 6, 1708, in *CSP Col*, 1708–9, no. 19. For another description see Belknap, *History*, 3: 130–33.

8. This entire complex from the Salmon Falls River to the Atlantic Ocean has sometimes been known as the Piscataqua. For comments on its suitability for trade see Belknap, *History*, 3: 147–48.

9. Ibid., pp. 145–46. For an excellent description of the harbor see Howard T. Oedel, "Portsmouth, New Hampshire: The Role of the Provincial Capital in the Development of the Colony (1700–1775)" (Ph.D. diss., Boston University, 1960), pp. 4–8.

10. Gorges' life and correspondence are found in James P. Baxter, ed., *Sir Ferdinando Gorges and His Province of Maine*, 3 vols. (Boston: Prince Society, 1890); Mason's in John W. Dean, ed., *Captain John Mason, the Founder of New Hampshire . . . Together with a Memoir by C. W. Tuttle* (Boston, 1887).

11. Jeremy Belknap, *The History of New-Hampshire*, ed. John Farmer (Dover, N.H., 1831), p. 13. This one-volume condensation of Belknap's *History* is hereafter cited as Belknap, *History* (Farmer ed.).

12. Belknap, *History*, 3: 25. This region was generally known as the Blue Hills.

13. This was especially true near Hampton (Belknap, *History* [Farmer ed.], pp. 20-21).

14. Primary sources relating to these early settlers are collected in *NHPP*, 1: 1-153; 25: 661-747. Significant studies on New Hampshire during this era are William H. Fry, *New Hampshire as a Royal Province*, Studies in History, Economics, and Public Law, vol. 29, no. 2 (New York, 1908), pp. 17-51; Bailyn, *New England Merchants*, pp. 5-15, 50-51; R. A. Preston, "The Laconia Company of 1629: An English Attempt to Intercept the Fur Trade," *Canadian Historical Review* 31 (1950): 125-44; Fairchild, *Messrs. William Pepperrell*, pp. 2-6; Belknap, *History* (Farmer ed.), pp. 3-52; Nathaniel Adams, *Annals of Portsmouth* (Exeter, N.H., 1825), pp. 1-20; Charles M. Andrews, *The Colonial Period of American History*, 4 vols. (New Haven, 1934-38), 1: 89-97, 320-43, 400-429, 476-85; Elwin L. Page, *Judicial Beginnings in New Hampshire, 1640-1700* (Concord, N.H., 1959), pp. 3-11, 183-203d; and Charles E. Clark, *The Eastern Frontier: The Settlement of Northern New England, 1610-1763* (New York: Knopf, 1970), pp. 3-51.

15. Bailyn, *New England Merchants*, pp. 5-9.

16. Discussion of David Thomson, a Plymouth fisherman who was the first settler in New Hampshire, has been omitted because he moved to an island in Boston harbor by 1628. But it should be noted that in 1623 he established a small settlement at Little Harbor known as Pannaway, which by 1630 had come under the control of the Laconia Company grantees (*NHPP*, 25: 661-73).

17. The exact date is uncertain, but Hilton was at Dover Neck by 1628 (Belknap, *History* [Farmer ed.], p. 5n; *NHPP*, 25: 669-72). During this period Dover Neck had several names: Hilton's Point, Dover Point, and Dover Neck were the most common. Technically, Dover Neck refers to the entire neck of land between Back River and the Piscataqua River, while Dover Point is the tip of Dover Neck; but in this period the words were used interchangeably.

18. *NHPP*, 25: 699. Hlton's patent is printed in ibid., pp. 698-700.

19. Ibid., p. 698; Fairchild, *Messrs. William Pepperrell*, p. 4.

20. Preston, "The Laconia Company," pp. 125-44. For a list of the merchants involved see *NHPP*, 1: 29-30. They claimed that they spent £3,000 in the undertaking. Their charter is printed in *NHPP*, 29: 33-38.

21. Present-day Portsmouth and South Berwick.

22. The full patent is in *NHPP*, 29: 39-43. The bounds are outlined in Map 1, which has been constructed from ibid., 25: 678.

23. Ibid., 25: 701.

24. Ibid., 1: 68-69, 81-82.

25. Several who withdrew had found the business unprofitable; see ibid., pp. 89-93, 97; *Transcripts of Original Documents in the English Archives Relating to the Early History of New Hampshire*, comp. John S. Jenness (New York, 1876), p. 18; Page, *Judicial Beginnings*, pp. 188, 190.

26. *NHPP*, 1: 91.

27. Ibid., 29: 63. The council had given Mason three earlier indefinite general grants: March 9, 1621/22; August 10, 1622; and November 7, 1629 (ibid., pp. 19-23, 23-28, 28-32).

28. Ibid., 1: 97-98. At his death Mason owned three-eighths of the Laconia grant, but all lying northeast of the Piscataqua River in Maine (at Newichewannock Falls). Gorges also owned one-eighth there. The other half of the grant, lying south of the Piscataqua, was owned in common by the Laconia Company; and it never divided these lands. Thus, Mason as an individual had no legal claim to lands south of the Piscataqua—that is, to New Hampshire. For further detail see Page, *Judicial Beginnings*, pp. 188-91, 203a-203d.

29. Preston, "The Laconia Company," pp. 141-43, discusses their plight. He feels that the death of Mason, the leader in Laconia Company affairs, was instrumental in its collapse.

30. By 1638, Mason's widow had abandoned the Laconia Company settlers to their own resources (*NHPP*, 1: 45; Belknap, *History* [Farmer ed.], pp. 22-23; Fry, *New Hampshire as a Royal Province*, p. 37).

31. Quoted in Emory Battis, *Saints and Sectaries* (Chapel Hill: University of North Carolina Press, 1962), p. 143. For further discussion of Wheelwright see Battis, pp. 110-55, 182-86; *NHPP*, 1: 128-31.

32. *Mass. Records*, 1: 189, 207; Andrews, *The Colonial Period*, 1: 485.

33. *NHPP*, 1: 134-36. Other clauses in these deeds extended the lands to the Merrimack River and from there to the Atlantic, and also granted meadows northeast one mile to the Oyster River.

34. Ibid., 1: 132-33. Some excellent material on Exeter can be gleaned from Charles H. Bell, *History of the Town of Exeter, New Hampshire* (Exeter, 1888).

35. Belknap, *History* (Farmer ed.), p. 20; *NHPP*, 1: 146, 148; *Mass. Records*, 1: 167, 236.

36. *Mass. Records*, 1: 259; *NHPP*, 1: 148. These privileges included election of a constable and town officers, control over town affairs, and electing a representative to the Massachusetts General Court.

37. There were about forty-five men in Hampton at this time, with thirteen of them freemen. See Belknap, *History* (Farmer ed.), pp. 21-22n; *NHPP*, 1: 151-52.

38. Belknap, *History* (Farmer ed.), pp. 20-22.

39. There were other settlements closely related to Strawbery Banke, but they were located north of the Piscataqua in Maine. Byron Fairchild properly treats the Laconia Company settlements both north and south of the Piscataqua as a unit reacting to the Piscataqua environment; but such a treatment does not give a full understanding of the diversity within New Hampshire's society, so it has not been adopted here. Fairchild's primary interest lay in Maine, which perhaps explains in part his lapses in describing the earliest settlements on the Piscataqua. He does not use the excellent source material relating to these settlements printed in the *NHPP*. See Fairchild, *Messrs. William Pepperrell*, pp. 5-6, and compare it with the excellent discussion presented by John S. Jenness in "Notes on the First Planting of New Hampshire and on the Piscaqua patents," *NHPP*, 25: 663-739. See also Clark, *The Eastern Frontier*, pp. 36-47.

40. Henry Sherburne from Hampshire and Thomas Walford from Essex were instrumental in establishing an Anglican ministry at Strawbery Banke in 1640. The glebe grant and appointment of Richard Gibson as minister is in *NHPP*, 1: 111-13. Of the twenty who signed the grant, eleven were Laconia Company servants or related to them, nine were newer settlers.

41. Ibid., 1: 61-65, 68, 81-82, 92.

42. Ambrose Gibbons to Laconia Company, July 13, 1633, *NHPP*, 1: 81-82.

43. Ambrose Gibbons to Capt. Mason, August 6, 1634, ibid., pp. 91-92.

44. Ibid., pp. 90, 91, 93; ibid., 29: 40.

45. Adams, *Annals*, pp. 18-19. Godfrey later moved north to Maine where he served as Gorges' governor in 1649. See also *NHPP*, 1: 68-69.

46. *NHPP*, 1: 68, 81-82; Mason to Gibbons, May 5, 1634, ibid., pp. 89-91.

47. Ibid., pp. 111-13. There is no record of this land division or of the civil compact because the town selectmen later destroyed all town records previous to 1652. For abundant indirect evidence see ibid., 17: 504-6; Brewster, *Rambles about Portsmouth*, pp. 22-23; Belknap, *History* (Farmer ed.), p. 28. Gibbons settled near Oyster River and apparently continued a profitable fur trade.

48. For the English origins of Hampton settlers see Charles Banks, *Topographical Dictionary of 2885 English Emigrants to New England, 1620-1650* (Philadelphia, 1937).

49. *NHPP*, 24: 845-47. Hampton's northern bounds were not established until 1652 (ibid., p. 868). See also ibid., 1: 46.

50. Quoted from Winthrop's *History* in *NHPP*, 1: 46.

51. Quoted in ibid., p. 148.

52. Joseph Dow, *History of Hampton, New Hampshire* (Hampton, N.H., 1883), pp. 12, 20-22; *NHPP*, 1: 152. The General Court sent three men to help the citizens of Hampton order their affairs (*NHPP*, 1: 150). This is not to say, however, that Hampton had no controversies: in 1644, for example, the town divided sharply over the practices of the minister (Belknap, *History* [Farmer ed.], p. 34n). Relatively speaking, though, security and stability were more prevalent at Hampton than elsewhere among the four towns.

53. *NHPP*, 1: 152, 153.

54. Ibid., p. 152.

55. For the origins of Exeter's settlers see Banks, *Topographical Dictionary*; John Wentworth, *Wentworth Genealogy* (Boston: Little, Brown and Company, 1878). For land controversies see *NHPP*, 1: 147–48; 24: 845–48.

56. For the forms of government see Bell, *History of Exeter*, p. 18. The Exeter Combination is printed in *NHPP*, 1: 131–33.

57. *NHPP*, 25: 698.

58. Ibid., p. 676. The Dover settlers had probably located on Bloody Point before the Laconia Company took out its patent. Nevertheless, technically they were squatters.

59. Quoted from Winthrop's *History* in *NHPP*, 1: 104. For evidence of the friendship between Wiggin and Winthrop, see ibid., pp. 105–6.

60. Apparently, Bloody Point received its name from this encounter (ibid., 1: 65n; 25: 682).

61. Ibid., 1: 157; 25: 682.

62. Ibid., 1: 106.

63. Hilton moved across the river at this time and developed one of the largest landed estates in the whole region. At his death in 1671 he was one of the richest men in New Hampshire. His inventory of £2,204 is in *NHPP*, 31: 124.

64. Ibid., 1: 170; 24: 836–42.

65. Ibid., 25: 683. The Crown had granted the Council for New England only the land; it had reserved governmental and jurisdictional rights to itself.

66. Wiggin had been appointed to this office by the new Puritan patentees. Once in his new office, Anglican George Burdett sent a letter to the Archbishop of Canterbury pointing out the lack of stable government on the Piscataqua, its geographical and strategic advantages, and the designs of Massachusetts toward the region. He asked that the archbishop use his influence to bring the Piscataqua under royal jurisdiction. See ibid., 17: 497–98; Belknap, *History* (Farmer ed.), pp. 18–19. The discovery of this correspondence probably led to his removal from office.

67. Belknap, *History* (Farmer ed.), p. 24. Underhill had been banished from Massachusetts.

68. *NHPP*, 1: 122–23, 126–28. This political crisis was complicated further by a religious scandal involving the immorality of two ministers of the Dover church, Hansard Knollys and Thomas Larkham. See Belknap, *History*, 1: 41–45; Clark, *The Eastern Frontier*, pp. 40–42.

69. The compact with signatures is printed in *NHPP*, 17: 501–2. Edward Hilton and some other Anglicans did not sign it.

70. Ibid., 1: 126–28. Twenty-three of the twenty-five signers of this letter had also signed the Combination. This letter suggests that the Combination was already in operation and was not entirely satisfactory. It also demonstrates that their main antagonism was directed toward the Hilton patentees in England.

71. Printed in ibid., pp. 155–56. The conveyance of jurisdiction was void, for only the Crown could do so in such patents.

72. Ibid., pp. 155–56, 158. For more detailed discussions of this reinterpretation, see ibid., 25: 685–89; Fry, *New Hampshire as a Royal Province*, pp. 37–41.

73. *NHPP*, 1: 158.

74. This was the clearest statement of Massachusetts' claim, expressed in its answer to the complaint of Mason and Gorges in 1676 (ibid., pp. 328–29). The General Court's first clarification of these disputed boundaries was asserted in 1652 (ibid., p. 200).

75. Ibid., 1: 159–61; Belknap, *History* (Farmer ed.), pp. 30–31; Fry, *New Hampshire as a Royal Province*, pp. 38–39; Page, *Judicial Beginnings*, pp. 11–13. Apparently, Strawbery Banke could not send a deputy to the General Court despite the above promise; none were sent until 1654, although in 1643 the town deputized a Massachusetts minister, James Parker, to represent it. The probable reason for this situation was that according to Massachusetts law deputies had to be both freemen and members of a Congregational Church. Strawbery Banke had no such church until the 1650's. By 1653 the town made a town rate in support of such a minister (*Portsmouth Town Records, 1645–1807*, 7 vols. [Portsmouth, N.H., WPA Project, 1939], 1: 14; Adams, *Annals*, p. 37.

76. *NHPP*, 25: 685.

77. Ibid., 1: 169-70, 207.

78. Ibid., p. 172.

79. See their petition to Massachusetts in October 1651 for evidence of this hostility (ibid., pp. 192-93). Massachusetts' actions from 1641 on did not exactly excite their friendliness: the Anglican minister, Gibson, was ousted, and both Dover and Hampton had their bounds extended at Strawbery Banke's expense. See ibid., 1: 168, 172, 174-77; Belknap, *History* (Farmer ed.), p. 29.

80. *NHPP*, 1: 168. Only a fragment of the petition remains.

81. Ibid., pp. 170-71.

82. Ibid., p. 171; Bell, *History of Exeter*, p. 44. Wheelwright and a few friends left Exeter for Maine rather than live under Massachusetts' control.

83. Massachusetts organized all four towns as part of the County of Norfolk after Exeter's submission (*NHPP*, 1: 169, 171; *Mass. Records*, 2: 38). Strawbery Banke remained especially aloof through the 1640's and early 1650's; see *NHPP*, 1: 195-96.

84. Belknap, *History* (Farmer ed.), p. 66.

85. *NHPP*, 1: 66, has a trade invoice of the Laconia Company. For Exeter see ibid., p. 139.

86. Page, *Judicial Beginnings*, pp. 122-26, found drunkenness, assault, and fornication the most common social crimes in seventeenth-century New Hampshire.

87. *NHPP*, 1: 147.

88. Ibid., p. 105. For other examples of lawlessness on the Piscataqua in the 1630's, see ibid., pp. 103-7, 122-24.

89. Ibid., p. 155.

90. For a list of the more important Massachusetts laws relating to New Hampshire, see *NH Laws*, 1: 749-71. For the laws enacted under the Cutt Commission from 1679 to 1681 that were very similar to those of Massachusetts, see ibid., pp. 11-47; Page, *Judicial Beginnings*, p. 23.

91. Throughout the colonial period New Hampshire people regarded England as home and Massachusetts as a sister colony. But there were also times of strong antagonism toward both these "relatives," and in these situations they were regarded as outsiders.

92. New Hampshire's exact population at this time cannot be accurately stated. Estimating from the number of signatures on various civil compacts and town records, Hampton had about 300 inhabitants; Dover, 250 to 300; Strawbery Banke, 100 to 150; and Exeter, about 200. See *NHPP*, 1: 151, 152, 126, 113, 132-33.

Chapter II

1. Exeter and Hampton first granted town lands in 1639. The inhabitants of Dover and Strawbery Banke undoubtedly occupied the best available land in the 1630's, but they received no town grants until the 1640's.

2. For the freemen see *NHPP*, 1: 150-51; for the grants see Dow, *History of Hampton*, pp. 17-18. The grants to Bachiler and Dalton accorded economic status equivalent to existent social status.

3. Dow, *History of Hampton*, p. 18; *Mass. Records*, 1: 376. For the freemanship oath and qualifications see *Mass. Records*, 1: 353-54. Because Hampton had been originally settled by a Massachusetts township grant, its settlers did not obtain the liberal suffrage extended to the other Piscataqua towns when they accepted Massachusetts' jurisdiction in 1641. Hampton's suffrage did not change until 1647, when the Massachusetts General Court allowed town inhabitants who were not freemen to vote for town officers and hold town offices. Even then, however, the town inhabitants could not vote on such issues as "ordering of schools, herding of cattle, laying out of highways, and distribution of lands" (ibid., 1: 197). Freemen still had the privilege of electing all local magistrates and deputies to the General Court. In 1658 the suffrage was extended to those "setled inhabitants" of "good and honest conversation" who owned an estate assessed at £20 or more in a single "country rate"

(ibid., 4, pt. 1: 336). In 1664 the General Court lowered barriers further by extending the franchise to all churchmen and to those nonchurchmen who paid at least ten shillings tax per annum and were freeholders and householders approved by a local minister (ibid., 4, pt. 2: 118; HTR, 1: 38). This emphasis upon both property and responsibility as qualifications for local suffrage continued through the remainder of the seventeenth century. For example, in 1680 the General Assembly of New Hampshire stipulated that only freeholders and "settled inhabitants" who were at least twenty-four years old, possessed a £20 ratable estate, had taken the oath of loyalty to the king, and were not "vicious in life but of honest and good conversation" could vote for town and province officers (NHPP, 1: 396; NH Laws, 1: 25).

4. HTR, 1: 326-27; Dow, History of Hampton, pp. 31-33. Both these factors evidently were established criteria for land grants.

5. For the grants based on cow commons ownership see HTR, 1: 345 (for 1669), 340-43 (for 1697), 585-89 (for 1714); 2: 93-99 (for 1722), 101, 325-28 (for 1738). By 1723 Hampton had proprietors for five separate land divisions, each receiving grants on the basis of his right in the commons.

6. NHPP, 1: 153.

7. Between 1681 and 1713 the value of one share of cow commons varied between £2 and £10, while the value of one unimproved acre in Hampton varied between 1s. and £1 7s. Thus, any new settler possessed at least a certain minimum of wealth. These figures are drawn from a survey of the inventories of estates scattered throughout NH Probate Records.

8. HTR, 1: 367-68, 372.

9. NHPP, 1: 132-34.

10. Ibid., p. 142. By 1641 Exeter's freemen were Richard Bulgar, Thomas Wardell, Thomas Wilson, Henry Elkins, and Thomas Weight (Mass. Records, 1: 171-79). Exeter's settlers at first opposed freemanship because of their opposition to Massachusetts' institutions in general. Evidence of conflict between those who claimed suffrage through freemanship and the other inhabitants can be seen in the 1640's. When Massachusetts assumed jurisdiction in 1643, both Bulgar and Wardell were elected selectmen. But they never held an important office in the town after that year and probably left the town. When Exeter came under Massachusetts' jurisdiction, all Exeter inhabitants who had formerly voted could do so and were thenceforth called freemen. After 1643, "freemen" and "inhabitants" were synonymous in Exeter. Its new form of government established in 1644 paralleled Hampton's and can be found in ETR, 1: 160.

11. ETR, 1: 144-45; NHPP, 1: 138; Bell, History of Exeter, pp. 435-38.

12. ETR, 1: 164; Bell, History of Exeter, pp. 131, 444.

13. ETR, 1: 144, 162; Bell, History of Exeter, pp. 131, 446.

14. ETR, 2: 147; Bell, History of Exeter, pp. 69, 129-46; NHPP, 31: 37. The land grants are scattered throughout the town records with the bulk of them in vol. 2. Charles Bell, however, has copied all the land grants and listed them according to year granted.

15. ETR, 1: 164, has the grant of January 1644/45; ibid., p. 180, has that of 1648; and ibid., p. 191, has that of January 1650/51.

16. Ibid., p. 254.

17. Between 1664 and 1702 three lumberers acquired over 2,400 acres of land through town grants: John Gilman was given 890 acres; Moses Gilman, 970 acres; and Peter Coffin, 560 acres.

18. This grant is in ETR, 1: 79-84. The lands were not actually given out until 1740, so that from 1725 to 1740 all the inhabitants were referred to as town proprietors in the town records. Also see Bell, History of Exeter, pp. 141-44.

19. The agreement with Massachusetts is in DTR, 1: 632-33, and more completely in NHPP, 1: 158-59, 161, 168-69.

20. NHPP, 1: 172, 174-77.

21. DTR, 1: 603-5.

22. New England Historical and Genealogical Register, 4: 246-47.

23. DTR, 1: 301, 630.

24. The individual grants are scattered throughout DTR, vol. 1. The tax list of 1648 is in ibid., pp. 590-96.

25. Ibid., pp. 344, 392-93, 412; *NHPP*, 1: 207.

26. Generally, almost all single grants of 200 acres or more went to the lumberers, in return for a £5 to £20 rent payment per year. See, for example, the grants to Valentine Hill in DTR, 1: 249-51, 263, 410; the grants to Thomas Wiggin (ibid., pp. 244-45, 246); and to Richard Waldron (ibid., pp. 233-35, 261-62, 268, 369). One exception before 1660 was the grant of 400 acres in 1656 to Dover's new minister, John Reyner.

27. Ibid., 1: 316-17, 620, 325-26; 2: 56.

28. Ibid., 1: 357, 358.

29. Ibid., p. 359.

30. Ibid., pp. 359-60. The oath of fidelity was one part of the freemanship requirement. As of 1655 thirty-one people had taken this oath who were not freemen. In 1653 Dover had twenty-four freemen (*New England Historical and Genealogical Register*, 4: 247).

31. DTR, 1: 358, 359-62.

32. Ibid., p. 393.

33. Ibid., 2: 50.

34. In the 1650's Dover had the largest population in the Piscataqua region. The Piscataqua men most prominent in Massachusetts politics lived there (Thomas Wiggin, Valentine Hill, and Richard Waldron), the courts were held there, and town economic resources had been more rapidly utilized there than elsewhere. Yet from the 1660's onward, Portsmouth gradually replaced Dover as the economic, social, and political capital of the Piscataqua region.

35. For the report of the New Hampshire General Assembly see *NHPP*, 9: 163-67.

36. Richard Cutt and Brian Pendleton were the two most prominent of these Puritans. Joseph Mason represented the claims of Ann Mason, Captain John Mason's widow, and served as her resident agent in Strawbery Banke from 1651 to 1667.

37. *NHPP*, 1: 192-93.

38. Ibid., pp. 195-96.

39. Ibid., pp. 193-94.

40. Ibid., p. 200.

41. Ibid., p. 201.

42. Ibid., pp. 207-8. Naturally enough, the petitioners somewhat overstated their case. Massachusetts responded by permitting the change of name to "Portsmouth" (*Mass. Records*, 2: 309).

43. The inhabitants had early established some form of government, but its exact nature is not clear. There was an elected "ruler" in the early 1640's, and the inhabitants kept some orderly records (Belknap, *History* [Farmer ed.], pp. 28-29; *Portsmouth Records, 1645-1656*, ed. Frank Hackett [Portsmouth, 1856], p. 58). The transfer of authority was as follows: "And we do fully agree, that these before named townsmen shall have full power to order all our town affairs, as though ourselves the whole town were present" (Hackett, *Portsmouth Records*, p. 2).

44. Hackett, *Portsmouth Records*, p. 16.

45. Ibid., p. 21; PTR, vol. 1. The earliest town book has never been found.

46. In 1665 one of the complaints of a disaffected faction at Portsmouth was that "some that have had lands given and laid out to them, the said contrary party have disowned the grants, and laid it out to others" (*NHPP*, 17: 511). Compare Hackett's interpretation (*Portsmouth Records*, pp. 66-67) and his detailed statement of the interpretative problems arising from this event (pp. 50-68).

47. Portsmouth had between fifty and sixty families at this time (*NHPP*, 1: 207). Those who were left out were probably anti-Massachusetts.

48. The grants are listed in Hackett, *Portsmouth Records*, pp. 20, 23-27.

49. Ibid., pp. 28-29.

50. PTR, 1: 66.

51. Ibid., pp. 143-44, 145, 146, 179, 191.

52. Hackett, *Portsmouth Records*, p. 35; and PTR, 1: 92, contain the exact holdings of Henry Sherburne, Anthony Brackett, and Richard Cutt—the town's leading public figures. Champernoun was a nephew of Sir Ferdinando Gorges, the Maine proprietary claimant.

53. *NHPP*, 1: 221-24.

54. PTR, 1: 90-91. The entire transaction is conveniently recorded in Brewster, *Rambles about Portsmouth*, 1st ser., pp. 25-27. Richard Cutt, John Cutt, and Bryan Pendleton held at least 350 acres each and at least 26.8 percent of the total property granted at this time.

55. PTR, 1: 182.

56. Ibid., 2: 17.

57. Dover was the exception, as there were no new town grants there after 1665. There were none in Portsmouth after 1699, none in Hampton after 1700, nor any in Exeter after 1725.

58. Dow, *History of Hampton*, pp. 20-21; Samuel Maverick, "A Briefe Description of New England and the Several Towns Therein" (1660), *Proceedings of the Massachusetts Historical Society*, 2d ser. 1 (October 1884): 233-35.

59. The shipping returns for New Hampshire are found in CO5 967, 968, and 969 at the British Public Record Office. Vol. 967 contains returns for 1723 and for 1752-60; vol. 968 contains returns for 1694-95, 1723-27, 1741-51; and vol. 969 has returns for 1761-69. For livestock exports, see Table 8. There is no record of vegetable importation before 1742; however, corn and wheat were imported regularly.

60. HTR, 1: 40, December 1639.

61. Ibid., p. 47. He received 100 acres of land.

62. Ibid., p. 10.

63. For instance, in 1652 the town ordered that all inhabitants could make pine staves from the commons. In 1653 no one was allowed to fell any commons oak trees for staves, bolts, or headings within two miles of any house. In 1655 no one could fell any commons timber for bolts and staves without a license from the selectmen. In 1657 and 1658 the use of commons timber for bolts and staves was completely halted. This continuing legislation suggests ineffective regulation and enforcement. See ibid., pp. 10, 82, 94, 95.

64. Ibid., pp. 119-21.

65. Ibid., pp. 129, 130. This referred particularly to trade or sale outside the town.

66. For instances see ibid., pp. 131, 362, 386-87, 401.

67. Hackett, *Portsmouth Records*, p. 15.

68. PTR, 1: 73.

69. For special grants see Hackett, *Portsmouth Records*, pp. 21, 22, 37. The town's attempt at theft regulation in January 1660/61 is recorded in PTR, 1: 82.

70. DTR, 1: 220.

71. For examples see ibid., pp. 216, 233-35, 244, 249-51, 257, 263, 269, 285-86. By 1653 eleven men owned sawmills in Dover: Hatevil Nutter, Edward Starbuck, Richard Waldron, Thomas Wiggin, Valentine Hill, William Furber, Ambrose Gibbons, William Wentworth, Henry Langster, Thomas Canney, and Joseph Austin.

72. Ibid., p. 218.

73. Ibid., p. 257.

74. See ibid., pp. 303-5 for these provisions.

75. Ibid., p. 324. The town records do not reveal the longevity of these procedures, but when Robert Wadleigh received a sawmill grant of 120 acres in 1669, the same limitations applied (ibid., pp. 468-69).

76. Bell, *History of Exeter*, pp. 51-52, 438, 440, 443, 447; ETR, 1: 147, 160, 161, 163.

77. The agreement is in ETR, 1: 175; and Bell, *History of Exeter*, p. 319. Edward Gilman, Jr. (?-1653), was the son of Edward Gilman (?-1681) of Hingham, England, who in 1638 brought his family to Boston, where he invested in the lumber trade. After Edward, Jr., received his mill grant in Exeter in 1647, the entire family moved there, including father Edward and two brothers, Moses (1630-1702) and John (d. 1708). The Gilmans soon became the leading family in Exeter's economy and politics and held this leadership throughout the colonial period. The most significant members before 1740 were John (above) and his sons John (1676-1720) and Nicholas (1672-1749), and their sons Peter (1703-88), Samuel (1698-1785), Daniel (1702-80), and Nicholas (1707-48). See the *Wentworth Genealogy* for more information.

78. ETR, 1: 183; Bell, *History of Exeter*, p. 320.

79. ETR, 1: 184. The town order also indicates the lack of an adequate medium of exchange.

80. Ibid., pp. 195–99 passim; Bell, *History of Exeter*, pp. 321–22.

81. ETR, 1: 196, 217.

82. Ibid., p. 216; Bell, *History of Exeter*, p. 53.

83. ETR, 1: 229; *NHPP*, 1: 303–4.

84. ETR, 1: 245, March 1673/74.

85. It should be noted that these seventeenth-century communities generally pursued exploitive timber policies—"forest-mining." They showed no concern for replenishment or for other conservation policies.

86. The town of Rochester held its first town meeting in 1737 but did not become a sizable settlement until after 1763. Chester had about 150 taxpayers in 1741 (about 600 people in all), while Londonderry contained between 750 and 800 people.

87. For the basis of land grants at Londonderry see LTR, 1: 177, 208, 211. The list of original proprietors is in ibid., pp. 62–63, and *NHPP*, 25: 275–77.

88. LTR, 1: 220.

89. See *NHPP*, 27: 513–14.

90. *Mass. Records*, 4, pt. 2: 546–47.

91. For a comparison with Massachusetts' approach to township grants, see Jonathan Belcher's letter to the Secretary of the Board of Trade, read on November 19, 1729, in *CSP Col*, 1728–29, no. 985.

92. The new townships were Kingston, Londonderry, Chester, Nottingham, Barrington, Rochester, Bow, Canterbury, Gilmanton, Barnstead, Chichester, Epsom, and Kingswood. This list does not include the eleven towns which incorporated from the original four: New Castle, Rye, and Greenland from Portsmouth; Hampton Falls, Kingston, and Kensington from Hampton; Newington, Somersworth, and Durham from Dover; and Stratham and Newmarket from Exeter. For a detailed description of the town charters see Fry, *New Hampshire as a Royal Province*, pp. 275–86. The town charters are printed in *NHPP*, vols. 24 and 25. For more information see Roy H. Akagi, *The Town Proprietors of the New England Colonies* (Philadelphia: University of Pennsylvania Press, 1924), pp. 207–8; Charles B. Kinney, *Church and State: The Struggle for Separation in New Hampshire, 1630–1800* (New York: Columbia University Press, 1955), pp. 50–54.

93. This last clause appeared in all the township charters. Kingston's charter had neither time limitations nor any other limiting requirement: apparently in 1694 Lieutenant Governor Usher (in the proprietory claimant Allen's interest) attempted to put something over on the Hampton townspeople by granting this new township within Hampton's boundaries on the premise that it was "given and granted . . . as far as in us lies" (*NHPP*, 25: 180–81). During the 1720's this method was successfully utilized against the proprietary claims to the forests and wastelands of New Hampshire, as the provincial government granted lands to the timber-hungry, land-hungry New Hampshire lumberers, farmers, and speculators.

Chapter III

1. The most recent scholarly discussion of the Masonian claim in the seventeenth century is Page, *Judicial Beginnings*, pp. 183–234. Other analyses may be found in Fry, *New Hampshire as a Royal Province*, pp. 17–65; Otis G. Hammond, "The Mason Title and Its Relations to New Hampshire and Massachusetts," *The Proceedings of the American Antiquarian Society* 26 (1916): 245–63; and Dean, *Captain John Mason*. The various land grants and other documents pertinent to the proprietary claims are in *NHPP*, 29: 19–218; Jenness, *Transcripts*.

2. All these grants may be found in *NHPP*, 29: 19–43; 1: 10–26. Also see Page, *Judicial Beginnings*, pp. 183–84.

3. Page, p. 187. "Severalty" is a legal term denoting property owned by individual right.

4. The division is printed in Jenness, *Transcripts*, pp. 18–19.

5. The patent is in *NHPP*, 29: 59–66. For the English background of the dissolution of the Council for New England, see Andrews, *The Colonial Period*, 1: 400–429.

6. Page, *Judicial Beginnings*, pp. 188–91. Only under the Laconia Company patent did Mason have any valid land claims in New England, but this patent was never used in defense of the title after 1659. For further support for this interpretation see *NHPP*, 1: 97–98; 17: 521–23; 29: 97; and Jenness, *Transcripts*, pp. 18–19, 42.

7. This will was probably not a conscious act of deception because it is possible that the land along the Newichewannock River comprised 7,000 acres, but Mason's claiming of this land within New Hampshire is incompatible with his 1635 patent description of New Hampshire. His will is in *NHPP*, 29: 88–95. Gorges had acknowledged Mason's ownership of the lands along the Newichewannock, though, in a deed of September 1635 (ibid., pp. 85–87). Mason's will, which represented his hopes rather than reality, was less than straightforward in defining New Hampshire, leaving it to his heirs to obtain what they could from it. It was probated on December 22, 1635.

8. *Mass. Records*, 4, pt. 1: 138; *CSP Col*, 1574–1660, p. 402; Jenness, *Transcripts*, pp. 38, 79; *NHPP*, 17: 502–6. Mason based his suits on the Laconia patents.

9. *NHPP*, 1: 193–96, 200, 205–6, 207–8; 17: 502–6. John and Richard Cutt and Brian Pendleton led at Portsmouth in encouraging acceptance of the protection and jurisdiction of Massachusetts.

10. *CSP Col*, 1574–1660, pp. 478–79; *NHPP*, 17: 506–7.

11. *CSP Col*, 1661–68, nos. 53, 64, 80.

12. Ibid., no. 1103; 1669–74, no. 687; *NHPP*, 1: 321–26; 17: 516–20, 533–38; 29: 100–104. His most flagrant lies were that Captain John Mason had spent £22,000 in settling people and erecting forts in New Hampshire, that in 1629 Mason and Gorges were given lands called the "Province of Laconia," that in the 1640's New Hampshire had experienced great population growth so that new townships were established there in 1646, that in 1652 Massachusetts invaded New Hampshire and forced the settlers to accept its authority and jurisdiction, that Joseph Mason had in that year claimed title to the province of New Hampshire, and that the majority of New Hampshire people both accepted and welcomed Mason's proprietorship.

13. Evidence of these tactics is readily available. See *CSP Col*, 1661–68, nos. 53, 64, 80, 1009, 1021, 1024, 1485, 1588, 1651; 1669–74, nos. 687, 907; *NHPP*, 17: 510–20, 533–38.

14. *CSP Col*, 1661–68, nos. 1021, 1103, 1485, pp. 346–47; *NHPP*, 1: 252–55; 17: 509–10.

15. *CSP Col*, 1661–68, no. 1024i; *NHPP*, 1: 284–86; 17: 510–13. Before calling their meeting at Portsmouth, the commissioners had declared Maine a royal colony and appointed justices of the peace there. One of these officers was Abraham Corbett, a Portsmouth innkeeper, who probably organized the Portsmouth meeting for the commissioners. He was later convicted of sedition by the Massachusetts government for his part in the episode. The people who signed the petition were a combination of the richest and poorest in the town. Going by the land grant of 1660, the last in a land-scarce town, fifteen of the thirty-two inhabitants who signed the petition were poor (eleven owned no land and four owned the minimum grant of thirteen acres), and most of the thirty-two were newcomers to the town. Then there were five relatively well-to-do men (John Pickering, Anthony Brackett, John Sherburne, George Walton, and George Wallis) owning over 100 acres each. Bernard Bailyn has suggested that this petition represented in part a strong division among merchants in New Hampshire—some looking toward Massachusetts connections, others toward London (Bailyn, *New England Merchants*, pp. 124–25). But he has overemphasized the extent of this division in 1665. New Hampshire colonists were confronted with a difficult dilemma in this situation, fearful of antagonizing either the Crown or Massachusetts. Rather than being influenced primarily by a mercantile conflict, those who signed this petition had local religious reasons (some were Quakers, some Anglican), economic reasons (about half were land-poor), and sociopolitical reasons (failure to obtain high social or political status in the town) for signing the petition. They hoped Mason would improve their status. It was incidental that some of them were merchants.

16. The attorney general's opinion is in *NHPP*, 29: 106–7. The sale offer is in *CSP Col*, 1669–74, no. 651.

17. For Mason's case in 1674–75 see *NHPP*, 17: 516–20. Captain Wyeborn's report is in *CSP Col*, 1675–76, no. 721.

18. *NHPP*, 29: 108–9.

19. Randolph's report, best known as "The Present State of New England, 1676," may be found in the British Museum, Additional Manuscripts, 28089, F. 5-20. Some extracts from this report are in *NHPP*, 1: 339-45.

20. *CSP Col*, 1677-80, nos. 342, 343; *NHPP*, 29: 109-10.

21. *NHPP*, 17: 529-30.

22. For more background see Michael G. Hall, *Edward Randolph and the American Colonies* (Chapel Hill: University of North Carolina Press, 1960), pp. 36-45.

23. These events can be traced through *CSP Col*, 1677-80, nos. 693, 996, 1036, 1041, 1053, 1054, 1058; *APC Col*, 1: 851-56. President John Cutt's commission is in *NHPP*, 1: 373-82. This commission received the Great Seal of England on September 18, 1679.

24. For examples see *NHPP*, vol. 40; *CSP Col*, 1661-68, nos. 1485, 1588, 1651; Page, *Judicial Beginnings*, pp. 25-26.

25. *NHPP*, 17: 524-28, October 22, 1677.

26. Ibid., 1: 393.

27. For the laws see ibid., pp. 382-408; for the letters of 1680, see ibid., pp. 409-13.

28. See, for instance, Mason's appointment of Richard Otis, Sr., as steward of his lands at Dover and Oyster River in ibid., pp. 429-30; and in *NHHS Coll*, 8: 63. See also *NHPP*, 17: 551-55.

29. Chamberlain to Blathwait, May 14, 1681, and Chamberlain to Lords of Trade, May 16, 1681, in *NHPP*, 17: 544-46, 546-51.

30. *NHPP*, 17: 559-62.

31. Richard Chamberlain was a close friend of Mason whom William Blathwayt, the auditor general of revenue for the colonies, had appointed secretary of New Hampshire in 1680.

32. *NHPP*, 17: 551-55. Richard Waldron (1615-89) was Dover's richest and most prominent citizen, and probably the most noted individual in upper New England. He was a farmer, fur trader, fisherman, lumber merchant, mariner, and shipbuilder. He served as a judge for Portsmouth and Dover, as Dover's deputy to the Massachusetts General Court from 1654 to 1679, and as Speaker of the Massachusetts House of Representatives in 1666-68, 1673-75, and 1679. From 1674 to 1679 he was appointed as major in command of the militias of upper New England. He served from 1679 to 1685 on the New Hampshire Council, where he led the opposition to the Masonian claims. The most famous and powerful of his colonial descendants were Colonel Richard Waldron (1650-1730); his son, Richard Waldron, Jr. (1694-1753); and his son, Thomas Westbrook Waldron (1721-85).

33. *NHPP*, 1: 517; *CSP Col*, 1681-85, nos. 346, 1800.

34. The Cranfield Commission is in *NHPP*, 1: 433-43. See p. 442, especially.

35. Cranfield's letter completely supported the New Hampshire Council's position, probably because the General Assembly had approved a tax for the colony. See Cranfield to Lords of Trade, December 1, 1682, ibid., 17: 570-74, 574-75; *NH Laws*, 1: 491-96.

36. For Cranfield's change of heart see his letters to the Lords of Trade between December 30, 1682, and June 19, 1683, in *NHPP*, 17: 575-78, 580-82, 582-84, 584-91; *CSP Col*, 1681-85, no. 870. Also Randolph to Lords of Trade, 1683, *NHPP*, 1: 491-96.

37. *NHPP*, 1: 449.

38. The best discussion of these irregular tactics is Page, *Judicial Beginnings*, pp. 208-21, 224-25. The manuscript court papers involved are deposited in the New Hampshire Historical Society. Also see *NHPP*, 1: 521.

39. The best contemporary description of Cranfield's activities is a letter of William Vaughan, a Portsmouth merchant, to Nathaniel Weare, the New Hampshire agent sent to England in 1684 to combat Mason's claims, dated February 4, 1683/1684, in *NHPP*, 1: 519-33. William Vaughan (d. 1719) of Wales was a protégé of Sir Josiah Child, a prominent London merchant. He arrived in Portsmouth by 1666. He married Richard Cutt's daughter Margaret in 1668 and became a partner in the Cutt fishery trade, which he inherited after Cutt's death in 1676. By the 1680's Vaughan was a leading merchant and politician in Portsmouth and remained so until his death. His daughter married Colonel Richard Waldron. His son, George (1676-1725), served as lieutenant governor of New Hampshire from 1715 to 1717; and George's son, William, carried on the Vaughan fish and lumber trade in Maine and was one of the planners and leaders of the Louisbourg expedition of 1745. See

NHHS Coll, 8: 318-25. Nathaniel Weare (1631-1718) moved to Hampton from Newbury, Massachusetts, in 1662, and became a prominent farmer-lumberer and political leader of the town. During the 1680's and 1690's Weare served as a member of the New Hampshire Council and was an attorney for Vaughan and others against the Masonian suits. In 1694 he was appointed chief justice of the Supreme Court of Judicature in New Hampshire. He remained a member of the council until 1715, when he retired from politics. His two sons, Peter and Nathaniel, and his grandson, Mesech (1713-86), also had distinguished political careers. See *NHHS Coll*, 8: 380-94.

40. For the complaints and briefs against Mason, see *NHPP*, 1: 511-14, 515-19; *CSP Col*, 1681-85, no. 1800. Cranfield's answer is in *CSP Col*, 1681-85, no. 1895. See R. N. Toppan and A. S. Goodbrick, eds., *Edward Randolph; Including His Letters and Official Papers*, Prince Society Publications, vols. 24-28, 30-31 (Boston, 1898-1909), 4: 15, 17, for Randolph's change of heart.

41. Cranfield to Lords of Trade, October 16, 1684, *CSP Col*, 1681-85, no. 1895.

42. *NHPP*, 1: 569-75.

43. This incident is colorfully related in Belknap, *History* (Farmer ed.), pp. 114-15; Page, *Judicial Beginnings*, p. 225.

44. *NHPP*, 1: 573-74; Page, *Judicial Beginnings*, p. 224. The technicality was that Vaughan had not asked Cranfield to reconcile the differences between Mason and himself in the case, as required in Cranfield's Commission.

45. For example, during the course of a debate over the validity of Mason's patents in the New Hampshire Council, Richard Waldron angrily remarked: "We are not the more bound to believe it because the King hath writt it" (Page, *Judicial Beginnings*, p. 199, quoting from the manuscript court papers). For other examples, see *NHPP*, 1: 519-33, 544-54, 578-82.

46. Allen's deed and purchase from the Masons is in *NHPP*, 29: 148-52. For the numerous petitions, appearances, and the final decision on New Hampshire's status, see *CSP Col*, 1689-92, nos. 1377i, 1450, 1668, 1729, 1740, 1745, 1751, 1998, 2006, 2018, 2078, 2102, 2104.

47. *NHPP*, 2: 57-69.

48. Ibid., 3: 176; *NH Laws*, 1: 534-35. The law became effective in October 1692.

49. Usher to Lords of Trade, October 29, 1692, *CSP Col*, 1689-92, no. 2586.

50. *NH Laws*, 1: 541-44; *NHPP*, 3: 183-87.

51. *NHPP*, 29: 155.

52. The Kingston charter is in ibid., 9: 431-32. For the Hampton response see HTR, 1: 367-68, 372. See also the earlier discussion of this issue in chapter 2 above.

53. *CSP Col*, 1696-97, no. 1222.

54. The continual harassment of Usher and his ultimate removal from office (1692-97) can be followed in ibid., 1693-96, nos. 108, 1097, 1306, 1599, 1917, 1922, 1936, 2105, 2142; 1696-97, nos. 294, 303, 341, 396, 500, 672, 730.

55. Ibid., 1697-98, no. 145.

56. Usher to Board of Trade, February 16, 1696/97, ibid., 1696-97, no. 730. Also see nos. 742, 1061, 1095, and 1096.

57. *CSP Col*, 1696-97, nos. 1220-23; 1697-98, no. 145; *NHPP*, 2: 260-61.

58. For a description of these cases see Page, *Judicial Beginnings*, pp. 230-32. Evidently Allen selected the judge but not the jury in these cases. In both cases the defendants won postponements on technicalities. See the letter of Partridge, Waldron, Jaffrey, and Penhallow to Leverett and Newton, July 14, 1699, Saltonstall Papers, Folio XI-D, MHS.

59. Saltonstall Papers, Folio XI-D.

60. Bellomont to Board of Trade, September 9, 1699, and June 22, 1700, in *CSP Col*, 1699, no. 769; 1700, nos. 580, 582ii.

61. *NH Laws*, 1: 657-58, 660-66.

62. Bellomont to Board of Trade, June 22, 1700, *CSP Col*, 1700, no. 580. Also see no. 354.

63. *CSP Col*, 1702-3, no. 68. For the background of Allen's successful appeal see ibid., 1700, no. 953 (p. 670); 1701, nos. 271, 365, 366.

64. *NH Laws*, 1: 681-82, 693, 695-96. These laws were passed under Lieutenant Governor William Partridge's administration, as Bellomont had died in May 1701.

65. Bellomont had described Partridge as unfit for his post: he was "a mean man . . . preferring a little sordid gain before the interest of England" and "a millwright by trade, which is a sort of carpenter, and to set a carpenter to preserve woods is like setting a wolf to keep sheep" (Bellomont to Board of Trade, April 23, 1700, *CSP Col*, 1700, no. 354). For Usher's reappointment see ibid., 1702-3, no. 590.

66. The marriage occurred in March 1698/99; the mortgage was signed on October 14, 1701. *NHPP*, 29: 159-62; 2: 118; *APC Col*, 2: 847.

67. *CSP Col*, 1702-3, nos. 501, 564, 565, 580, 649.

68. For the grants see *NH Laws*, 2: 45-46, 57. Dudley found it easy to justify his political actions to the Board of Trade because Usher had been instructed by the Crown not to disturb the existing courts, judges, or juries, so as to ensure a fair trial of the land controversy. Dudley took care to promote himself as favorable to Allen's claims in his letters to royal authorities, but his actions tended to favor the antiproprietary elements (particularly his failure to appear before the New Hampshire Council to order the juries to bring in special verdicts). See for instance his letters to the Board: *CSP Col*, 1702-3, no. 315; 1704-5, nos. 600, 1109; 1710-11, no. 491. For Usher's objections to him see ibid., 1704-5, nos. 35, 120, 260; 1706-8, no. 1592; 1708-9, no. 663; 1710-11, no. 335. Kimball in his biography of Dudley suggests that Dudley intentionally favored and sympathized with the New Hampshire settlers in this controversy. The evidence suggests, however, that Dudley consistently sought a pragmatic compromise settlement of the controversy. See Everett Kimball, *The Public Life of Joseph Dudley* (New York: Longmans, Green & Company, 1911).

69. *NHPP*, 29: 162-63. Kingstown was the fifth town.

70. *CSP Col*, 1704-5, nos. 600, 982.

71. *NHPP*, 29: 164-65. A list of the members of each subscription committee is in ibid., 17: 693.

72. In this compromise offer the New Hampshire settlers were in fact giving Allen 6,500 acres and £2,000 for his guarantee of land titles within the existing towns. From their point of view, if the Crown wanted to give Allen all Crown lands beyond the existing settlements for his own profit, that was its privilege; they would not oppose it. See ibid., 29: 165-67.

73. Dudley to Blathwait, May 9, 1705, *CSP Col*, 1704-5, nos. 120, 1109.

74. On Waldron see *CSP Col*, 1706-8, no. 1592. The mortgage is in *NHPP*, 29: 167-72.

75. The documents relating to *Allen* v. *Waldron* are in *NHPP*, 2: 514-62; for the specific arguments of both sides see pp. 522-28. The forged Wheelwright deed is in ibid., 1: 56-60.

76. Ibid., 2: 560-61.

77. Governors Bellomont and Dudley had warned the Board of Trade that New Hampshire juries would never accept Allen's claims. Dudley wrote: "It is most certain there is not one person in the Province of New Hampshire, Councilor, Judge, or Juryman, who will ever be found to do that title right, being so concerned in the lands of the Province" (*CSP Col*, 1704-5, no. 1422). For Bellomont's views see ibid., 1699, no. 769; 1700, no. 580. Bellomont claimed that New Hampshire colonists would start a rebellion if Allen ever attempted a forcible entry upon his claims.

78. For the creation of Vaughan's agency and the petition, see *NHPP*, 3: 353-55; *CSP Col*, 1708-9, no. 65.

79. Joseph H. Smith, *Appeals to the Privy Council from the American Plantations* (New York: Columbia University Press, 1950), p. 157.

80. *NHPP*, 3: 377-78; Usher to Board of Trade, July 1709, and July 3, 1710, in *CSP Col*, 1708-9, no. 663; 1710-11, no. 283. Dudley to Board of Trade, November 15, 1710, ibid., 1710-11, no. 491.

81. The deed is in *NHPP*, 29: 213-17. The political and economic interests involved in this deal were very complex, but land speculation was the guiding motive. See Fry, *New Hampshire as a Royal Province*, pp. 301-13; Oedel, "Portsmouth," pp. 456-60; Jere Daniell, "Politics in New Hampshire under Governor Benning Wentworth, 1741-1767," *William and Mary Quarterly*, 3rd ser. 23 (January 1966): 87-88.

82. *CSP Col*, 1708-9, no. 392 (March 1, 1708/9).

83. *NHPP*, 29: 173-75.

84. Ibid., pp. 175-77.

85. See the numerous petitions addressed to the New Hampshire government between 1715 and 1740 requesting new township grants (*NHPP*, 3: 655, 707, 725, 765, 773-74, 777, 781, 791, 793, 799-800; 4: 29, 84, 197, 222, 239, 541, 777, 778, 790, 832; 9: 168-72).

86. For examples of the boundary controversy, see ibid., 24: 822-924. A committee was chosen to establish town boundaries in 1715 (ibid., 3: 618-19, 760). The law of 1719 is in *NH Laws*, 2: 340-45.

87. *NHPP*, 29: 177-88; for the Massachusetts quitclaim see ibid., pp. 189-93; for the tripartite agreement of April 6, 1739, see ibid., pp. 193-96.

88. Mason was the party of the first part to this tripartite agreement; the five New Hampshire men—John Rindge, Theodore Atkinson, Andrew Wiggin, George Jaffrey, and Benning Wentworth (all socially prominent landed merchants)—were parties of the second part; and John Thomlinson, an ambitious and aggressive London merchant, was the party of the third part.

89. The deed and quitclaim are in *NHPP*, 29: 213-17. This agreement did not end all controversy about the Masonian claims. The final settlement of all claims did not occur until 1790, well after the American Revolution. But the proprietary claims were never an important political issue or economic threat in New Hampshire after the 1740's. See Hammond, "The Mason Title," pp. 261-62.

Chapter IV

1. Clark, *The Eastern Frontier*, pp. 9-10, has an excellent discussion of these factors.

2. *Historical Statistics of the United States, Colonial Times to 1957* (Washington, D.C.: Government Printing Office, 1960), p. 756.

3. For examples see *NHPP*, 1: 199, 299-301; 24: appendices.

4. New Hampshire Council to Board of Trade, May 7, 1681, ibid., 17: 541-43.

5. The Pennacooks accepted white supremacy, while the Abnaki tended to be hostile. Actually, there were relatively few Indians south of the Piscataqua River because a smallpox epidemic had wiped most of them out.

6. For more detailed descriptions of the actual warfare in New Hampshire, including many colorful and grisly incidents, see Belknap, *History* (Farmer ed.), pp. 71-85, and Everett S. Stackpole, *History of New Hampshire*, 4 vols. (New York: The American Historical Society, 1916), 1: 91-99. The best concise general history of King Phillip's War is Douglas E. Leach, *Flintlock and Tomahawk: New England in King Phillip's War* (New York: Little, Brown, 1958), though it slights events in northern New England. Leach also provides a short summary of the war in *The Northern Colonial Frontier, 1607-1763* (New York: Holt, Rinehart & Winston, 1966), pp. 53-61. Also see Alden T. Vaughan, *New England Frontier: Puritans and Indians, 1620-1675* (Boston: Little, Brown, 1965), pp. 309-20.

7. Richard Waldron to Governor Leverett, September 25, 1675, *NHPP*, 1: 354-57.

8. *NHPP*, 1: 318-19; *Mass. Records*, 5: 53, 55, 76.

9. Belknap, *History* (Farmer ed.), p. 74; *Mass. Records*, 5: 72; Leach, *Flintlock and Tomahawk*, p. 213.

10. The story of this deception—by means of a "sham" battle or a "training," in which the Indians, under the impression they were playing a game, discharged their weapons and then were easily captured at Waldron's home—can be found in Belknap, *History* (Farmer ed.), pp. 76-86, and in Stackpole, *History of New Hampshire*, 1: 93-94. Supporting documents are in *NHPP*, 1: 357-58, 360. Most of the 200 Indians captured were sold into slavery.

11. Waldron, Cutt, Daniel, Pike, Martyn, and Vaughan to Governor Leverett, October 19, 1676, *NHPP*, 1: 358-59. I have modernized the spelling of this letter.

12. Ibid., pp. 358-59, 361, 363.

13. A formal treaty with the Eastern Indians was signed at Casco Bay (ibid., 1: 365). See Belknap, *History* (Farmer ed.), p. 83.

14. *Mass. Records*, 5: 144-45.

15. Andros had strengthened the frontier in 1688 by building at least ten forts in Maine and garrisoning them with English and colonial troops. But by May of 1689 these troops had

been recalled. *CSP Col*, 1689-92, nos. 242, 285, 336, 407, 901, 906, 912, 913; Viola Barnes, *The Dominion of New England* (New Haven: Yale University Press, 1923), p. 218.

16. See the "Journal of Reverend John Pike of Dover," *NHHS Coll*, 3: 40-67, especially p. 43 (hereafter cited as "Pike Journal"). Pike had moved from Massachusetts to Dover in 1681 and remained in Dover and Portsmouth until his death in 1710. The most colorful account of this famous attack is Belknap, *History* (Farmer ed.), pp. 124-30. Also see Stackpole, *History of New Hampshire*, 1: 171-76, and Thomas Hutchinson, *The History of the Colony and Province of Massachusetts-Bay*, ed. L. S. Mayo (Cambridge: Harvard University Press, 1936), 1: 355ff.

17. "Pike Journal," *NHHS Coll*, 3: 43; Belknap, *History* (Farmer ed.), p. 131.

18. For the towns' petition see *NHPP*, 2: 34-39. For the attempts to create an independent or royal government, see ibid., pp. 30-34, 43-46; *CSP Col*, 1689-92, nos. 883-85.

19. *NH Laws*, 1: 372-73, 409-10; *NHPP*, 2: 40-42.

20. "Pike Journal," *NHHS Coll*, 3: 43; Belknap, *History* (Farmer ed.), pp. 132-33.

21. *Collections of the Maine Historical Society*, 2d ser., vol. 5, contains many letters describing the chaotic and difficult conditions prevalent in the Piscataqua region at this time. For specific comments concerning New Hampshire, see ibid., pp. 105, 157; Belknap, *History* (Farmer ed.), p. 133; *CSP Col*, 1689-92, nos. 904-6, 1911, 1918, 2569, and p. 729.

22. John Usher to Robert Treat, May 8, 1693, *NHPP*, 2: 105.

23. Richard Waldron and William Vaughan to William Wallis, October 21, 1692, Toppan, *Randolph*, 2: 414-15. For details of the petition's failure see *CSP Col*, 1693-96, no. 2057. In 1693 the New Hampshire General Assembly sent further petitions, but the Lords of Trade dismissed them because they had not been presented by a "duly authorized person" (ibid., no. 250).

24. "Pike Journal," *NHHS Coll*, 3: 45; Belknap, *History* (Farmer ed.), pp. 138-41.

25. *NHPP*, 2: 136-38, 140, 141, 158.

26. *CSP Col*, 1693-96, no. 1306.

27. *NHPP*, 2: 180.

28. New Hampshire House of Representatives to Lieutenant Governor Usher, September 24, 1696, ibid., 3: 47. For more details on the tax and salary conflict see pp. 44-46, 195-96. Usher was both the Crown's appointee and the proprietary claimant's agent, and as such he never received any salary from the General Assembly. The harvest of 1696 was bountiful, so famine conditions disappeared (ibid., p. 228).

29. New Hampshire Council to Lieutenant Governor Staughton, March 26, 1697, ibid., 2: 225.

30. "Pike Journal," *NHHS Coll*, 3: 43-50. The tax laws are in *NHPP*, 3: 164-67, 188-89, 195-96, 203-4, 207.

31. *NHPP*, 2: 324, 325, 346-47, 362-63, 366; 3: 100, 108, 110-11, 162, 238-39; 19: 727, 736, 738; *CSP Col*, 1700, no. 155.

32. Rawlinson Manuscripts, C. 128, F. 15, Bodleian Library; *CSP Col*, 1702-3, nos. 225, 265.

33. *CSP Col*, 1702-3, nos. 611, 687*ii*.

34. 1710 was the only year with no rumors of a large invasion. "Pike Journal," *NHHS Coll*, 3: 50-61; Samuel Penhallow, *The History of the Wars of New England with the Eastern Indians* (Boston, 1726); Hutchinson, *Massachusetts-Bay*, 2: 102-51; Belknap, *History* (Farmer ed.), pp. 166-81; Leach, *Northern Colonial Frontier*, pp. 117-25.

35. *NHPP*, 2: 415-18, 425-28, 438, 442, 452-54, 492, 584, 585; 3: 290-91, 294, 315, 328-29, 392, 436, 462-63, 497, 511, 530; Kimball, *Joseph Dudley*, pp. 134-40.

36. *NHPP*, 3: 328. See also the General Assembly's petition of October 22, 1707, to the Queen, praising Dudley's "prudent foresight and good intelligence" and his "great care and good conduct" (ibid., pp. 350-52, 455).

37. The taxes are in *NH Laws*, 2: 60-116 passim.

38. Ibid., pp. 55-56. There were a few exceptions—ministers, selectmen, Crown officers, and members of the council. Provisions were to be purchased by each town.

39. *NHPP*, 2: 457. For other evidences of hardship during the war see ibid., 3: 395, 507, 520.

40. Ibid., 2: 476.

41. Ibid., 3: 349. George Vaughan of Portsmouth was chosen agent for New Hampshire. He presented petitions in June and July of 1708 describing the New Hampshire people as "few and inconsiderable . . . and daily lessening by the murders of the savage enemy" and "reduced to great poverty." He asked for 200 English soldiers, a "fourth rate man of war," and "stores of all sorts" (*CSP Col*, 1706-8, no. 1514; 1708-9, no. 19).

42. The list of military stores is in *NHPP*, 2: 599-600. The Order in Council is in *CSP Col*, 1708-9, no. 332. See nos. 354, 797; Rawlinson Mss., C. 128, F. 7.

43. New Hampshire House of Representatives to Usher, June 27, 1709, *NHPP*, 3: 386. These war petitions undoubtedly exaggerated the realities for effect.

44. *NHPP*, 3: 410-11; *NH Laws*, 2: 94-96.

45. On the war alone, the New Hampshire government spent about £2,600 in 1710 and £2,300 in 1711 (*NHPP*, 3: 467-71, 525-28). For the issuance of paper currency see *NH Laws*, 2: 94-96, 102-4, 105, 111-12, 117.

46. *NHPP*, 2: 119, 131-32, 405, 496, 570, 588, 598; 3: 307-8, 369, 465, 511, 520-21, 555.

47. The peace treaty signed with the Indians on July 13, 1713, is in ibid., 3: 543-46. For Governor Dudley's designation of frontier towns see *CSP Col*, 1711-12, no. 375.

48. *CSP Col*, 1720-21, no. 447. Norridgewock was a French mission on the Kennebec River.

49. Dudley to Board of Trade, March 1, 1708/9, ibid., 1708-9, no. 392.

50. *NHPP*, 2: 645.

51. Belknap, *History* (Farmer ed.), pp. 202-12; Penhallow, *History of the Wars*. Most of the new townships were not yet settled by 1722; only Londonderry and Chester had settlers during this war. Penhallow described the Piscataqua frontier as including Dunstable, Exeter, Oyster River, Cochecho, and Wells. He attributed the war to the establishment of new towns along the Kennebec River, which threatened Indian land use, and also to the sharp trading practices of New England frontier traders (Penhallow, pp. 83-89).

52. For a definitive discussion of Father Rale's work at Norridgewock, see James P. Baxter, *The Pioneers of New France and New England* (Albany: Munsall, 1894). A brief but significant analysis of Rale is F. H. Eckstrom, "The Attack on Norridgewock, 1724," *New England Quarterly* 7 (September 1934): 541-78.

53. For examples see Penhallow, *History of the Wars*; Belknap, *History* (Farmer ed.), pp. 200-202; *New England Historical and Genealogical Register*, 32: 21-27; *NHPP*, 3: 693-701, 740; 2: 731, 743, 745; *CSP Col*, 1722-23, no. 73.

54. *CSP Col*, 1722-23, nos. 184, 242, 322, 805. War was declared on July 25, 1722.

55. Ibid., 1724-25, no. 360; *NHPP*, 4: 91, 128, 169, 182-83.

56. *NH Laws*, 2: 366-68, 372-73, 382, 386-87; *NHPP*, 4: 148.

57. *NHPP*, 9: 435. For a contrary view of the effect of the war in New Hampshire, see Lieutenant Governor Wentworth to Board of Trade, September 12, 1724, *CSP Col*, 1724-25, no. 360.

58. The new townships were Bow, Canterbury, Gilmanton, Barnstead, Epsom, and Chichester. These grants comprised most of the remaining unclaimed land legally recognized as part of New Hampshire.

59. Most of the documents relating to the boundary dispute are in *NHPP*, 19: 179-646. For the extracts of these charters see ibid., pp. 601, 608, 609.

60. The Massachusetts government interpreted the charter as a crooked line three miles across the river along its entire course regardless of its direction. New Hampshire's government objected that this interpetation violated the Massachusetts Charter, that a literal interpretation of the charter would be even more absurd, and that, therefore, some other solution should be found, such as a line run due west from the Atlantic coast three miles north of the Merrimack River's mouth.

61. Examples of both tax evasion and double taxation can be found in *NHPP*, 19: 196-99, 206-10, 249. In January 1732/33 Governor Belcher represented the situation to the Board of Trade as follows: "The poor borderers on the lines . . . live like toads under a harrow, being run into Goals [*sic*] on the one side and the other, as often as they please to quarrel . . . they pull down one another's houses, often wound each other, and I fear it will end in bloodshed" (ibid., 4: 649).

62. Ibid., 19: 180-81. The conflict revolved around where to start the line and whether it should be straight or crooked.

63. Ibid., pp. 182–85. The Hampton petition complained not only of tax evasion by "borderers" but also of the theft of Hampton masts and timber by Massachusetts inhabitants (ibid., 2: 166). The surveyors turned in a map establishing a crooked line following the course of the Merrimack three miles northward from the ocean through Kingston (ibid., 29: 609).

64. Ibid., 3: 321, 414–15, 548–49; 19: 185–86. John Wentworth, Mark Hunking, and John Plaisted served on a committee with persons from Massachusetts to settle the problem of which town should tax which borderers so that no one would pay double taxes.

65. The New Hampshire government created eight separate parishes from the original four towns between 1714 and 1740, marking only the beginning of a general trend. The eight were Newington in 1714, Stratham in 1716, Hampton Falls and Rye in 1726, Newmarket in 1727, Somersworth in 1729, Durham in 1732, and Kensington in 1737. For the various petitions concerning new townships see above, chap. 3, n. 85. Also see Map 3.

66. *NHPP*, 3: 626, 632. The dispute again concerned the location of the starting point for the boundary line.

67. Ibid., pp. 755–56, 779–80; 9: 480–81; 19: 188, 195. For reiteration of this new position, see 19: 199. This area lay between the Merrimack and Connecticut Rivers, west of New Hampshire's traditional bounds. See Map 2.

68. John Wentworth to Board of Trade, December 26, 1720, *CSP Col*, 1720–21, no. 333.

69. This situation is further analyzed in chapter 7. Wentworth's letters are quite enlightening as to the ambitions and motivations behind these attacks, particularly his interest in obtaining control of the best mast trees for the mast trade and of good land for speculative purposes. See *CSP Col*, 1720–21, no. 333; 1724–25, nos. 45*i*, 121, 204, 476, 714; 1726–27, nos. 95, 300, 498; 1728–29, nos. 59, 898; 1730, no. 148. For the 1731 decision to seek a separate governor, see *NHPP*, 19: 223–25. After Wentworth's death in 1730 the mantle of leadership fell upon Lieutenant Governor David Dunbar's shoulders, but the real leaders of the faction were Theodore Atkinson, Benning Wentworth, George Jaffrey, Andrew Wiggin, Joshua Peirce, and John Rindge—ably supported by John Thomlinson of London. For the efforts of this group see the Atkinson-Thomlinson correspondence in *NHPP*, 4: 833–65; 5: 915–31; 18: 149–73; the correspondence of David Dunbar with various royal officials in *CSP Col*, 1730–37; Benning Wentworth to Joshua Peirce, March 22, 1730/31, Peirce Papers, Portsmouth (N.H.) Athenaeum; the various messages of the New Hampshire House of Representatives to the governor and council from 1731 to 1741 in *NHPP*, vols. 4–5; and the boundary line papers in *NHPP*, vol. 19.

70. *NHPP*, 24: 31–62, 748–819.

71. The pro-Massachusetts element can most clearly be understood by reading the correspondence of Governor Belcher with the Secretary of New Hampshire, Richard Waldron, Jr., who more or less ran New Hampshire political affairs during Belcher's absences in Massachusetts; see the Waldron Papers and the Belcher Papers, NHHS, and the Belcher Letterbooks, MHS. The petition asking that New Hampshire be annexed to Massachusetts (*NHPP*, 9: 349–56) is evidence of the rather strong pro-Massachusetts sentiment in the outlying New Hampshire towns in 1739. For the leaders of the two factions, see *NHPP*, 19: 223–25; the Belknap Papers, MHS; and C05 10, 880, pp. 92–93. One of the more representative petitions against Belcher and in favor of the Wentworth version of the boundary is New Hampshire House of Representatives to the King in Council, November 4, 1737, Weare Papers, vol. 1, NHHS.

72. Although New Hampshire had contended for a due west line starting three miles north of the Merrimack at the coast, the award had the line parallelling the southwestern meandering of the river until it turned north and from there a due west line extending to New York, which extended the southern and western boundaries of New Hampshire. In addition, the colony was awarded its due north line claims for the northern boundary. See Map 2.

73. Francis Wilks to Secretary Willard, March 20, 1739/40, *NHPP*, 19: 468–70. The award is in ibid., pp. 476–79. Actually, the activities of John Thomlinson and his connections in England were more crucial in determining the Privy Council's decision.

74. Thomlinson was an agent of Ralph Gulston, the naval mast contractor, and an extensive trader with such New Hampshire lumberers and merchants as Rindge, Atkinson, Wibird, and the Wentworths (ibid., 18: 166, 168–69).

75. Ibid., 19: 471–74.

76. The best analysis of the foundations for his political power is Daniell, "Politics in New Hampshire," pp. 76–105.

77. The grants of 1722 were to Londonderry, Barrington, Chester, Rochester, and Nottingham. Those of 1727 were to Gilmanton, Barnstead, Canterbury, Bow, Chichester, and Epsom. Several motives impelled these grants. Londonderry's had a communitarian objective. Barrington's was a government subsidy to would-be iron manufacturers. But perhaps the most important reason for the grants lay in the Parliamentary act of 1722 which threatened New Hampshire's extensive lumber trade by forbidding the cutting of white pines outside township bounds (8 George I, C. 12). Genuine land hunger and desires for land speculation were important motives as well.

78. Kingswood's charter is in *NHPP*, 9: 456–58. This grant appears to have been a reward to Belcher's political friends. When the new Masonian proprietors quitclaimed the lands of the various towns in 1746, they ignored the Kingswood grant (most of them were Wentworth supporters) on the grounds that no settlement existed. Later they regranted the lands to others.

79. In Chester, for instance, only 13 of the original 125 grantees became actual settlers, yet the town had few conflicts with the nonresident proprietors. In Londonderry almost all the inhabitants were proprietors—over 120 out of 135—so the town followed the patterns of the older towns.

80. *NHPP*, 9: 722. The other towns that petitioned were Nottingham (ibid., p. 634), Canterbury (p. 87), Chichester (pp. 126–27), Barrington (p. 45), and Epsom (p. 247).

81. Ibid., pp. 126–27.

82. *NH Laws*, 2: 530–31, 557–58, 578.

83. *CSP Col*, 1716–17, nos. 249*i*, 286, 291, 301, 302, 582–84, 591, 592, 599. For the estate inventories see Probate Records, New Hampshire State Archives.

84. John Wentworth to⸺, June 15, 1730, John Wentworth Manuscripts, Box 1, Folder 1, NHHS.

Chapter V

1. Paul C. Phillips, *The Fur Trade*, 2 vols. (Norman, Oklahoma: University of Oklahoma Press, 1961), 1: 121. For other general discussions of the New England fur trade see Francis X. Maloney, *The Fur Trade in New England* (Cambridge: Harvard University Press, 1931); Vaughan, *New England Frontier*, pp. 211–34; Bailyn, *New England Merchants*, pp. 23–32, 49–60; Leach, *Northern Colonial Frontier*, pp. 90–108, 144–62.

2. *NHPP*, 1: 139.

3. Ibid., 1: 61–98, 100–101.

4. *Mass. Records*, 2: 60; DTR, 1: 249–51, 410. For the various methods of fur trade regulation used by the Massachusetts government, see *Mass. Records*, 1: 179, 298, 322–24; 2: 83; 3: 424; 4, pt. 1: 354, 355; 4, pt. 2: 365; 5: 5, 345.

5. For evidence on Waldron and the fur trade see *Mass. Records*, 4, pt. 2: 242, 414; *NHPP*, 1: 348; John Scales, *History of Dover, New Hampshire* (Manchester, N.H., 1923), pp. 325, 349. For Samuel Hall of Exeter, another probable licensed fur trader, see *NHPP*, 40: 474–76.

6. Robert Mason to Lords of Trade, December 11, 1671, *CSP Col*, 1669–74, no. 687. Mason's exaggerations were an attempt to attract official attention to New Hampshire.

7. *NHPP*, 2: 80. Shipping Returns, CO5 968, p. 6; also see CO5 967, 968, and 969 passim.

8. *NHPP*, 2: 656. Wentworth probably told Shute that the post was unnecessary, as there were no Indians in the colony. For an analysis of the Massachusetts truckhouse system see Ronald O. McFarlane, "The Massachusetts Bay Truck-houses in Diplomacy with the Indians," *New England Quarterly* II (March 1938): 48–65.

9. The New Hampshire General Assembly foresaw this possibility when it passed a law in 1713 that required all Indian traders to obtain a license from the Massachusetts Governor (*NH Laws*, 2: 199–200).

10. In 1743 Governor Benning Wentworth attempted to establish a truckhouse near Lake Winnipesaukee but gave it up when he ran into opposition from both the Indians (over its projected location) and the House of Representatives (over patronage). *NHPP*, 5: 95, 209, 219–25 passim.

11. Saltonstall, *Ports of Piscataqua*, p. 12; ETR, 1: 162; *NHPP*, 40: 454–55. The recipients of these grants were Richard Waldron, Edward Starbuck, and William Furber of Dover, and Christopher Lawson of Exeter.

12. The best studies of the seventeenth-century development of the New England and North American fisheries are Harold Innis, *The Cod Fisheries* (Toronto: University of Toronto Press, 1954); Raymond McFarland, *A History of the New England Fisheries* (New York: Appleton & Company, 1911); Charles B. Judah, Jr., *The North American Fisheries and British Policy to 1713*, Illinois Studies in the Social Sciences, vol. 18, nos. 3–4 (Urbana: University of Illinois, 1933); Bailyn, *New England Merchants*. For the special climate of the Isles of Shoals see Jenness, *The Isles of Shoals*. Jenness describes the curing process which produced the famous "dunfish" as "a process of alternate drying and sweating, without salt." He estimated the market price of these fish to be three or four times that of Newfoundland cod. See also Belknap, *History*, 3: 130–33; Samuel J. McKinley, "The Economic History of Portsmouth, New Hampshire, from its First Settlement to 1830" (Ph.D. diss., Harvard University, 1931), pp. 298–303; and Clark, *The Eastern Frontier*, pp. 27–32.

13. John Winthrop noted that seventeen fishing ships had visited the Isles of Shoals between January and March of 1633/34. *Winthrop's Journal*, ed. James K. Hosmer, 2 vols. (New York: Barnes & Noble, 1908), 1: 120. Charles L. Woodbury, *The Relation of the Fisheries to the Discovery and Settlement of North America* (Boston, 1880), pp. 25–26, emphasizes the role of the New England "winter fishery" both in developing farmer-fishermen and attracting new immigrants to New England. Matthew Gyles, the wealthiest taxpayer of Dover in 1648, was an example.

14. The Cutts, Seeleys, Hunkins, Christopher Jose, John Davis, John Moore, and Philip Babb, for example, emigrated to New Hampshire and Maine (*NHPP*, 40: 47, 94, 116, 471; Judah, *North American Fisheries*, pp. 90–91; Bailyn, *New England Merchants*, pp. 77–78).

15. Another possible cause for their relocation lay in the fact that after 1647 women were forbidden to live on the Isles (*Mass. Records*, 2: 57). For Tobias Langdon see *NHPP*, 40: 148. The Cutts were probably the most significant of these families. John Cutt (d. 1681) was the son of Richard Cutt, a member of the House of Commons from Wales during Cromwell's rule. John and his two brothers, Robert (a shipbuilder) and Richard (d. 1676), came to New England before 1646 and invested in the fisheries at the Isles of Shoals. John and Richard moved into Portsmouth, received large land grants and a sawmill grant from the town, began exporting lumber as well as fish, and emerged as wealthy mariner-merchants by the 1670's. Both men held the significant town offices in the 1660's and 1670's, and in 1679 John was appointed president of the new royal colony of New Hampshire. At that time he was probably the wealthiest man in the colony. The daughters (four in all) of these two brothers obtained good marriages within the emerging mercantile community of New Hampshire, marrying Richard Waldron, William Vaughan, Samuel Penhallow, and Thomas Daniel, respectively. See *NHHS Coll*, 8: 308–11; Jenness, *Isles of Shoals*, pp. 86–88.

16. Families such as the Vaughans, Sherburnes, Joses, Daniels, Hills, Jaffreys, Pepperrells, Penhallows, Gerrishes, and Elliotts exemplify this trend.

17. For a more general discussion of the role of the fisheries in recruiting a merchant class in New England, see Bailyn, *New England Merchants*, pp. 82–83; Innis, *The Cod Fisheries*, pp. 80–81.

18. *NHPP*, 17: 520–21; *CSP Col*, 1669–74, no. 687. In colonial trade, a quintal of fish was equal to 100 pounds.

19. New Hampshire Council to Lords of Trade, May 7, 1681, *NHPP*, 17: 541–43; Cranfield to Lords of Trade and Cranfield to Blathwayt, October 23, 1682, ibid., pp. 567–70, and Toppan, *Edward Randolph*, 6: 115–17.

20. Jenness, *Isles of Shoals*, pp. 105–7, suggests that Massachusetts' purchase of Maine was the crucial factor in the decline of the Shoals fishery because the northern islands (those under the jurisdiction of Massachusetts) were abandoned to avoid high taxes and differing

religious approaches. Fairchild, *Messrs. William Pepperrell*, pp. 18-19, accepts this thesis and develops the further one that the opening of a fishing trade with Newfoundland in the late seventeenth century was more important in this decline. Nevertheless, the Indian wars were probably the most significant factor in both the hasty withdrawal from the northern islands and the expansion of the Newfoundland fishery before the 1690's. Also see Lyman V. Rutledge, *The Isles of Shoals in Lore and Legend* (Barre, Mass.: Barre Publishers, 1965), pp. 26-27.

21. William Vaughan, for example, went so far as to obtain a license from the French allowing him to fish off Nova Scotia (*CSP Col*, 1681-85, no. 1985). For other Newfoundland traders see *NHPP*, 2: 79; Shipping Returns, August 1694-August 1695, C05 968, pp. 2, 4; Noyes, pp. 315-16. For a general discussion of the growth of the Newfoundland fishery see Judah, *North American Fisheries*, pp. 106-76, and McFarland, *New England Fisheries*.

22. For the customs returns see C05 968, pp. 1-9. The 160 quintals of fish were imported from Newfoundland.

23. Bellomont to Board of Trade, November 1700, *CSP Col*, 1700, p. 678; McFarland, *New England Fisheries*, p. 69; *NHPP*, 2: 356.

24. Bellomont to Board of Trade, April 23, 1700, *CSP Col*, 1700, no. 354; see also ibid., p. 676.

25. George Vaughan to Board of Trade, July 6, 1708, ibid., 1708-9, no. 19 (italics mine); see Thomas Dudley to Board of Trade, April 8, 1712, ibid., 1711-12, no. 375. For further discussion of the role of the wars upon the New England fishery see William B. Weeden, *Economic and Social History of New England, 1620-1789*, 2 vols. (Boston, 1891), 1: 373; McFarland, *New England Fisheries*, pp. 74-75, 80-81.

26. For the roles of Mark Hunking, John Penhallow, and William Pepperrell (a resident of Kittery who owned property in New Castle, New Hampshire) see Fairchild, *Messrs. William Pepperrell*, p. 80. For Sampson Sheafe see Saltonstall, *Ports of Piscataqua*, p. 28. The NH Shipping Returns of the 1720's, while incomplete, reveal the importance of Joshua Peirce, Richard Wibird, and William Pepperrell. They are complete for 1723, 1725, and 1727. In those years Pepperrell exported significant quantities of fish in at least five vessels, Peirce did so in at least four vessels, and Wibird in at least six vessels (CO5 968, pp. 1-17, 29-43). The largest single fish export from New Hampshire was undertaken by Samuel Deering, a resident of York in Maine, who sent 1,587 quintals to England in one vessel in 1727. William Vaughan was involved in the Canso fisheries off Nova Scotia by 1719 and remained active in this area through 1744, when he played a significant role in the successful plan of attack on Louisbourg in that year (*CSP Col*, 1719-20, no. 236; Belknap, *History* [Farmer ed.], pp. 269-70; McFarland, *New England Fisheries*, p. 91). For Wentworth and Reed see *CSP Col*, 1724-25, no. 401*vi*.

27. The 1742 Shipping Returns are in CO5 968, pp. 44-53.

28. *CSP Col*, 1720-21, no. 94*ii*. The New Hampshire agent, Henry Newman, described New Hampshire's fisheries to the Board of Trade in similar terms in 1721 but reduced the number of those employed in the fishery to about 300 (Rawlinson Mss., C. 128, no. 14). Also see McFarland, *New England Fisheries*, p. 83, and Innis, *The Cod Fisheries*, p. 161.

29. For figures on the 1718 fish export see Joseph J. Malone, *Pine Trees and Politics* (Seattle: University of Washington Press, 1964), p. 153. Joshua Peirce's activities in the Canso fishery are revealed in the Peirce Papers, Barrett Wendell Collection, Baker Library, Harvard University; see also McKinley, "Portsmouth, New Hampshire," pp. 300-303. The Shipping Returns show Peirce involved in both the Canso and Newfoundland fisheries; in 1727 he imported 560 quintals from Canso and 250 quintals from Newfoundland. The port of Piscataqua imported a total of 1,155 quintals of fish in 1727 (CO5 968, pp. 29ff.). For the Pepperrells' activities in both areas see Fairchild, *Messrs. William Pepperrell*, pp. 97-105. For Wentworth's opinion see John Wentworth to Board of Trade, August 7, 1727, *CSP Col*, 1726-27, no. 661; Popple to Wentworth, February 28, 1727/28, ibid., 1728-29, no. 71.

30. Wentworth wrote that "the trade of this country has been five times more within these last ten years than before" (*CSP Col*, 1726-27, no. 661). He attributed this growth to the use of paper currency and wanted authority from the Board of Trade to issue more of it.

31. *NHPP*, 3: 820; 9: 561-62.

32. These figures are only approximations and do not reflect the total fish exportation of the New Hampshire fish traders; however, they are based upon the only records available for New Hampshire. In 1725, out of a total of 8,810 quintals, some 6,400 quintals went to Spain and Portugal, 2,200 to Marblehead, and 200 to the Caribbean. In 1727, out of a total of 8,165 quintals, about 3,500 went to Spain and Portugal, 3,550 to England, and 1,030 to the Caribbean. CO5 968, pp. 25-41, 42-43.

33. Jonathan Belcher to Board of Trade, April 4, 1737, CO5 880, Cc. 54, pp. 1-4; Belknap, *History* (Farmer ed.), p. 234.

34. NH Shipping Returns, 1742, CO5 968, pp. 45-53. Theodore Atkinson commented on the hard times in a letter of May 19, 1742, to John Thomlinson: "This year has been exceedingly expensive, provisions of all kinds having advanced near 100%" (*NHPP*, 18: 175). For New Hampshire fish prices see McKinley, "Economic History of Portsmouth," pp. 359-60, 383, 421.

35. The French had never accepted either English or New England claims in the Canso area, and they attempted to break up New England's exploitation of the fisheries there when the war began. Belknap, *History* (Farmer ed.), pp. 265-81, has an account of the rivalry and the New England expedition against Louisbourg.

36. In 1727, for example, sixteen out of thirty Piscataqua-based traders exported fish, while in 1742 the figures were twenty-two out of forty-five. By 1752 further specialization occurred, as only twenty-eight out of eighty-five exported fish—a drop from one-half to one-third (CO5 967, pp. 7-20). In 1752 New Hampshire exported 7,860 quintals of fish, of which 5,300 went to Spain and Portugal (67.4 percent), an indication of the importance of Catholic Europe as a market for New Hampshire.

37. For evidence of Massachusetts' dominance of the fisheries see Innis, *The Cod Fisheries*, pp. 70, 118-19, 161; *CSP Col*, 1700, p. 678. As an example, when in 1721 New Hampshire had about 100 fishing vessels, Marblehead alone had about 120. Or again, in 1699 Boston exported 50,000 quintals of fish, as compared to the Piscataqua export of 1,300 quintals.

38. See Table 2, which shows lumber exportation in the early eighteenth century, for evidence of its importance. For an extended description of New Hampshire lumber resources see Belknap, *History*, 3: 56, 73-88.

39. *NHPP*, 1: 45, 91-93.

40. For Exeter, see Bell, *History of Exeter*, pp. 318-24; Noyes, pp. 237-38. Dover mill-owners are listed in DTR, vol. 1. For a discussion of Hampton's mill-owners, see Dow, *History of Hampton*, pp. 531-43. For Portsmouth, see DTR, vol. 1. A list of Exeter and Dover mill-owners may be found in David E. Van Deventer, "The Emergence of Provincial New Hampshire, 1623-1741" (Ph.D. diss., Case-Western Reserve University, 1969), p. 191.

41. *CSP Col*, 1661-68, no. 1103, p. 347. *NHPP*, 40: 3-14 passim, 22, 35, 55, 63, 91, 132, 196; 31: 13-15, 32-33, 219-22. These men included Captain John Underhill, Richard Waldron, Hatevil Nutter, Edward Colcord, Clement Campion, George Durrell, Richard Bulgar, James Johnson, Valentine Hill, William Payne, William Waldron, William Bellew, Edward Starbuck, Christopher Lawson, Joseph Miller, Henry Roby, Philip Chesley, William Roberts, Ralph Hall, Thomas Canney, Philip Lewis, Thomas Wiggin, John Pickering, Thomas Wilson, Ambrose Gibbons, and Richard Cummings. This list includes only those who came before the courts from 1640 to 1653.

42. *NHPP*, 40: 134. Hill had close mercantile connections with his brother, John Hill, a London merchant, and in the early 1640's had engaged in both the fur trade and the fisheries (Bailyn, *New England Merchants*, pp. 35, 51, 80). During the 1650's he built a sawmill, purchased a large farm, and probably engaged in shipbuilding as well. Bryan Pendleton had become a leading Portsmouth fish merchant and politician during the 1650's and 1660's (Noyes, p. 537). He died by April of 1681; his will is in *NHPP*, 31: 191-93.

43. Pp. 95, 98-99, 101. Bailyn's citation of the Hutchinsons' nineteen sawmills on the Great Works River must be discarded, since that river is in Maine, not New Hampshire.

44. DTR, 1: 220, 303-5; ETR, 1: 147, 160-63, 184, 216; HTR, 1: 10, 82.

45. Scales, *History of Dover*, p. 66; Bell, *History of Exeter*, p. 336; Fairchild, *Messrs. William Pepperrell*, p. 9; PTR, 1: 73. In 1650 Thomas Trickett (or Trickey) of Dover built a

forty-ton vessel (Noyes, p. 694). Lumber was so widely utilized that it served as the basic medium of exchange in New Hampshire throughout the seventeenth century (*NHPP*, vol. 40).

46. New Hampshire Council to Lords of Trade, May 7, 1681, *NHPP*, 17: 541–43. For further evidence of this dependence see ibid., pp. 578–79; Toppan, *Edward Randolph*, 7: 410; *CSP Col*, 1700, no. 354.

47. *CSP Col*, 1699, no. 769*xiv*; Bridger to Board of Trade, October 24, 1706, ibid., 1706–8, no. 552.

48. Maverick is quoted in Bailyn, *New England Merchants*, p. 124. Also see *NHPP*, 18: 922–23; *CSP Col*, 1681–85, no. 98, p. 46. These ship owners included Thomas Daniel, John Cutt, Jr., William Vaughan, Richard Waldron, John Hunking, Robert Elliott, Reuben Hull, Richard Martin, Nathaniel Fryer, Thomas Harvey, George Jaffrey, John Partridge, Peter Coffin, Samuel Wentworth, and John Hinckes. Three of the nineteen owners were widows.

49. NH Shipping Returns, August 1, 1694–September 1, 1695, CO5 968, pp. 1–2, 7–9. Unfortunately, the records list only the masters and not the owners of the vessels, so that it is impossible to determine accurately either the proportion or the names of the New Hampshire traders involved in the lumber trade. Judging from the basis of familiar New Hampshire names among the masters, perhaps thirty of them were based at Piscataqua, representing twenty to twenty-five New Hampshire lumber traders.

50. The classic work on the New England mast trade is Robert G. Albion, *Forests and Sea Power* (Cambridge: Harvard University Press, 1926); however, Malone is indispensable as well.

51. Bailyn, *New England Merchants*, p. 133; Albion, *Forests and Sea Power*, pp. 50–52.

52. According to *CSP Col*, 1661–68, no. 1333, only one out of five ships carrying masts had any contract with naval suppliers.

53. These men and their families were all in New Hampshire before 1660. See Noyes; *NHPP*, vol. 40; NH Probate Records.

54. For Randolph's masting activities see Toppan, *Edward Randolph*, 1: 6–8; 5: 71–73. For Allen see *CSP Col*, 1696–97, no. 141.

55. *NHPP*, 1: 424–28. At least nine out of the thirteen councillors of the 1680's were lumber and mast traders, as were at least six out of eleven members of the first House of Representatives and seven out of eight councillors of the 1690's (Richard Waldron, William Vaughan, Robert Elliott, Peter Coffin, Henry Green, Nathaniel Weare, and John Hinckes). For Vaughan's background see above, chapter III, n. 39.

56. See Table 2. Significantly enough, in this year 25 percent of the masts exported went to the Caribbean islands rather than to the mother country—another indication of the unspecialized nature of the trade in the seventeenth century. That this exportation was comparatively low may be seen by a comparison with Robert Mason's testimony of 1671 on New Hampshire trade. Mason claimed that New Hampshire exported "20,000 tons of deals and pipestaves" and "10 shiploads of masts." In 1695, only three ships exported masts. On the other hand, Mason consistently exaggerated New Hampshire's prospects to English officials as part of his efforts to obtain proprietary rights in the area. He stated, for example, that New Hampshire was the "most populated" and "best improved for land" in all New England, "having a great trade to all parts" (*NHPP*, 17: 515).

57. In his correspondence with the Board of Trade, Governor Bellomont referred to Partridge's trade with Catholic Europe repeatedly, but perhaps the best single example is his letter of April 23, 1700, *CSP Col*, 1700, no. 354. The lumber trade with Spain and Portugal dropped precipitately in 1718–20, in 1726–27, and after 1739 because of wars and was illegal for most of the remainder of the colonial period as a result of the two wars and the Sugar Act of 1764, which forbade the export of lumber to any part of Europe except Great Britain. The customs returns show only one vessel clearing for Catholic Europe in 1741 (it returned with 1,000 hogsheads of salt) and show no trade with Catholic Europe in 1742.

58. For evidence of early shipbuilding in New Hampshire see *NHPP*, 40: 64–65, 71; Saltonstall, *Ports of Piscataqua*, pp. 12–13; Bell, *History of Exeter*, pp. 66, 336. Across the Piscataqua in Kittery, Robert and Richard Cutt, John Diamond, and Samuel Winkley were

also engaged in shipbuilding before 1660. After 1660 John Bray and his son-in-law, William Pepperrell, built their fortunes on shipbuilding and trade (Fairchild, *Messrs. William Pepperrell*, pp. 13-14).

59. Belknap, *History*, 3: 147; Saltonstall, *Ports of Piscataqua*, p. 17; *APC Col*, 2: 299; George H. Preble, "Vessels of War Built at Portsmouth, New Hampshire, 1690-1868," *New England Historical and Genealogical Register*, 22: 393-403.

60. For detailed descriptions of the various types of vessels, see John Robinson and George Dow, *Sailing Ships of New England, 1607-1901* (Salem, Mass., 1922), pp. 9-33. Briefly, a sloop was a small single-masted vessel; ketches were somewhat larger, with two masts; a brigantine was a still larger two-masted vessel; ships (with three masts) were usually the largest vessels in the colonial trade; barks and pinks also had three masts and varied greatly in size. The returns of 1681 are in *NHPP*, 18: 922-23. For significant discussions of tonnage see Bernard Bailyn and Lotte Bailyn, *Massachusetts Shipping, 1697-1714* (Cambridge: Harvard University Press, 1959), pp. 8-9; Christopher French, "Eighteenth-Century Shipping Tonnage Measurements," *Journal of Economic History* 33 (June 1973): 434-43. Of forty-seven entries between June 1680 and April 1681, twenty-two were ships and eighteen were ketches (Belknap, *History* [Farmer ed.], p. 96).

61. These vessels include only those which were indicated in the records as built in New Hampshire or at Kittery. They were found in the incomplete Piscataqua returns of 1692, the returns of 1695, and the Massachusetts Shipping Records, 1686-88, CO5 848, pp. 16, 17, 23, 24. These statistics are not a complete list of New Hampshire ships built or used between 1680 and 1696; however, no duplications have occurred, so that these figures do represent the minimum number built.

62. Unfortunately, it is impossible to determine accurately either ownership, building location, tonnage, or the home port of the 134 vessels in these returns. The Bailyns found that the Massachusetts fleet of 1698 had 171 vessels, of which 42.7 percent were sloops, 20.5 percent were brigs, and 18.7 percent were ships; they found, too, that the New Hampshire–registered vessels trading in Massachusetts were almost all sloops, averaging 16.7 tons; they also found that between 1678 and 1700 New Hampshire had built sixteen vessels, averaging 52.7 tons, whose home port was in Massachusetts (Bailyn and Bailyn, *Massachusetts Shipping*, pp. 19, 82-83, 88, 106). The latter statistic indicates the trend toward larger vessels by the 1690's.

63. This total comprises the 26 vessels of August 1681, the 34 vessels that were both built and based at Piscataqua from 1687 to 1695, the 16 vessels built between 1678 and 1700 that were based in Massachusetts, and the 2 warships that were built for the Royal Navy.

64. These markets are listed in accordance with the volume of lumber products they received from Piscataqua in the 1690's. In 1695, 131 vessels cleared for Boston, in 1713 there were 129 clearances, 128 in 1714, 118 in 1723, but 197 in 1724 as new expansion occurred. Fairchild has compiled these clearances of 1713 on from the *Boston News-Letter* (Fairchild, *Messrs. William Pepperrell*, p. 84n). Figures such as these reflect only relative consistency because there is the strong possibility that the vessels involved in the coastal trade had increased in average size, thereby increasing the actual volume of trade. The records provide neither tonnage nor import volume statistics, so this factor cannot be accurately established.

65. Archibald MacPhaedris (1690?-1729) was a mariner who came to New Hampshire from Scotland by 1712 and supplied lumber goods to his various friends and connections —James Caldwell and Robert Wilson & Co. in Ireland, and Robert Fenwick in Cadiz. He married Sarah Wentworth, the daughter of Lieutenant Governor John Wentworth, in 1718, by which time he had at least six vessels engaged in overseas trade. His estate at his death was inventoried at £6,330, including his mansion (now known as the Warner House), which was valued at £2,500. MacPhaedris Letterbook, Warner House, Portsmouth, New Hampshire.

Richard Wibird (1680?-1732) came to Portsmouth about 1700, having been an understeward on a British man-of-war, and set up a shop as a retail merchant. He soon became involved in the fishery, then became a mariner-merchant in both wholesale and retail of fish and lumber. By the 1720's he was one of the richest merchants in Portsmouth: he paid the highest tax in the town in 1727 and owned five houses, three slaves, and two forty-ton vessels which traded with the West Indies. His estate at his death was valued at more than £3,800. Brewster, *Rambles about Portsmouth*, 1st ser., p. 157; 2d ser., pp. 66–67; Clifford Shipton, *Sibley's Harvard Graduates* (Boston: Massachusetts Historical Society, 1873–), 7: 139.

John Frost (1681–1733) was the son of Major Charles Frost of Kittery. John was captain of a British warship before 1701. In 1702 he married William Pepperrell's daughter and moved to New Castle, where he became a mariner-merchant. By 1720 he was third in wealth in the town, and in 1725 he paid the highest taxes in New Castle. He was appointed to the New Hampshire Council in 1723. By 1727 he was shipping lumber and naval stores to Newfoundland. His estate was probably worth around £10,000 at his death. See *NHPP*, 32: 395–400.

Captain Daniel Warner (1699–1778) moved to Portsmouth from Ipswich, Massachusetts, by 1720. He married Sarah Hill, a granddaughter of Valentine Hill, and by 1727 was a mariner-merchant owning two vessels of 40 and 50 tons, respectively, and trading with the West Indies. By the 1740's he had expanded his enterprise to four vessels, carrying lumber and livestock to Newfoundland and Barbados and masts to England, and acting as both a wholesale and retail merchant in Portsmouth. By 1725 he and his son, Jonathan, were second among New Hampshire-based traders in total volume of overseas trade. Shipping Returns, CO5 967, 968, passim.

Joshua Peirce (1670–1743) moved to New Hampshire from New Jersey and settled in Portsmouth in 1700. He married into the Hall family of Greenland and began working the fishery, opening a retail store in his home. After 1713 he engaged in large-scale fishing at Canso and gradually entered into the wholesale trade in lumber and fish with the West Indies. By 1742 he and his son, Joshua, Jr., owned at least four vessels engaged in trade with the West Indies, North Carolina, and Newfoundland, not to mention their many fishing vessels at Canso. At his death he was worth about £6,000. *NHPP*, 33: 31–36.

66. For evidence of Jaffrey's trade in West Indian slaves see CO5 968, p. 43. Biographical sketches of the Jaffreys are given in Shipton, *Harvard Graduates*, 5: 156–66; Noyes, pp. 375–76; Brewster, *Rambles about Portsmouth*, 2d ser., pp. 68–69, 156–58. The Odiornes (Jotham Odiorne, 1675–1748, and Jotham Odiorne, Jr., 1703–51) had experiences quite similar to those of the Jaffreys as they established themselves in the fishery business at New Castle, became retail merchants, and then expanded into the lumber trade by the 1730's, purchasing sawmills and woodlands in the process. By 1742 they owned at least six vessels and were among the top six New Hampshire-based traders; by 1747 they owned at least seventeen vessels. See *NHPP*, 34: 129–31.

67. In 1727 Henry Sherburne owned 200 tons of shipping (four vessels) and carried on 9 percent of the total trade of the Piscataqua region. Samuel Waldo was the top trader with 450 tons (10.3 percent), while William Pepperrell was the third highest with 230 tons of shipping (seven vessels), carrying on 8.6 percent of the total trade. Sherburne traded lumber primarily, but also some fish, livestock, and naval stores to the southern colonies, Newfoundland, and the West Indies and returned with rum, sugar, and provisions for New Hampshire consumption. CO5 968, pp. 42–43.

68. Mark Hunking Wentworth owned five vessels to the Sherburnes' six in 1742, but three of Wentworth's vessels were mast ships of 300 to 400 tons each. Wentworth's mast contracts eventually made him the richest man in New Hampshire until his brother, Governor Benning Wentworth, began appropriating 500 acres in every new township grant to himself. Strangely enough, ten years later neither of the Sherburnes engaged any vessels in trade, though both were very rich men. Brewster, *Rambles about Portsmouth*, 2d ser., pp. 44–50, 53–56, 71.

69. The merchants holding the mast contracts between 1691 and 1742 were John Taylor, Samuel Allen, Francis Collins, Ralph Gulston, William Wallis, and John Thomlinson (Albion, *Forests and Sea Power*, p. 235; Malone, *Pine Trees and Politics*, p. 65; Theodore Atkinson to John Thomlinson, November 26, 1740, in *NHPP*, 18: 165–67; Curtis P. Nettels, *The Money Supply of the American Colonies before 1720*, University of Wisconsin Studies, no. 20 [Madison, Wis., 1934], p. 74n). As early as 1700 Bellomont saw the mast trade monopolized by "ten or twelve private men" (*CSP Col*, 1700, no. 354).

70. These changes and policies are well outlined in Malone, *Pine Trees and Politics*, pp. 47–53, 70–76, 98–99; and in Laurence H. Gipson, *The British Empire before the American Revolution*, 15 vols. (New York: Knopf, 1958–70), 3: 39–42.

71. Malone, p. 66, saw that it had little effect but did not explain why. For the law see *NH Laws*, 2: 82–83. The stated purpose of the act was to preserve white pines which were 24 inches in diameter at 12 inches from the ground from unauthorized cutting. The real point was that there were no trees that the surveyor of the woods could authorize for cutting under the given definition of private property.

72. Malone, *Pine Trees and Politics*, pp. 70, 75–76.

73. This is particularly true of the boundary controversy. The pro-Massachusetts people in New Hampshire—the Waldrons, Gilmans, Vaughans, and Weares, for example—had close connections with Massachusetts mast traders (Westbrook and Waldo) and political leaders in the 1720's and 1730's (these families all owned timberlands in Maine), while the pro–New Hampshire group—the Wentworths, Jaffreys, and Atkinsons—had connections with both Massachusetts merchants (David Jeffries) and London merchants (Thomlinson) but not directly with the mast agents or the Massachusetts political leadership. Naturally enough, the latter group sought larger boundaries and less dependence upon Massachusetts so that they could enjoy more freedom of action. Since this approach also appealed to other outsiders in the lumber economy of New Hampshire, it emerged as the more popular approach. Thus, the desire for a more open economy played an important role in the Wentworth clan's ultimate success.

74. The coastal trade with Massachusetts, consisting almost entirely of lumber products, did not expand significantly between 1689 and 1723; but with the granting of new New Hampshire townships in 1722, this trade increased by about 60 percent in the mid-1720's, with 118 vessels in 1723 and 197 vessels in 1724. Little evidence remains of the quantity of Piscataqua trade with Boston between 1725 and 1742, but it probably rose proportionately with the rest of Boston's coastal trade. See Fairchild, *Messrs. William Pepperrell*, p. 88. In 1730 the value of the Piscataqua-Boston trade was estimated at £5,000 sterling, while the value of Piscataqua's exports to the West Indies and Europe was estimated at £1,000 sterling (Belcher to Board of Trade, January 22, 1730/31, *NHPP*, 4: 532). These figures, if accurate, reflect a relative decline in the importance of the coastal trade in the Piscataqua's total exportation during the 1720's.

75. These statistics are drawn from the New Hampshire tax summary for 1753 in the Weare Mss., vol. 2.

76. It is difficult to evaluate the effect of Dummer's War on the mast trade, since many merchants were smuggling masts to Spain, and the New England mast contractors probably did not send all their vessels through the Piscataqua customs office in the 1720's. The mast exportation statistics for 1742 (see Table 4) are probably reliable because all the mast contracting agents were exporting through Piscataqua customs. For a list of mast and lumber prices in the 1740's see Belknap, *History*, 3: 80.

77. Shipping Returns, 1742–68, CO5 967, 968, 969, passim.

78. Jonathan Belcher to Board of Trade, April 4, 1737, CO5 880, Cc. 54, pp. 1–4.

79. The NH Shipping Returns show that at least seven new vessels were built in 1722, twenty-four in 1723, fourteen in 1724, twenty-two in 1725, ten in 1726, and seventeen in 1727. Shipbuilding expanded rapidly in the 1720's. The twenty-two vessels built in 1725 totaled only 1,130 tons, for a 51.4 ton average per vessel, but the seventeen vessels of 1727 totaled 2,010 tons, for a 118.2 ton average. Five of the 1727 vessels were ships of 200–400 tons.

80. These names have been culled from the NH Probate Records and *NHPP*, vol. 17. The best treatment of shipbuilding at Portsmouth is McKinley, "Economic History of Portsmouth," pp. 272–97, but he did not use the customs records of the colony.

81. At least twelve vessels were built in 1740, eighteen in 1741, thirty in 1742, thirty-three in 1743, fifteen in 1744, twenty-six in 1745, and eight others sometime between 1740 and 1745. Building costs in the 1740's ranged from £11 to £16 per ton, as compared to £5–£6 per ton of the 1720's.

82. CO5 968, p. 42. The only other finished wood products exported in 1727 were two parcels of "woodenware." The total figure for a number of these exports is unknown

because the customs official did not record the total of such exports carried by three of the vessels (ibid., p. 53).

83. "Overseas ports" means ports located outside New England. The five vessels involved carried either ballast, fishing stores, or fish.

Chapter VI

1. For some general discussions of the New England economy of the seventeenth and eighteenth centuries, see Weeden, *Economic and Social History*; Nettels, *The Money Supply*; Bailyn, *New England Merchants*; Fairchild, *Messrs. William Pepperrell*; and Eleanor C. Lord, *Industrial Experiments in the British Colonies of North America*, Johns Hopkins University Studies in Historical and Political Science, vol. 17 (Baltimore, 1898).

2. Bell, *History of Exeter*, p. 49; ETR, 1: 175. For other examples of land grants for this purpose see the grant to Daniel Maud, a teacher and pastor at Dover (DTR, 1: 220), and also the excerpts of Dover's town records in Alonzo H. Quint, *Historical Memoranda Concerning Persons and Places in Old Dover, New Hampshire* (Dover, 1900), p. 151.

3. *NH Laws*, 2: 349–50.

4. Peagrum to Popple, April 30, 1736, *CSP Col*, 1735–36, no. 297. John Wentworth exemplified this approach when he wrote a new grantee about his son's grants of land in the New Hampshire townships: "I pray God he may live to reap the benefit of them. It will be a fine estate in time" (John Wentworth Mss., Box 1, Folder 1).

5. By "earlier settlers" I mean anyone in New Hampshire before 1645 or anyone coming into New Hampshire before 1660 who had no connections with or interest in mercantile activities with either England or another colony at the time of his immigration. Among the more prominent newcomers were Valentine Hill, Bryan Pendleton, William Vaughan, John and Richard Cutt, Francis Champernoune, Richard Martyn, John Hunking, George Jaffrey, Nathaniel Fryer, William Partridge, John Hinckes, Walter Barefoote, Thomas Graffort, Thomas Daniel, and Reuben Hull.

6. There are numerous examples of prominent older settlers intermingling with mercantile immigrants. Richard Waldron became an ally of Valentine Hill and William Vaughan, while his son married John Cutt's daughter; Peter Coffin of Dover was another ally of Hill; John Tuttle, a Dover shipbuilder and lumberer, had married his daughter to Richard Martyn; Samuel Wentworth, the eldest son of Elder William Wentworth of Dover, married Mary Benning, the daughter of a prominent Boston merchant; Samuel's eldest son, John, was employed by both William Partridge and William Pepperrell in the 1690's. One could go on and on, taking almost any mercantile name in New Hampshire and checking marriages in Noyes. Bernard Bailyn found this general pattern of alliances among mercantile elements to be prevalent throughout New England by the end of the seventeenth century (*New England Merchants*, pp. 191–97).

7. Noyes, p. 17; *CSP Col*, 1700, no. 336; *APC Col*, 1680–1720, pp. 298–99, 303–5. The Gilmans worked through Elisha Hutchinson of Boston, while another Boston merchant and mast supplier carried accounts with Richard Waldron, Sr., and Richard Waldron, Jr., Peter Coffin, Thomas Daniel, William Vaughan, and Reuben Hull of New Hampshire (*NHPP*, 31: 269; Noyes, p. 16). For the shipping returns of 1681 see *NHPP*, 18: 922–23.

8. Bailyn, *New England Merchants*, pp. 61–74, discusses the failures of New England capitalists who attempted iron and wool manufacturing.

9. They were a failure in the sense that New Hampshire exported limited quantities of iron goods and no woolen manufactured goods at all. They did, however, export large quantities of sheep by the 1740's (305 sheep in 1742, for example). The nature of these policies will be discussed below.

10. In 1660, Samuel Mavericke noted "Mutch Tar hath been made at Cochecho Creek" (*New England Historical and Genealogical Register*, 39: 33). Waldron's fur trading activities and sawmills were located along the Cochecho River.

11. The earliest innkeepers were Henry Sherburne, Robert Tuck, Henry Roby, Henry Deering, Walter Abbott, Anthony Stanyon, Thomas Trickey, and Thomas Beard. By 1671, however, almost all the mercantile-minded had obtained liquor licenses; these included Richard Waldron, Peter Coffin, James Weymouth, Richard Wilcom, Richard Cutt, John Cutt, Thomas Daniel, Richard Martyn, Richard Stileman, Nathaniel Fryer, Edward West, Samuel Wentworth, and William Vaughan. In 1672, William Cotton, Bryan Pendleton, and Joachim Harvey joined this group. By 1677, John Partridge, Robert Elliott, George Jaffrey, Roger Kelly, Edward Gilman, Moses Gilman, Andrew Wiggin, and John Fabes had obtained licenses. In 1686, the New Hampshire courts divided license holders into two categories: the innkeepers and the "retailers out of doors." These special retailers provided rum for the lumberers and fishermen as part of their wages; they included such prominent merchant-traders as Richard Waldron, Edward Hilton, Richard Stileman, William Partridge, Peter Coffin, Richard Gerrish, Reuben Hull, John Hinckes, Robert Elliott, Walter Barefoote, William Vaughan, John Fabes, Thomas Harvey, and Thomas Graffort. The innkeepers were Samuel Sherburne, Thomas Diamond, Richard Wilcomb, Edward Gilman, John Young, Charles Gleeden, Joseph Beard, James Smith, John Partridge, Edward Bickford, Joshua Purmut, Henry Crown, Edward Cater, John Johnson, and Francis Mercer. *NHPP*, 40: 283, 338, 404.

12. Elwin Page in his study of the seventeenth-century courts suggests that drunkenness was the most common criminal offense prosecuted in the courts of that era (*Judicial Beginnings*, p. 123). See also *NHPP*, 1: 391, for testimony that in 1680 drunkenness did "greatly abound."

13. Though masts and ship timbers are included in any list of naval stores, they are not included in this discussion because there was no problem exporting them. The naval stores which enterprisers had difficulty producing and exporting were pitch, tar, turpentine, resin, flax, and hemp. For extended treatment of the imperial approach to naval stores production see Lord, *Industrial Experiments*; Albion, *Forests and Sea Power*; Andrews, *The Colonial Period*, vol. 4; Malone, *Pine Trees and Politics*.

14. For Partridge's proposals see *CSP Col*, 1697-98, no. 987; 1699, no. 817; 1704-5, nos. 396, 464. The best discussion of Bridger is Malone, *Pine Trees and Politics*, pp. 21ff., 164-65; see also Bridger to Board of Trade, October 18, 1706, *CSP Col*, 1706-8, no. 544, in which he writes that if the new premiums are not paid, the whole project will collapse. For Usher's view see Malone, p. 167n.

15. 3 & 4 Anne, c. 10. Malone, pp. 26-27, discusses the more relevant clauses. The act placed premiums on merchantable pitch and tar at £4 per ton; resin and turpentine at £3 per ton; hemp at £6 per ton; and masts, yards, and bowsprits at £1 per ton.

16. *NH Laws*, 2: 330-31. The act expired after three years and was not renewed.

17. Malone, *Pine Trees and Politics*, pp. 20-27, 46; Partridge to Board of Trade, November 11, 1698, *CSP Col*, 1697-98, no. 987; Partridge and Jackson to Board of Trade, September 25, 1699, ibid., 1699, no. 817; Bellomont to Board of Trade, April 23, 1700, ibid., 1700, no. 354. Partridge had recommended that tar and pitch could be produced in Maine if 1,000 garrison troops were sent there along with emigrating poor families.

18. Joseph Dudley to Board of Trade, March 1, 1708/9, ibid., 1708-9, no. 392.

19. John Wentworth to Board of Trade, December 30, 1723, ibid., 1724-25, no. 45*i*. Also, between 1715 and 1740 a number of letters and testimonials were presented to the Board of Trade in support of bounties upon hemp and flax as an encouragement to their production in New Hampshire. See, for example, ibid., 1734-35, no. 613; 1735-36, nos. 94, 313.

20. The naval authorities, convinced of the inferiority of New Hampshire pitch and tar, never supported the bounty system and obtained its temporary removal in 1724 and a permanent reduction in the premiums in 1729 (8 George I, c. 12; 2 George II, c. 35; Malone, *Pine Trees and Politics*, pp. 38-43).

21. Table 6 is relatively self-explanatory. New Hampshire's change from a net importer of naval stores to a net exporter occurred some time between 1727 and 1742, probably in 1741 with the change in mast agents, though this conclusion is mainly supposition, since evidence is lacking. The mast agents who dominated the trade by 1742 were Ralph Gulston and Mark H. Wentworth. Together they exported 82.4 percent of the pitch, 96.4 percent of the tar, and 69.3 percent of the turpentine leaving Piscataqua in 1742.

22. No general study has ever been done on labor conditions in New Hampshire, probably because of the inadequate sources. New England labor conditions are discussed, however, in Richard Morris, *Government and Labor in Early America* (New York: Columbia University Press, 1946); Carl Bridenbaugh, *Cities in the Wilderness* (New York: Ronald Press, 1938); Abbott E. Smith, *Colonists in Bondage* (Chapel Hill: University of North Carolina Press, 1947).

23. Bellomont to Board of Trade, April 17 and September 9, 1699, and June 22, 1700, in *CSP Col*, 1699, nos. 262, 769; 1700, no. 580. Bellomont wrote with amazement that three shillings a day was "the least that's ever paid to a common laboring man" and suggested that hemp be raised in Ireland, where labor wages were "cheaper 3/4" than in New Hampshire. On February 17, 1719/20, Governor Shute wrote the Board that "considering the excessive price of labor, the merchant can afford what is imported cheaper than what is made in the country" (ibid., 1719–20, no. 564*i*).

24. George Vaughan to Board of Trade, May 10, 1715, ibid., 1714–15, no. 389*i*.

25. Belcher to Duke of Newcastle, June 28, 1735, ibid., 1734–35, no. 613.

26. Bell, *History of Exeter*, pp. 439, 442, 446, and DTR, 1: 343, provide examples.

27. Page, *Judicial Beginnings*, p. 121; Belknap, *History* (Farmer ed.), p. 75. For an example of an Indian servant in 1671 see *NHPP*, 31: 127, the will of Thomas Leighton of Dover.

28. *NH Laws*, 1: 570.

29. Ibid., 1: 679; 2: 128, 138–39, 152–53, 196–98.

30. Ibid., 2: 152–53. Since there is almost no evidence on the number of Indian servants and slaves in New Hampshire, it is impossible to judge the effect of the £10 tax, except in very general terms. According to the act itself the number of Indian servants and slaves had increased during the long wars from 1689 to 1713 with the French and Indians.

31. Indian slaves were still prevalent in the 1720's; they were rated for tax purposes at £20 per head in 1728 (*NHPP*, 4: 301). Other evidence suggests that there were enough present for them to be listed among "others" counted in the new listing of ratable polls and estates in 1753 (ibid., 6: 175).

32. Pendleton owned two Negroes in 1663 (Noyes, p. 537). Other owners of Negroes in the 1670's and 1680's were John Hall of Dover; Seaborn Cotton of Hampton; and Jane Jose, Joanna Severett, Richard Martyn, Richard Cutt, Jethro Furber, and Reuben Hull of Portsmouth (*NHPP*, 31: 161–67, 195–98, 274–81, 330–31, 345–46, 376–80). References to the last three names above are found in the estate inventories in NH Probate Records. The wills and estate inventories reveal the existence of only five slaveholders between 1690 and 1713—Bridget Graffort, the Portsmouth widow of a fish merchant; Nicholas Follett, a Portsmouth mariner; Augustine Bullard, another Portsmouth mariner; Richard Martyn, a Portsmouth merchant; and David Laurence, an Exeter lumber trader (*NHPP*, 31: 376–80, 473–81, 649–51). Any conclusion about the social background of slaveholders must be extremely tentative.

33. *NH Laws*, 1: 570; 2: 292. The reasons for the Crown's veto are found in ibid., 1: 861, and in *CSP Col*, 1706–8, no. 369.

34. *NH Laws*, 2: 128, 138–39, 196–98.

35. For population statistics on Negroes see *Hist. Statistics of U.S.*, p. 756, and Table 1. It was not at all uncommon for Negroes to be imported into New Hampshire from the West Indies while children (thus assuring the master that he was not receiving planter "rejects") to serve until age twenty-four and then be given their freedom. In his will, Robert Briscoe provided that "Negro Boy Cato" should serve either his wife or Reverend John Odlin until "he comes to the full age of twenty-four years," at which time he would be given £20, a cow, and his freedom (*NHPP*, 32: 351). Thomas Hansen willed that his "black Slave pegg" should be given her freedom in two years; Robert Elliott willed "Bess" to be free three years after his death and willed her two-year-old daughter the promise of freedom at age twenty (ibid., pp. 74–75, 343). For two entertaining but somewhat naïve accounts of slavery in Portsmouth in the mid-eighteenth century, see Brewster, *Rambles about Portsmouth*, 1st ser., pp. 208–11; Oedel, "Portsmouth," pp. 713–19. In 1728, John Wentworth noted that there had been a great increase in the importation of Negro slaves in the previous year and

attributed it to the fact that Massachusetts had an import duty on Negroes while New Hampshire did not (Wentworth to Board of Trade, February 20, 1727/28, *CSP Col*, 1728–29, no. 59).

36. That Negro slaves had become a sign of social status is evidenced by their increasingly widespread usage and their population growth from less than 200 to about 500 between 1730 and 1740. For an indication of the families owning them see Brewster, *Rambles about Portsmouth*, 1st ser., p. 157; and Inventories of the Polls and Estates in the Province of New Hampshire, 1727–1773, NHHS. Also see the wills in *NHPP*, 32: 73–75, 197–202, 341–45, 350–52, 356–58, 500–504, 523–24, 556–58, 625–29, 724–28, 774–75, 785–801 passim; 33: 45. Those owning two to four slaves included George and William Vaughan, George Walker, Richard Waterhouse, and Richard Wibird—all of Portsmouth. Doctors and mariners seemed to have had more of a real need for slaves because slaves were relatively prevalent among these groups of middling wealth. Some ministers also had Negro slaves in the 1720's and 1730's.

37. Stackpole, *History of New Hampshire*, 1: 76. In 1658 alone Dover admitted ten such servants—Richard Hubbard, Thomas Lundall, Henry Browne, Patrick Jameson, Edward Erwin, Walter Jackson, James Murray, Thomas Dowty, James Air, and James Middleton (DTR, 1: 357). For evidence of servant ownership see *NHPP*, 31: 87–95, 245–52, 376–80; and the Portsmouth tax list of 1681 in ibid., 1: 428. In 1670 Richard Cutt had five indentured servants (*NHPP*, 40: 223, 263). Among the Exeter servants who became inhabitants before 1680 were John Sinclair, John Bean, Alexander Gordon, John Barber, and Richard Bray (Stackpole, 1: 76; Bell, *History of Exeter*, pp. 59–61).

38. For an excellent general discussion of the apprentice system see Morris, *Government and Labor*, pp. 22, 42, 310, 363–89. Traditional examples can be found in the New Hampshire wills; see, for example, *NHPP*, 31: 132, 182, 361, 506, 787; 32: 96, 694; also 17: 747–49. For an atypical example more akin to indentured servitude, see ibid., 40: 511–12, 515. For some examples of those desiring to find a good trade see ibid., 31: 132, 182, 506, 787; 2: 96.

39. *NHPP*, vol. 32, and 40: 240, 329. These informal guardian apprenticeships were typical after 1715; in fact, only two of the more formal apprenticeships are recorded between 1716 and 1740 (ibid., 32: 96, 694). Orphans were often apprenticed out as well (ibid., 31: 125, 182, 198–99, 234).

40. *NH Laws*, 1: 537–41, 678; 2: 115, 254–55; *NHPP*, 3: 179.

41. *NH Laws*, 1: 537–41, 692; 2: 55–56, 359–60. For direct evidence of "draft avoidance" among New Hampshire colonists, see ibid., 2: 61–62. New Hampshire responded by sending unpaid volunteers who would receive bounties on scalps of Indian men, women, and children (ibid., 2: 106–7).

42. Ibid., 2: 123.

43. *NHPP*, 13: 246.

44. The Scotch-Irish settlers who eventually settled in Londonderry in 1722 had first sought land grants from Massachusetts in 1719. In his letter to the Board of Trade, June 1, 1720, *CSP Col*, 1720–21, no. 94*ii*, Governor Shute reported that there were "very few" white servants in New Hampshire.

45. John Wentworth to_____, June 15, 1730, John Wentworth Mss., Box 1, Folder 1.

46. ETR, 1: 160, quoted in Bell, *History of Exeter*, p. 443.

47. DTR, 1: 390–91; *NH Laws*, 1: 537–41, 692; 2: 55–56, 284–91, 359–61; Ralph May, *Early Portsmouth History* (Boston, 1926), p. 167. Although the number of exemptions from militia service had increased greatly by 1718, nevertheless, the principle of mass military training continued. For the exemptions see *NH Laws*, 2: 284–91. A money payment might also serve as a substitute, depending upon the severity of the labor shortage and the need for the completed project. These labor services also were reflections of cash shortages in the colony.

48. *NHPP*, vol. 31. For the Massachusetts law of 1649 see ibid., p. xii.

49. See the acts of 1693 and 1718 in *NH Laws*, 1: 566; 2: 295–98. The reason for the Crown's repeal is in *CSP Col*, 1706–8, no. 369. Similar arguments were expressed before the Board of Trade in 1730 (ibid., 1730, no. 171*i*).

50. The lack of wage and price regulation is somewhat puzzling, particularly since such regulation was common in Massachusetts. But the Massachusetts government turned wage regulation over to the various towns in 1636, and there are no wage regulations in the New Hampshire town records or in the provincial laws. Perhaps the towns feared such legislation would keep prospective settlers away. For a discussion of the Massachusetts act of 1636 see Morris, *Government and Labor*, p. 63.

51. DTR, 2: 57 (May 8, 1667); PTR, 1: 96, 151 (March 9, 1667/68). In 1680 Portsmouth added "corders of wood," and in 1691, "cullers of fish" (PTR, 1: 224, 272). Such regulations also revealed the local concern for improved quality of products.

52. *NH Laws*, 1: 687-89. In 1714, the government took a somewhat similar action on frauds in the sale of cordwood (ibid., 2: 141). For a similar act regulating shingle sales see ibid., pp. 403-4.

53. Ibid., 2: 143. The act of May 15, 1714, forbade such activities in the colony and stipulated a £20 fine for each offense.

54. Ibid., pp. 255-56, May 14, 1718. Penalties were similar to the act of 1714, but this act had no time limitation and was therefore permanent.

55. Ibid., 1: 570, 691-92. For an excellent short discussion of colonial maritime labor relations see Morris, *Government and Labor*, pp. 224-78. For the experience of William Pepperrell, a leading Piscataqua trader, in maritime labor relations, see Fairchild, *Messrs. William Pepperrell*, pp. 145-59.

56. *NH Laws*, 2: 301-2.

57. The wills and estate inventories provide innumerable examples of such adjustments.

58. Nettels, *The Money Supply*, p. 8; Bailyn, *New England Merchants*, p. 182. For a New Hampshire explanation see William Partridge to Board of Trade, December 2, 1700, and George Vaughan to Board of Trade, May 10, 1715, *CSP Col*, 1700, no. 961; 1714-15, no. 389*i*.

59. That the lack of an adequate medium was a continuous reality in New Hampshire in its first century of development can be seen in the use of commodities in place of money throughout the seventeenth century (for examples, see DTR, 1: 306; *NHPP*, 1: 399, 448; *NH Laws*, 1: 64, 70, 138, 524-26, 585-86); in the concern of both Massachusetts and New Hampshire that none of the coins produced in the Massachusetts mint be exported from New England (Henry Sherburne, Hercules Hunking, and Elias Stileman held the office of "searchers of money" between 1654 and 1679 [*Mass. Records*, 4: 198; 4, pt. 2: 421]); in the great concern of Sam Hall, an Exeter trader, that he not be labeled a cheat in trade, for "no man will credit a man that is a cheating knave and a cozening knave" (1661; *NHPP*, 40: 474-76, 491); in the fact that a group of New England merchants, including Richard Waldron and John Hinckes, recommended the creation of a credit bank in 1685 (Barnes, *Dominion of New England*, p. 64); and in the fact that in 1682 anyone who paid his taxes in currency received a 33.3 percent discount (*NHPP*, 1: 448). In 1694 the New Hampshire House of Representatives pointed out that almost everyone depended upon cattle and corn as the medium of exchange for payment of taxes (*CSP Col*, 1693-96, nos. 1, 119*ii*). In 1708, Usher wrote that whatever coin came into New Hampshire was soon exported (ibid., 1706-8, nos. 1, 592; also, Partridge to Board of Trade, December 2, 1700, ibid., 1700, no. 961). Governor Dudley pointed out that "the perfect want of money" in wartime was the primary reason for printing of paper currency in Massachusetts and New Hampshire (Dudley to Board of Trade, December 1, 1713, ibid., 1712-14, no. 509). George Vaughan saw the "want of a medium of exchange" pinching New Hampshire's economy in 1715 (ibid., 1714-15, no. 389*i*); and between 1715 and 1740 the assembly journals and New Hampshire letters to the Board of Trade are full of this problem. For examples see ibid., 1726-27, no. 64; *NHPP*, 2: 733; 3: 814; 4: 174, 264, 297, 592, 602, 634-35, 643-44, 693-98; 5: 18, 70, 72-73, 76. In 1732 the New Hampshire Assembly reported to the governor that "our circumstances are so that if there should be an additional tax upon the polls and estates of the inhabitants of this province, it would have a greater tendency to fill the public Gaols than supply the Treasury" (*NHPP*, 4: 618). Belcher responded by seeking the Board of Trade's permission to issue more paper currency based on gold and silver because New Hampshire was in such "great distress" for an adequate medium of exchange that without "speedy help" it would be "almost impossible for that little province to support any trade" (ibid., p. 649).

60. Other items specified as acceptable in payment of taxes before 1713 included butter, cheese, and barley malt (DTR, 1: 306, 595; NHPP, 1: 399, 448; NH Laws, 1: 64, 70, 138, 524-26, 585-86; 2: 60-61, 548-50). In 1708 a special act made tar acceptable for taxes. Hemp and bar iron were added in 1737. New Hampshire did not generally accept commodity money in payment of provincial taxes between 1709 and 1742 except for customs imposts. Nevertheless, one could always sell his produce for bills of credit, which could then be used for taxes (NHPP, 3: 411, for example). In 1743 the New Hampshire treasury began accepting commodity money again and issued a greatly enlarged list, including bar iron, rye, hemp, flax, pitch, tar, turpentine, beeswax, bayberry wax, tallow, and tanned sole leather (ibid., 5: 684). Compare this with 1737, when one could pay taxes only in bills of credit, silver, hemp, flax, or bar iron (ibid., 4: 724). Nettels, The Money Supply, pp. 202-28, has an excellent general discussion of colonial commodity money.

61. NH Laws, 1: 526-27, 531-33; 2: 141, 265-66, 317-19, 345-47, 403-4. The General Assembly always required that commodities used as money be either "good sound" products or "merchantable" products; but this was the only regulation aimed at protection against spoilage. There was generally a shortage of grain in the colony.

62. NH Laws, 2: 61.

63. Masts and ship timber were never listed as commodity money, while hemp, flax, and tar received special encouragement as well as being listed as commodity money. See ibid., pp. 82-83, 87, 330-31, 363, 541-42, 548-50; NHPP, 5: 684.

64. Many of these practices have been discussed earlier in other connections. For exemptions from taxes see NHPP, 1: 399 (exempting the president, council members, ministers, and church elders in 1680); NH Laws, 1: 524-26 (exempting ministers, school teachers, and members of the council in 1692); ibid., pp. 554-55, 563 (exempting ministers). For provision of free servants, see ibid., 2: 115, 286-87. For exemptions from military service see ibid., 1: 541; 2: 55-56, 286-87.

65. NH Laws, 2: 55. The act did provide that each town should provide food for the troops through its taxes. An act of 1704 ordered every householder to provide his own snowshoes and moccasins for winter military service (ibid., p. 63). For an institutional analysis of New Hampshire military organization see Fry, New Hampshire as a Royal Province, pp. 473-85.

66. NH Laws, 2: 94, 106-7; NHPP, 1: 414. With the disappearance of hostile Indians from New Hampshire borders, the danger declined and so did the need for universal military service, with the result that this unpopular policy was changed (NH Laws, 2: 61-62). The bounties included £60 on adult Indian male scalps, £30 on Indian female scalps, and £15 on scalps of all Indians under age 20. The law required that a bounty hunter must serve at least four months and show each scalp to the treasurer before receiving payment. See also NH Laws, 2: 284-91; for continuing difficulties of enforcement see ibid., pp. 347-49; for wage payments see NHPP, 19: 163, 166; 4: 335, 362. For new bounties in 1723 see NH Laws, 2: 373-74. Wage payments in paper currency were one method of disbursing a medium of exchange throughout the colony.

67. NH Laws, 1: 65, 70, 82-83; also see Nettels, The Money Supply, pp. 229-49, for a more general discussion. It is not clear why the New Hampshire government reduced the value of the piece of eight: local economic dependence dictated a different direction. Perhaps the Massachusetts threat of high import duties on New Hampshire products forced it to retreat to the Massachusetts standard, for Massachusetts was New Hampshire's chief market; or perhaps it was just a matter of adjusting the local economic situation to the changed conditions. Evidence of trading friction between the two colonies may be found in NHPP, 1: 421, 464. For the early action of Massachusetts see Mass. Records, 2: 20, 29 (1642), 262 (1652); 4, pt. 2: 533-34 (1672).

68. Nettels, The Money Supply, pp. 240n, 243-48. In 1739 the New Hampshire secretary, Richard Waldron, Jr., testified that "the rate of silver and exchange between this currency and Sterling has always been the same as at Boston, which is the Grand Mart of New England, and in that respect governs the whole country" (NHPP, 5: 46).

69. For descriptions of the "impoverishment," "decay of trade," and military insecurity in New Hampshire just before its adoption of paper currency in 1709, see Dudley to Board of Trade, March 1, 1708/9; George Vaughan to Board of Trade, July 6, 1708; and Henry

Newman to Privy Council, December 16, 1708 (*CSP Col*, 1708-9, nos. 19, 392; Rawlinson Mss., C. 128, no. 7). Also see *CSP Col*, 1706-8, no. 1592, for Usher's views and *NHPP*, 3: 386, for the New Hampshire Assembly's view in 1709.

70. *NHPP*, 3: 348-410. For an excellent summary of the varied difficulties New Hampshire colonists confronted in 1709, see Fry, *New Hampshire as a Royal Province*, pp. 345-46. The stated purpose of the act was the payment of the colony's debts, most of which involved soldiers' wages; but it also provided money for an agent to be sent to England against the proprietary claimant. The agent was also to ask for a new military expedition against Canada. Governor Dudley probably persuaded the General Assembly to use paper currency by offering his support to any agent chosen by them and by threatening them with the loss of the Queen's favor unless they paid their debts. To a colony that had just received powder and arms from the Crown in 1708, such a threat was taken seriously. See Dudley to Vaughan, *NHPP*, 3: 392, 401-3, 412-13, 415-16.

71. New Hampshire politicians were not original in this realization. The Massachusetts government had been using bills of credit successfully since 1690 and by 1714 had created a public land bank, as had South Carolina. See Theodore Thayer, "The Land-Bank System in the American Colonies," *Journal of Economic History* 13 (Spring 1953): 145-59; George Billias, *The Massachusetts Land Bankers of 1740*, University of Maine Studies, 2d ser., no. 74 (Orono, Maine: University of Maine Press, 1959), pp. 1-7. Five out of the six leaders in the New Hampshire House of Representatives and all the councillors were involved in trade between 1709 and 1716. The six House leaders were Mark Hunking, Richard Gerrish, Theodore Atkinson, George Jaffrey, Jr., Ezekial Wentworth, and the nontrader Joseph Smith (*NHPP*, 19: 9-67). For an understanding of the method used in evaluating political leadership in the lower House, see Jack P. Greene, "Foundations of Political Power in the Virginia House of Burgesses, 1720-1776," *William and Mary Quarterly*, 3rd ser. 16 (October 1959): 502-3. The only difference in method stems from the fact that the New Hampshire House journals never reveal which members were chairmen of committees.

72. *NH Laws*, 2: 102-5, 111-12, 116, 117, 153, 156, 199-200; *NHPP*, 3: 563-64; Dudley to Board of Trade, December 1, 1713, *CSP Col*, 1712-14, no. 509; Vaughan to Board of Trade, May 10, 1715, ibid., 1714-15, no. 389*i*.

73. *NHPP*, 3: 688-89; *NH Laws*, 2: 249-51. The leading members of the New Hampshire House between 1717 and 1722 were all merchants and lumber traders with the exception of Ephraim Dennett, a Portsmouth tanner. These leaders included Joshua Peirce, Colonel John Gilman, Colonel James Davis, Jotham Odiorne, Thomas Packer, Peter Weare, Andrew Wiggin, Henry Sherburne, Ephraim Dennett, and John Plaisted. The men most directly connected to the paper currency decisions were all merchants—Mark Hunking, George Jaffrey, Richard Wibird, and John Wentworth in the council; and Joshua Peirce, John Gilman, Jotham Odiorne, Peter Weare, James Davis, Ephraim Dennett, and Thomas Packer in the House.

74. *NHPP*, 3: 735, 793, 835; 19: 120, 145, 146, 161, 165; 4: 100, 105, 157, 167, 194, 205, 341, 342, 343; *NH Laws*, 2: 366-68, 372-73, 382, 386-87, 391, 393. The General Assembly also postponed payment of the £15,000 loan (ibid., 2: 554).

75. For the Instruction see *NHPP*, 3: 814. John Wentworth to Board of Trade, August 7, 1727, *CSP Col*, 1726-27, no. 661.

76. *CSP Col*, 1728-29, no. 303.

77. *NHPP*, 4: 289, 293, 298, 490, 491, 502. Undoubtedly, the Board of Trade's opposition was the deciding factor in this rejection (*CSP Col*, 1728-29, no. 755).

78. For the new emission see *NH Laws*, 2: 518, 524-25, 548-50, 559, 579-81. Two thousand pounds was issued in 1730, £7,100 in 1737, and £2,700 in 1740. For evidence of the political nature of the currency question see *NHPP*, 4: 592, 602, 607-8, 632, 634-98 passim, 771-72, 835-36; 5: 9, 18, 24, 45, 70, 73, 76. In this conflict the members of the House strongly supported paper currency; their leadership—particularly Andrew Wiggin, Theodore Atkinson, Joshua Peirce, John Rindge, James Clarkson, Thomas Packer, and Jotham Odiorne —was almost entirely mercantile. As much at stake as paper money was the political question as to whether the council and governor could have a voice in choosing the New Hampshire agent in London. When the governor and council were willing to pay the House's agent a respectable salary (in 1737 and 1740—though he was working for Belcher's dismissal) and accept bills of credit, the House would vote the money. Given these political

machinations, it is not difficult to explain the political antagonism engendered by this complex issue. Moreover, Belcher had received royal instructions to forbid emissions over £6,000 in bills of credit and not to allow any more than that amount to be current "at one and the same time" (*NHPP*, 18: 25). Considering the fact that about £22,000 was current in 1730 and at least £12,500 in 1739, Belcher faced an impossible situation (ibid., 5: 46).

79. Theodore Atkinson to John Thomlinson, February 28, 1733/34, *NHPP*, 4: 835. Also see ibid., pp. 602, 635, 688. A year earlier Belcher had asked permission to issue bills of credit based on gold and silver in New Hampshire (Belcher to Board of Trade, January 13, 1732/33, ibid., p. 649).

80. These bankers included Theodore Atkinson, George Jaffrey, William Parker, John Rindge, Jonathan Warner, Thomas Phipps, James Jaffrey, John Pray, Richard Wibird, Thomas Wibird, "three wentworths," Jotham Odiorne, and Thomas Wright (Richard Waldron to Jonathan Belcher, April 2, 1734, Waldron Mss., vol. 1).

81. *Boston Weekly Post-Boy*, April 21, 1735. This newspaper was closely allied with the Belcher administrations in Massachusetts and New Hampshire, as its editor was Ellis Huske, the New Hampshire naval officer and postmaster. Richard Waldron, Jr., submitted a number of pro-Belcher articles to it, particularly on the currency issue: see ibid., May 12, 1735, May 26, 1735, and May 11, 1741, for examples. Also see *NHPP*, 4: 685. The penalty for acceptance of this currency was forfeiture of the currency plus a threefold fine in Massachusetts currency.

82. *Boston Weekly Post-Boy*, May 26, 1735; *NHPP*, 4: 685, 688, 697. According to the *Post-Boy* of May 11, 1741, the New Hampshire notes "died in infancy."

83. *NHPP*, 5: 152, 652, 668, 669, 672; 18: 140, 147–48. New Hampshire merchants justified the emission on the grounds of defending and settling their large new frontier. The New Tenor emission was set for 6s. 8d. = 1 oz. of foreign silver and was given a 1 : 4 ratio with the Old Tenor bills of credit which had been circulating since 1709 (*NH Laws*, 2: 684). The turning point in the Crown's decision to approve this emission occurred when a petition from "the principal merchants trading to New Hampshire" (organized by Thomlinson), stating that the money was "absolutely necessary" to carry on business, to defend the colony and the mast ships, to keep out "base" currency of other colonies, and to secure to each creditor the true value of his debt, thus benefiting the English merchant, was presented to the Board of Trade and the Privy Council (*APC Col*, 1720–45, pp. 745–47).

84. *NH Laws*, 2: 106 (1711), 563–64 (1738); *NHPP*, 3: 751, 797; 4: 107, 117; 5: 2, 4, 8, 22, 55, 56, 212. Between 1709 and 1711, £6,500 in bills of credit had been issued, as had £15,000 in 1717, over £10,000 in 1722, and £7,000 in 1737.

85. Belknap, *History*, 3: 168 and elsewhere.

86. McKinley, "Economic History of Portsmouth," app. I, table II, p. 376; Nettels, *The Money Supply*, pp. 240n, 243, 246–48; *NH Laws*, 2: 94–96. "Proclamation money" and "lawful money" represented the relationship between New England currency and the English pound sterling as established by Massachusetts after the Royal Proclamation of 1704. By 1709 the Massachusetts and New Hampshire ratio was £155 in paper currency and "lawful money" to £100 sterling. In addition, 1 oz. of foreign (Spanish) silver was equal to 8s. of "lawful money."

Given the present state of knowledge about the impact of paper currency on the colonial economies, it is impossible to assess accurately how much inflation had occurred in New Hampshire during this period. For further discussion of this problem, see Joseph A. Ernst, *Money and Politics in America, 1755–1775* (Chapel Hill: University of North Carolina Press, 1973), pp. 3–30, 353–59.

87. Among this group were some members of the political faction supporting Belcher in New Hampshire during the 1730's, particularly Henry Sherburne, Ephraim Dennett, Richard Waldron, Jr., Benjamin Gambling, and the Reverend Hugh Adams. Belcher himself was in this category. Waldron to Belcher, July 12, 1731, April 2, 1734, Waldron Manuscripts, vol. 1. Also see *NHPP*, 5: 33–34, 37; Belcher to Sherburne, November 22, 1736, December 12, 1740, in the Belcher Letterbook, 1736–1738, MHS; Belcher Papers, *MHS Coll*, 6th ser., 7: 330.

88. *CSP Col*, 1720–21, no. 665; 1728–29, no. 303; Belcher Papers, 6: 227. Belcher wrote Waldron in October 1742: "I cannot persuade myself to believe what they talk about a Loan; but will say once for all, if the King's Ministers are cajoled and blinded as far as to put it into

the power of Governors of the plantations to open the flood gates at their pleasure, and to make such delusive, fraudulent emissions of paper for money as in years past, this country must be deluged with the waters of the vilest iniquity and injustice" (Belcher Letterbook, 1736–38).

89. Belcher himself attributed his defeat to the land bank issue. Billias, *Massachusetts Land Bankers*, p. 37, agrees. But the most influential factor in his dismissal was his loss of patronage in England and the triumph of William Shirley and his patron, the Duke of Newcastle. See John A. Schutz, *William Shirley, King's Governor of Massachusetts* (Chapel Hill: University of North Carolina Press, 1961).

90. *NHPP*, 4: 540, 543.

91. For debtors before 1660 see *NHPP*, 40: 3–23 passim, 61, 66, 168. Lumber traders in this group included Peter Weare, William and Richard Waldron, Thomas Wiggin, George Walton, William Hilton, Morgan Lewis, John Tare, and John Redman. For creditors before 1660 see ibid., pp. 4–19 passim, 35, 44, 45, 61, 92, 136. They included Bryan Pendleton, Francis Williams, William Beard, William Hilton, Francis Champernoune, John Pickering, Henry Roby, Edward Gilman, George Walton, William Waldron, and James Wall.

92. These figures have been obtained by combining information from the wills in *NHPP*, vol. 31, and the inventories in NH Probate Records to 1690. Wills and/or inventories were made by 231 people, of which 19 were creditors and 83 were debtors. These wills and inventories probably represent approximately 40 percent of the total deaths, but whether or not this is a representative sample cannot be determined. See Kenneth Lockridge, "A Communication," *William and Mary Quarterly*, 3rd ser. 25 (July 1968): 516, for an analysis of this problem with wills and estate inventories.

93. Noyes, p. 17. See above, p. 000.

94. *NHPP*, 31: 41–43, 103–5, 161–67, 245–52, 259, 266–67, 328–29, 376–80, 514–19, 634, 759–63, 814–18; Noyes, pp. 178, 182, 375–76.

95. The Gilmans, Waldrons, Sherburnes, Vaughans, and Ellis Huske traded through the Usher-Jeffries mercantile house in Boston after 1715. By the 1730's John Rindge had established profitable relationships with John Thomlinson, and before long the Wentworth clan followed suit. For other local relationships see Fairchild, *Messrs. William Pepperrell*, pp. 45–47, 77–82.

96. The interpretation presented here owes much to Richard Bushman, *From Puritan to Yankee* (Cambridge: Harvard University Press, 1967), pp. 107–34. Both indebtedness and new enterprise were increasing, as may be seen from the new laws regulating debt, insolvency, and new enterprises between 1701 and 1718 (*NH Laws*, 1: 683–91 passim; 2: 61–62, 74–75, 123, 126, 130–32, 139–40, 143, 192–96, 247, 249, 252, 255–56, 282–84, 315–17, 326–27). Most of these enterprises were in mercantile activities. The laws sought to deal with those who encroached on the town commons, sold liquor without license, went to sea, or acted as peddlers and "petty chapmen" in the country towns.

97. *NH Laws*, 2: 126, 192–96. The bankruptcy act distinguished between honest and fraudulent bankruptcy, rewarding the honest bankrupt with an allowance (besides personal effects) of between five and fifty pounds, depending upon the value of the estate. For bankruptcy petitions see *NHPP*, 17: 729, 730; 2: 634, 691, 708. Twelve out of twenty-eight insolvent estates in the New Hampshire wills between 1640 and 1735 occurred between 1713 and 1723.

98. *NH Laws*, 2: 199–200, 246, 247, 249–51, 252, 255–56.

99. Ibid., pp. 282–84, 315–17, 326–27.

Chapter VII

1. These merchants included William Vaughan, Richard Waldron, William Partridge, William Pepperrell, Thomas Daniel, John Cutt, Samuel Penhallow, Robert Elliott, Reuben Hull, Richard Martyn, Nathaniel Fryer, Joseph Smith, Henry Deering, Peter Coffin, George Walton, Samuel Wentworth, John and Mark Hunking, Moses Gilman, Thomas Harvey,

John Sherburne, George Jaffrey, Thomas Graffort, John Gerrish, Thomas Diamond, and Sampson Sheafe. The term "merchant" is used loosely to include lumber traders, fish traders, wholesalers, retailers, and mariners who engaged in overseas and local trade. For a lower estimate of New Hampshire vessel ownership see Bellomont to Board of Trade, 1700, *NHPP*, 2: 356.

2. *CSP Col*, 1700, no. 354. The incomplete 1692 Shipping Returns provide some indication of the materials imported from Boston (*NHPP*, 2: 77-84).

3. *NHPP*, 2: 82-83; Fairchild, *Messrs. William Pepperrell*, p. 39.

4. The West Indies (Barbados, Antigua, and Jamaica) provided sugar, molasses, rum, and cotton; Madeira and Fayal provided the wine; Saltatude and Tortuga supplied the salt. For general patterns of New England trade in the late seventeenth century see Bailyn, *New England Merchants*, pp. 124-34. For New Hampshire see Tables 2, 6-10.

5. For verification of these statistical generalizations from the Shipping Returns, 1694-95, see Tables 7 and 9. For the trade patterns of Pepperrell see Fairchild, *Messrs. William Pepperrell*, pp. 31-40. It is unlikely that Pepperrell was the foremost trader at Piscataqua in the 1690's, as Fairchild suggests. Although evidence is sparse, William Partridge and William Vaughan probably outranked him. The Shipping Returns of 1694-95 do not contain ownership information on the vessels engaged in trade.

6. Toppan, *Edward Randolph*, 3: 76, 138, 181, 216-19, 343; 4: 96, 98, 168-69; 5: 40, 41, 81, 216, 238-39; 6: 313; 7: 363. Bailyn, *New England Merchants*, pp. 126-27, 134-37, 143, 177.

7. See the correspondence in *NHPP*, 17: 513-15, and in *CSP Col*, 1661-68, nos. 1485, 1588, 1651; 1669-74, nos. 651, 687; 1689-92, no. 1377i; 1700, no. 42. See also Toppan, *Edward Randolph*, 1: 1-10; 2: 187-88; 5: 71-73; Hall, *Randolph*, pp. 2-4.

8. See chap. 3.

9. These local merchants had been chosen by the Lords of Trade from a list of names submitted by Sir William Warren, one of the mast contractors trading with New Hampshire. Warren had recommended John Gilman and John Folsom of Exeter; Richard Waldron, Peter Coffin, John Gerrish, and Anthony Nutter of Dover; Nathaniel Weare, Christopher Hussey, Samuel Dalton, and John Sanborn of Hampton; and Sampson Sheafe, Elias Stileman, John Cutt, Thomas Daniel, Richard Martyn, Nathaniel Fryer, and William Vaughan of Portsmouth. *CSP Col*, 1677-80, nos. 1053, 1054.

10. *NHPP*, 1: 382-408, 409-11. The councillors even established exact lists of those who should vote for members of the House in 1680, thus controlling the general character of the first House of Representatives (ibid., 19: 655-60). Eight out of eleven members of the House were lumber traders.

11. Toppan, *Edward Randolph*, 3: 76, 84, 211; *NHPP*, 19: 662-68 passim. After 1680 the Navigation Acts did not prohibit trade in enumerated articles to Ireland, as a clause doing so had just lapsed (Andrews, *The Colonial Period*, 4: 65-66, 124-29).

12. Toppan, *Edward Randolph*, 3: 76; 5: 216, 238; 6: 313; 7: 363.

13. Ibid., 3: 181, 211, 347, 350; 4: 96, 98, 168-69; 5: 41, 81.

14. Noyes, pp. 375-76; Toppan, *Edward Randolph*, 3: 217-19; 6: 313; 7: 363. For the special status of Scotland and Scotch traders in the colonies see Andrews, *The Colonial Period*, 4: 69-73.

15. Severett's will is in *NHPP*, 40: 328-29. He was a target of Randolph in the 1680's (Toppan, *Edward Randolph*, 3: 347; 4: 168-69; 5: 41).

16. *NHPP*, 19: 665-84 passim; *NHHS Coll*, 8: 69-71; Toppan, *Edward Randolph*, 3: 76, 138, 165, 181; 6: 95-98. When one of the deputies called the councillors "rebels" who "would deny the King himself, if he were here," the council fined him £20 and sent him to jail.

17. For Mason's efforts see *CSP Col*, 1681-85, no. 98, pp. 44-46, nos. 420, 422, 424.

18. Chamberlain to Blathwayt, May 14, 1681, *NHPP*, 17: 544-46; 19: 688, 689, 691. "Opportunists" is not used here in a derogatory sense. See Cranfield to Lords of Trade, December 1, 1682, ibid., pp. 570-71; Toppan, *Edward Randolph*, 6: 120-29, 130-33.

19. Scotch residents of the colonies had all the rights and privileges of Englishmen. Since Randolph did not mention enumerated commodities in any description of the case, they must not have been part of the cargo; for they would have strengthened his case (Toppan, *Edward Randolph*, 3: 216-19, 256-58).

20. Ibid., 3: 255-61; 6: 130-33; *NHPP*, 17: 615-16.

21. Cranfield dismissed Waldron, Martyn, and Gilman and appointed Nathaniel Fryer and his two sons-in-law, Robert Elliott and John Hinckes, in their places. The mercantile leaders who undermined Cranfield in England were Nathaniel Weare, William Vaughan, Elias Stileman, Richard Waldron, and the Congregational minister, Joshua Moodey. They worked with Sir Josiah Child, an eminent London merchant. *NHPP*, 1: 491-578, provides evidence of their efforts. See also Toppan, *Edward Randolph*, 4: 3-4, 17, 227; 6: 252-53, 265. For Gove, see *NHPP*, 1: 458-61.

22. The council helped appoint merchants to such lucrative offices as captain of the fort, naval officer, secretary, treasurer, judge, recorder, and justice of the peace. It also helped establish legal fees, exempted its members from taxation, protected local interests as the highest court of appeals, and served as the primary voice of local interests in relation to England and Massachusetts' competition.

23. Cranfield's dissolution of the lower House revealed that body's limitations, but "taxation without representation" was one of the charges that led to Cranfield's dismissal. The House was dominated by antiproprietary lumber traders in the early 1680's. The election of Richard Waldron (the son of Colonel Richard Waldron) as Speaker of the House each time a new House met was an indication of that domination.

24. The council and House sent Nathaniel Weare in 1684, Samuel Penhallow and William Partridge in the 1690's, William Vaughan and George Vaughan between 1700 and 1715, and John Rindge in the 1730's. *NHPP*, 1: 515-19; 17: 663-64, 680-81; 4: 617, 644; Rawlinson Mss., C. 128, no. 15; *CSP Col*, 1702-3, no. 225; 1708-9, no. 19; 1714-15, no. 389*i*.

25. Sir William Warren, Sir Josiah Child, William Wallis, Sir Henry Ashurst, John Taylor, Ralph Gulston, Henry Newman, and John Thomlinson were among the more effective London merchants who acted as agents for New Hampshire or for its mercantile interests.

26. The proposed constitution is in *NH Laws*, 1: 260-61. The commissioners involved were William Vaughan, Richard Waldron, Nathaniel Fryer, Robert Elliott, John Pickering, and Thomas Cobbett of Portsmouth; Nathaniel Weare, Henry Green, Samuel Sherburne, Morris Hobbs, Henry Dow, and Edward Gove of Hampton; John Woodman, John Gerrish, John Tuttle, John Roberts, Thomas Edgerly, and Nicholas Follett of Dover; and Robert Wadleigh, Samuel Leavitt, William Hilton, and Jonathan Thing of Exeter. For the various town meetings see *NHHS Coll*, 8: 396-402; *NHPP*, 2: 30-34.

27. Nathaniel Weare to Robert Pike, March 15, 1689/90, *NHPP*, 2: 43-46. The petition, in ibid., pp. 34-39, contains 373 names.

28. The petition is in *CSP Col*, 1689-92, nos. 883, 884; a full list of signers is in Noyes, p. 43. Known traders among the fifty-six signers included John Hinckes, John Lewis, Nathaniel Fryer, Robert Elliott, Thomas Cobbett, Shadrach Walton, John West, John Diamond, John and Robert Tufton, and Pheasant Eastwick.

29. *APC Col*, 1680-1720, pp. 298-99.

30. *CSP Col*, 1696-97, no. 1196; 1697-98, nos. 108, 186, 324, 586, 1022. Usher, a Massachusetts merchant who had supported Randolph in the 1680's, found ready friends in New Hampshire among a few of the merchants in the 1690's, which encouraged merchant disunity.

31. Samuel Penhallow to Bellomont, November 25 and December 7, 1698, *NHPP*, 17: 680-81. For Bellomont's support against the Usher-Allen faction see ibid., 2: 345, 351-53, 355.

32. Bellomont to Board of Trade, April 23, 1700, *CSP Col*, 1700, no. 354; May 25 and June 22, 1700, *NHPP*, 2: 347-48, 348-55, 357; Bellomont to Commissioners of Customs, May 28, 1700, ibid., p. 348. Bellomont commented that Partridge "is of the country, and the interest of England is neither in his head nor his heart, like the generality of the people in these Plantations." He also said that all the King's officers should be Englishmen of "undoubted probity and well born." Partridge wrote the Board of Trade in reply to Bellomont's attack on trade with Spain and Portugal, pointing out that it was in England's interest to allow trade in lumber and fish with Portugal, as it helped provide returns for English manufactured goods (*CSP Col*, 1700, no. 961).

33. Andrews, *The Colonial Period*, 4: 102-3.

34. Both factions consisted of lumber and fish merchants. Usher gained support from George Jaffrey (who married his daughter), Joseph Smith, Sampson Sheafe, Richard

Wibird, Theodore Atkinson, Thomas Phipps, Thomas Packer, John Wentworth, Richard Gerrish, and Peter Weare. The opposing, antiproprietary faction included William and George Vaughan, Richard Waldron, Samuel Penhallow, William Partridge, Mark Hunking, John Hinckes, John Plaisted, and Thomas Westbrook. Both factions were unstable. Usher's Boston connections, the Usher-Jeffries mercantile house, provided economic benefits for those merchants who supported him.

35. Belcher to Waldron, May 28 and June 4, 1739, Belcher Papers, 3: 52, 54; Belcher to Duke of Newcastle, July 13, 1731, *CSP Col*, 1731, no. 296; Belcher to Shadrach Walton, July 18, 1731, ibid., no. 377*iv*, in which he wrote: "I thank you for a list of the restless and uneasy. If some people might enjoy all the places of profit and honor in the Province, as they have for many years past, they would be well content. But I think it time and very reasonable some other families should share in the advantages of the Government."

36. Andrews, *The Colonial Period*, 4: 204-10; Thomas C. Barrow, *Trade and Empire* (Cambridge: Harvard University Press, 1967), pp. 76-78.

37. For Usher's problems with the council and assembly see *NHPP*, 2: 161-86; 3: 28-38; *CSP Col.*, 1693-96, nos. 1569, 2105, 2137, 2142; 1696-97, nos. 282-85.

38. Usher later grounded his case on the fact that the masters of the vessels had not registered entries with the naval officer. Yet at the time of the first vessel's entry no officer had been appointed. This episode can be traced in *NHPP*, 2: 122-45 passim; *CSP Col*, 1693-96, no. 1151 and enclosures, no. 1569 and enclosures.

39. The evidence of customs seizures is sparse; but where there is evidence of such seizures after 1696, in almost every case local rivalries were the paramount motivation. In 1698 Usher and Randolph seized William Partridge's bond on a vessel carrying sugar to Newfoundland (Toppan, *Edward Randolph*, 5: 216; *CSP Col*, 1701, no. 180). In 1698 Allen seized European wines imported by James Meinzies (*NHPP*, 2: 284-85; *CSP Col*, 1699, nos. 89*xx*, 831). In 1699 Partridge's vessel carrying lumber to Portugal was seized by Sheafe and Bellomont on information from Allen (*CSP Col*, 1699, no. 986). In 1701 Partridge and Sheafe seized four bags of cotton wool (*NHPP*, 2: 394-99). In 1723 John Wentworth and Collector Butts Bacon seized William Pepperrell's vessel, the *Prosperous*, for carrying small masts to Spain (*CSP Col*, 1722-23, no. 806; Fairchild, *Messrs. William Pepperrell*, p. 71). There was a seizure in 1735 by Ellis Huske (*Boston Weekly Post-Boy*, August 25, 1735, November 10, 1735; Belcher Papers, 2: 137, 139, 187, 189, 205, 207, 211) and another by Huske (of the *Caesar*) in 1739 ("Belcher Papers," *MHS Coll*, 6th ser., 7: 203, 205, 239, 370, 493, 496, 541). The only other seizure between 1696 and 1740 seems to have been motivated by lawful zeal: Sampson Sheafe, the collector, seized the *Hopewell* in 1699 for importing ivory tusks and wine directly from Fayal. But because he did not give the master of the vessel twenty-four hours leeway for obtaining water and provisions, he lost the case in the courts (Bellomont to Board of Trade, October 25, 1699, *CSP Col*, 1699, no. 894; Randolph to Board of Trade, July 24, 1701, ibid., 1701, no. 669).

40. For example, under Usher (1692-97) Pheasant Eastwick, Thomas Cobbett, and Charles Story served as customs collector, naval officer, and vice-admiralty judge, respectively. Under Bellomont (1699-1701) Robert Armstrong served as both collector and naval officer and Wait Winthrop as vice-admiralty judge. Under Lieutenant Governor Partridge (1701-3) Sampson Sheafe (who had received appointment as deputy collector under Governor Allen in 1698) became collector; Theodore Atkinson, naval officer; and Thomas Newton, vice-admiralty judge. Under Governor Dudley (1703-15) Sheafe and Atkinson continued until 1710, when Robert Armstrong was appointed from England and held both offices until 1723; Charles Story was appointed vice-admiralty judge until 1715, when John Meinzies, a local merchant, took his place. Lieutenant Governor John Wentworth, holding executive authority from 1723 to 1731, obtained Theodore Atkinson as deputy customs commissioner to Butts Bacon, who held the collectorship until his death in 1725, at which time Atkinson took over, Richard Wibird was appointed naval officer, and George Jaffrey, vice-admiralty judge. When Belcher became governor (1730-41), he removed these people and appointed Wibird as collector, Ellis Huske as naval officer, and Benjamin Gambling to the vice-admiralty post. The Collector's post, however, was taken out of Belcher's hands in the 1730's as patronage politicians in England used this post to meet local obligations, appointing Anthony Reynolds, John Gray, Benjamin Plummer, and Samuel Solly to this post between 1732 and 1740. Solly became a supporter of the Wentworth faction upon his

arrival in 1740; and Huske, the naval officer, also came to terms with the Wentworths, holding his post until at least 1755. These appointments are recorded in *NHPP*, vols. 2-5, and in *CSP Col*, 1696-1737.

41. Bellomont to Board of Trade, October 25, 1699, *CSP Col*, 1699, no. 894; Randolph to Board of Trade, July 24, 1701, ibid., 1701, no. 699. Dudley reported that he felt Sheafe was justified in his seizure; but since the owner had died, there was no one to sue, and the case was closed (ibid., 1702-3, no. 315).

42. Ibid., 1702-3, nos. 315, 343; *NHPP*, 2: 384, 390, 394-99, 412, 414.

43. Bellomont to Lords of Treasury, September 8, 1699, quoted in Barrow, *Trade and Empire*, p. 97; *CSP Col*, 1699, no. 769xiv.

44. Joseph Dudley to Board of Trade, February 11, 1702/3, *CSP Col*, 1702-3, no. 315; Sampson Sheafe to Board of Trade, February 28, 1703/4, ibid., 1704-5, no. 141. The fact that Thomas Holland's wife was the defendant in the case was crucial for its origin, as Holland was a rival to Partridge and Sheafe.

45. This political case in 1723 was a conflict between mercantile rivals John Wentworth and William Pepperell (*CSP Col*, 1722-23, no. 806; Fairchild, *Messrs. William Pepperrell*, p. 71; Malone, *Pine Trees and Politics*, pp. 86-87). On complaints of violations, in 1708 Usher wrote that all the vessels entered and cleared at New Castle instead of Portsmouth and imported large quantities of silk and fruit from Lisbon and Newfoundland. Undoubtedly, he exaggerated. See *CSP Col*, 1706-8, no. 1592. By 1717 the Board of Trade had become so aware of smuggling that it asked Governor Shute to send "exact accounts" of the imports and exports of Massachusetts and New Hampshire for the last three years. In the meantime John Wentworth was writing the Board that New Hampshire had the least smuggling of all the colonies because of Robert Armstrong's "great care." But Armstrong was submitting a list of exports to Spain and Portugal for the last six years, intimating that the Spanish fleet had been greatly increased from New Hampshire's naval stores. Five years later the Board heard petitions against Armstrong for ignoring his duties as collector, accepting bribes, allowing the rivals of the petitioners—relatives of John Wentworth (Archibald MacPhedris, George Jaffrey, Henry Sherburne, Mark Hunking)—to cut mast trees into logs, and also allowing them to export large masts to Spain (*CSP Col*, 1716-17, no. 579; 1717-18, nos. 277, 307, 810; 1722-23, nos. 329, 340, 344, 356, 703). Wentworth's rebuttal indicated that local political antagonists were behind the petitions and complaints (ibid., 1719-20, no. 313).

46. *CSP Col*, 1722-23, no. 685.

47. Ibid., 1724-25, no. 141. For a discussion of Whipple's case in Boston, where the witnesses were so intimidated that Governor Shute recommended using British troops, see Barrow, *Trade and Empire*, pp. 89-90, 95.

48. See Tables 7 and 9. The designation "West Indies" could also indicate that a vessel's destination included many of the West Indian islands, but multiple West Indian destinations had been common before 1727, so why change the traditional approach if not to cover up illicit trade? See Pepperrell's trade patterns in the 1720's and 1730's, particularly with the French West Indies and his Madiera-West Indies triangle before 1733 (Fairchild, *Messrs. William Pepperrell*, pp. 93, 109-23, 126-30, 133-37). Fairchild found no evidence that the Pepperrells traded with the French islands after 1733, though they smuggled naval stores there before that year.

49. Peirce Papers, Baker Library, Harvard University; McKinley, "Economic History of Portsmouth," pp. 317-18; Shipping Returns, CO5, 967, p. 5; 968, pp. 39-41.

50. Waldron to Belcher, November 5, 1731, Waldron Papers, vol. 1, no. 38, NHHS. Dunbar to Popple, August 20, 1731, *CSP Col*, 1731, nos. 377, 410; *NHPP*, 4: 614.

51. Belcher to Waldron, September 24, October 1, October 8, October 15, October 22, October 30, November 5, November 6, and November 9, 1739; Belcher to Ellis Huske, September 17, September 24, October 15, November 5, November 26, and December 24, 1739; April 21, June 23, and July 7, 1740; Belcher to Lords of Admiralty, January 31, 1740/41; "Belcher Papers," *MHS Coll.*, 6th ser., 7: 203-8, 222, 239, 306, 370, 491, 493, 495-96, 497, 504, 511.

52. Barrow, *Trade and Empire*, p. 133. Whereas only two or three vessels from Piscataqua traded with Newfoundland in 1695, 1723, and 1725, this number increased to ten in 1727, nine in 1735, twenty in 1742, and thirty-two in 1752. Although these increases do not of necessity indicate smuggling activity, the opportunities were present at Newfoundland; and

it is unlikely that some of these traders failed to take advantage of them. The statistics for 1735 have been culled from the *Boston Weekly Post-Boy*, May 22, 1735–April 23, 1736.

53. The best analyses are in Albion, *Forests and Sea Power*; Malone, *Pine Trees and Politics*; Bailyn, *New England Merchants*, pp. 132–34, 142.

54. DTR, 1: 324; *Mass. Records*, 4, pt. 2: 384.

55. *NH Laws*, 1: 592. The act contained a clause exempting mast trees for the Royal Navy from its provisions, but the inference was that the surveyor of the woods could search only that land outside the townships for such masts. For evidence of earlier trespasses see *NHPP*, 40: 6, 233, and elsewhere; HTR, 1: 361; Quint, *Old Dover*, p. 149.

56. That the laws were inadequate to stop trespassing may be seen in the repeated attempts in the acts of 1707, 1718, 1724, and 1739 to attain this goal (*NH Laws*, 2: 82–83, 257–58, 380–82, 572–74).

57. For excellent discussions of both these policies in New England, see Malone, *Pine Trees and Politics*; Lord, *Industrial Experiments*; Nettels, *The Money Supply*, pp. 140–61.

58. *CSP Col*, 1693–96, no. 1922; 1699, no. 817; *APC Col*, 1680–1720, pp. 299, 303–5; Malone, *Pine Trees and Politics*, pp. 20–22.

59. For petitions of English merchants see *CSP Col*, 1702–3, nos. 579, 581, 1033; Rawlinson Mss., C. 379. Vaughan's petition of January 2, 1702/3 is in Rawlinson Mss., C. 128. Also see *NHPP*, 3: 158–62.

60. *Journal of the Commissioners for Trade and Plantations*, 14 vols. (London: His Majesty's Stationery Office, 1920–38), 1704–9, 30. 3 and 4 Anne, c. 10.

61. For petitions see *CSP Col*, 1714–15, nos. 389i, 422, 505, 550; 1716–17, no. 22; *NHPP*, 2: 719; 3: 741, 744, 753, 780; 4: 123.

62. Bridger to Board of Trade, May 1, 1722, *CSP Col*, 1722–23, no. 123.

63. For the statistics see Table 7. Although part of this increase represented an increase in naval stores exports, the increase in other lumber products can be seen from the growing number of vessels after 1723 that went to London and nonnaval ports and were not carrying masts. In 1723 there were two, in 1725 there were five, in 1727 there were six, in 1735, eleven. Although there were only four in 1742, this number is misleading because by 1742 the vessels carrying masts and naval stores to the naval ports also carried large quantities of other lumber products. In fact, this statistic for 1742 reflects a trend toward monopolization of the English lumber trade by the mast contractors and their agents in the Piscataqua region.

64. Wentworth to Board of Trade, December 27, 1723, *CSP Col*, 1722–23, no. 806.

65. Francis N. Thorpe, ed., *The Federal and State Constitutions, Colonial Charters, and Other Organic Laws of the States*, 7 vols. (Washington, D.C.: Carnegie Institution, 1909), 3: 1875–87. Legally, this charter had no force in New Hampshire (3 and 4 Anne, c. 10). Also see Malone, *Pine Trees and Politics*, pp. 10–28.

66. *NH Laws*, 2: 82–83; *NHPP*, 2: 576–77. The other provisions were similar to those of the Massachusetts Charter.

67. Bridger to Board of Trade, July 23, 1711, *CSP Col*, 1711–12, no. 41; Usher to Stanhope, November 25, 1710, CO5 10, 880, p. 20; John Wentworth to Board of Trade, August 20, 1723, *CSP Col*, 1722–23, nos. 685, 806; Dunbar to Popple, January 12, 1730/31, ibid., 1731, no. 12; Board of Trade to Duke of Newcastle, February 10, 1730/31, ibid., no. 45. For Benning and John Wentworth, see Malone, *Pine Trees and Politics*, pp. 128, 133.

68. Daniell, "Politics in New Hampshire," pp. 76–105; Malone, *Pine Trees and Politics*, pp. 124–32.

69. 9 Anne, c. 17; 8 George I, c. 12.

70. 2 George II, c. 35.

71. William Vaughan to Board of Trade, January 2, 1702/3, Rawlinson Mss., c. 128.

72. *NH Laws*, 1: 592; 2: 82–83, 257–58, 380–82, 572–74. The acts were passed in 1697, 1708, 1718, 1724, and 1739, respectively.

73. For examples, see Bridger to Board of Trade, March 9, 1707/8; Board of Trade to Bridger, July 7, 1708; Bridger to Board of Trade, July 14, 1718; Bridger to Popple, June 20, 1720; Armstrong to Board of Trade, 1722; Board of Trade to King George, March 20, 1727/28; Peter Weare v. Dunbar, May 9, 1730; Shute to Board of Trade, December 12, 1720 (*CSP Col*, 1706–8, no. 1384ix; 1708–9, no. 24; 1717–18, no. 616; 1720–21, nos. 118, 319; 1722–23, no. 132; 1728–29, no. 118; 1730, no. 224). See Malone, *Pine Trees and Politics*, pp. 57–123.

74. Joseph Smith to John Usher, January 25, 1715/16, *CSP Col*, 1716-17, no. 19*i*; John Wentworth to Board of Trade, May 22, 1720, ibid., 1720-21, no. 82.

75. *NHPP*, 4: 24, 40; John Usher to Lord Carteret, *CSP Col*, 1722-23, no. 703; Armstrong to Board of Trade, September 1, 1724, ibid., 1724-25, no. 352; Ralph Gulston to Treasury, January 24, 1726/27, ibid., 1726-27, no. 450*ii*; Armstrong to Jeremiah Dunbar, November 23, 1728, ibid., 1728-29, nos. 37, 118, 359, 517. The role of Lieutenant Governor Wentworth in these grants is uncertain. While he was a greedy grantee, receiving 500 acres per township grant, nevertheless, he saw to it that clauses were included in each charter upholding the Crown's rights to the white pines; it is possible that he hoped to enforce these clauses. He wrote the Board of Trade in April 1727 that royal rights to the pines were protected in the new townships and that if the surveyor performed his duties, they would be secure in New Hampshire. It is more likely, however, that Wentworth was trying to discredit the surveyor so that he could obtain the post.

76. There are a number of descriptions of this riot, but the best short analysis is in Malone, *Pine Trees and Politics*, pp. 111-13. See also Schutz, *William Shirley*, p. 18; Belknap, *History* (Farmer ed.), pp. 233-35; Bell, *History of Exeter*, pp. 72-75; Belcher to Board of Trade, July 1, 1734, "Belcher Papers," *MHS Coll.*, 6th ser., 7: 78-85; Waldron to Belcher, April 26, 1734, Waldron Papers, vol. 1, no. 49. The two letters imply that Dunbar's actions and the Exeter response were primarily political in motivation.

77. The case of *Frost* v. *Leighton* in Maine in 1735, with its direct challenge to the trespass charges the New Hampshire and Maine lumbermen had utilized effectively in the past, was the last important case Dunbar sued in New England. Until its outcome was enforced in the early 1740's, the surveyor's office had little authority (Malone, *Pine Trees and Politics*, pp. 114-18; Smith, *Appeals to Privy Council*, pp. 328-32). This case became a part of Dunbar's general feud with Belcher over politics and forest policies.

78. Waldron to Belcher, September 16, 1748, Waldron Papers, vol. 2, no. 156.

79. Bellomont to Board of Trade, September 9 and November 22, 1699, *CSP Col*, 1699, nos. 769, 986. Also see ibid., 1701, no. 631; 1706-8, no. 113.

80. Bridger's deputies included Richard Waldron, Ichabod Plaisted, Robert Coffin, Richard Gerrish, Ezekial Wentworth, and Benjamin Wentworth (*CSP Col*, 1706-8, nos. 709, 1384*v*).

81. With Theodore Atkinson as deputy surveyor and George Jaffrey as judge of Vice-Admiralty Court in the late 1730's, the Wentworth faction dominated royal timber policy in the Piscataqua, while the opposition supported the governor and dominated New Hampshire's local political offices. John Wentworth had furthered local antagonisms when he lowered Thomas Westbrook's rank in the New Hampshire Council in 1726 (*NHPP*, 4: 221, 223, 770). For further evidence of conflicts see Dunbar to Wentworth, January 9, 1730; Thomas Westbrook to Wentworth, January 13, 1729/30, CO5 880, 54-58; Waldron to Belcher, September 20, 1742, Waldron Papers, vol. 2, no. 94.

82. Daniell, "Politics in New Hampshire."

83. For evidence of these problems see *NHPP*, 1: 346-66; 2: 53-55, 128-29, 289; 3: 35, 36, 45, 47, 101; 17: 541-43; Toppan, *Edward Randolph*, 7: 410; *CSP Col*, 1689-92, nos. 242, 336, 407, 513, 802, 906, 1911, 1918; 1696-97, no. 570; 1700, no. 580; 1706-8, no. 1592; 1708-9, nos. 19, 392, 458; 1714-15, no. 389*i*; 1722-23, no. 795; 1724-25, nos. 95, 476. The existence of these problems should not obscure the fact that war also stimulated portions of New Hampshire's economy (see pp. 000, 000).

84. McKinley, "Economic History of Portsmouth," pp. 248-49; *Mass. Records*, 4 pt. 2: 496; *NHPP*, 1: 299-302.

85. *NHPP*, 2: 34-35, 43. A small clique of pro-Masonian people opposed acceptance of Massachusetts' authority. See *NH Laws*, 1: 409-10, 420, 425, 441-76 passim.

86. For the new laws see *NH Laws*, 1: 524-31, 537-41. For Usher's petitions see Usher to Board of Trade, 1694, *CSP Col*, 1693-96, nos. 39, 40, 1119; Richard Waldron to William Wallis, October 21, 1692, in Toppan, *Edward Randolph*, 7: 414-15. Usher had begged the Crown for money and troops to no avail. In fact in 1695 the New Hampshire Council refused to petition the Crown for aid (*NHPP*, 2: 171; 3: 47). For a petition to Massachusetts in 1697 for military aid see *NHPP*, 2: 225.

87. *NHPP*, 2: 346, 411, 435-36; *CSP Col*, 1700, nos. 580, 580*ix*; William Vaughan to Board of Trade, January 21, 1702/3, ibid., 1702-3, no. 225.

88. For petitions for aid see *CSP Col*, 1704-5, no. 141; 1706-8, nos. 552, 1592; 1708-9, nos. 19, 392; 1724-25, no. 360; 1726-27, no. 300; Rawlinson Mss., C. 128, no. 7; *NHPP*, 3: 780.

89. *NHPP*, 3: 378-411. The merchants who dominated the House were Mark Hunking, Richard Gerrish, Theodore Atkinson, and George Jaffrey, Jr.

90. Ibid., pp. 415-16, 438, 445-46, 452-55, 493-94, 507-8, 509.

91. Vaughan to Board of Trade, May 10, 1715, CO5 914, 13-21. Vaughan was seeking the post of lieutenant governor of New Hampshire, and this petition probably influenced his appointment. It also influenced his dismissal, as Sir William Ashurst thought it "a monstrous offense" and obtained his dismissal in 1717 (Belknap, *History*, 3: 258).

92. For piracy at Piscataqua in the 1630's see *NHPP*, 1: 105; for the 1660's and 1670's see Rutledge, *The Isles of Shoals*, p. 20; George F. Dow and John Edmonds, *The Pirates of the New England Coast, 1630-1670* (Salem, Mass., 1923); for the two intercolonial wars see *Coll. Maine Hist. Soc.*, 5: 140, 277-79; Dow and Edmonds, *Pirates*, pp. 31-32; Jenness, *Isles of Shoals*, p. 174; Fairchild, *Messrs. William Pepperrell*, pp. 106-8; *CSP Col*, 1704-5, no. 1456; *NHPP*, 2: 437; and for the period frm 1717 to 1722 see *NHPP*, 2: 702-3, 707, 735; 4: 2-3; 17: 730-32.

93. Between 1702 and 1709, John Wentworth, Richard Gerrish, Thomas Holland, Thomas Packer, and George Jaffrey engaged in privateering in the Caribbean (*NHPP*, 2: 578; *APC Col*, 1680-1720, pp. 415, 545).

94. The 1699 law (*NH Laws*, 1: 653) was vetoed by the Crown and never renewed. For the embargo see *NHPP*, 2: 701; Saltonstall, *Ports of Piscataqua*, p. 27. While the Massachusetts government maintained an armed galley for protection against pirates, the New Hampshire government felt that the expense of such a precaution far overbore any danger from pirates.

95. *NHPP*, 2: 234, 244-45.

96. Ibid., pp. 641, 643.

97. An exception to this conclusion occurred in 1740/41, when the New Hampshire government was forced to place an embargo on the export of provisions outside the British Empire as a result of the new war with Spain, but the embargo probably cut into New Hampshire's trade with the French West Indies as well. See ibid., 5: 76; *NH Laws*, 2: 584-85.

98. Usher to Lords of Trade, November 1694, *CSP Col*, 1693-96, no. 1569. Morris, *Government and Labor*, pp. 272-78, has an excellent general discussion of colonial impressment.

99. New Hampshire Council to Usher, May 1696, *NHPP*, 17: 659-60; New Hampshire Council to Captain Robert Hancock, 1697, ibid., 2: 255.

100. Ibid., 2: 586. Usually, ownership of an impressed vessel brought lucrative spoils to the New Hampshire treasurer's political friends and was a sought-after honor.

101. Bailyn, *New England Merchants*, p. 128. For later New England clashes with Britsh diplomatic policies see Archibald Cummings to Board of Trade, August 2, 1716, *CSP Col*, 1716-17, no. 297. In 1717 the Board sent circular letters to the colonial governors forbidding trade with French colonies and asking for their cooperation in enforcement of this ban (ibid., no. 571). In 1719, George Vaughan defended New Hampshire economic interests before the Board, arguing that the Isles of Canso (below Nova Scotia) belonged to Britain, not France (ibid., 1719-20, no. 236).

102. The Molasses Act of 1733, by placing prohibitive duties on the colonial importation of French colonial sugar and molasses, threatened one of New Hampshire's more lucrative markets for lumber and fish when these products glutted the British West Indian markets. While the act did regulate imperial trade, it adversely affected New Hampshire opportunities for obtaining both "returns" and goods useful in other trade patterns. For evidence of violations see the Peirce Papers, Baker Library, Harvard University; McKinley, "Economic History of Portsmouth," pp. 317-18; Fairchild, *Messrs. William Pepperrell*, p. 129. For an example of illicit trade with Spain see Benning Wentworth to John Rindge, March 29, 1735, Peirce Papers, Portsmouth Athenaeum; also Albion, *Forests and Sea Power*, p. 264.

103. Of course, British diplomatic approaches were not always antagonistic to New Hampshire interests. The capture of Port Royal and the opening of Nova Scotia to New Hampshire trade after 1713 were beneficial, as were the British attempts to protect New England sources of logwood and salt at Campeche and Tortuga (*CSP Col*, 1719-20, no. 578; Andrews, *The Colonial Period*, 4: 91-92).

104. None of these policies were followed by all the merchants. In fact, some were quite content with the status quo and worked within the existing system to better themselves economically. They obtained land grants in Maine, for example, or strengthened ties with the Massachusetts mercantile community.

105. *NHPP*, 1: 421-22; 9: 685; 17: 611, 613-15.

106. *NH Laws*, 1: 83-84.

107. Ibid., pp. 527-31; *NHPP*, 3: 168-73; *CSP Col*, 1693-96, nos. 192, 197, 205, 247, 258, 262, 372, 453-55.

108. *NH Laws*, 1: 566, 588, 592. After 1696 Massachusetts traders were not exempted from these duties and complained of it often (*NHPP*, 2: 147, 509; 3: 90, 104; 19: 725).

109. *NH Laws*, 2: 150-52. The act reduced import duties substantially, as might be expected after the war, but the export duty on lumber was 1s. per 1,000 feet of boards, 2s. per 1,000 feet of pine planks, 3s. per 1,000 feet of oak planks, 1s. per 1,000 pipestaves, and some other lesser duties. See the conflicts between the New Hampshire House and Council from 1704 to 1714 in *NHPP*, 2: 291, 294-95, 305, 373, 445, 518; 19: 22, 25, 31, 38, 52, 54-55. The new merchants were Mark Hunking, George Jaffrey, Jr., Richard Gerrish, Theodore Atkinson, John Wentworth, and Richard Wibird.

110. Jeremiah Dummer to Board of Trade, January 17, 1714/15, *CSP Col*, 1714-15, no. 167; E. Ames and A. C. Goodell, eds., *Acts and Resolves of the Province of Massachusetts Bay*, 17 vols. (Boston, 1869-1910), 9: 418; *NHPP*, 3: 597.

111. New Hampshire Council to Lords of Trade, May 7, 1681, *NHPP*, 1: 541-43.

112. *NH Laws*, 2: 361-63, 365, 366; Ames and Goodell, *Acts and Resolves*, 10: 83, 120-21; *CSP Col*, 1720-21, no. 333. Wentworth complained bitterly to the Board of Trade of Massachusetts' "unneighborly" duties, saying "they despise and lay heavier burden on us . . . they impose double duties for all merchandise we send there. . . . I would once more renew my petition for the settling of the line between us, it's the only thing that can make this Province thrive" (Wentworth to Board of Trade, March 27, 1726, ibid., 1726-27, no. 95). Wentworth attacked Massachusetts in almost every letter he wrote to London officials.

113. Popple to Shute, August 18, 1721, *CSP Col*, 1720-21, no. 618; *NH Laws*, 2: 404-5; Belcher to Board of Trade, April 4, 1737, CO5 880, Cc. 54, 1-4. The government did enact a small powder duty to be paid by all vessels entering the port of Piscataqua.

114. Wentworth to Board of Trade, January 21, 1724/25, *CSP Col*, 1724-25, no. 476. For further evidence of this growing timber shortage see ibid., 1725-27, no. 95; 1728-29, no. 638, 670; 1730, no. 502. For example, one deputy surveyor wrote that the New Hampshire woods were "quite destroyed" except for about 3,000 trees "fit for masts" and that the people had "turned their fury" on Maine.

115. Dunbar to Board of Trade, August 19, 1730, ibid., 1730, no. 402. Westbrook had established his masting activities in Maine as early as 1718. By the 1720's Falmouth was an important masting center. For these activities see Leonard Chapman, "The Mast Industry of Old Falmouth," *Coll. Maine Hist. Soc.*, 2d ser., 7: 390-405. Waldron's Casco activities can be found scattered throughout the Waldron Papers, NHHS, but particularly in vol. 2.

116. Dunbar noted upon his arrival in New Hampshire that he found "many forests of large white pines" in Exeter, Dover, Newmarket, Nottingham, and Rochester which he thought would "serve the Navy for several years." But these trees were on private property, according to provincial law, and could be utilized in whatever manner the owner desired. Dunbar to Popple, February 3, 1729/30, *CSP Col*, 1730, no. 45.

117. See the Atkinson to Thomlinson correspondence in *NHPP*, 4: 833-65; 5: 921-30; 18: 149-86; and Benning Wentworth's correspondence with Thomlinson in the Ayer Mss., Newberry Library, Chicago. See also the London merchants' petition for a separate governor in New Hampshire (*APC Col*, 1720-45, pp. 637-39). Other members of the clan included Henry Sherburne, Jr., George Jaffrey, Thomas Packer, Andrew Wiggin, and Richard Wibird, Jr.

118. Dunbar was the lieutenant governor of New Hampshire; his patron was Martin Bladen at the Board of Trade. Shirley was seeking promotion in Massachusetts under the patronage of the Duke of Newcastle. The Gulstons, Thomlinson, and Chapman were London merchants either holding mast contracts or desiring such contracts. Thomlinson especially was on the "make," which in large part explains his support of the Wentworth

clique. By 1740 he had obtained a mast contract from the navy and was working with Mark H. Wentworth in New Hampshire, supplying masts. Ferdinand John Paris was a skilled English solicitor.

119. Thomlinson to Atkinson, June 23, 1740, *NHPP*, 18: 161-63; Thomlinson to Atkinson, February 6, 1740/41, ibid., p. 169; Daniell, "Politics in New Hampshire," p. 79; Schutz, *William Shirley*, pp. 34-35.

120. Governor Dudley to Board of Trade, March 1, 1708/9, *CSP Col*, 1708-9, no. 392, wrote of the hardships at Piscataqua that had caused people to leave the colony. He said that New Hampshire had thirty vessels in trade, which was an increase of only six over the trade of 1700 (ibid., no. 953, p. 676).

121. Usher to Board of Trade, February 25, 1704, in Nettels, *The Money Supply*, p. 105. In 1695, 134 vessels engaged in this coastal trade; in 1713, 128 were involved.

122. The lumber market was exhausted, too (*NHPP*, 2: 578; 3: 162; *APC Col*, 1680-1720, p. 415).

123. Such merchant-traders as William Partridge, Samuel Penhallow, Mark Hunking, George Jaffrey, Sampson Sheafe, John Usher, Richard Waldron, John Pickering, William Vaughan, and William Pepperrell are examples. For Pepperrell, see Fairchild, *Messrs. William Pepperrell*, pp. 40-47.

124. These included John Plaisted, George Vaughan, Richard Gerrish, John Frost, Andrew Pepperrell, John Wentworth, Henry Sherburne, George Jaffrey, Jr., Richard Hilton, Nathaniel Weare, and John and Nicholas Gilman.

125. These included Tobias Langdon, Thomas Phipps, Richard Wibird, Joshua Peirce, Theodore Atkinson, Thomas Packer, Samuel Weeks, George Walker, John Knight, Theophilus Dudley, Jonathan Thing, Joshua Wingate, Thomas Westbrook, Archibald MacPhaedris, and Joseph Newmarch.

126. The additions to the lumber traders and mariner-merchants between 1713 and 1723 included Ephraim Dennett; Benjamin Gambling; Ellis Huske; Daniel Bell; William Knight; Richard Waldron, Jr.; John Newmarch; Peter Weare; Morris Hobbs; Paul Gerrish; Joseph, Edward, and Kingsley Hall; and Paul and Benjamin Wentworth. Additions between 1723 and 1730 included John Rindge, Jotham Odiorne, Daniel Warner, Joseph Sherburne, Hunking Wentworth, Benning Wentworth, Bartholemew Thing, and Jonathan Wadleigh. Additions between 1730 and 1742 included John Moffatt, Jacob Sheafe, Theodore Atkinson, Richard Wibird, Jr., Henry Sherburne, Jr., Thomas Bell, Thomas Peirce, Mark Hunking Wentworth, Thomas Wibird, Thomas Wright, David Wentworth, Charles Frost, Joshua Peirce, Jr., Thomas Wallingsford, Ebenezer Wentworth, William Moor, John McEllwin, Jacob Wendell, Robert Rae, Thomas Millet, John Wingate, and Tristram Coffin. This list is by no means complete.

127. Shute to Popple, June 1, 1720, *CSP Col*, 1720-21, no. 94*ii*. Evidence of this "pinch" can be seen in New Hampshire's attempts to discriminate against Massachusetts vessels carrying Piscataqua lumber and in its acceptance of free port status. The main area of low demand for lumber was in the West Indies.

128. As Table 7 indicates, there was no trade with Europe in 1695, but by 1725 almost 17 percent of the export trade went to southern Europe. By 1742, however, this area received less than 1 percent of the export trade. For trade with Ireland, Amsterdam, and Spain between 1712 and 1730, see the MacPhaedris Letterbook, Warner House, Portsmouth; the Peirce Papers, Portsmouth Athenaeum; *CSP Col*, 1716-17, no. 19*i*; 1719-20, no. 410*i*; 1722-23, nos. 329, 344, 356, 703; 1728-29, nos. 108, 517.

129. Table 7 indicates the great increase in trade with England in the 1730's and early 1740's, from about 10 percent to 45 percent. For the increase in naval stores production before the 1720's see Lord, *Industrial Experiments*, p. 86 and elsewhere; Bridger to Board of Trade, June 23, 1719, *CSP Col*, 1719-20, no. 245. The act in the early 1720's which removed bounties on naval stores decreased this trade in pitch, tar, and turpentine with the mother country during the 1720's.

130. Fairchild, *Messrs. William Pepperrell*, pp. 126-29.

131. See above, Chapter V, and also *NHPP*, 9: 709-12; Belknap, *History*, 3: 159.

132. *NHPP*, 3: 754, 759; *NH Laws*, 2: 336, 349; Saltonstall, *Ports of Piscataqua*, pp. 170-72. The causes of the failure of iron manufacturing included the shortage of skilled

labor, the inferior quality of the ore beds, lack of adequate water power, and the cold climate.

133. By 1742 New Hampshire was exporting skillets, guns, shot, handspikes, kettles, and axes. The sources of iron appear to have been Spain, Sweden, and England. In 1742, for example, one of the mastships brought in 48 tons of junk, some of which was probably used in production of iron goods.

134. *NH Laws*, 2: 335; *NHPP*, 4: 596; Shipping Returns, 1742, CO5 968, p. 53; Belcher to Board of Trade, November 6, 1734, "Belcher Papers," *MHS Coll*, 6th ser., 7: 150. By 1720 the common law courts of New Hampshire had prohibited the Vice-Admiralty Court from hearing cases involving illegal importations of wool in New Hampshire (Armstrong to Board of Trade, July 19, 1720, *CSP Col*, 1720-21, no. 699*iii*). See also ibid., no. 466.

135. In 1742 over 37,000 bricks were exported. For a discussion of Dover's brick manufacturing see Scales, *History of Dover*, pp. 56-60.

136. John Wentworth to Board of Trade, 1774, Wentworth Mss., NHHS; Richard Waldron's deposition, 1739, *NHPP*, 5: 46. For the valuation of 1730 see *NHPP*, 4: 532.

137. Shipping Returns, 1742, CO5 968, p. 48. Mark H. Wentworth's vessel was appropriately named the *New Hampshire*.

138. See Table 7. The export volume for 1735 is an estimate based proportionately on the number of vessels and trade volume of 1727. This increased trade with England was undertaken by a relatively few New Hampshire traders, particularly the few local merchants involved in the mast trade. Note, too, the dominance of Samuel Waldo, George Craddock, Ralph Gulston, and Mark H. Wentworth in the total trade volume (see Table 13).

139. The primary lumber exports to the West Indies were pine boards, barrel and hogshead staves, shingles, hoops, and clapboards. By 1742 about one-fifth of the vessels engaged in this direct trade made two round trips a year.

140. The sale of vessels and cargoes carrying sugar and molasses to England did not become a significant part of Piscataqua's trade until the 1740's and 1750's. Note that in 1727 the percentages of export and import volume with the West Indies were relatively equal (Tables 7 and 9). This began to change in the 1730's, and by 1742 New Hampshire exported approximately 34 percent of its tonnage to the West Indies but returned only 25 percent. By 1752 the export was 53 percent, but importation was only 36 percent.

141. MacPhaedris Letterbook, Warner House, Portsmouth. MacPhaedris owned at least six vessels in trade by 1717, and he married Sarah, the daughter of Lieutenant Governor John Wentworth, in 1718.

142. Shipping Returns, 1742, CO5 968, pp. 44-53. For example, Daniel Warner's vessels the *Black Swallow* and *Ranger* followed this pattern.

143. Fairchild, *Messrs. William Pepperrell*, pp. 160-62. Because William Pepperrell was one of the leading Piscataqua traders from the 1690's to the 1720's, Fairchild's discussion of the trade patterns and shipping practices in these years is excellent and is amply supported by the extant Shipping Returns for Piscataqua.

144. See the economic framework outlined by Douglass C. North and Robert P. Thomas, eds., *The Growth of the American Economy to 1860* (New York: Harper and Row, 1968), pp. 1-9, to which I am indebted.

145. The year 1727 was chosen primarily because it had shipping returns that provided full information on vessels and ownership. Perhaps the returns of 1723 would have been a somewhat more accurate representation of this growth (see Table 12). The 1723 returns would have reflected a somewhat greater increase in trade volume than that of 1727.

146. Dudley to Board of Trade, March 1, 1708/9, *CSP Col*, nos. 391, 392, estimated the trade of Massachusetts at about £50,000 and New Hampshire's as one-tenth that of Massachusetts. For 1720 see Governor Shute to William Popple, June 1, 1720, ibid., 1720-21, no. 94*ii*; Henry Newman to Board of Trade, Rawlinson Mss., C. 128, no. 14. The number of New Hampshire-based traders for 1695 given in the text is only an estimate. The shipping Returns for 1695 give the names only of the ship captains, not the owners; hence, Table 11 does not indicate the number of such traders for 1695.

147. See Table 13. These statistics reflect only the Shipping Returns for 1727 and are minimum rather than maximum estimates.

148. See Table 1. The population increase between 1730 and 1740 was about 116 percent.

149. See Table 11. The volume increase between 1742 and 1752 matched the increase of 1727–42 in quantity but not in percentage. In 1754 Governor Wentworth estimated the value of New Hampshire's export trade at £80,000 sterling. In that year the Piscataqua port exported 9,297 tons, as compared to the 7,633 tons of 1742. Using the £40,000 sterling estimate of 1721 and the £80,000 sterling estimate of 1754 as a base, New Hampshire's export trade in 1742 was probably about £70,000 sterling—more evidence of extensive economic growth in New Hampshire. For further crude evidence, note the comparative increase in population between 1720 and 1750 in relation to the increase in export trade volume between 1723 and 1752 (see Tables 1 and 7). Population increased from 9,375 to 27,505, a 193 percent increase, while export volume tonnage increased from 3,116 to 10,231, a 228 percent increase.

150. Mast traders increasingly dominated Piscataqua trade by the 1740's. In 1727 they carried on about 19 percent of the total trade; in 1742 they controlled 37 percent, almost doubling their influence. By 1752, however, their trade volume had dropped to 23 percent, as increasing numbers of masts were exported from Falmouth and ports farther north.

151. Shipping Returns, 1742–47, CO 5 968.

152. With the exception of the few top traders, the dominant pattern followed by the vast majority was to maintain a relatively stable level of trade volume or fall into a very gradual decline. Note, for example, the declining volume of trade and vessel tonnage of the Pepperrells, Peirces, Bells, and Henry Sherburne, Sr. (Table 13). Other traders—such as the Warners, John Moffatt, George Jaffrey, and the Sheafes—maintained relative consistency.

Chapter VIII

1. The divergent attitudes of Dover, Exeter, Hampton, and Portsmouth have already been discussed in chap. 1. They included religious conflicts among Anglicans, Antinomians, and Congregationalists, and differences in the primary goals of the settlers. One manifestation of these differences can be seen in the fact that Dover, dominated by ministers and religious conflict during the 1630's, chose five different ministers between 1634 and 1642 in the following order: a pro-Massachusetts Puritan, an Anglican, an anti-Massachusetts Puritan, an Anglican, and a pro-Massachusetts Puritan (William Leveridge, George Burdett, Hansard Knollys, Thomas Larkham, and Daniel Maud, respectively). See Robert F. Lawrence, *The New Hampshire Churches* (Claremont, N.H., 1856), pp. 318–20; George Burdett to Archbishop of Canterbury, November 29, 1638, *NHPP*, 17: 497–98. While Dover and Strawbery Banke settlers came to New England to catch fish and get rich in the fur trade, the settlers of Exeter and Hampton had special religious goals and were oriented toward agriculture.

2. *NHPP*, 1: 126. The Dover Combination was established in 1640.

3. Ibid., p. 132. The Exeter Combination was established in 1639. Hampton was already organized as a township under Massachusetts Congregationalism. Strawbery Banke (Portsmouth) had a town government by 1638 under an elected Anglican governor, Francis Williams. Ibid., pp. 111–13; 17: 504–6; Belknap, *History* (Farmer ed.), p. 28.

4. *NHPP*, 1: 126–28, 158, 170–71, 192–93. Other considerations also guided the towns. By 1643, Exeter's religious unity had declined as John Wheelwright moved into Maine and the townspeople sought new settlers. Portsmouth's Anglicanism was tempered by an influx of Massachusetts settlers during the 1640's and 1650's and the appearance of a Puritan missionary-preacher, Joshua Moodey, who became its first permanent Congregational minister from 1658 to 1697. Moodey, however, was not ordained at Portsmouth until 1671, was forced to leave New Hampshire in 1684 by Anglican Governor Cranfield, and did not return until 1693.

5. Of 105 New Hampshire wills written between 1640 and 1690, only 12 (11 percent) expressed the concept of stewardship. Ten of those twelve were Hampton wills. *NHPP*, 31: 43, 108, 118, 127, 129, 142, 217, 236, 263, 271, 274, 308. Only 4 percent of New Hampshire wills written between 1680 and 1740 emphasized stewardship. All together, from 1640 to 1740, only 27 of 459 wills (5.9 percent) were phrased in support of Christian stewardship.

6. This conclusion rests upon such indirect evidence as the special political privileges and land grants given to freemen in Dover and Hampton; the comparatively large number of

individual wills from these towns expressing stewardship concepts; the relatively close relationship there between religion and education; the existence of strong, established town churches in Dover, Hampton, and Exeter (for example, the harsh treatment of Quakers in Dover, the special role of religious piety among Hampton's local politicians, and the crucial role of the Reverend John Wheelwright in Exeter); and the special emphasis placed upon religion in the early political covenants of these towns. For evidence of the special power of selectmen as rulers see HTR, 1: 121; DTR, 1: 214, 218, 220, 247. As an example of the special cohesiveness of Exeter, when the harvest of 1642 failed, the Exeter selectmen ordered a committee to search all homes for surplus corn not needed by a family to subsist upon until the next harvest and to buy that corn at the prevailing market price and distribute it among those most in need in return for whatever they could pay (Bell, *History of Exeter*, p. 444.) Further discussion and documentation of these patterns in the three towns can be found above in chapter 2.

7. The best discussion of this general pattern is in Michael Zuckerman, "The Social Context of Democracy in Massachusetts," *William and Mary Quarterly*, 3rd ser. 25 (October 1968): 523–44. The pattern was significant in Portsmouth after 1652; all male inhabitants could vote and hold public office, and the Congregational Church played a relatively minor role in the town until it obtained town tax support in 1671. By the 1690's perhaps half Portsmouth's inhabitants attended the Congregational Church, for it had about 140 male members in 1693, and 255 people had paid taxes in the town in 1688 (PTR, 1: 252–55, 306–7). For the role of inhabitants at town meetings see the Portsmouth records in Hackett, pp. 13, 16, 21, 28, 33, 34, 35, 37, where such phrases as "it is generally concluded and agreed upon," "the inhabitants do generally acknowledge," and "it is ordered by the common consent" were frequent. Originally, the status of freeman had no special significance in Portsmouth, but by the 1660's, as Portsmouth leaders wanted a voice at the Massachusetts General Court, a number of the townspeople became freemen.

8. Exeter had no settled minister between 1643 and 1650. The town enjoyed the services of a preacher-lumberer, Samuel Dudley, from 1650 to 1683 but did not have a formal church. There was no minister in the town between 1683 and 1698, but finally, with the ministry of John Clark from 1698 to 1705, Exeter formally established its first Congregational Church with twenty-eight members, perhaps 25 percent of the male adult population (Lawrence, *New Hampshire Churches*). Also, in Exeter all free male adult inhabitants could exercise the franchise; and although the town selectmen initiated some policies, all decisions were voted upon at the town meetings. The creation of a comprehensive timber usage policy (discussed in chap. 2 above) represents one example of the blending of individual self-interest and the needs of the community that developed in Exeter through this town-meeting consensus approach.

9. This interpretation should be contrasted with that of Kenneth A. Lockridge and Alan Kreider, "The Evolution of Massachusetts Town Government, 1640 to 1740," *William and Mary Quarterly*, 3rd ser. 23 (October 1966): 549–74, who found that the town inhabitants of Massachusetts did not take an active part in town politics until the era between 1680 and 1720, when ministerial vacancies and sectional rivalries destroyed earlier political stability and consensus. Political crises of another sort appeared in New Hampshire before 1680, with similar but earlier results.

10. DTR, 1: 358, 360. For further analysis of Dover's crisis see above, chap. 2. In Exeter the shift began as early as 1640 (NHPP, 1: 137–45; ETR, vol. 1).

11. By the new £20 ratable estate definition of freeman in the Cutt Code, only one taxpayer out of 119 male taxpayers did not qualify to vote (NHPP, 1: 396, 424). For examples of the freemen's authority see HTR, 1: 119, 121; NHHS Coll, 8: 40.

12. PTR, 1: 181–83. The town then appointed a special committee of two merchants to aid the selectmen in establishing the tax rates. Economic and social rivalries, pitting an established group of merchants against a number of newcomers to trade, probably played a minor part in this episode as well. The former group included the Cutts, Elias Stileman, Nathaniel Fryer, and Richard Martyn; the latter, Henry Deering, Walter Neale, John Hunking, and John Pickering. These events can be traced in ibid., pp. 161–83.

13. The Quakers threatened the religious orthodoxy of Dover and Hampton and were prosecuted in the courts as criminals during the 1660's (NHPP, 1: 226–30, 239, 243–44; ibid.,

vol. 40; Page, *Judicial Beginnings*, pp. 120–21; Stackpole, *History of New Hampshire*, 1: 61–73. The proprietary claimant's appearance in Portsmouth in 1651 caused a change in its town government and a closer alliance between the Portsmouth inhabitants and Massachusetts from 1652 to 1679, as they sought stable land titles and a more acceptable legal system.

14. For the list of voters see *NHPP*, 19: 659–60. In Hampton only 57 names were listed, out of 120 male taxpayers; in Exeter, only 20 out of 64; in Dover, 61 out of 114; and in Portsmouth, 71 out of 117. Comparing the list of voters with the tax lists of 1680, it is clear that the suffrage was not based upon economic wealth (ibid., 1: 424–28). For a discussion of the New Hampshire General Assembly, 1679–82, see above, pp. 00–00, 000–00.

15. *NHPP*, 1: 382, 557–58.

16. Ibid., p. 383. The Cutt Code is printed in ibid., pp. 382–408. Most of these laws, particularly the capital and criminal laws, were copied from the Massachusetts statutes. In 1682, however, this code was voided by the Crown.

17. For examples, see ibid., pp. 384–85, 387–88, 398–99, 403. A guarantee of the town meeting's local autonomy was the most important protection of these institutions. This guarantee was renewed in 1692 (*NH Laws*, 1: 526–27). For the law concerning religion see ibid., pp. 560–61; it exempted only the Quakers from payment of the town minister's salary but gave each town religious autonomy.

18. *NHPP*, 1: 386. This law was a direct imitation of the Massachusetts suffrage act of 1658 (see *Mass. Records*, 4, pt. 1: 336). The property qualification was reduced to a £15 taxable estate in 1682 (*NH Laws*, 1: 63). The freemanship suffrage qualification adopted in the Cutt Code represented the past experience of Hampton and Dover. Both Portsmouth and Exeter had granted suffrage to all town freeholders of twenty-one years of age (PTR, 1: 245; ETR, 1: 160). The new suffrage qualification must therefore have appeared restrictive to them.

19. Stackpole, *History of New Hampshire*, 1: 114; Belknap, *History* (Farmer ed.), p. 92; Page, *Judicial Beginnings*, pp. 34–35.

20. Kinney, *Church and State*, p. 82.

21. In Portsmouth and Exeter before 1680 all free male inhabitants of twenty-one years or older had qualified as voters in town elections. Applying the £20 ratable estate qualification (an estate which would bring in £3 6s. 8d. per year in rent over a six-year period) to the 1680 tax lists of the four towns shows that only 20 male taxpayers (18 of them from Dover) out of 415 could not meet this requirement. This was less than 5 percent of the taxpayers and meant increased power for the resident voters of each town, as they could now have a direct voice in their provincial government, whereas before, only freemen who were church members could elect deputies to the Massachusetts General Court.

22. *NHPP*, 1: 393, 397–98, 403, 408. Also, the town served as the unit of political representation in the New Hampshire House of Representatives; each town had its own court session and elected a slate of jurors; and the town selectmen were in charge of local taxation. No supervisory officials, such as justices of the peace or sheriffs, were created; instead, the necessary functions of such officials were given to the elected town constables or to the New Hampshire president and council members, who were leading men of each town. The continuing strength of localistic attitudes can be seen in the events of 1689–90, when, in the wake of the Glorious Revolution, the New Hampshire town leaders drew up a republican constitution which gave the suffrage to all town inhabitants (male and 21) and allowed each town equal representation in the Assembly, only to have Hampton's inhabitants veto it because of their fear of being dominated by the other three towns (ibid., 2: 43–46; Dow, *History of Hampton*, pp. 116–18).

23. Lieutenant Governor Usher wrote the Board of Trade on June 28, 1708, describing this approach as follows: "Pity things are carried on as they are for sake of money, most persons holding their places by reason thereof" (*CSP Col*, 1706–8, no. 1592). See also his letter of July 1, 1694, ibid., 1693–96, no. 1119, for evidence of localism, factionalism, and suspicion of executive authority.

24. From 1715 to 1741, the legislative journals reflect such values as various factions argued over land policies, suffrage requirements, paper money, taxation, the location of provincial courts, the areal representation of the councillors, the New Hampshire boundary

location, the governor's salary, the appointment of the provincial agent to London, and so on (*NHPP*, vols. 2-4).

25. See above, chap. 2.

26. The importance of this characteristic varied somewhat from town to town, having lesser significance in such agricultural towns as Hampton and Hampton Falls and in towns which lacked water transportation to the Piscataqua River.

27. The Oyster River settlement and Kingston were partially abandoned during these wars. For the impact of the wars on land utilization see chap. 4 above.

28. None of the frontier towns, for example, provided education for their children during the war years. See *NH Laws*, 1: 561, for example.

29. Many leading families in frontier towns obtained military commissions from the provincial government and achieved higher social status with military successes. The Gilman family of Exeter and the Hiltons and Waldrons of Dover are examples. The various appeals to England and Massachusetts have been discussed in chaps. 4 and 7.

30. In 1693 the provincial government required each town to build a school and appoint and pay a teacher. In 1708 a free Latin grammar school was authorized at Portsmouth for the whole province, with each town contributing to its expenses. *NH Laws*, 1: 560-61; 2: 85-86, 143-44. The latter law was revised in 1710 so that Portsmouth alone paid the costs of the grammar school. By 1712 the problem of illiteracy among children led to legislation allowing selectmen to supervise the schooling of children over ten years of age who could not read or write. Ibid., 2: 98, 115, 336-37, 358. In the 1693 act concerning religion each town was authorized to choose and pay its own minister. The minister and church would be supported through town taxes, but those who conscientiously and regularly attended a church of another persuasion were exempted from support of the town's established church. Ibid., 1: 660-61. Some laws were enacted "to keep Sunday holy" (pointing out that everyone should apply himself to the duties of religion and piety) and forbidding business negotiations, labor, play, travel, and recreation on the Sabbath. Ibid., 1: 564, 672-74. Of course, the provincial government also carried on such traditional functions as establishing courts, suffrage requirements, and a system of taxation, and defining crimes and the extent of punishment for those crimes.

31. Ibid., 2: 121-366. Significantly, these assertions of the General Assembly's authority were coincidental with the increased political power of the mercantile community, the rise of a new generation of merchants in politics, and the domination of the New Hampshire Council by Portsmouth merchants.

32. For the provincial government's role in solving ministerial problems at Portsmouth and Dover between 1713 and 1720 see ibid., 2: 154-56, 189, 252-53.

33. This is not to say that local practices were abolished by these assertions of central authority. In the majority of cases the new legislation tended to ratify existing local practices of the major towns. Nevertheless, the assertion of provincial jurisdiction and authority in these realms was the most significant change during and after the war years. Also, while this change occurred during the war, other factors, products of conflict and dissent at the local level, played a causative role as well.

34. The problems had first appeared in Dover during the 1660's and Portsmouth in the 1670's when the parishes of Oyster River and New Castle sought separation from their respective towns. The Indian wars postponed a solution. *NHPP*, 1: 236, 308-10, 318; 9: 566; 12: 670-78.

35. Generally, the wealthier people of the community consolidated their holdings near the center of the town by the meetinghouse or moved to Portsmouth and invested in trade and commerce, leaving the outlying areas to the younger, poorer, and newer settlers.

36. "Outlivers," a term describing those who lived outside the central area of a town, has been borrowed from Richard Bushman. His discussion of town parishes in Connecticut generally works for New Hampshire as well. See Bushman, *From Puritan to Yankee*, pp. 52-74.

37. See New Castle's experience with Portsmouth in the 1680's (*NHPP*, 12: 672-73, 675-76). For Greenland parish see ibid., 9: 320-24; 12: 64-67; for Newington parish see ibid., 3: 549-51; 9: 710; for Rye parish see ibid., 9: 734-40; for Durham parish see ibid., 1: 308-10, 318; 9: 234-41; for Somersworth parish see ibid., 9: 761-62; 13: 426; for Stratham see ibid., 9:

777-84; for the North Hill parish of Hampton see ibid., 12: 117-22; for Hampton Falls parish see ibid., 9: 338-39, 343-45, 347-49; 12: 133-35; for Brentwood parish see ibid., 9: 76-79, 252-90; for Londonderry and Derry see ibid., 9: 495-506; 12: 435-40. Also see ibid., 9: 690-93.

38. For examples see n. 37 above and ibid., 9: 261, 284, 349.

39. Significantly, between 1713 and 1720, when the provincial government extended its power, only two parishes had any representation in the House of Representatives. The colony's provincial politics was dominated by the established political leaders of the older towns.

40. He removed the political and social leaders of various towns from the council, forced two Puritan ministers to flee the colony, attacked the role of the Congregational Church in the colony, and sought to redistribute property in the colony. See *NHPP*, 1: 433-575, and the discussion of Cranfield's administration in chaps. 3 and 7.

41. Ibid., pp. 378, 439; *NH Laws*, 1: 560-61.

42. Stackpole, *History of New Hampshire*, 1: 73, 221. In 1741, the General Assembly exempted Quakers from taking oaths (*NH Laws*, 2: 584).

43. *NHPP*, 4: 727-29; 9: 105-6; Kinney, *Church and State*, pp. 55-56, 58-59.

44. Among New Hampshire's mercantile elite the ideal and style of life of the English gentry class had become dominant by the 1730's, modifying earlier Puritan concepts.

45. The letter from the Portsmouth members of the Anglican Church to the Society for the Propagation of the Gospel in Foreign Parts (SPGFP), December 26, 1734, lists the members (SPGFP Transcripts, Library of Congress). Also see *NHPP*, 4: 837, 841-42, 845-46, 847, 851. The leading members were George Jaffrey, Theodore Atkinson, John Wentworth, Joshua Peirce, Daniel Warner, Henry Sherburne, Jr., James Jaffrey, Henry Sherburne, Benning Wentworth, Ellis Huske, Hunking Wentworth, Mark H. Wentworth, John Penhallow, Samuel Sherburne, and Pierce Long.

46. For example, in 1739 Greenland exempted Thomas Packer, Thomas Marston, and William Simpson because they attended the Portsmouth Anglican Church (*NHPP*, 12: 67). For the Portsmouth agreement see Dunbar to Bishop of London, December 2, 1735, SPGFP Transcripts, LC. Approximately sixty families, less than 10 percent of the Portsmouth population, belonged to the Anglican church in 1741 (Reverend Arthur Browne to SPGFP, 1741, ibid.).

47. See the treatment of the Exeter "New Lights" during the 1740's (*NHPP*, 9: 278-97). They argued that their separation into new churches was a "Sacred Right" and a liberty of all Englishmen and that it was "every man's duty to follow the dictates of his own conscience" (ibid., pp. 287-90).

48. New Hampshire actually contained twenty-six towns by 1740, but eight of them were sparsely settled speculative grants of the 1720's (see Map 3). Portsmouth had 551 "ratable polls" in 1741 and paid almost twice as much proportionately of the province tax as any other town (*NH Laws*, 2: 724).

49. The exceptions were three of the new towns along the Merrimack River—Londonderry, Chester, and Rochester—which traded down the river to Newburyport in Massachusetts.

50. For a crude indication of comparative town populations, multiply the number of taxpayers shown in Table 14 by six. Also see Map 3. Of the other twelve continental colonies, only Delaware and Georgia had smaller populations than New Hampshire (19,870 and 2,021, respectively). New Hampshire's population quadrupled between 1710 and 1740 (see Table 1).

51. PTR, vols. 15-16, contain numerous examples in the tax records. I have compiled a profile of Portsmouth's economic elite by determining the top twenty to thirty taxpayers (less than 5 percent of the total taxpayers) in the town for each year from 1713 to 1741. While this profile is not completely accurate, the results had 100 men filling 676 possible slots. At least three new men (on the average) reached the top ranks every year, an indication of the open economy and upward mobility in Portsmouth. Of the 100 at the top (the economic elite), at least 20 were farmers, while about 70 were entrepreneurs (either retail merchants, shopkeepers, overseas traders, mariners, or craftsmen-retailers). The richest of these top taxpayers were always wholesale and/or retail merchants; they included John Wentworth,

George Jaffrey, Richard Wibird, Samuel Penhallow, Henry Sherburne, Joshua Peirce, Thomas Westbrook, John Rindge, Richard Waldron, Jr., Samuel Sherburne, John Moffatt, Archibald MacPhaedris, and Mark H. Wentworth.

52. See Table 14. While the probate wills and inventories do not provide a cross-section of either occupations or estate ownership in each town, they do give some crude information concerning the variety of occupations in each town. These statistics come from the NH Probate Records and the New Hampshire wills in *NHPP*, vols. 31–32. These records indicate economic tendencies in Portsmouth, for they contain more laborers of various types from Portsmouth (85) than from any of the other towns (which combined had 121). Also, Portsmouth's records contain a larger number of mariners (38) and merchants (21). Adding in the shopkeepers (13), all three entrepreneurial classes comprise almost 40 percent of Portsmouth's wills; only 15 percent of Portsmouth's wills were written by farmers. For economic structure, the tax records are far more reliable than probate records. See Tables 15–20. In 1732 the richest third of Portsmouth's taxpayers owned about 90 percent of the real property, but they had owned over 80 percent of the land as early as 1660. Stratification in land ownership had occurred as early as the 1650's and continued to exist throughout the colonial period. More important for understanding Portsmouth's economic stratification are Tables 18–20. Note especially the contrasts in Table 19 between various years. Under such a fluctuating economic situation, choosing any two single years for comparison is an arbitrary situation. I have chosen 1735 as the most typical economic year in the 1730's. Contrasting the structure in 1681 with that of 1735, there are fewer poor people in 1735 than there were in 1681; there are far more people in the middle area (£30–£100) and more and richer people in 1735 than in 1681. Whereas in 1681 the upper 10 percent of Portsmouth's taxpayers controlled 39 percent of the taxable wealth of the town, in 1735 they controlled 32 percent. This, however, is the only major difference. The upper two-thirds of the taxpayers owned 88 percent of the wealth in 1681 and 90 percent in 1735. Considering that the lowest third of Portsmouth's taxpayers in 1735 included at least twenty-five (15 percent) nonresidents who owned small quantities of the town's taxable wealth, there was no significant difference in total wealth owned between the lower elements of the economic structure (those taxed under £15) of 1681 and of 1735. See Table 20. While there is a possibility that mercantile wealth was underassessed (which could skew the tax lists toward a more equalitarian economic structure than really existed), I have found no evidence that such was the case.

53. In 1731 Exeter had 48 men (about 20 percent) out of about 250 taxpayers "doomed" (an estimated tax) for trade income (*NHPP*, 11: 648; NH Inventories, 1727–1773, NHHS). Hampton had 36 out of 185 male taxpayers "doomed" for trade, while Hampton Falls did so for only 10 out of 190 taxpayers.

54. See Tables 15 and 16 for crude comparative statistics of real estate ownership. Note the variety of profiles among the towns. These lists understate the holdings of most of the settlers, for they are based only upon improved property. Note that Portsmouth had the richest landholders as well as most of the poorest. For the assessed values assigned to various types of property see *NHPP*, 4: 244–45, 304. Generally, I have assumed (Portsmouth and New Castle excepted) that anyone who owned real property taxed at £5 or more was at least a subsistence farmer. The figures for Portsmouth in Tables 15 and 16 do not reflect true wealth, as they do not include trade income or property. Contrasting Tables 15 and 16 with Tables 20 and 21, the richest 10 percent of Portsmouth's taxpayers possessed only 34.3 percent of the taxable property and income, while the richest 10 percent of real estate owners possessed 57.6 percent of the taxable real estate. Unfortunately, Dover's inventory for 1732 has disappeared.

55. *NHPP*, 9: 561–62. Note the similarities in the 1720 economic profiles of mercantile New Castle and prosperously agricultural Greenland as shown in Tables 21 and 22, and compare these statistics with those of Boston in 1687 as compiled by James M. Henratta, "Economic Development and Social Structure in Colonial Boston," *William and Mary Quarterly*, 3d ser. 22 (January 1965): 80. In Boston the top 10 percent owned 42 percent of the taxable property, and the lowest 33.3 percent, only about 6 percent of the taxable property. One can see relatively more equalitarian economic structures present in New Castle, Portsmouth, and Greenland of the 1720's and 1730's than present in the Boston of

1687. There are varied problems in using tax records and probate records as evidence of economic and social stratification, but one which became clear in working with Portsmouth bears directly upon the research of Henratta. The Portsmouth tax profile varied significantly from year to year (see Tables 18 and 19), so that one could support almost any conclusion one wished by choosing a yearly profile favoring that conclusion. What is true for Portsmouth may be true for Boston as well and for any of the other New Hampshire town profiles used in this study. Thus, all my conclusions concerning economic structure can only be suggestions when based upon these records alone.

It is interesting to compare the economic structures of the New Hampshire towns with those of the agriculturally prosperous Chester County, Pennsylvania, between 1693 and 1748, as compiled by James T. Lemon and Gary B. Nash, "The Distribution of Wealth in Eighteenth-Century America: A Century of Change in Chester County, Pennsylvania, 1693-1802," *Journal of Social History* 2 (Fall 1968): 11-13. (See Tables 20, 21, 23, and 31 for the economic profiles of Portsmouth, Dover, Exeter, and New Castle.) In all the New Hampshire towns surveyed, the economic profiles are roughly equal to or more economically democratic (less concentration of property among the upper economic classes) than the 1730 and 1748 profiles of Chester County. Where Lemon and Nash found economic prosperity, a rising standard of living, and a continuing "drift toward greater concentration of wealth" from 1715 onward in Chester County (as manifested by changes at the top and the bottom of the economic structure), the patterns of economic structure of the four New Hampshire towns in the early eighteenth century remained relatively constant or became less concentrated at the top, suggesting a continuing high degree of economic opportunity amidst economic growth and prosperity.

56. Town suffrage was based upon possession of a £20 taxable estate (*NH Laws*, 2: 340-45). After 1727 the standard for election to the provincial House of Representatives differed from that of town elections (ibid., pp. 402-3).

57. Below Portsmouth and Dover in assessed trade income were such towns as Exeter, Newmarket, Kingston, and Londonderry, which were assessed at £428, £160, £100, and £100, respectively (NH Inventories, 1727-73, p. 63). In 1732 the 256 taxpayers of Hampton Falls owned 1,531 farm animals, and Dover's taxpayers owned 1,582 farm animals. Contrast this with Portsmouth's 484 comparatively urban taxpayers who owned 1,116 farm animals (NH Inventories, 1727-73). Table 14 gives comparative statistics for 1732 on all the towns.

58. Compare the tax profiles of 1741 for Portsmouth and Dover in Tables 18 and 23. Note the comparative changes in the two town profiles over what had existed in 1680 (see Table 24). Dover's economic position in comparison with Portsmouth had markedly improved by 1741 over its position in the 1680's. It is clear that from time to time each town experienced economic fluctuations and crises that had no effect in other towns. Consequently, it is difficult to compare various town economic profiles of differing years with any accuracy. The safest comparisons appear to be among various towns in the same year. For a crude comparison of the average taxable wealth per person by towns, see Table 14.

59. As Table 23 indicates, the most significant changes occurred at the top and bottom strata in the profile.

60. The wills and estate inventories in the New Hampshire probate records are a biased sample for a variety of reasons. They represent the older people in the population, excluding slaves and indentured servants; they do not adequately represent people in the outlying towns; 707 wills and inventories are a very small sample of the total population between 1640 and 1740. Nevertheless, these sources can provide crude indications of some general tendencies among the more successful families of the older towns. With this in mind, I have compiled statistics based on all inventories in the probate records of 1640 to 1740, comparing general tendencies in the period from 1640 to 1715 with developments from 1715 to 1740. See Tables 25-29. For the general occupational structure found in the probate records among wills and inventories see Table 17.

61. See Tables 25 and 26. All values are expressed in Old Tenor currency. Before 1716, the men possessing inventoried estates over £2,000 were Andrew Pepperrell, George Jaffrey, Edward Hilton, and John Gerrish. After 1716, they included John Rindge, George Vaughan, John Gilman, Bartholemew Thing, Thomas Phipps, Jonathan Wiggin, Hugh Ramsay, John Pickering, Jacob Gilman, Joseph Chase, Samuel Banfield, William Knight,

John Emerson, Kingsley Hall, Samuel Emerson, Nathan Longfellow, Nathaniel Batchelder, Henry Sherburne, Samuel Cutt, John Jenness, Samuel Shaw, Chase Wiggin, Benjamin Hilliard, Thomas Wiggin, Thomas Trickey, and Richard Calley. For the exact amounts involved see Van Deventer, "The Emergence of Provincial New Hampshire," p. 437. These records did not include some of the very rich men without inventories, such as Richard Waldron and John Wentworth, who both possessed about £20,000 in estates, and such others after 1716 as Theodore Atkinson, Samuel Penhallow, Mark Hunking, John Frost, John Knight, Simon Wiggin, Eliphalet Coffin, Morris Hobbs, Richard Gerrish, John Sherburne, Thomas Packer, George Walker, Samuel Winkley, and Archibald MacPhaedris. There were also a number of wealthy men without inventories before 1716: Richard Cutt, Richard Martyn, Thomas Daniel, Richard Waldron, William Vaughan, Nathaniel Fryer, Moses Gilman, Edward Gilman, Thomas Wiggin, Theophilus Dudley, Elias Stileman, Robert Elliott, and Reuben Hull. Much of this information has been obtained from the various town tax records and the wills in *NHPP*, vols. 31-32.

62. The problems relating to land shortages are discussed above in chaps. 2-4. The inventories reveal that land prices had risen rapidly in some areas. In Hampton, unimproved land was worth 5s. per acre in the 1680's and £6 in the 1720's. Meadow acreage worth £2 in the 1680's was worth £10 in the 1720's. In Portsmouth in the 1690's an unimproved acre was worth 10s.; by 1727 it was worth between £6 and £10. The cost of farms had doubled in these years, from £6 to £12 per acre. Exeter, however, was an exception to these rising land prices. Because land was plentiful there until the 1730's, land prices rose much more slowly. For example, the cost of farms rose only from £4 to £6 per acre between the 1690's and the 1720's. In 1725 every adult male in the town received a share of the last town commons. The grants were based generally upon the proportion of taxes each person paid. In Table 30 I have compiled the total of all Exeter town land grants between 1670 and 1725 and created a chart showing the total town land grant holdings of adult males by 1725, by which time each person had received at least 20 acres of town land. This table does not show the actual amount of property owned by Exeter inhabitants, for they could have either acquired more land or sold out their holdings privately by this time. For Exeter tax profiles see Table 31.

63. This conclusion contrasts somewhat with that of Charles S. Grant in his study of Kent, Connecticut, between 1732 and 1800. He found similar population pressures and declining opportunities there by the late eighteenth century and concluded that these conditions led to a great increase in social stratification (*Democracy in the Connecticut Frontier Town of Kent* [New York: Columbia University Press, 1961], pp. 82-103, 169-73). Similar conclusions were formulated for eastern Massachusetts by Kenneth A. Lockridge, "Land, Population, and the Evolution of New England Society, 1630-1790," *Past and Present* 39 (April 1968): 62-80.

64. New Hampshire retail prices for agricultural commodities doubled between the early 1720's and the early 1740's, reflecting in part currency inflation (see the Retail Price Series chart in McKinley, "Economic History of Portsmouth," pp. 390-407). For evidence of transportation improvements see *NHPP*, 3: 803; 9: 89; Weeden, *Economic and Social History*, 2: 509; *Boston Weekly Post-Boy*, February 7, 1740/41. For evidence of gradual wage increases among laborers see Fairchild, *Messrs. William Pepperrell*, pp. 145-46. For an estimate of the normal cost of living for a three-person family see *Sibley's Harvard Graduates*, 7: 341, on Nicholas Gilman of Durham in 1742.

65. One of the interesting by-products of increasing land scarcity was a marked trend toward parceling out one's estate to one's sons before death. Between 1640 and 1690, 14 out of 79 men with eligible heirs (17.7 percent) gave land to their sons before death; from 1690 to 1717, 29 out of 88 men with eligible heirs (33 percent) gave land to their sons before death; and from 1718 to 1740, 60 out of 160 men with eligible heirs (40 percent) did so. These wills provide evidence of a trend caused both by the desire of sons for land in periods of scarcity and by the desires of parents to keep the family within the community as new land beckoned. See *NHPP*, vols. 31-32.

66. Examples are legion. In Portsmouth the most prominent examples before 1660 were Henry Sherburne, John Pickering, Richard Cutt, and Bryan Pendleton; in Dover they included Richard Waldron, Elder William Wentworth, Thomas Wiggin, Hatevil Nutter, Valentine Hill, and Ralph Hall; in Exeter, John Wheelwright, Moses and John Gilman, Anthony Stanyon, John Legat, and Christopher Lawson; in Hampton, Stephen Bachilor,

Timothy Dalton, Deacon Christopher Hussey, Deacon Robert Page, Roger Shaw, and Samuel Dalton. Short genealogical references for most of these men may be found in Noyes. Also see *NHHS Coll,* 8: 327-41, 244-46.

67. Others, such as John and Richard Cutt, could have been analyzed here. See chap. 5 above.

68. For more on Thomas Wiggin see Page, *Judicial Beginnings,* pp. 3, 12, 13, 15, 16, 43-45; Scales, *History of Dover,* pp. 94-95, 102-4. His sons and grandsons maintained the family's social status while following agricultural and lumbering pursuits in Stratham. Andrew Wiggin (1671-1753), Thomas's grandson and a brother-in-law to the Wentworths, served as Speaker of the House from 1727 to 1744 and as judge of probate from 1741 until his death (Noyes, pp. 751-53).

69. Noyes, p. 537; *NHPP,* 31: 191-93; Bailyn, *New England Merchants,* p. 82; Brewster, *Rambles about Portsmouth,* 1st ser., pp. 23, 25, 27, and elsewhere.

70. *NHPP,* 31: 124; Noyes, pp. 331-32, 336-37. Bell, *History of Exeter,* p. 435, prints the land agreement between Hilton and the Exeter townspeople. Hilton's more notable progeny were Captain William Hilton, Edward Hilton, and Colonel Winthrop Hilton (1671-1710), all of whom held significant political and military positions before 1740.

71. For short biographical sketches of Waldron and his descendants see *NHHS Coll,* 8: 332-41; Noyes, pp. 711-12. *NHPP,* 1: 370-72, gives a list of all New Hampshire politicians elected to the Massachusetts General Court from 1641 to 1679. Waldron missed election to only two sessions in twenty-five years. The most famous and powerful of his colonial descendants were Colonel Richard Waldron (1650-1730), Richard Waldron, Jr. (1694-1753), and Thomas Westbrook Waldron (1721-85).

72. During the latter part of the seventeenth century, 149 selectmen held 518 offices in the four towns, an average of 3.5 offices per man. But in the early eighteenth century, 331 selectmen held 940 offices, averaging 2.8 offices per man. Compare these statistics with those compiled on other New England towns in the mid-eighteenth century by Edward M. Cook, Jr., "Local Leadership and the Typology of New England Towns, 1700-1785," *Political Science Quarterly* 86 (December 1971): 605-6. For a list of the most popular selectmen in the four towns in the seventeenth and early eighteenth centuries see Van Deventer, "The Emergence of Provincial New Hampshire," p. 449n.

73. Bailyn, *New England Merchants,* pp. 194-95.

74. The town offices that remained attractive included assessor, selectman, clerk, moderator, and lot layer.

75. This was the case with such men as George Jaffrey, Richard Gerrish, Richard Wibird, Benjamin Gambling, and Ephraim Dennett, whose activities in the House of Representatives so impressed the royal executive and his friends that each received appointment to the council. Each one was a leader of the first rank during his tenure in the House. See *NHPP,* vols. 3-4.

76. For the exact relationships among these families see Noyes; Brewster, *Rambles about Portsmouth;* Bell, *History of Exeter;* Scales, *History of Dover;* Wentworth, *Wentworth Genealogy;* and Charles H. Pope, *The Pioneers of Maine and New Hampshire* (Boston, 1908).

77. Bailyn, *New England Merchants,* pp. 133-34. The role of the Waldrons, Vaughans, Partridges, Plaisteds, Gilmans, Wiggins, Hiltons, Jaffreys, Westbrooks, Wentworths, Atkinsons, and John Rindge in their quest for masts has been discussed in chaps. 5 and 7.

78. This pattern was typified, with minor variations, by Richard Waldron, John and Richard Cutt, the Gilmans, Peter Coffin, Samuel and John Wentworth, the Partridges, George Jaffrey, the Plaisteds, Thomas Westbrook, the Hiltons, William Vaughan, and Richard Wibird. In some cases this general pattern took two generations to work out. See Richard Waldron, Jr., to Jonathan Belcher, July 1, 1748, Waldron Papers, vol. 2, no. 142, NHHS.

79. The most famous men of these families were Colonel Winthrop Hilton, Captain John Gilman, and Lieutenant John Gilman (Noyes, pp. 336-37). See the attempts of Thomas Westbrook Waldron to obtain a military command in the 1740's (Waldron Papers, vol. 2). The letters in the Waldron Papers also provide evidence of William Vaughan's efforts in this direction.

80. Chase's inventory of estate of January 12, 1717/18 is in NH Probate Records, vol. 9.

81. Knowledge of the law was useful in land and trade contracts as well as in politics. Such knowledge helped these men obtain royal political offices—judge, deputy surveyor of the woods, secretary, sheriff, treasurer, and justice of the peace.

82. Short but excellent biographies of these individuals are given in *Sibley's Harvard Graduates*, vols. 4-7. For a few of these individuals, medicine or some other subject provided their main fare at Harvard. Nineteen of the twenty Harvard graduates from New Hampshire lived in Portsmouth or New Castle. The three who did not obtain significant political posts were Sherburne, Rindge, and Hinckes. As early as 1669 Portsmouth's merchants took the lead in promoting education (*Mass. Records*, 4, pt. 2: 432-33). Also see *NH Laws*, 2: 85-86, 98.

83. In 1740 slaves comprised 2 percent and servants probably between 2 and 3 percent of the total population of New Hampshire. See Table 1.

84. *CSP Col*, 1696-97, nos. 283*i*, 1096; 1697-98, no. 186; Atkinson to Thomlinson, 1735, *NHPP*, 4: 844. The dominant role of the mast traders has been analyzed in chap. 7.

85. Nathaniel Weare to Robert Pike, March 15, 1689/90, *NHPP*, 2: 45; New Hampshire Council to House of Representatives, January 28, 1616/17, ibid., 3: 678-79; Penhallow to Cotton Mather, December 27, 1716, "Diary of Cotton Mather," *MHS Coll*, 7th ser., 8: 422.

86. For a discussion of titles in seventeenth-century New England see Norman H. Dawes, "Titles as Symbols of Prestige in Seventeenth-Century New England," *William and Mary Quarterly*, 3rd ser., 6 (January 1949): 69-83.

87. See the New Hampshire wills in *NHPP*, vol. 32. These men held the largest estates in New Hampshire, ranging from £5,000 to £20,000; and most of them served on the New Hampshire Council as well.

88. Men who used the titles "Merchant," "Captain," "Mister," and even "Esquire" also called themselves "Gentleman." See ibid.

89. The use of the title "Yeoman" was more than twice as prevalent in the wills and inventories after 1715 than before that date. "Captain" referred to the captain of a sailing vessel. In general, the use of titles, particularly those denoting skilled laborers and craftsmen, increased during the later era.

90. *NHPP*, 3: 732; 4: 323. For a more general discussion of these various badges of distinction see Oedel, "Portsmouth," p. 720; *CSP Col*, 1732, no. 87, p. 61; Brewster, *Rambles about Portsmouth*, 1st ser., p. 105. Samuel Penhallow scorned such funeral practices and instead gave money to the poor (*NHPP*, 32: 285). See also *NHPP*, 31: 552; 32: 67, for other examples.

91. Quoted from *Sibley's Harvard Graduates*, 6: 114, which is taken from Robert Hale, *Journal of an Expedition to Nova Scotia*.

92. Richard Waldron to Jonathan Belcher, April 8, 1751, Waldron Papers, vol. 2, no. 218, NHHS.

93. The best discussion of this crisis is in Oedel, "Portsmouth," pp. 334-38. Also see the *Portsmouth Town Records*, WPA Project, vol. 2, f. 41*BA* ff.; *NHPP*, 3: 715, 717; 13: 244-48; *NH Laws*, 2: 252-53.

94. George Vaughan's ideas have been extensively discussed in chap. 7, above. The new council appointees were Richard Gerrish, Theodore Atkinson, George Jaffrey, and Richard Wibird; Archibald MacPhaedris, Thomas Packer, and Thomas Westbrook soon followed. Nathaniel Weare and Richard Waldron, members from Hampton and Dover, were dismissed.

95. *NHPP*, 3: 675-76, 677-79.

96. The Triennial Act, 1728, had the ostensible purpose of obtaining three-year terms for General Assemblies, but it also legalized plural voting by dropping residence requirements for town voting for the House of Representatives. This allowed land speculators to vote in any town where they had £50 of real estate. Ibid., 4: 263-66, 468-70, 474-75; *NH Laws*, 2: 402-3.

97. See Table 14 for Portsmouth and New Castle in 1732. In order to qualify for suffrage one had to own between £5 and £10 of taxable estate. In terms of actual property this translated into ownership of at least a house, one acre, and a cow; or a house, one horse, and two cows; or five improved acres of land. These figures are based on land values as compared to assessed valuations, whose sources are in the NH Probate Records and in the NH

Inventories, 1727-73. Actually, town moderators, elected by those men attending a town meeting, tended to allow all adult males to vote.

98. A crude quantification of this conclusion has been attempted by comparing taxable property ownership of those people who lived in Portsmouth for at least twenty years with the property owned by those who lived there less than twenty years. See Table 33. Generally, the longer one lived in a town, the more likely he was to possess a relatively high economic status.

99. Belcher to Duke of Newcastle, July 13, 1731, *CSP Col*, 1731, no. 296.

100. Belcher to Shadrach Walton, July 1, 1731, ibid., no. 377*iv*.

101. *NHPP*, vols. 3-5 passim.

102. See, for example, the Waldron Papers, NHHS; Penhallow, *History of the Wars*; and the petitions signed by the Gilmans, Weares, and over 650 other people to have New Hampshire annexed to Massachusetts (*NHPP*, 9: 349-56). On October 29, 1731, Richard Waldron wrote to Belcher: "I really believe . . . that a union of the Provinces would at this junction be vigorously opposed, yet I can't but flatter myself we may see an Assembly ere long that will fall into any reasonable scheme to obtain such a happiness" (Waldron Papers, vol. 1, no. 37).

103. While the Wentworth faction won a great political victory in 1741, obtaining their desired land augmentation and the political separation from Massachusetts, this did not stop Richard Waldron's political machinations against the "clan." Only death brought his efforts to an end. The Waldron Papers, vol. 2, are full of his efforts to remove Governor Benning Wentworth from the political scene during he 1740's. Also see Daniell, "Politics in New Hampshire."

104. See Table 32. For Benning Wentworth's testimony about the prevalence of suffrage among all town freeholders in the choice of members to the House of Representatives see Benning Wentworth to John Thomlinson, June 11, 1749, Ayer Manuscripts, no. 622, Newberry Library, Chicago.

105. PTR, 2: 149. The town officials for 1730 to 1740 are in ibid., pp. 146-49.

106. *NHPP*, 11: 517; 12: 432; 13: 12-13, 254, 259. For a Portsmouth suffrage controversy in 1745 see ibid., 9: 698-703. Also see ibid., 12: 711, 713, 714.

107. See Table 32, comparing Londonderry with the other town selectman statistics, and Table 34, comparing total officeholding in Portsmouth with that of Londonderry, a relatively new town.

WORKS CITED

Primary Sources

Manuscripts

Ayer Manuscripts. Newberry Library, Chicago, Illinois.

Belcher Letterbook, 1736–38. Massachusetts Historical Society, Boston, Massachusetts.

Belcher Papers: Letters of Jonathan Belcher to Richard Waldron. 3 vols. New Hampshire Historical Society, Concord, New Hampshire.

Belknap Manuscripts. Massachusetts Historical Society.

Dover Town Records. New Hampshire State Library, Concord, New Hampshire.

Excerpts from the Journals (24 vols., 1700–1787) of the Society for the Propagation of the Gospel in Foreign Parts and from the Bishop of London's Fulham Palace Manuscripts Relating to New Hampshire, As Revealed in the Indices in the Library of Congress. A typescript in the Portsmouth Public Library, Portsmouth, New Hampshire.

Exeter Town Records. New Hampshire State Library.

Hampton Town Records. New Hampshire State Library.

Inventories of the Polls and Estates in the Province of New Hampshire, 1727–73. New Hampshire Historical Society.

Londonderry Town Records. New Hampshire State Library.

MacPhaedris-Warner Letterbook. Warner House, Portsmouth, New Hampshire.

Massachusetts Shipping Returns, 1686–88. British Public Record Office, London, England.

New Hampshire Miscellaneous Manuscripts. Library of Congress, Washington, D.C.

Peirce Papers. Portsmouth Athenaeum, Portsmouth, New Hampshire.

Peirce Papers. Wendell Collection. Baker Library, Harvard Business School, Boston, Massachusetts.

Portsmouth Miscellaneous Papers. New Hampshire Historical Society.

Portsmouth Town Records. New Hampshire State Library.

Probate Records of New Hampshire. 26 vols. New Hampshire State Archives, Concord, New Hampshire.

Randolph, Edward. "The Present State of New England." Additional Manuscripts. British Museum, London, England.

Rawlinson Manuscripts. Bodleian Library, Oxford, England.

Saltonstall Papers. Massachusetts Historical Society.

Shipping Returns for the Port of Piscataqua. New Hampshire Customs Records. British Public Record Office, London, England.

Vaughan Papers. New Hampshire Historical Society.

Waldron Papers. 2 vols. New Hampshire Historical Society.

Weare Manuscripts. New Hampshire Historical Society.

Wentworth Manuscripts. New Hampshire Historical Society.

Miscellaneous (Diaries, Histories, Correspondence, Journals)

"Belcher Papers." *Collections of the Massachusetts Historical Society*, 6th ser., vols. 6–7.

Gorges, Sir Ferdinando. "A Brief Narration of the Original Undertakings of the Advancement of Plantations into the Parts of America." *Collections of the Maine Historical Society*, 1st ser., vol. 2, pt. 2.

Hutchinson, Thomas. *The History of the Colony and Province of Massachusetts-Bay.* Edited by L. S. Mayo. 3 vols. Cambridge: Harvard University Press, 1936.

"Journal of Reverend John Pike of Dover." *Collections of the New Hampshire Historical Society* 3: 40–67.

Maverick, Samuel. "A Briefe Description of New England and the Several Towns Therein" (1660). *Proceedings of the Massachusetts Historical Society*, 2d ser. 1: 233–35.

Penhallow, Samuel. *The History of the Wars of New England with the Eastern Indians. . . .* Boston: T. Fleet and Cornhill, 1726.

Prince, Thomas. *A Chronological History of New England in the Form of Annals*, 1736. Boston: Cummings, Hilliard & Company, 1826.

Smith, John. *A Description of New England . . . 1615.* Boston: W. Veazie, 1865.

———. *The Generall Historie of Virginia, New-England, and the Summer Isles.* London, 1632.

Travels and Works of Captain John Smith. Edited by A. G. Bradley. Edinburgh: J. Grant, 1910.

Winthrop's Journal. Edited by James K. Hosmer. 2 vols. New York: Barnes & Noble, 1908.

Public Documents and Collections

Acts and Resolves of the Province of Massachusetts Bay. Edited by E. Ames and A. C. Goodell. 17 vols. Boston, 1869–1910.

Acts of the Privy Council of England, Colonial Series. Edited by William L. Grant and James Monro. 6 vols. London: His Majesty's Stationery Office, 1908–12.

Calendar of State Papers, Colonial Series: America and West Indies, 1574–1736. Edited by W. M. Sainsbury et al. London, 1850–1953.

Collections Historical and Miscellaneous; and Monthly Literary Journal. Edited by John Farmer and J. B. Moore. 3 vols. Concord, N.H., 1823–24.

Collections of the Maine Historical Society.

Collections of the Massachusetts Historical Society.

Collections of the New Hampshire Historical Society.

Edward Randolph; Including His Letters and Official Papers. . . . Edited by R. N. Toppan and A. S. Goodrick. 7 vols. Prince Society Publications, vols. 24–28, 30–31. Boston, 1898–1909.

The Federal and State Constitutions, Colonial Charters, and Other Organic Laws of the States. Edited by Francis N. Thorpe. 7 vols. Washington, D.C.: Carnegie Institution, 1909.

Journals of the Commissioners for Trade and Plantations, 1704–1782. 14 vols. London: His Majesty's Stationery Office, 1920–38.

Laws of New Hampshire. Edited by Albert S. Batchellor. 10 vols. Manchester, N.H., 1904–22.

Portsmouth Records, 1645–1656. Edited by Frank Hackett. Portsmouth, 1856.

Portsmouth Town Records, 1645–1807. Bound typescript. 7 vols. W.P.A. Project, 1939, Portsmouth Public Library.

Proceedings of the Massachusetts Historical Society.

Proceedings of the New Hampshire Historical Society.

Provincial and State Papers: Documents and Records Relating to the Province and State of New Hampshire. Edited by Nathaniel Bouton et al. 40 vols. Concord, N.H., 1867–1943.

Records of the Governor and Company of the Massachusetts Bay in New England. Edited by Nathaniel B. Shurtleff. 5 vols. Boston, 1853–54.

Transcripts of Original Documents in the English Archives Relating to the Early History of New Hampshire. Compiled by John S. Jenness. New York, 1876.

Periodicals

Boston Newsletter
Boston Weekly Post-Boy
New England Historical and Genealogical Register

Secondary Works

Books

Adams, Nathaniel. *Annals of Portsmouth*. Portsmouth, N.H., 1825.

Akagi, Roy H. *The Town Proprietors of the New England Colonies: A Study of Their Development, Organization, Activities, and Controversies, 1620-1770*. Philadelphia: University of Pennsylvania Press, 1924.

Albion, Robert G. *Forests and Sea Power: The Timber Problem of the Royal Navy, 1652-1862*. Cambridge: Harvard University Press, 1926.

Andrews, Charles M. *The Colonial Period of American History*. 4 vols. New Haven: Yale University Press, 1934-38.

Bailyn, Bernard. *The New England Merchants in the Seventeenth Century*. Cambridge: Harvard University Press, 1955.

Bailyn, Bernard, and Bailyn, Lotte. *Massachusetts Shipping, 1697-1714: A Statistical Study*. Cambridge: The Belknap Press of Harvard University Press, 1959.

Banks, Charles. *Topographical Dictionary of 2885 English Emigrants to New England, 1620-1650*. Philadelphia, 1937.

Barnes, Viola. *The Dominion of New England: A Study in British Colonial Policy*. New Haven: Yale University Press, 1923.

Barrow, Thomas C. *Trade and Empire: The British Customs Service in Colonial America, 1660-1775*. Cambridge: Harvard University Press, 1967.

Battis, Emory. *Saints and Sectaries: Anne Hutchinson and the Antinomian Controversy in the Massachusetts Bay Colony*. Chapel Hill: University of North Carolina Press, 1962.

Baxter, James P. *The Pioneers of New France and New England, with Contemporary Letters and Documents*. Albany, N.Y.: Munsall, 1894.

―――, ed. *Sir Ferdinando Gorges and His Province of Maine*. 3 vols. Boston: Prince Society, 1890.

Belknap, Jeremy. *The History of New-Hampshire*. 3 vols. 2d ed. Boston, 1813.

―――. *The History of New-Hampshire*. Edited by John Farmer. Dover, N.H., 1831.

Bell, Charles H. *History of the Town of Exeter, New Hampshire*. Exeter, 1888.

Billias, George A. *The Massachusetts Land Bankers of 1740*. University of Maine Studies, 2d ser., no. 74. Orono, Me.: University of Maine Press, 1959.

Brewster, Charles W. *Rambles about Portsmouth*. 2 series. Portsmouth, N.H., 1859, 1869.

Bridenbaugh, Carl. *Cities in the Wilderness: The First Century of Urban Life in America, 1625-1742*. New York: Ronald Press, 1938.

Bushman, Richard L. *From Puritan to Yankee: Character and the Social Order in Connecticut, 1690-1765*. Cambridge: Harvard University Press, 1967.

Clark, Charles E. *The Eastern Frontier: The Settlement of Northern New England, 1610-1763*. New York: Knopf, 1970.

Dean, John W., ed. *Captain John Mason, the Founder of New Hampshire . . . Together With a Memoir by C. W. Tuttle*. Boston, 1887.

Dow, George F., and Edmonds, John. *The Pirates of the New England Coast, 1630–1670*. Salem, Mass.: Marine Research Society, 1923.

Dow, George, and Robinson, John. *Sailing Ships of New England, 1607–1901*. Salem, Mass., 1922.

Dow, Joseph. *History of Hampton, New Hampshire*. Hampton, 1883.

Ernst, Joseph A. *Money and Politics in America, 1755–1775: A Study in the Currency Act of 1764 and the Political Economy of Revolution*. Chapel Hill: University of North Carolina Press, 1973.

Fairchild, Byron. *Messrs. William Pepperrell: Merchants at Piscataqua*. Ithaca, N.Y.: Cornell University Press, 1954.

Fry, William H. *New Hampshire as a Royal Province*. Studies in History, Economics, and Public Law, vol. 29, no. 2. New York, 1908.

Gipson, Lawrence H. *The British Empire before the American Revolution*. 15 vols. New York: Knopf, 1958–70.

Grant, Charles S. *Democracy in the Connecticut Frontier Town of Kent*. New York: Columbia University Press, 1961.

Hall, Michael G. *Edward Randolph and the American Colonies, 1676–1703*. Chapel Hill: University of North Carolina Press, 1960.

Historical Statistics of the United States, Colonial Times to 1957. Washington, D.C.: Government Printing Office, 1960.

Innis, Harold. *The Cod Fisheries: The History of an International Economy*. Toronto: University of Toronto Press, 1954.

Jenness, John S. *The Isles of Shoals*. 2d ed. Boston, 1915.

Judah, Charles B., Jr. *The North American Fisheries and British Policy to 1713*. Illinois Studies in the Social Sciences, vol. 18, nos. 3–4. Urbana: University of Illinois, 1933.

Kimball, Everett. *The Public Life of Joseph Dudley: A Study of the Colonial Policy of the Stuarts in New England, 1660–1715*. New York: Longmans, Green & Company, 1911.

Kinney, Charles B. *Church and State: The Struggle for Separation in New Hampshire, 1630–1800*. New York: Columbia University Press, 1955.

Lawrence, Robert F. *The New Hampshire Churches*. Claremont, N.H., 1856.

Leach, Douglas E. *Flintlock and Tomahawk: New England in King Philip's War*. New York: Little, Brown, 1958.

———. *The Northern Colonial Frontier, 1607–1763*. New York: Holt, Rinehart & Winston, 1966.

Lord, Eleanor. *Industrial Experiments in the British Colonies of North America*. Johns Hopkins University Studies in Historical and Political Science, vol. 17. Baltimore, 1898.

McFarland, Raymond. *A History of the New England Fisheries*. New York: Appleton & Company, 1911.

McKinley, Samuel J. "The Economic History of Portsmouth, New Hampshire, from its First Settlement to 1830, Including a Study of Price Movements There, 1713–1770 and 1804–1830." Ph.D. dissertation, Harvard University, 1931.

Malone, Joseph J. *Pine Trees and Politics: The Naval Stores and Forest Policy in Colonial New England, 1691–1775.* Seattle: University of Washington Press, 1964.

Maloney, Francis X. *The Fur Trade in New England.* Cambridge: Harvard University Press, 1931.

May, Ralph. *Early Portsmouth History.* Boston: Goodspeed & Company, 1926.

Morgan, Edmund S. *The Puritan Dilemma: The Story of John Winthrop.* Boston: Little, Brown, 1958.

Morris, Richard B. *Government and Labor in Early America.* New York: Columbia University Press, 1946.

Nettels, Curtis P. *The Money Supply of the American Colonies before 1720.* University of Wisconsin Studies, no. 20. Madison, 1934.

North, Douglass C., and Thomas, Robert P., eds. *The Growth of the American Economy to 1860.* New York: Harper and Row, 1968.

Noyes, Sybil; Libby, Charles; and Davis, Walter. *Genealogical Dictionary of Maine and New Hampshire.* Portland, Me., 1928–39.

Oedel, Howard T. "Portsmouth, New Hampshire: The Role of the Provincial Capital in the Development of the Colony (1700–1775)." Ph.D. dissertation, Boston University, 1960.

Osgood, Herbert L. *The American Colonies in the Seventeenth and Eighteenth Centuries.* 7 vols. New York, 1904–7, 1924–25.

Page, Elwin L. *Judicial Beginnings in New Hampshire, 1640–1700.* Concord, N.H.: Evans Printing Company, 1959.

Phillips, Paul C. *The Fur Trade.* 2 vols. Norman: University of Oklahoma Press, 1961.

Pope, Charles H. *The Pioneers of Maine and New Hampshire, 1623–1660.* Boston, 1908.

Quint, Alonzo H. *Historical Memoranda Concerning Persons and Places in Old Dover, New Hampshire.* Dover, 1900.

Rutledge, Lyman V. *The Isles of Shoals in Lore and Legend.* Barre, Mass.: Barre Publishers, 1965.

Saltonstall, William G. *Ports of Piscataqua.* Cambridge: Harvard University Press, 1941.

Scales, John, *History of Dover, New Hampshire.* Manchester, N.H., 1923.

Schutz, John A. *William Shirley, King's Governor of Massachusetts.* Chapel Hill: University of North Carolina Press, 1961.

Shipton, Clifford S. *Sibley's Harvard Graduates: Biographical Sketches of Those Who Attended Harvard College. . . .* Boston: Massachusetts Historical Society, 1873–.

Smith, Abbot E. *Colonists in Bondage: White Servitude and Convict Labor in America, 1607–1776.* Chapel Hill: University of North Carolina Press, 1947.

Smith, Joseph H. *Appeals to the Privy Council from the American Plantations.* New York: Columbia University Press, 1950.

Stackpole, Everett S. *History of New Hampshire.* 4 vols. New York: The American Historical Society, 1916.

Van Deventer, David E. "The Emergence of Provincial New Hampshire, 1623–1741." Ph.D. dissertation, Case-Western Reserve University, 1969.

Vaughan, Alden T. *New England Frontier: Puritans and Indians, 1620–1675.* Boston: Little, Brown and Company, 1965.

Weeden, William B. *Economic and Social History of New England, 1620–1789.* 2 vols. Boston, 1891. Reprint. New York: Hillary House Publishers Ltd., 1963.

Wentworth, John. *Wentworth Genealogy.* Boston: Little, Brown & Company, 1878.

Woodbury, Charles L. *The Relation of the Fisheries to the Discovery and Settlement of North America.* Boston, 1880.

Articles

Chapman, Leonard. "The Mast Industry of Old Falmouth." *Collections of the Maine Historical Society*, 2d ser., 7: 390–405.

Cook, Edward M., Jr. "Local Leadership and the Typology of New England Towns, 1700–1785." *Political Science Quarterly* 86 (December 1971): 586–608.

Daniell, Jere. "Politics in New Hampshire under Governor Benning Wentworth, 1741–1767." *William and Mary Quarterly*, 3rd ser., 23 (January 1966): 76–105.

Dawes, Norman H. "Titles as Symbols of Prestige in Seventeenth-Century New England." *William and Mary Quarterly*, 3rd ser., 6 (January 1949): 69–83.

Eckstrom, F. H. "The Attack on Norridgewock, 1724." *New England Quarterly* 7 (September 1934): 541–78.

French, Christopher. "Eighteenth-Century Shipping Tonnage Measurements." *Journal of Economic History* 33 (June 1973): 434–43.

Greene, Jack P. "Foundations of Political Power in the Virginia House of Burgesses, 1720–1776." *William and Mary Quarterly*, 3rd ser., 16 (October 1959): 485–506.

Hammond, Otis G. "The Mason Title and Its Relations to New Hampshire and Massachusetts." *The Proceedings of the American Antiquarian Society* 26 (1916): 245–63.

Henratta, James M. "Economic Development and Social Structure in Colonial Boston." *William and Mary Quarterly*, 3rd ser., 22 (January 1965): 75–92.

Jenness, John S. "Notes on the First Planting of New Hampshire and on the Piscataqua Patents." *New Hampshire Provincial Papers*, 25: 663–739.

Lemon, James T., and Nash, Gary B. "The Distribution of Wealth in Eighteenth-Century America: A Century of Change in Chester County, Pennsylvania, 1693–1802." *Journal of Social History* 2 (Fall 1968): 1–24.

Lockridge, Kenneth A. "Land, Population, and the Evolution of New England Society, 1630–1790." *Past and Present* 39 (April 1968): 62–80.

Lockridge, Kenneth A., and Kreider, Alan. "The Evolution of Massachusetts Town Government, 1640 to 1740." *William and May Quarterly*, 3rd ser., 23 (October 1966): 549–74.

Lounsbury, Robert G. "Yankee Trade at Newfoundland." *New England Quarterly* 3 (October 1930): 607–26.

MacFarlane, Ronald O. "The Massachusetts Bay Truck-Houses in Diplomacy with the Indians." *New England Quarterly* 11 (March 1938): 48–65.

Preston, R. A. "The Laconia Company of 1629: An English Attempt to Intercept the Fur Trade." *Canadian Historical Review* 31 (1950): 125–44.

Thayer, Theodore. "The Land-Bank System in the American Colonies." *Journal of Economic History* 13 (Spring 1953): 145–59.

Zuckerman, Michael. "The Social Context of Democracy in Massachusetts." *William and Mary Quarterly*, 3rd ser., 25 (October 1968): 523–44.

INDEX

Abbot, Walter, 96, 255 n.11
Abnaki, 63–66, 68, 71–72, 89. *See also* Indians
Adams, Rev. Hugh, 126, 261 n.87
Agriculture, 4, 32, 225; patterns of, 32–33, 85, 191, 280 n.64; products of, 33, 236 n.59, 254 n.9. *See also* Trade
Air, James, 257 n.37
Allen, Samuel: claims New Hampshire, 51, 59, 132, 137; compromise offer by, 56–57, 241 n.72; and customs case, 265 n.39; economic activities of, 95, 97, 108, 132, 140, 252 n.69; as governor, 51, 53–55, 138; and proprietary cases, 53, 54, 240 n.58. *See also* Masonian proprietary controversy
Allen, Thomas, 51, 56–58
Allen v. Waldron, 57
Andros, Sir Edmund, 66, 136, 242 n.15
Anglican Church, 190, 277 nn.45–46. *See also* Religion
Anglo-Dutch wars, 44
Apprentices, 115, 116, 120
Apprenticeship, 115, 257 nn.38–39
Armstrong, Robert: as customs collector, 266 n.45; politics of, 138, 141, 146, 149, 265 n.40
Ashurst, Sir Henry, 108
Ashurst, Sir William, 53, 143, 264 n.25
Atkinson, Theodore: as Anglican, 277 n.45, as councillor, 282 n.94; economic activity of, 161, 215, 242 n.88, 249 n.34; politics of, 142, 159, 216, 245 n.69, 260 nn.71 and 78, 261 n.80, 265 nn.34 and 40, 268 n.81, 269 n.89, 270 n.109, 271 n.125; status of, 212, 213, 280 n.61; values of, 221. *See also* Factions
Atkinson, Theodore (son), 271 n.126

Auchmuty, Robert, 142
Austin, Joseph, 236 n.71
Ayers, Edward, 108, 191

Babb, Sampson, 191
Bachiler, Rev. Stephen, 8, 22, 280 n.66
Bacon, Butts, 265 nn.39 and 40
Bailyn, Bernard: on lumber trade, 94–95, 249 n.43; on Portsmouth town meeting, 238 n.15; on role of trade, 109; on social structure, 213
Banfield, Samuel, 279 n.61
Bankruptcy, 128, 262 n.97
Barber, John, 257 n.37
Barefoote, Walter, 50, 97, 134, 254 n.5, 255 n.11. *See also* Masonian proprietary controversy
Barrington, 193, 246 n.77
Batchelder, Nathaniel, 280 n.61
Bean, John, 257 n.37
Beard, Joseph, 255 n.11
Beard, Thomas, 255 n.11
Bedford Galley, 98
Belcher, Jonathan: and boundary dispute, 77–78; factionalism of, 138–39, 216, 220–21; as governor, 77, 92, 104, 111, 123, 126, 142, 159, 262 n.89; and paper currency, 123–26, 258 n.59, 261 nn.78, 79, 81, 87, and 88, 262 n.89; status of, 213
Bell, Daniel, 174, 271 n.126, 273 n.152
Bell, Thomas, 177, 271 n.126, 273 n.152
Bellomont, Earl of (Richard Coote): as governor, 53, 90, 110–11, 131, 138, 141, 151, 256 n.23; and Masonian proprietary controversy, 53–55, 241 n.77; opinion of Partridge on, 138, 241 n.65, 264 n.32
Bickford, Edward, 255 n.11

293